Kubernetes for Generative AI Solutions

A complete guide to designing, optimizing, and deploying Generative AI workloads on Kubernetes

Ashok Srirama

Sukirti Gupta

Kubernetes for Generative AI Solutions

Portfolio Director: Kartikey Pandey
Relationship Lead: Prachi Rana
Project Manager: Sonam Pandey
Content Engineer: Sarada Biswas
Technical Editor: Simran Ali
Copy Editor: Safis Editing
Indexer: Manju Arasan
Proofreader: Sarada Biswas
Production Designer: Shankar Kalbhor
Growth Lead: Shreyans Singh

First published: June 2025

Production reference: 1230525

Published by Packt Publishing Ltd.
Grosvenor House
11 St Paul's Square
Birmingham
B3 1RB, UK

ISBN 978-1-83620-993-5

`www.packtpub.com`

To my mother, my wife, and everyone whose presence shaped the person I've become.

To my special needs children, thank you for teaching me life's true meaning: empathy, resilience, and humility.

– Ashok Srirama

To my wife and children, whose love fills my life with purpose and joy. To my parents, for all their guidance and unwavering support, and to my brother, for always being my ally, offering constant encouragement and strength.

– Sukirti Gupta

Foreword

Over the past few years, I've had the privilege of working closely with organizations that are pushing the limits of what's possible with cloud-native technologies. From Serverless modernization to Kubernetes-scale container orchestration, one thing has become abundantly clear—Generative AI is no longer a futuristic concept. It's here, it's powerful, and it's redefining how we build, deploy, and scale intelligent systems.

When I first reviewed this manuscript, I was struck by how comprehensive yet hands-on it is. *Kubernetes for Generative AI Solutions* does more than teach you how to run LLMs or deploy state-of-the-art models—it gives you a production-grade blueprint. From observability to cost optimization, from secure scaling to HA/DR patterns, this book meets developers, architects, and product leaders where they are—and takes them forward with confidence.

I've had the privilege of working with **Ashok Srirama** and **Sukirti Gupta**, who are recognized thought leaders in cloud-native technologies. Their combined experience at AWS and in modernizing large-scale systems is evident throughout this book. Ashok's deep technical expertise in EKS and GenAI infrastructure, paired with Sukirti's strategic perspective on product development and GTM expertise, make this book both visionary and grounded.

What I especially appreciated is the pragmatic tone—not just code, but also battle-tested patterns, modular Terraform stacks, observability practices, and real-world tips that could save you weeks, if not months, of trial and error. As someone who spends a lot of time enabling teams to scale with Kubernetes and Serverless on AWS, I found myself nodding along and learning from the practical insights this book delivers.

Whether you're a solutions architect trying to productionize LLM apps, a start-up founder exploring OpenAI and Amazon Bedrock, or an enterprise leader looking to make sense of GPUs on Kubernetes, this book is a must-have on your desk.

Ashok and Sukirti have given us a gift—a guide not just to building GenAI systems, but to building them right.

Rajdeep Saha

Principal Solutions Architect, AWS

Bestselling Author, Mentor, Speaker at KubeCon, AWS re:Invent

Contributors

About the authors

Ashok Srirama is a principal specialist solutions architect at AWS, where he leads initiatives to architect scalable, secure, and cost-efficient container-based solutions for enterprise customers. With over 19 years of experience in IT, Ashok brings profound expertise in cloud architecture, Kubernetes, container platforms, and, most recently, Generative AI.

Before joining AWS, Ashok held pivotal cloud architecture roles at AIG and IBM, where he led digital transformation initiatives and cloud migration projects across insurance and communication sectors. His technical acumen spans across designing distributed architectures, infrastructure automation, and application modernization using containers and serverless technologies.

As a recognized thought leader in cloud-native architecture, Ashok has authored numerous technical publications, including 20+ official AWS blogs and technical guides on Amazon EKS networking, observability, security, and container CI/CD pipelines. He has presented at over 25+ public events, including AWS re:Invent, AWS Summits, and start-up CTO cohorts, sharing his expertise with the broader technical community.

Ashok's commitment to technical excellence is reflected in his extensive certification portfolio, which encompasses all 12 AWS technical certifications and the complete suite of Kubernetes certifications from the Linux Foundation. His achievements have earned him the coveted AWS Gold Jacket and Kubestronaut accreditation.

Beyond his architectural work, Ashok is passionate about enabling developers to simplify the complexity of running GenAI workloads at scale using cloud-native tools.

Sukirti Gupta is a technologist and product management leader at **Amazon Web Services** (**AWS**), where he leads the adoption of Generative AI technologies across start-up ecosystems. With over 15 years of experience in cloud computing, AI/ML, and data center technologies, he has played influential roles in shaping product narratives and engineering solutions for high-impact workloads across AWS, AMD, and Intel.

At AWS, Sukirti leads initiatives that help start-ups integrate GenAI into their product strategy, enabling them to innovate with powerful infrastructure and tools. His previous roles include leading cloud product development at AMD and managing GTM strategy for Intel's flagship computing platforms, where he helped drive billion-dollar revenue programs.

Sukirti holds a B.Tech. from IIT (BHU), Varanasi, an M.S. in electrical engineering from the University of Cincinnati, and an MBA in strategy and marketing from Santa Clara University.

In addition to his corporate work, Sukirti loves to mentor AI start-ups through IIT's accelerator programs and frequently writes on Medium about GenAI trends and product leadership.

About the reviewers

Swati Tyagi is an AI/ML leader with over a decade of experience, specializing in Generative AI, **large language models** (**LLMs**), and responsible AI. She has contributed to impactful AI initiatives across finance, healthcare, and education, including in her current role as a senior machine learning engineer at JPMorgan Chase, where she focuses on deploying scalable and ethical AI solutions.

Swati's expertise spans large-scale model deployment, explainability, bias mitigation, and hyper-personalization. She brings together deep technical knowledge in AI/ML with hands-on experience in MLOps, cloud-native architectures (AWS), and production-grade model development. Her leadership extends to advisory roles with LLM start-ups and AI education initiatives. She actively serves on technical program committees, editorial boards, and advisory panels across the AI community.

Swati holds a Ph.D. in statistics and machine learning from the University of Delaware, a master's in business analytics from IIT Delhi, and a bachelor's degree in computer science. A committed lifelong learner and IEEE Senior Member, she continues to advance the field of responsible AI through cutting-edge research, mentorship, and active community engagement.

Dhirendra Kumar is a seasoned IT professional with over 22 years of diverse industry experience, including healthcare and infrastructure companies, currently serving as a senior cloud architect for a hedge fund company, building and designing distributed systems. His passion lies in crafting innovative solutions, showcasing a commitment to lifelong learning. Beyond his professional endeavors, Kumar is an enthusiastic contributor to open source projects within the Cloud Native Computing Foundation and other cloud-native initiatives. In his free time, he actively supports cutting-edge solutions that drive the industry forward.

He has also worked on books such as *Implementing GitOps with Kubernetes*, *Cloud Native Development with Azure*, and *AWS Cloud Engineering Guide*.

I would like to thank my wife, Geethashri, and my parents, for the patience and support they provided during my review of this book.

Table of Contents

Preface xiii

Free Benefits with Your Book xix

Part 1: GenAI and Kubernetes Foundation

1

Generative AI Fundamentals 3

Artificial Intelligence versus GenAI 3
Evolution of machine learning 6
Transformer architecture 9
GenAI project life cycle 12
GenAI deployment stack 16
GenAI use cases 19
Summary 21
Appendix 1A – RNNs 22
Appendix 1B – Transformer mathematical models for the self-attention mechanism 23
Understanding the temperature parameter for GenAI use cases 24

2

Kubernetes – Introduction and Integration with GenAI 25

Understanding containers 25
Container terminology 27
Creating a container image 28
Why containers for GenAI models? 29
Building a GenAI container image 31
What is Kubernetes (K8s)? 36
Kubernetes architecture 37
Why K8s is a great fit for GenAI models 40
Summary 43
Appendix 43

3

Getting Started with Kubernetes in the Cloud 45

Advantages of running K8s in the cloud 46
Setting up a K8s cluster in the cloud 48
Prerequisites 51
Provisioning the Amazon EKS cluster 51
Deploying our first GenAI model in the K8s cluster 59
Summary 63

Part 2: Productionalizing GenAI Workloads Using K8s

4

GenAI Model Optimization for Domain-Specific Use Cases 67

Technical requirements 67
The need for domain-specific optimization 68
LLM model selection 69
The LangChain framework 69
Understanding RAG 71
How RAG works 72
Running a query 72
Model fine-tuning 76
Fine-tuning example 77
Summary 84
Further reading 85

5

Working with GenAI on K8s: Chatbot Example 87

Technical requirements 87
GenAI use cases for e-commerce 88
Experimentation using JupyterHub 89
Fine-tuning Llama 3 in K8s 96
Data preparation 97
Creating a container image 97
Deploying the fine-tuning job 99
Deploying the fine-tuned model on K8s 102
Deploy a RAG application on K8s 105
Deploying a chatbot on K8s 112
Summary 115

6

Scaling GenAI Applications on Kubernetes 117

Scaling metrics 117
Conventional metrics 118
Custom metrics 118
HorizonalPodAutoscaler (HPA) 119
VerticalPodAutoscaler (VPA) 122
Combining HPA and VPA 124
KEDA 124
Cluster Autoscaler (CA) 127
Karpenter 128
Summary 134

7

Cost Optimization of GenAI Applications on Kubernetes 135

Understanding the key cost components 135
Kubecost 136
Cost optimization techniques 140
Compute best practices 140
Networking best practices 144
Storage best practices 146
Summary 151
Join the CloudPro Newsletter with 44000+ Subscribers 152

8

Networking Best Practices for Deploying GenAI on K8s 153

Understanding the Kubernetes networking model 154
Selecting the CNI networking mode for GenAI applications 156
Service implementation in K8s 157
Service health checks 158
Advanced traffic management with a service mesh 160
Securing GenAI workloads with Kubernetes' network policies 162
Implementing network policies in a chatbot application 163
Service mesh versus K8s network policies 165
Optimizing network performance for GenAI 165
Kube-Proxy – IPTables versus IPVS 166
eBPF and SR-IOV 167
CoreDNS 168
Network latency and throughput enhancements 168
Summary 171

9

Security Best Practices for Deploying GenAI on Kubernetes 173

Technical requirements 173
Defense in depth 174
K8s security considerations 175
Supply chain security 176
Host security 179
Container runtime security 180
Network security 182
Secrets management 183
Additional considerations for GenAI apps 184
Data privacy and compliance 184
Secure model endpoints 188
Implementing security best practices in a chatbot app 189
Summary 195

10

Optimizing GPU Resources for GenAI Applications in Kubernetes 197

Technical requirements 198
GPUs and custom accelerators 198
Allocating GPU resources in K8s 200
Understanding GPU utilization 203
NVIDIA Data Center GPU Manager (DCGM) 203
GPU utilization challenges 206
Techniques for partitioning and sharing GPUs 207
NVIDIA MIG 207
NVIDIA MPS 209
GPU time-slicing 211
Scaling and optimization considerations 215
NVIDIA NIM 216
Summary 217

Part 3: Operating GenAI Workloads on K8s

11

GenAIOps: Data Management and the GenAI Automation Pipeline 221

Technical requirements 221
Overview of GenAI pipelines 222
GenAIOps on K8s 224
KubeFlow 224
MLflow 226
Argo Workflows 227
Ray 228
Deploying KubeRay on a K8s cluster 229
Comparing KubeFlow, MLFlow, and Ray 233

Data privacy, model bias, and drift monitoring 234
Methods to test bias and variance 234
Summary 238
Join the CloudPro Newsletter with 44000+ Subscribers 238

12

Observability – Getting Visibility into GenAI on K8s 239

Observability key concepts 239
Logs 240
Metrics 241
Traces 242
Monitoring tools in K8s 242
Fluentd and Fluent Bit 243
Loki 244
OpenTelemetry 245
Prometheus 246
Visualization and debugging 254
Grafana 254
LangChain observability 262
LangFuse 264
Summary 265

13

High Availability and Disaster Recovery for GenAI Applications 267

Designing for HA and DR 267
Resiliency in K8s 269
DR strategies in K8s 274
Additional K8s DR considerations 277
Summary 278

14

Wrapping Up: GenAI Coding Assistants and Further Reading 279

Technical requirements 279
GenAI-powered coding assistants 280
GenAI-powered observability and optimization 281
Amazon Q Developer walk-through with EKS 283
References for further reading 289
Summary 290
Stay Sharp in Cloud and DevOps – Join 44,000+ Subscribers of CloudPro 291

15

Unlock Your Exclusive Benefits 293

Index 297

Other Books You May Enjoy 314

Preface

Generative AI (GenAI) is revolutionizing the way organizations build intelligent systems by enabling machines to create content, code, text, images, and more. As demand for large-scale AI applications continues to grow, **Kubernetes (K8s)** has become the de facto platform to manage these workloads with scalability, resilience, and efficiency.

This book provides a comprehensive, hands-on guide for building, deploying, monitoring, and scaling GenAI applications on Kubernetes using Amazon EKS and other open source and cloud-native tools. From foundational concepts to advanced GPU optimization, the book addresses the lifecycle of GenAI projects with practical examples, deployment patterns, and industry best practices.

Who this book is for

This book is for the following people:

- Solution architects
- Engineering leaders
- DevOps engineers
- GenAI developers
- Product managers
- Students and researchers exploring GenAI and Kubernetes

You should have a basic understanding of cloud computing and AI/ML concepts. No prior experience with Kubernetes is required—the book provides a gradual learning curve through real-world examples.

What this book covers

Chapter 1, Generative AI Fundamentals, gives an overview of GenAI fundamentals, covering the distinction from traditional AI, the evolution of machine learning from CNNs/RNNs to transformers, outlines the GenAI project lifecycle, and explores diverse industry applications.

Chapter 2, Kubernetes – Introduction and Integration with GenAI, explores the challenges of running GenAI workloads at scale and why containerization and Kubernetes are ideal solutions. You will build and run your first GenAI container image locally.

Chapter 3, Getting Started with Kubernetes in the Cloud, introduces cloud-based Kubernetes deployment options and provides step-by-step guidance for setting up Amazon EKS using Terraform and deploying an LLM model.

Chapter 4, GenAI Model Optimization for Domain-Specific Use Cases, delves into optimizing general-purpose GenAI models for domain-specific applications, emphasizing techniques such as **retrieval-augmented generation** (**RAG**), fine-tuning, and the use of LangChain for enhanced performance and efficiency in tasks such as chatbots and personalized recommendations.

Chapter 5, Working with GenAI on K8s – Chatbot Example, demonstrates deploying and fine-tuning GenAI models on Kubernetes using Amazon EKS, exemplified by setting up Jupyter Notebook for experimentation, fine-tuning the Llama 3 model, and deploying a RAG-powered chatbot for personalized e-commerce recommendations.

Chapter 6, Scaling GenAI Applications on Kubernetes, explores various scaling strategies and best practices for Kubernetes applications, focusing on efficient resource utilization and optimal performance using HPA, VPA, KEDA, Cluster Autoscaler, and Karpenter.

Chapter 7, Cost Optimization of GenAI Applications on Kubernetes, explores cost optimization strategies for GenAI applications on Kubernetes, focusing on compute, storage, and networking. It emphasizes right-sizing resources, efficient storage management, and networking best practices, and introduces tools such as Kubecost and Goldilocks for monitoring and optimizing resource utilization.

Chapter 8, Networking Best Practices for Deploying GenAI on K8s, covers essential networking components such as CNI, Kubelet, and CRI, overlay and native networking methods, and delves into advanced features such as Service Mesh and NetworkPolicy to ensure secure, efficient, and scalable network performance.

Chapter 9, Security Best Practices for Deploying Gen AI on Kubernetes, provides a comprehensive framework for securing GenAI applications on Kubernetes through a defense-in-depth approach, covering critical security domains including supply chain, host, network, and runtime security, while also addressing secret management best practices and IAM.

Chapter 10, Optimizing GPU Resources for GenAI Applications in Kubernetes, explores strategies for maximizing GPU efficiency in Kubernetes for GenAI applications, discussing GPU resource management, partitioning techniques such as MIG and MPS, GPU monitoring, and auto-scaling solutions to optimize performance and cost.

Chapter 11, GenAIOps – Data Management and GenAI Automation Pipeline, introduces GenAIOps, detailing the tools and workflows for deploying, monitoring, and optimizing GenAI models, with a focus on data management, privacy, bias mitigation, and continuous model monitoring.

Chapter 12, Observability – Getting Visibility into GenAI on K8s, explains the importance of observability in monitoring GenAI applications on Kubernetes, detailing the use of Prometheus, Grafana, and NVIDIA DCGM to build a robust monitoring framework for real-time insights and debugging.

Chapter 13, High Availability and Disaster Recovery for GenAI Applications, explores high availability and disaster recovery strategies for GenAI applications on Kubernetes, detailing architectural patterns that enable automatic scaling and continuous service during outages. It covers redundancy approaches, key metrics (RPO, RTO, and MTD), and implementation strategies ranging from backup-restore to multi-region deployments.

Chapter 14, Wrapping up: GenAI Coding Assistants and Further Reading, highlights the transformative impact of GenAI coding assistants such as Amazon Q Developer, GitHub Copilot, and Google Gemini Code Assist to automate IaC, optimize workloads, and manage Kubernetes clusters. It also discusses AI-driven improvements in security, cost efficiency, and scalability, and provides a list of further reading resources for mastering Kubernetes and GenAI tools.

To get the most out of this book

You'll benefit most if you're familiar with basic programming (Python preferred), cloud fundamentals, and the concepts of machine learning. No in-depth Kubernetes experience is needed, as setup and configuration steps are covered in detail.

Software/hardware covered in the book	**Operating system requirements**
Operating system	Linux, macOS, Windows (via WSL)
Kubernetes	Amazon EKS, kind (for local testing)
AI/ML frameworks	Hugging Face Transformers, PyTorch, TensorFlow
Accelerators	NVIDIA GPUs, AWS Trainium/Inferentia
Observability	Prometheus, Grafana, OpenTelemetry, Loki
Automation	Kubeflow, MLflow, Ray, Argo Workflows
Security tools	OPA, Kyverno

You'll need the following:

- An AWS account with sufficient quota for EC2 instances (especially GPU nodes)
- Basic CLI tools (kubectl, eksctl, Terraform, and Helm)
- A Hugging Face account for model access

If you are using the digital version of this book, we advise you to type the code yourself or access the code from the book's GitHub repository (a link is available in the next section). Doing so will help you avoid any potential errors related to the copying and pasting of code.

Download the example code files

You can download the example code files for this book from GitHub at `https://github.com/PacktPublishing/Kubernetes-for-Generative-AI-Solutions`. If there's an update to the code, it will be updated in the GitHub repository.

We also have other code bundles from our rich catalog of books and videos available at `https://github.com/PacktPublishing/`. Check them out!

Conventions used

There are a number of text conventions used throughout this book.

`Code in text`: Indicates code words in text, database table names, folder names, filenames, file extensions, pathnames, dummy URLs, user input, and X/Twitter handles. Here is an example: "This can be achieved by adding the `service.beta.kubernetes.io/aws-load-balancer-nlb-target-type: ip` annotation to the K8s service, as shown here:"

A block of code is set as follows:

```
...
  metadata {
    name = "gp2"
...
```

When we wish to draw your attention to a particular part of a code block, the relevant lines or items are set in bold:

```
metadata {
    name = "gp3"
    annotations = {
      "storageclass.kubernetes.io/is-default-class": "true"
  ...
```

Any command-line input or output is written as follows:

```
$ terraform init
$ terraform plan
$ terraform apply -auto-approve
```

Bold: Indicates a new term, an important word, or words that you see onscreen. For instance, words in menus or dialog boxes appear in **bold**. Here is an example: "Select **Savings** from the left-hand side menu in the Kubecost UI console to view the cost savings recommendations."

> **Tips or important notes**
> Appear like this.

Get in touch

Feedback from our readers is always welcome.

General feedback: If you have questions about any aspect of this book, email us at `customercare@packtpub.com` and mention the book title in the subject of your message.

Errata: Although we have taken every care to ensure the accuracy of our content, mistakes do happen. If you have found a mistake in this book, we would be grateful if you would report this to us. Please visit `www.packtpub.com/support/errata` and fill in the form.

Piracy: If you come across any illegal copies of our works in any form on the internet, we would be grateful if you would provide us with the location address or website name. Please contact us at `copyright@packt.com` with a link to the material.

If you are interested in becoming an author: If there is a topic that you have expertise in and you are interested in either writing or contributing to a book, please visit `authors.packtpub.com`.

Share Your Thoughts

Once you've read *Kubernetes for Generative AI Solutions*, we'd love to hear your thoughts! Scan the QR code below to go straight to the Amazon review page for this book and share your feedback.

`https://packt.link/r/1-836-20993-2`

Your review is important to us and the tech community and will help us make sure we're delivering excellent quality content.

Stay Sharp in Cloud and DevOps – Join 44,000+ Subscribers of CloudPro

CloudPro is a weekly newsletter for cloud professionals who want to stay current on the fast-evolving world of cloud computing, DevOps, and infrastructure engineering.

Every issue delivers focused, high-signal content on topics like:

- AWS, GCP & multi-cloud architecture
- Containers, Kubernetes & orchestration
- Infrastructure as Code (IaC) with Terraform, Pulumi, etc.
- Platform engineering & automation workflows
- Observability, performance tuning, and reliability best practices

Whether you're a cloud engineer, SRE, DevOps practitioner, or platform lead, CloudPro helps you stay on top of what matters, without the noise.

Scan the QR code to join for free and get weekly insights straight to your inbox:

https://packt.link/cloudpro

Free Benefits with Your Book

This book comes with free benefits to support your learning. Activate them now for instant access (see the "*How to Unlock*" section for instructions).

Here's a quick overview of what you can instantly unlock with your purchase:

PDF and ePub Copies

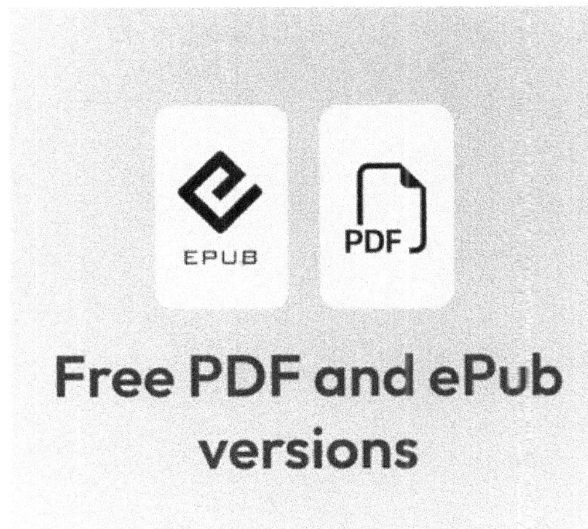

- Access a DRM-free PDF copy of this book to read anywhere, on any device.
- Use a DRM-free ePub version with your favorite e-reader.

Next-Gen Web-Based Reader

- **Multi-device progress sync**: Pick up where you left off, on any device.
- **Highlighting and notetaking**: Capture ideas and turn reading into lasting knowledge.
- **Bookmarking**: Save and revisit key sections whenever you need them.
- **Dark mode**: Reduce eye strain by switching to dark or sepia themes

How to Unlock

Scan the QR code (or go to `packtpub.com/unlock`). Search for this book by name, confirm the edition, and then follow the steps on the page.

Note: Keep your invoice handly. Purchase made directly from packt don't require one.

Part 1: GenAI and Kubernetes Foundation

This section introduces **Generative AI (GenAI)** fundamentals, tracing its evolution from traditional neural networks to transformers, and outlines the complete GenAI project life cycle. It explores how containers and Kubernetes address the challenges of GenAI workloads, and provides a guide to getting started with Kubernetes in the cloud.

This part has the following chapters:

- *Chapter 1, Generative AI Fundamentals*
- *Chapter 2, Kubernetes – Introduction and Integration with GenAI*
- *Chapter 3, Getting Started with Kubernetes in the Cloud*

1

Generative AI Fundamentals

Generative AI (GenAI) has revolutionized our world and has grabbed everyone's attention since the introduction of ChatGPT in November of 2022 by OpenAI (`https://openai.com/index/chatgpt/`). However, the foundational concepts of this technology have been around for quite some time. In this chapter, we will introduce the key concepts of GenAI and how it has evolved over time. We will then discuss how to think about a GenAI project and align it with the business objectives, covering the entire process for developing and deploying GenAI workloads, along with potential use cases across different industries.

In this chapter, we're going to cover the following main topics:

- Artificial intelligence versus GenAI
- The evolution of machine learning
- Transformer architecture
- The GenAI project life cycle
- The GenAI deployment stack
- GenAI project use cases

Artificial Intelligence versus GenAI

Before we dive deeper into GenAI concepts, let's discuss the differences between **Artificial Intelligence** (**AI**), **Machine Learning** (**ML**), **Deep Learning** (**DL**), and GenAI, as these terms are often used interchangeably.

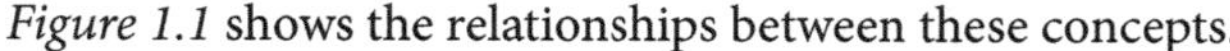

Figure 1.1 shows the relationships between these concepts.

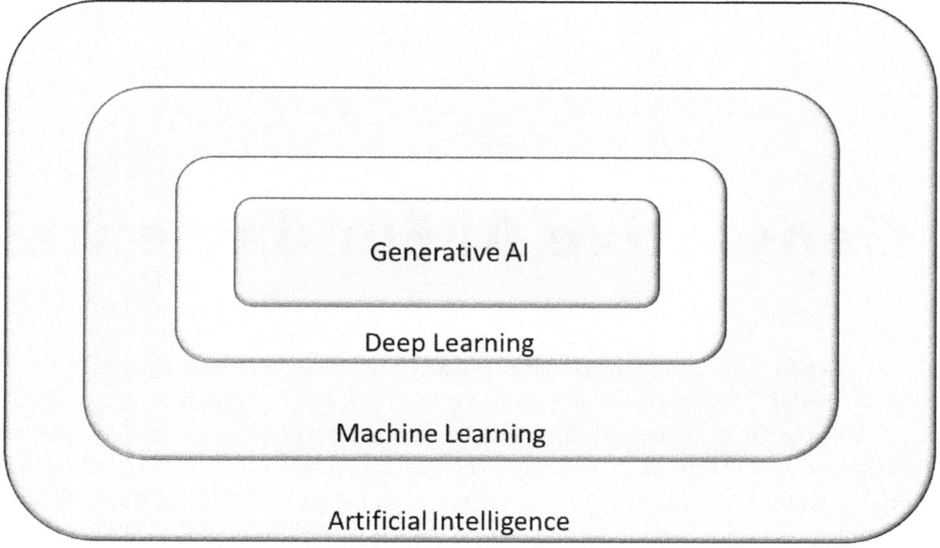

Figure 1.1 – Relationships between AI, ML, DL, and GenAI

Let's learn more about these relationships:

- **AI**: AI refers to a system or algorithm that is capable of performing tasks that would otherwise typically require human intelligence. These tasks include reasoning, learning, problem-solving, perception, and language understanding. AI is a broad category and can include rule-based systems, expert systems, neural networks, and GenAI algorithms. The evolution of AI algorithms has provided machines with human-like senses and capabilities, such as vision to analyze the world around them, listening and speaking to understand natural language and respond verbally, and using sensor data to understand the external environment and respond accordingly.
- **ML**: ML is a subset of AI that involves algorithms and models that enable machines to learn from data and make predictions without requiring explicit coding. In traditional programming, developers write explicit instructions for a computer to execute, whereas in ML, algorithms learn from the patterns and relationships in data and make predictions. ML can further be divided into the following sub-categories:
  - **Supervised learning**: This uses labeled datasets to train the models. It can further be subdivided into classification and regression problems:
    - **Classification problems** use labeled data, such as labeled pictures of dogs and cats, to train the model. Once the model is trained, it can classify a user-provided picture using the classes it has been trained on.

    - **Regression problems**, on the other hand, use numerical data to understand the relationship between dependent and independent variables, such as house pricing based on different attributes. Once a model establishes a relationship, it can then forecast the pricing for different sets of attributes, even if the model has not been trained on these specific attributes. Some popular regression algorithms are linear regression, logistic regression, and polynomial regression.

- **Unsupervised learning**: This uses ML algorithms to analyze and cluster unlabeled datasets to discover hidden patterns in data. Unsupervised learning can further be divided into the following two sub-categories:

    - **Clustering algorithms** group data based on similarities or differences. A popular clustering algorithm is the **k-means clustering algorithm**, which uses Euclidian distances between data points to measure the similarity between data points and assign them in *k* distinct, non-overlapping clusters. It iterates to refine the clusters to minimize the variance within each cluster. A typical use case is segmenting customers based on purchasing behavior, demographics, or preferences to target marketing strategies effectively.

    - **Dimensionality reduction** is another form of unsupervised learning, which is used to reduce the number of features/dimensions in a given dataset. It aims to simplify models, reduce computational costs, and improve overall model performance. **Principal Component Analysis** (**PCA**) (`https://towardsdatascience.com/a-one-stop-shop-for-principal-component-analysis-5582fb7e0a9c`) is a popular algorithm used for dimensionality reduction. It achieves this by finding a new set of features called components, which are composites of the original features that are uncorrelated with one another.

- **Semi-supervised learning**: This is a type of ML that combines supervised and unsupervised learning by leveraging both labeled and unlabeled data for training. This is particularly useful when obtaining labeled data is time-consuming and expensive because you can use small amounts of labeled data for training and then iteratively apply it to the large amounts of unlabeled data. This can be applied in both classification and regression use cases, such as spam/image/object detection, speech recognition, and forecasting.

- **Reinforcement learning**: In reinforcement learning, there is an agent and reward system, and algorithms learn by trial and error to maximize the reward for the agent. An **agent** is an autonomous system, like a computer program or robot, that can make decisions and act in response to its environment without direct human instructions. **Rewards** are given from the environment when agent actions lead to a positive outcome. For example, if we want to train a robot to walk without falling over, positive rewards are given for actions that help the robot to remain upright, and negative rewards are given for actions that cause it to fall over. The robot begins by trying different actions randomly, such as leaning forward, moving its legs, or shifting its weight. As it performs these actions, it observes the resulting changes in its state. The robot uses feedback (rewards) to update its understanding of which actions are beneficial and thus learns to walk over time.

We have summarized the different categories of ML in *Figure 1.2*:

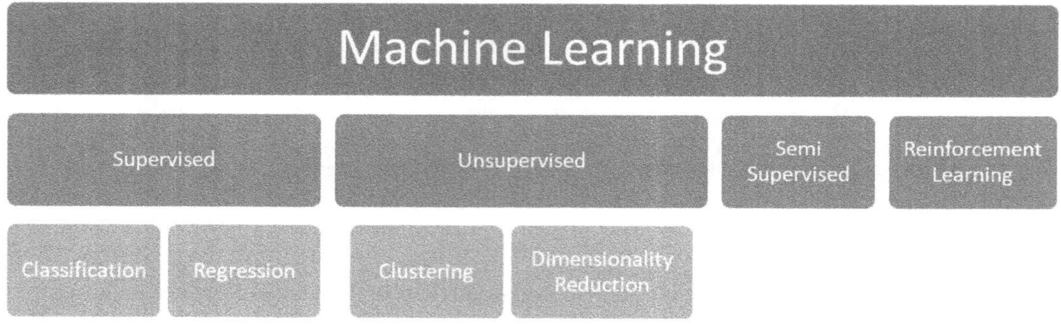

Figure 1.2 – Different categories of ML

- **DL**: DL is a subset of ML that involves deep neural networks with many layers. Conceptually, it is inspired by the human brain, which has billions of deeply connected neurons and provides humans with very advanced cognition. Some popular examples of deep neural nets are **Convolutional Neural Networks** (**CNNs**), used for image processing, and **Recurrent Neural Networks** (**RNNs**), which are used for analyzing time series data or natural language processing.
- **GenAI**: GenAI is a further subset of DL and focuses on creating new data, such as text, images, music, and other forms of content. Lots of generative applications are based on **Foundational Models** (**FMs**), which are large-scale AI models trained on vast amounts of diverse data, serving as a base for a wide range of downstream tasks. They are pre-trained on broad datasets and can be fine-tuned for specific applications. **Large Language Models** (**LLMs**) are a subset of FMs specifically designed for understanding and generating human language. GenAI is the primary focus of this book; we will be diving into its details later in the book.

Now that we understand the key differences between AI, ML, DL, and GenAI, let's explore the evolution of ML and how transformer architecture has revolutionized the ML landscape, particularly in the field of **Natural Language Processing** (**NLP**).

Evolution of machine learning

Since this book is about GenAI, what could be a better way to start it than asking ChatGPT to summarize the evolution of AI and ML over the last decade?

Prompt: `"Why did the chicken cross the road?" Describe how that question's answer evolved using AI/ML over the last decade.`

ChatGPT Response (ChatGPT-4o, June 16th, 2024):

```
The evolution of AI/ML responses to the question "Why did the
chicken cross the road?" over the past decade reflects significant
advancements in language processing and understanding. Here's a
detailed description of how these responses have evolved:
Early 2010s: Rule-Based Systems
```

```
Response Type: Traditional, rule-based
Example Answer: "To get to the other side."
Description: In the early 2010s, AI systems were primarily rule-
based. These systems relied on pre-defined patterns and rules coded
by developers. When asked "Why did the chicken cross the road?" the
AI would output the standard punchline "To get to the other side"
because it was programmed to recognize this classic joke and respond
accordingly. The response lacked creativity and was limited to what
was explicitly coded into the system.
Mid 2010s: Statistical and Early Machine Learning Models
Response Type: Basic machine learning-generated variations
Example Answer: "To find some food on the other side."
Description: As machine learning techniques began to develop, early
models could generate responses based on statistical patterns in
the data they were trained on. These models, such as simple neural
networks or early natural language processing (NLP) algorithms,
could create variations of the joke. However, the answers were still
relatively straightforward and sometimes nonsensical, as these models
had limited understanding of context and nuance.
Late 2010s: Advanced Neural Networks and NLP
Response Type: Context-aware and more sophisticated
Example Answer: "Because it wanted to explore the other side of the
road."
Description: The late 2010s saw the rise of advanced neural networks
and NLP (natural language processing) techniques, such as LSTM (Long
Short-Term Memory) networks and early transformer models. These models
had a better grasp of context and could generate more sophisticated
responses. They could recognize the structure of the joke but also
provide contextually appropriate variations that made sense and were
more engaging.
Early 2020s: Transformer-Based Models
Response Type: Highly fluent and creative
Example Answer: "To escape from the boredom of farm life and seek
adventure!"
Description: With the advent of transformer-based models like
GPT-3 and BERT, AI's ability to generate human-like text improved
dramatically. These models, trained on vast amounts of internet text,
could produce responses that were not only fluent but also creative
and contextually rich. They could understand humor better and generate
answers that went beyond the traditional punchline, incorporating more
complex wordplay or humor styles.
Present Day: LLMs and Personalization
Response Type: Personalized and contextually relevant
Example Answer: "Because its AI model predicted a 95% chance of
finding a better grain on the other side."
Description: Today's LLMs, such as GPT-4, are capable of highly
personalized and contextually aware responses. They can take into
account previous conversational history, the user's preferences, and
cultural context. The AI might generate responses that are tailored to
the individual user, offering a wide range of humorous and inventive
answers that reflect a deep understanding of language and context.
This level of personalization and creativity was unimaginable a decade
ago.
```

As can be seen from the preceding example, transformers revolutionized NLP by enabling parallel processing and improving scalability and efficiency; however, prior to transformers, deep neural networks, such as CNNs and RNNs, dominated the DL field since being introduced in the 1980s. Here are some brief descriptions of these neural networks:

- **CNNs** are similar in functionality to how our visual cortex functions. Our brain processes images from the retina by using specialized neurons that handle specific types of information or features. Similarly, the different filters in a CNN can detect various sets of features in an image or dataset. To learn more, refer to the paper by Yann LeCun et al. *Backpropagation Applied to Handwritten Zip Code Recognition* (`https://ieeexplore.ieee.org/document/6795724`), presented in 1989. CNNs are still commonly used for image analysis.
- **RNNs** are commonly used for sequences of data, or time series data, to analyze patterns and potentially forecast future events, such as analyzing historical stock market data to predict future trade options. RNNs are also frequently used in NLP, as natural language is a sequence of words where the order matters and can significantly impact the meaning.

  The concept of RNNs was introduced in the 1986 paper by *David Rumelhart, Geoffrey Hinton, et al., Learning representations by back-propagating errors (*`https://www.nature.com/articles/323533a0`*)*. This seminal paper introduced the concept of the backpropagation algorithm, based on the gradient descent concept, which is an essential technology for training neural networks and has revolutionized the entire AI field. In *Appendix 1A*, we have included a brief mathematical introduction to RNNs and their popular variants, such as **Long Short-Term Memory** (**LSTM**) networks and **Gated Recurrent Units** (**GRUs**).

In 2007, Fei-Fei Li, then a professor of Computer Science at Stanford University, started the ImageNet competition (`https://www.image-net.org/`), which included a massive dataset of images available on the internet that were labeled for training and testing. Every year, different AI/ML teams try to automate the prediction and improve the accuracy of their models using this training dataset.

Until 2011, the state-of-the-art technologies in the ImageNet competition were based on classical ML approaches, such as **Support Vector Machines** (**SVMs**), which tried to create an isolation plane between two different categories with the maximum margin in between. A breakthrough came with the introduction of AlexNet in 2012, developed by Alex Krizhevsky, Ilya Sutskever, and Geoffrey Hinton. This paper (`https://papers.nips.cc/paper_files/paper/2012/hash/c399862d3b9d6b76c8436e924a68c45b-Abstract.html`) won the ImageNet competition using deep CNNs and brought GPU programming to the forefront of AIML development.

- **Transformers**: In 2017, the transformer architecture was introduced by Vaswani et al. in their seminal paper *Attention Is All You Need* (`https://arxiv.org/abs/1706.03762`). It revolutionized NLP by enabling parallel processing and improving the scalability and efficiency of NLP. **Bidirectional Encoder Representations from Transformers** (**BERT**), developed by Google, significantly improved the understanding of context in language models. Since then, there have been lots of LLMs introduced by different companies, such as the GPT series by OpenAI and Claude by Anthropic.

Over the last two decades, ML has evolved from basic algorithmic models that were rule-based and dependent on manually curated features to advanced, context-aware models using deep learning frameworks such as neural networks and transformers. Let's take a closer look at the transformer architecture now.

Transformer architecture

A **transformer model** uses an **encoder-decoder** architecture, where the encoder maps the input sequences/tokens through a self-attention mechanism. This mapped data is used by the decoder to generate the output sequence. The mapping of input tokens retains not only their intrinsic values but also their context and weight in the original sequence. Let's go through some key aspects of the encoder architecture in the following figure:

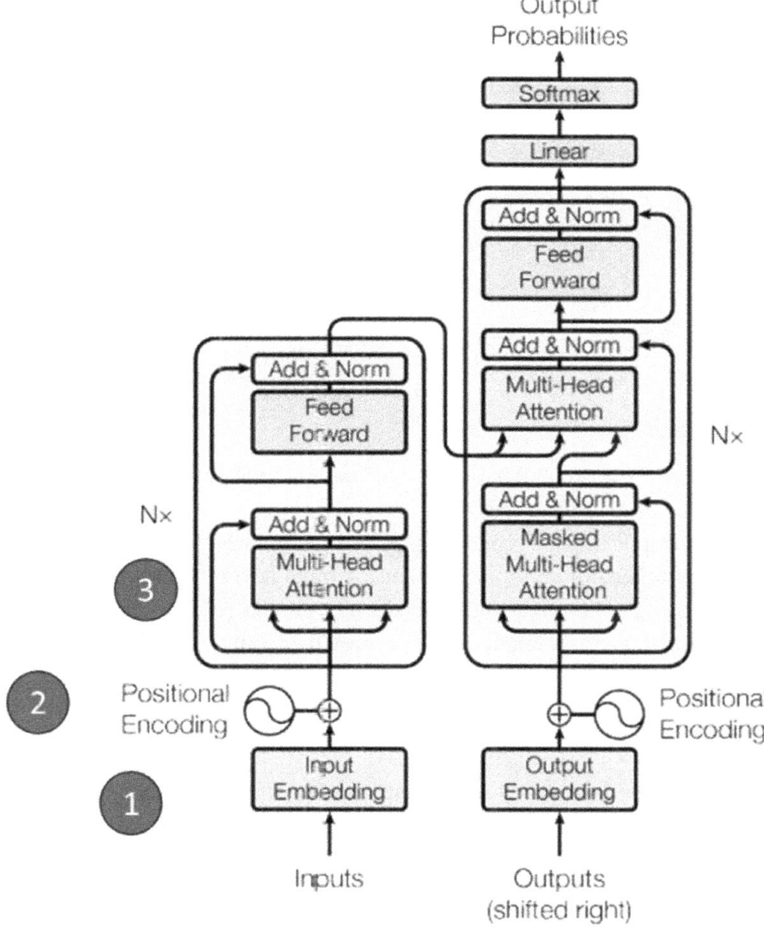

Figure 1.3 – Transformer architecture from the Attention Is All You Need paper

Here is a breakdown of the concepts highlighted in *Figure 1.3*:

- **Input embeddings**: Marked as **1** in the figure, this is a key part of the transformer model, which converts input sequences/tokens into high-dimensional vector embeddings. In real-world applications, output embeddings from a trained model may be stored in high-dimensional vector databases, such as Elasticsearch, Milvus, or PineCone. Vector databases help to find similar searches in high-dimensional space using either Euclidian distance or cosine similarity, and similar objects are assigned closer to each other in this high-dimensional vector space, as shown in the following figure.

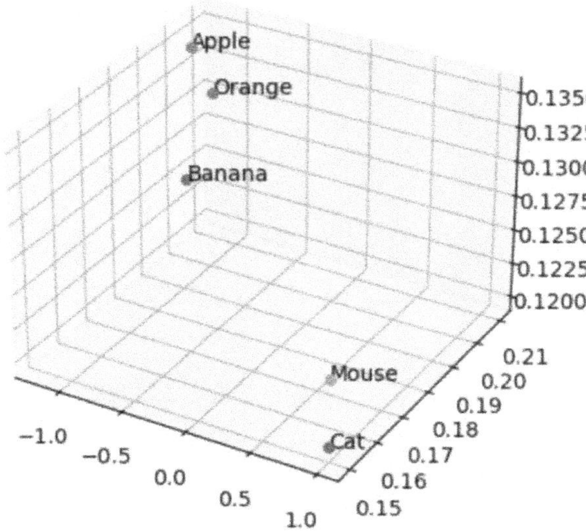

Figure 1.4 – Assignment of similar objects in high-dimensional space

- **Positional encoding**: Positional encoding, marked as **2** in *Figure 1.2*, provides information about the order of tokens in an input sequence. Unlike RNNs, which have the knowledge of time step *t* or the notion of the sequence, transformer models rely on self-attention mechanisms and lack awareness of intrinsic token order. Positional encoding injects sequential information into the token embeddings.

For example, if the input sequence is `The Brown hat`, here is how the mechanism would work:

- **Token embeddings**: Each word in the sentence is converted into a vector representation (embedding). Let's say we have these simple embeddings for demonstration:
  - `The` -> [0.1, 0.2]
  - `Brown` -> [0.3, 0.4]
  - `hat` -> [0.5, 0.6]

    - **Positional encoding vectors**: We generate positional encodings for each position in the sentence. Transformer models typically use sinusoidal functions for positional encoding, however for illustration purposes, let's use the following example:

        - **Position 0**: [0.01, 0.02]
        - **Position 1**: [0.03, 0.04]
        - **Position 2**: [0.05, 0.06]

    - **Adding positional encodings to token embeddings**: We add the positional encoding vectors to the token embeddings to incorporate positional information:

        - `The` + Position 0: [0.1, 0.2] + [0.01, 0.02] = [0.11, 0.22]
        - `Brown` + Position 1: [0.3, 0.4] + [0.03, 0.04] = [0.33, 0.44]
        - `hat` + Position 2: [0.5, 0.6] + [0.05, 0.06] = [0.55, 0.66]

    Now, each word has a unique vector that includes both the word's meaning and its position in the sentence.

- **Multi-head attention mechanism**: In a multi-head attention mechanism, marked as **3** in *Figure 1.2*, the model calculates the query, key, and value vectors for every I/P sequence and each attention head. A possible analogy for thinking about the multi-head attention mechanism is a team of detectives solving a very complex case, where each detective is an attention head. Every attention head has its own query vectors, which is an aspect of the case that a detective is focused upon, such as motive for the crime, weapon used, and so on. Finally, the key is the clues or pieces of evidence related to that given motive. So, if the query is the weapon used, the detective would investigate the crime scene for anything that could be used as a weapon, and the value would be the insights gained from each bit of evidence (e.g., fingerprints on a weapon). By having multiple attention heads, a model can focus on different parts of the input simultaneously, capturing various patterns or dependencies in the data, such as word meanings, words' relative positions, and sentence structures, similar to our analogy, where different detectives are focusing on different aspects of the case. Besides that, multi-head attention also allows the parallel processing of inputs, making it highly efficient and speeding up both training and inference by distributing them across different devices.

  In *Appendix 1B*, we cover the mathematical model and complexities of key-value pairs, as well as feed-forward networks and the concept of temperature in transformer models.

Now that we understand how transformer architecture has revolutionized DL by using an encoder-decoder framework that relies on self-attention mechanisms to enable the parallel processing of input data, let's explore a typical GenAI project life cycle.

GenAI project life cycle

Enterprise spending on GenAI projects has been growing exponentially since 2023, with c-suite executives planning to spend even more on GenAI projects (`https://www.gartner.com/en/newsroom/press-releases/2023-10-11-gartner-says-more-than-80-percent-of-enterprises-will-have-used-generative-ai-apis-or-deployed-generative-ai-enabled-applications-by-2026`). However, there is growing concern about how to quantify the **Return on Investment** (**ROI**) of these efforts, such as revenue impact, efficiency, and accuracy gains. Moving forward, ROI will become a critical part of the conversation, as enterprises look for new GenAI projects. So, before starting a new GenAI project, it is recommended to think about the entire project life cycle. In this section, we will be covering the project life cycle.

Let's first look at the following figure, which outlines the end-to-end GenAI project life cycle, starting from defining business objectives, or KPIs. This is followed by selecting or training FMs and optimizing them using techniques such as fine tuning and prompt tuning. Then, the model is evaluated, deployed, and continuously monitored to ensure that business goals are met.

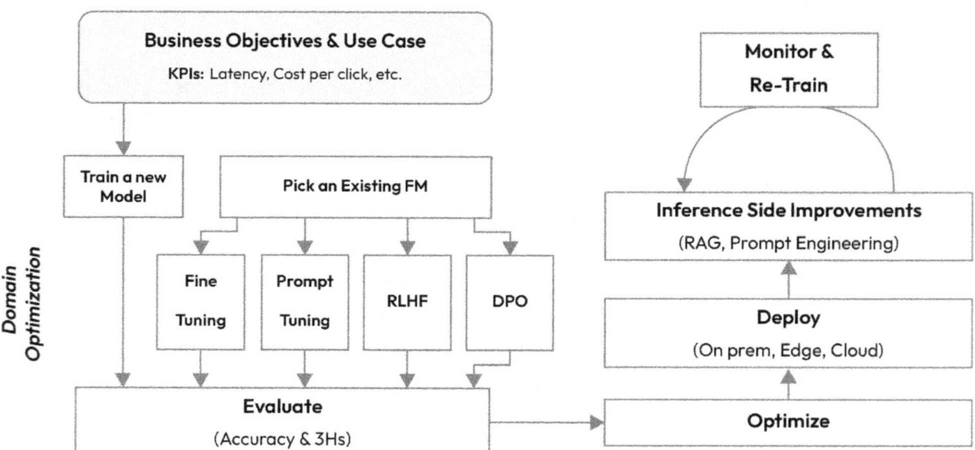

Figure1.5 – GenAI project life cycle

Let's take a closer look at each stage of the GenAI project life cycle:

- **Business objectives and FM selection**: The GenAI project life cycle starts with the business objective/problem statement we are trying to solve with GenAI. Business objectives could be increasing customer conversion or retention, creating personalized marketing campaigns, or creating a customer chatbox using enterprise internal data:
    - **Critical KPIs**: After the use case, the next consideration is business-critical KPIs, such as cost per inference. For example, if we are creating a personalized marketing campaign, we should ensure that the cost per customization is less than the product of the **Lifetime Value**

(**LTV**) of the customer and the probability of customer conversion. If the cost of inference is more than the business value the project is expected to deliver, the project might not have long-term sustainability. Other KPIs to think about could include latency, as sub-second response times might be needed for certain use cases or throughput, if a certain number of tokens is expected per second.

- **Selecting and training a FM**: The next step is to either pick an existing FM or train a new one. Training a new FM could be extremely resource intensive and cost billions of dollars and significant time, so in the majority of applications, it is better to pick an existing FM and do domain-specific optimization. When picking an existing model, you can select either an open source model or a proprietary model that can be accessed through web interfaces or over APIs, such as Claude or ChatGPT. It is always a good idea to check the licensing terms of these models to ensure that they meet application requirements and can scale with your enterprise needs.

- **Model optimization**: Once the FM is selected, the next step is to optimize the model for the business use case using techniques such as fine tuning, prompt tuning, Reinforcement Learning from Human Feedback (RLHF), and DPO:

  - **Fine tuning**: In fine tuning, a domain-specific labeled dataset with prompt and completion data is used to train the model for a specific domain or set of domains. Since all model weights can be updated in fine tuning, the compute requirements for fine tuning are similar to those for full training. However, the training time is smaller, as we are training the model on a smaller dataset. To reduce the training resources, there are options such as **Performance-Efficient Fine Tuning** (**PEFT**), which only updates a small set of weights and thus reduces the compute requirements. **Low Rank Adoption** (**LoRA**) is a very popular form of PEFT, where the original model matrix is reparametrized using a low-rank representation to significantly reduce the number of model parameters to be updated. As an example, in Vaswani's paper, each attention head has the dimensionality [512, 64], that is, 32,768 parameters to train per head. With LoRA, we train much smaller weight matrices to offer 80% or higher weight reduction. We will cover this topic in detail in *Chapter 4*. Another version of LoRA is **QLoRA** (**Quantized Lower Rank Adoption**). In QLoRA, we use quantization to compress the model weights from 32-bit precision to 8-bit or 4-bit precision, which dramatically reduces the model size and makes it easier to run on GPUs with less memory.

  - **Prompt tuning** is a low-cost technique where soft prompt tokens are added to the input query to optimize model performance for domain-specific tasks. These tokens are optimized as the model is retrained on the labeled domain-specific data. Unlike traditional fine tuning, which adjusts the model's parameters across numerous training iterations, prompt tuning focuses on refining the prompts to guide the model more effectively.

    - In **RLHF** (`https://huggingface.co/blog/rlhf`), human feedback is used to train LLMs to align with human preferences using RL techniques. In this approach, the LLM generates multiple responses to a variety of prompts, which humans evaluate and rank based on criteria such as accuracy, relevance, and ethical standards. Using the ranked responses, a reward model is trained to predict the human preference score for any given LLM response, and the LLM is fine-tuned using RL algorithms guided by the developed reward model.
    - In **Direct Preference Optimization** (**DPO**) (`https://huggingface.co/papers/2305.18290`), a policy is trained with a simple classification objective to best align with human preferences without using RL. Similar to RLHF, multiple outputs are generated by the LLM for a set of input prompts. Human evaluators compare these outputs in pairs and indicate which output they prefer. This creates a dataset of preference pairs, such as (Ap, Anp), where Ap indicates a preferred answer and Anp indicates a not-preferred answer. A loss function is then designed to maximize the probability that the preferred output is ranked higher than the less-preferred output as the LLM output. The model parameters are optimized to minimize this loss function over all collected preference pairs. This directly tunes the model to produce outputs that are more aligned with human preferences.
    - **Evaluation**: After the models are trained, you need to evaluate them for accuracy using metrics such as *ROUGE* (`https://huggingface.co/spaces/evaluate-metric/rouge`) or *BLEU* (`https://huggingface.co/spaces/evaluate-metric/bleu`), based on the use case:
        - **Bilingual Evaluation Understudy** (**BLEU**) measures how closely machine-generated text matches a set of reference texts. This metric was originally designed for machine translation and is also commonly used to evaluate text generation tasks, such as **n-grams** (contiguous sequences of *n* words) in generated text against reference texts.
        - **Recall-Oriented Understudy for Gisting Evaluation** (**ROUGE**) is a set of metrics used to evaluate the quality of summaries and translations generated by models. It compares the overlap between the generated text and a set of reference texts. ROUGE metrics are particularly popular in evaluating the performance of summarization systems.

Besides those metrics, developers should also evaluate generated responses against the **Honesty, Harmlessness, and Helpfulness** (**3H**) metric and ensure that training data is free of biases and harmful content.

- **Deployment optimization**: Once the model training/fine tuning is complete, the next step is to explore options to reduce the model size and optimize it for latency and cost. Some possible options are quantization, distillation, and pruning:
    - **Quantization**: In quantization, we can explore model precision tradeoffs, such as changing model weights from FP32 (floating point, 32 bit), which requires 4 bytes of memory per parameter, to FP16 or Bfloat16, which requires 2 bytes of memory per parameter, or even

Int 8, which requires only 1 byte per parameter. So, by moving from FP32 to Int8, we could reduce memory requirements by 4X; however, that could impact model accuracy. So, we need to evaluate model performance/accuracy to see whether these trade-offs are acceptable.

- **Distillation**: In distillation, we can train a student model with a smaller size than the original model by minimizing the distillation loss. The goal of distillation is to create a student model that approximates the performance of the teacher model, while being more efficient in terms of computational resources, such as memory and inference time.
- **Pruning**: In pruning, we try to reduce the size and complexity of a model by removing less important parameters, such as weights close to zero, while maintaining/improving the model's performance. The main goal of pruning is to create a more efficient model that requires fewer computational resources for inference and training without significantly affecting accuracy.

- **Deployment options**: Once the model is ready, the next choice is to pick the deployment options, such as cloud, on-premises, or hybrid approach. The selection depends on criteria such as hardware availability, cost, CapEx versus OpEx, and data residency requirements. Usually, cloud deployment offers the most simplicity due to the managed services and scalability; however, there could be data residency requirements, requiring either on-premises or hybrid deployments.
- **Inference size improvements**: After the model is ready and deployed, we can focus on imporving results on the inference side. Two options for this are **Retrieval Augmentation Generation (RAG)** and **prompt engineering**:
  - **RAG**: In RAG, we provide the model with relevant information and documents besides the prompt to fix knowledge cutoff issues. This technique provides real-time information within the prompt without the need for continuous model training, thus reducing the overall training costs. RAG combines the capabilities of retrieval-based models and generation-based models to improve the quality of text generation tasks. We will discuss RAG implementation in detail in *Chapter 4*.
  - **Prompt engineering**: In prompt engineering, we provide the model with some examples or context while asking a question. It could be zero-shot learning, where the model is given direct instructions without examples, such as `summarize this text`. In few-shot learning, the user includes a few examples within the input prompt, which helps the model learn the desired output format and style.

Once the model is deployed, we need to keep monitoring it to ensure that the model's results don't drift or get stale over time. We will explore model monitoring, performance, and drift in detail in *Chapter 11*.

In this section, we looked at the various stages of the GenAI project life cycle. It starts with defining the business objectives and KPIs, which is followed by model selection and various fine-tuning techniques. We evaluate model accuracy using metrics such as BLEU and ROGUE, and finally we deploy and continuously optimize the model. Now, let's look at the various layers of the GenAI deployment stack for deploying models.

GenAI deployment stack

As we discuss GenAI application development and deployment over Kubernetes, it is a good idea to understand the entire deployment stack, which can help us to think about the right infrastructure, orchestration platform, and libraries. The following figure shows the various layers of the GenAI deployment stack, from the foundational infrastructure layer comprising compute, storage, and networking through to the orchestration, tools, and deployment layers.

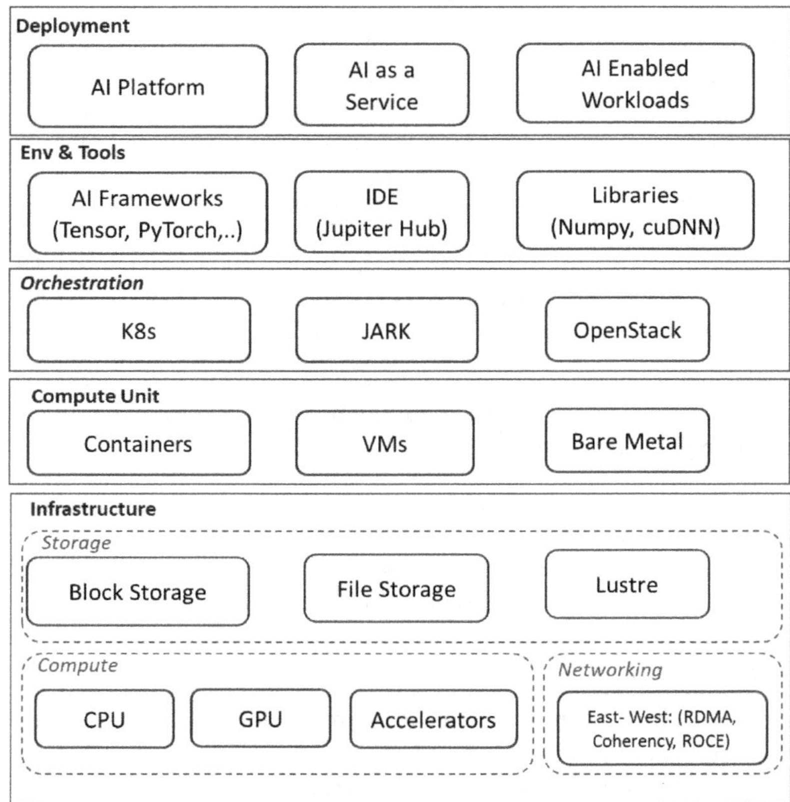

Figure1.6 – Deployment stack for GenAI applications

Let's a closer look at each of these layers:

- **Infrastructure layer**: We will start from the foundation layer of the stack and move upward. The foundation of this stack is the infrastructure layer, which covers compute, networking, and storage options:
    - **Compute**: For compute, we can use options such as CPUs, GPUs, custom accelerators, or a combination of these. As explained previously, LLMs are very computationally intensive.

GPUs offer massively parallel matrix multiplication capabilities and are mostly favored for training workloads. For inference, both CPUs and GPUs are used, but for LLMs with billions of model parameters, GPUs are often needed for inference as well. Besides CPUs and GPUs, there are custom accelerators, such as AWS Inferentia and Trainium, which are custom silicon chips specially designed for ML and highly optimized for mathematical operations.

- **Networking**: Networking is the next critical infrastructure component. For language models that are very large, both training and inference could become a distributed system problem. To explain this, let's look at recent LLM model trends:

Year	Model	Model Size (in billion parameters)
2018	BERT-L	0.34
2019	T5-L	0.77
2019	GPT2	1.5
2020	GPT3	175
2023	GPT4	Trillions

Table 1.1 – Evolution of GenAI model sizes

It's evident here that GenAI models are growing exponentially, and more parameters generally mean a more complex model that can capture more intricate patterns in data, thus requiring more computational resources for training and inference.

To clarify, if we say a model has 1 billion parameters, it usually refers to model weights after training has been completed. However, for training these models, we need the model weights, gradients, Adam Optimizers, activations terms, and some temporary variables throughout the training epochs (`https://huggingface.co/docs/transformers/v4.33.3/perf_train_gpu_one#batch-size-choice`).

So, during training, we might need to store up to *six parameters* per training weight, which could take up to 24 bytes at FP32 precision, 12 bytes at FP16 (or Bfloat16) precision, or 6 bytes at FP8 or Int8. Actual precision depends on the accuracy requirements versus the training cost.

Now, let's say we are training or fine tuning a 70B-parameter model, such as Llama3. It would require 840 GB (70B*12 bytes) of memory to store all the model weights and temporary variables with Bfloat16 or FP16 for precision. If we are using the latest NVIDIA H200 GPUs, which were introduced in 2024 and offer up to 141 GB of memory, we would still need about six GPUs to store these model parameters during training or full fine tuning, assuming the model is fully sharded.

In reality, the actual GPU count could be higher, if we would like to train these models in a reasonable time. This explains that East-West traffic, that is, the traffic flowing within the data center nodes or GPUs, could become a performance bottleneck for large model training or fine tuning. For this reason, non-blocking networking technologies such as **memory coherence** and **Remote Direct Memory Access** (**RDMA**) could help scale performance across nodes. RDMA is a technology that lets nodes in a distributed system access the memory of other nodes without involving either the core processor or operating system. Similarly, memory coherence technology ensures that all the caches in the system have up-to-date memory information and that write operations by one node to memory are visible to all the nodes/caches that are connected coherently. These two technologies result in lower latency and increased throughput for distributed training and fine-tuning problems.

- **Storage**: After networking, the next infrastructure choice is storage, with choices such as block storage, file storage, or Lustre. In a **block storage system**, such as Amazon S3, data is stored in data blocks. These block sizes range from 512 bytes to 64 KB, and multiple blocks can be accessed in parallel, which could provide higher I/O bandwidth. In a **file storage** system, data is stored in files and directories, making it easier to manage and structure the data. However, a file storage system creates an additional overhead of managing the file hierarchy and metadata. **Lustre** is a popular storage system that is now gaining traction for GenAI applications and has been in use for quite some time in high-performance computing. Lustre provides a massively parallel file storage system and can be scaled horizontally by adding more resources.

  If you are planning to store data in databases, you might choose SQL for fixed schema data or NoSQL databases for unstructured data, such as images and videos.

- **Compute unit**: After infrastructure, the next thing is to select the compute unit. The possible options are **bare-metal machines, Virtual Machines** (**VMs**), or **containers**. Containers pack all software dependencies, such as language runtimes and libraries, into an image, and multiple containers can share the same node/kernel. This allows much tighter bin packing or resource utilization as compared to VMs. For VMs, each VM requires a separate OS and runtime before the application can be deployed. Bare-metal machines are physical servers that are dedicated to a single tenant or customer, unlike VMs, which run on shared physical servers through a hypervisor.

- **Orchestration platform**: After compute unit selection, we choose the orchestration platform to manage the underlying infrastructure life cycle. This orchestration platform needs to be capable of scaling up or down based on workload demand and should be able to withstand network outages or hardware failures. **Kubernetes** (**K8s**) has emerged as a leading orchestration platform for containers and will be the primary focus in this book, as lots of leading companies, such as OpenAI (`https://openai.com/research/scaling-kubernetes-to-7500-nodes`) and Anthropic, are using it for their GenAI workload orchestration. OpenStack is an open source orchestration platform for VMs.

- **Frameworks**: After the orchestration platform comes the AI framework, such as TensorFlow or PyTorch. PyTorch **Fully Sharded Data Parallel** (**FSDP**) and TensorFlow distributed libraries allow model parameters and training data to be distributed across multiple GPUs and help the system to scale for large model sizes.
- **IDEs**: After orchestration, the next selection is what **Integrated Development Environment** (**IDE**) to use, such as JupyterHub, as well as what libraries to use, such as cuDNN, NumPy, or pandas, based on the infrastructure selection made earlier.
- **Endpoints**: Finally, the user can select the final deployment endpoint, such as offering models as an API, a platform, or a workload. Considering this stack for scalability, cost, latency, and disaster recovery could help users avoid very expensive rearchitecting once application use starts to scale. In our experience, data science teams often pick a simple architecture for proofs of concept, but these implementations sometimes don't scale well and are very expensive during deployment.

In this section, we discussed various layers of the GenAI deployment stack, from the foundational infrastructure layer to the high-level abstraction layer. We also looked at the challenges these models present as model sizes grow and the different ways to solve them. Let's take a look at GenAI use cases across industries.

GenAI use cases

GenAI is transforming all industries. As per McKinsey (`https://www.mckinsey.com/capabilities/mckinsey-digital/our-insights/the-economic-potential-of-generative-ai-the-next-productivity-frontier#key-insights`), it is expected to add trillions of dollars to the economy by 2030. The following are some of the industry verticals affected and use cases. It is by no stretch a comprehensive list, as the list of applications is growing very rapidly.

However, learning about some of these will give you an idea of the potential GenAI carries:

- **Retail/e-commerce**:
  - **Product design**: GenAI can be used with every stage of product design, such as summarizing market and user research, creating visuals/animations of possible product options, refining concepts based on user feedback, and creating product descriptions and marketing campaigns.
  - **Personalized recommendation**: GenAI can enable more natural engagement for e-commerce websites. Users can ask in natural language for product recommendations, such as `the best running shoes under $100 with red stripes`. GenAI can comprehend the user's request and provide recommendations accordingly.
  - **Review summarization**: GenAI can help summarize user reviews and overall sentiments, so users don't have to read through all the different reviews.

- **Finance**:
    - **Financial reporting/analysis:** GenAI can help create financial reports and summaries based on the data and trend analysis.
    - **Customer service**: GenAI can help with personalized marketing and chatbots to address user questions based on their data.
- **Healthcare**:
    - **Drug discovery**: GenAI models can predict how different drugs interact with various biological targets (proteins, enzymes, etc.) by analyzing existing interaction data. This can help in identifying promising drug candidates more efficiently. They can also propose novel molecular structures that have the potential to be effective drugs. These models can be further optimized for properties such as binding affinity, bioavailability, and toxicity.
    - **Personalized medicine**: LLMs can integrate and analyze diverse types of patient data, such as medical records, lab results, imaging data, and genetic information, to create comprehensive patient profiles and identify genetic biomarkers that predict a patient's response to particular treatments.
- **Education**:
    - **Personalized learning**: GenAI can help develop personalized learning paths, based on user journeys and responses.
    - **New language learning**: GenAI can help create personalized content and conversation examples.
- **Legal**:
    - **Document review and summarization**: GenAI can help automate the review and summarization of legal documents and prior similar cases for legal precedents.
    - **Contract generation**: GenAI can help create legal contracts based on the parameters provided.
    - **Customer interaction**: GenAI can help in developing chatbots for client inquiries and support.
- **Entertainment**:
    - **Content creation**: GenAI can help create scripts, music, artwork, and characters.
    - **Virtual reality**: GenAI can help create immersive VR environments and experiences.
    - **Personalized content**: GenAI can help in tailoring entertainment content and recommendations to individual preferences.

In this section, we looked at various GenAI use cases across different industries, from enhancing customer experience in retail to drug discovery and personalized medicine in healthcare. This is not an exhaustive list and it continues to grow as technology and models evolve.

Summary

In this chapter, we covered the differences between AI and GenAI. AI is a very broad term that refers to technologies that enable machines to emulate human intelligence and encompasses a broad range of applications, including GenAI, whereas GenAI specifically focuses on creating new content, such as text, images, and videos.

We then looked at the evolution of ML, understanding its progression from CNNs/RNNs to the transformer architecture introduced in 2017. Transformers have revolutionized AI with their ability to process sequences of data efficiently, making them fundamental to many GenAI applications, particularly in NLP.

The chapter also outlined the life cycle of a GenAI project, which includes business objectives and KPIs, foundational model selection, model training, evaluation, and deployment. Each stage is critical, with continuous iterations based on performance feedback.

Finally, the chapter covered various use cases of GenAI across different sectors, including retail/e-commerce, finance, healthcare, and legal, that can leverage GenAI for summarization, recommendation, and personalization. This exploration underscores the versatile and transformative potential of GenAI in augmenting human creativity and transforming our day-to-day lives. In the next chapter, we will introduce the concepts of containers, K8s, and cover how K8s can manage the deployment, scaling, and operations of containerized workloads We will also cover the specific advantages of using K8s in GenAI projects and what makes it attractive for GenAI applications.

Appendix 1A – RNNs

In this section, we will provide a basic overview of how RNNs work, including a mathematical explanation of their functionality. RNNs handle sequential data by maintaining a hidden state (or memory cell) that can capture information from previous time steps. The following is a very simplistic and mathematical representation of an RNN.

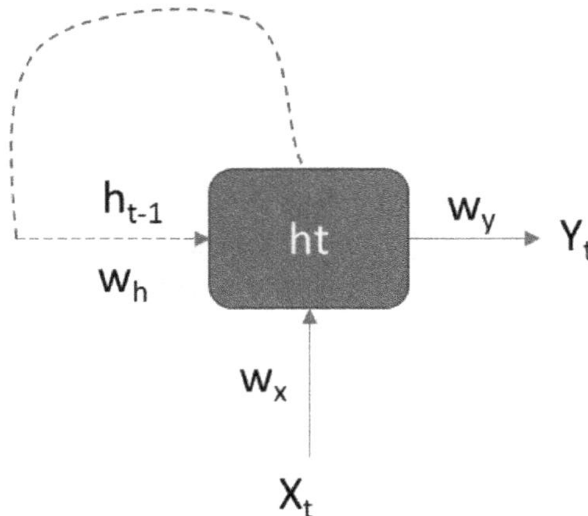

Figure 1.7 – Simple representation of an RNN

In this figure, **ht** represents the hidden state at a given time step **t** and can be presented as:

ht = f(wh * ht-1 +wx *Xt)

Where **wh** is the weight for the hidden stage and **ht-1** is the output of this hidden stage at step **t-1**. **Xt** is the input, **wx** is the weight of the input stage, and **f** is the activation function.

Output Yt = wy * ht + by

In RNNs, the output at time **t** depends upon the hidden stage, which includes the weighted output of the prior steps, such as **ht-1**, **ht-2**, and so on. This architecture can process inputs of any length, and the model size does not increase with the size of the input. However, this implementation is sequential in nature and can't be accelerated beyond a point through parallel processing.

There are four different types of RNN topologies:

- **Sequence-to-sequence RNN**: For this RNN topology, both input and output are a sequence, such as stock market analysis
- **Sequence-to-vector RNN**: This involves examples such as sentiment analysis by analyzing a statement or text
- **Vector-to-sequence analysis**: This includes practical scenarios, such as creating a caption from an image
- **Encoder-to-decoder**: This can be used for machine translation from one language to another

Significant advancements in RNNs came with the introduction of LSTM networks. LSTM networks addressed the problem of vanishing and exploding gradients in standard RNNs, making it possible to learn long-range dependencies in sequences more effectively. LSTM cells maintain separate short-term and long-term states. GRU is another optimization over LSTM and gives better training performance.

Appendix 1B – Transformer mathematical models for the self-attention mechanism

In this section, we will provide a basic overview of how the transformer model works, including a mathematical explanation of its functionality. We discussed the concepts of queues, keys, and values as part of transformer analysis earlier in this chapter. For a given attention head **i**, the following are the query, key, and value vectors:

$\mathbf{Q= X^{*}\, Wi^{Q}}$

$\mathbf{K= X^{*}\, Wi^{K}}$

$\mathbf{V= X^{*}\, Wi^{V}}$

Where W_i^Q, W_i^K, and W_i^V are the weight vectors for the attention head **i** for the query, key, and values. These weights are the parameters that we optimize as we train the model.

To understand the computational complexity of these calculations, let's look over the dimensionality of these vectors:

- $X= [n, d_{model}]$, where *n* is the number of tokens in the input sequence and d_{model} is the dimensionality of the multi-dimensional space.
- **Weight vectors**: $W_i^Q W_i^k W_i^v = [d_{model}, d_k]$, where $d_k = d_{model}$ / # of attention heads

In the *Attention Is All You Need* paper, d_{model} was 512 and the number of attention heads was 8, so d_k =512/8 =64.

During a forward pass, each of the Q, K, and V vector calculations would require ~262,144 multiplications (8*64*512) and 261,632 additions (8*64*511). During training, model goes through multiple forward and backward passes for each head across multiple sets of training data. This explains the complexity and compute resource requirements for these transformer models.

For each attention head, the attention score is calculated with the following equation:

$$\text{Attention}(Q, K, V) = \text{softmax}(\frac{QK^T}{\sqrt{d_k}})V$$

After computing the attention outputs for each head, they are concatenated to create multi-head attention, where W^o is the weight matrix for the output:

$$\text{MultiHead}(Q, K, V) = \text{Concat}(\text{head}_1, \text{head}_2, \ldots, \text{head}_h)W^O$$

This final output is then used in subsequent layers of the transformer model to perform various tasks, such as translation, text generation, or classification.

Understanding the temperature parameter for GenAI use cases

In the *softmax* function used as a part of the attention score, **temperature** refers to a parameter that controls the smoothness or sharpness of the probability distribution produced by the softmax function. Adjusting the temperature can influence how confident the model is about its prediction of the output:

$$\text{softmax}(z_i; T) = \frac{e^{z_i/T}}{\sum_{j=1}^{n} e^{z_j/T}}$$

Lower temperature settings make the softmax distribution sharper (more confident predictions), while higher temperatures make the distribution smoother (less confident predictions) and could lead to more creative responses.

The following is a sample response from ChatGPT for two temperature settings with the input prompt of `What is the purpose of Life?`

Temperature = **2.0**:

```
The purpose of life is like an ever-changing kaleidoscope, bursting
with colors and patterns that shift with every moment. For some,
it's about weaving tales of adventure and discovery, chasing after
the mysteries that lie just beyond the horizon. For others, it's the
serene pursuit of inner peace, finding harmony in the gentle ebb and
flow of existence.
```

Temperature = 0.75:

```
The purpose of life is a question that has intrigued humanity for
centuries, and it can be seen from various perspectives. For many,
the purpose of life is to seek happiness and fulfillment, to find and
pursue passions that bring joy and meaning. This can involve forming
deep connections with family and friends, contributing to the well-
being of others, and making a positive impact on the world.
```

2

Kubernetes – Introduction and Integration with GenAI

Deploying and managing GenAI workloads at scale presents significant challenges, including building the models, packaging them for distribution, and ensuring effective deployment and scaling. In this chapter, we will discuss the concepts of containers and **Kubernetes** (**K8s**) and why they are emerging as powerful solutions to address these complexities. They are becoming the de facto standard for companies such as OpenAI (`https://openai.com/index/scaling-kubernetes-to-7500-nodes/`) and Anthropic (`https://youtu.be/c9NJ6GSeNDM?si=xjei4T9VfZvejD5o&t=2412`) to deploy GenAI workloads. We will cover the following main topics:

- Understanding containers
- Why containers for GenAI models
- What is Kubernetes (K8s)?

Understanding containers

Containers have revolutionized the way we manage applications by standardizing the packaging format. With the portability of containers, applications are packaged as a standard unit of software that packages all of your code and dependencies to deploy consistently and reliably across various environments, such as on-premises, public, and private clouds. Containers are also considered an evolution of **Virtual Machine** (**VM**) technology, where multiple containers are run on the same operating system, sharing the underlying kernel to increase the overall server utilization. This is a massive advantage of containers as there is no overhead of multiple **Operating Systems** (**OSes**) and other OS-level components. So, containers can be started and stopped a lot faster while providing isolation.

The following figure illustrates the evolution of computing environments, highlighting a shift toward higher levels of abstraction and an increased focus on business logic.

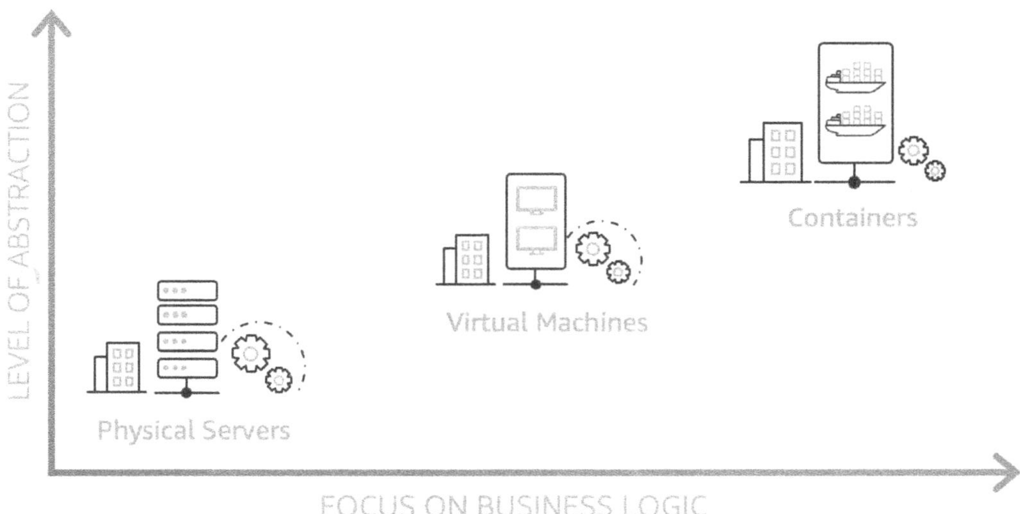

Figure 2.1 – Evolution of container technology

Physical servers offer the least abstraction, with extensive manual configuration, and resource inefficiencies. VMs provide a middle ground, by abstracting underlying hardware resources using hypervisor technology. This allows you to run multiple VMs on the same physical server, increasing the resource utilization and security. However, they are bulky and slow to boot up. Containers provide the highest level of abstraction by encapsulating applications and dependencies in portable units, allowing us to focus more on developing and optimizing business logic rather than managing infrastructure. *Figure 2.2* illustrates the high-level differences between VMs and containers.

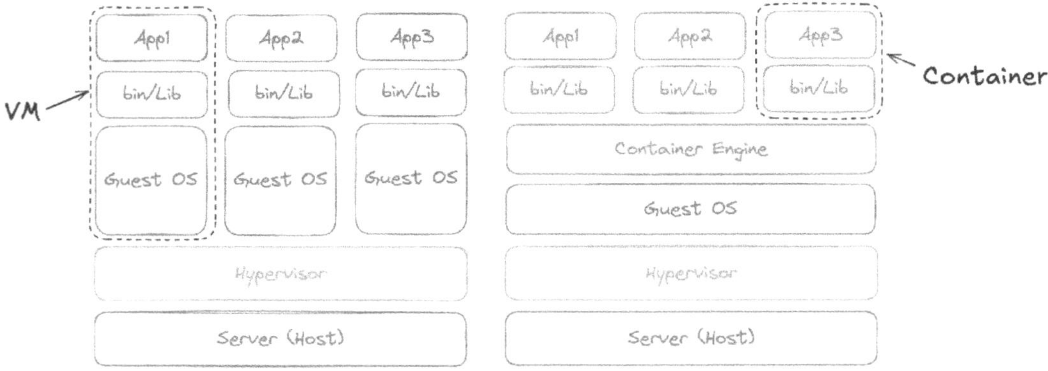

Figure 2.2 – Virtual machines versus containers

Container technology is made possible because of namespaces and cgroups (control groups) in the Linux kernel. They form the foundational building blocks to provide isolation and resource limits. A **Linux Namespace** (`https://man7.org/linux/man-pages/man7/namespaces.7.html`) is an abstraction over resources in the operating system. It partitions OS-level resources such that different sets of processes see a different set of resources (network, file system, etc.,) even though they are running on the same OS kernel. **Cgroups** (`https://man7.org/linux/man-pages/man7/cgroups.7.html`) govern the isolation and usage of system resources, such as CPU, memory, and network, for a group of processes and optionally enforce limits and constraints. These capabilities let containers abstract the operating system components for modern applications.

Container terminology

The following are some terms associated with containers that will be crucial in following along with this book:

- **Container runtime**: This is a host-level process that is responsible for creating, stopping, and starting containers. It interacts with low-level container runtimes such as runc to set up namespaces and cgroups for containers. Popular examples include containerd, CRI-O, and so on.
- **Container image**: This is a lightweight, standalone, executable package that includes everything needed to run a piece of software, including the code, runtime, libraries, environment variables, and configuration files. It is created using a Dockerfile, a plain text definition file that includes a set of instructions to install dependencies, applications, and so on. Typical characteristics of a container image include the following:
    - **Self-contained**: It encapsulates everything needed to run software applications.
    - **Immutable**: It is read-only in nature; any changes would require a new image.
    - **Layered**: Images are built in layers, each layer representing a file system. This is what makes images highly efficient as common layers can be shared across multiple images.
    - **Portable**: As the image packages the application and all its dependencies, they can be run on any system that supports a container runtime, making them highly portable in nature.
- **Container registry**: This is a tool used to manage and distribute container images. Popular registries include Docker Hub (`https://hub.docker.com/`), Amazon Elastic Container Registry (`https://aws.amazon.com/ecr/`), Google Artifact Registry (`https://cloud.google.com/artifact-registry`), and so on. Tools such as Artifactory and Harbor can be used to self-host a registry.
- **Container**: This is a running instance or process created from the container image by the container runtime.

Let's now understand the high-level container workflow using Docker, a software platform designed to help developers build, share, and run container applications. Docker follows traditional client-server architecture. When you install Docker on a host, it runs a server component called the Docker daemon and a client component – the Docker CLI. The **Daemon** is responsible for creating and managing images, running containers using those images, and setting up networking, storage, and so on. As depicted in *Figure 2.3*, the Docker CLI is used to interact with the Docker daemon process to build and run containers. Once the images are built, the Docker daemon can push and pull those images to/from a container registry. Storing the images in a container registry allows them to be portable and they can be run anywhere a container runtime is available.

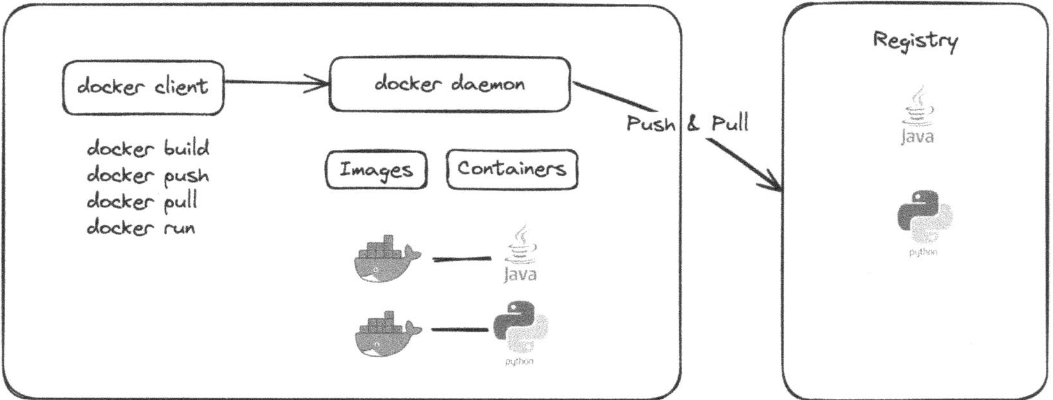

Figure 2.3 – Docker architecture overview

Creating a container image

Let's create our first hello world container image and run it locally. Use the Docker documentation page at `https://docs.docker.com/engine/install/` to install Docker Engine on your machine. The following are the links to install Docker Desktop for different operating systems:

- Docker Desktop for Linux: `https://docs.docker.com/desktop/install/linux-install/`
- Docker Desktop for Mac (macOS): `https://docs.docker.com/desktop/install/mac-install/`
- Docker Desktop for Windows: `https://docs.docker.com/desktop/install/windows-install/`

In the following Dockerfile, we are creating a simple hello world application using the `nginx` server. We will use `nginx` as the parent image and customize the `index.html` with our *Hello World!* message. Let's start by following these steps:

1. Create a Dockerfile with the following content:

```
FROM nginx
RUN echo "Hello World!" > /usr/share/nginx/html/index.html
```

2. Build a container image with a `v1` tag:

```
$ docker build -t hello-world:v1 .
```

   You can list the local container images using the following command:

```
$ docker images
REPOSITORY      TAG         IMAGE ID        CREATED         SIZE
hello-world     v1          7a5469eb898f    2 mins ago      273MB
```

3. Run a container using the `hello-world` image and bind nginx port `80` to the `8080` host port:

```
$ docker run -p 8080:80 hello-world:v1
```

4. Now that we have the image running, we can test the container by calling localhost `8080`:

```
$ curl http://localhost:8080/
Hello World!
```

As an optional step, you can also push the container image to an `xyz` container registry so that you can run it anywhere. Replace `xyz` with your container repository name. For example, follow the instructions at `https://www.docker.com/blog/how-to-use-your-own-registry-2/` to create the registry in Docker Hub:

```
$ docker tag hello-world:v1 xyz/hello-world:v1
$ docker push xyz/hello-world:v1
```

In this section, we learned about the evolution of computing environments, the benefits of using containers over traditional physical servers, and VMs. We gained an understanding of the overall Docker architecture and various key container terminology and built and ran our first hello-world container application. Let's explore why containers are a great fit for GenAI models.

Why containers for GenAI models?

A typical challenge with developing ML or GenAI applications involves using complex and continuously evolving open source ML frameworks such as PyTorch and TensorFlow, ML tool kits such as Hugging Face Transformers, ever-changing GPU hardware ecosystems from NVIDIA, and custom accelerators from Amazon, Google, and so on.

The following figure illustrates various components involved in creating and running an ML or GenAI container.

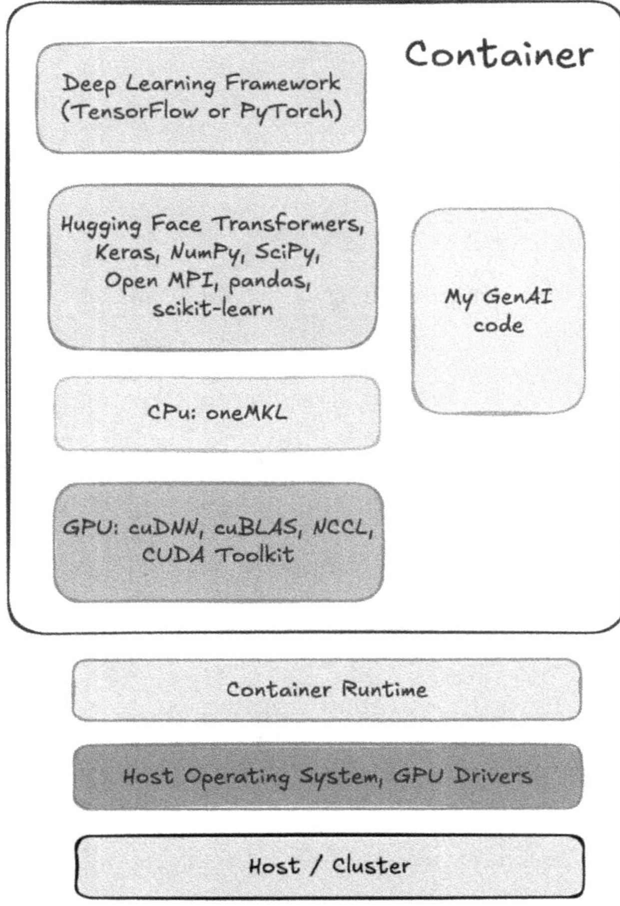

Figure 2.4 – A typical GenAI container image

At the top layers, the container encapsulates various software libraries, deep learning frameworks, and user-supplied code. The next set of layers contains hardware-layer-specific libraries to interact with GPUs or custom accelerators on the host. The container runtime can be used to launch the containers from the container image. Let's dive into the significant benefits of using containers for GenAI workloads:

- **Dependency management**: This could become crucial due to evolving frameworks and interdependencies on specific versions. With containers, we can encapsulate the GenAI application code and its dependencies in a container image and use it on a developer machine or in the test/production environment consistently.

- **Resource access**: GenAI/ML apps are computationally intensive, need access to single or multiple GPUs or custom accelerators, and adjust resource allocations dynamically based on the workload demand. Containers allow for fine-grained control over resource allocation, enabling efficient utilization of the available resources and avoiding noisy neighbor situations. Containers can also be scaled horizontally or vertically to handle increased demand in the applications.
- **Model versioning and updates**: Managing different versions of the model and keeping respective dependencies up to date without disrupting applications could be challenging. With containers, different images can be created and versioned, making it easy to track changes, manage different model versions, and seamlessly execute rollbacks if needed. We will also explore how to use container orchestration engines to automate these updates later, in *Chapter 11*.
- **Security**: Protecting data during the training and inference stages is crucial when developing GenAI apps. With containers, we can enforce strict access controls and policies for data access, minimize the attack surface by including only the necessary components in the container image, and they also provide a layer of isolation between the containers and the underlying host.

By providing isolated, consistent, and reproducible environments, containers can simplify dependency management, optimize resource efficiency, streamline model deployments, and improve overall system security. Container technology comprehensively addresses all challenges presented by GenAI application development, thus making it a de facto choice.

Building a GenAI container image

Let's get a first-hand experience of building our first GenAI container image and deploying it locally. To get started, we will download the model files from **Hugging Face** (`https://huggingface.co/`), an AI/ML platform that helps users build, deploy, and test machine learning models. Hugging Face operates the **Model Hub**, where developers and researchers can share thousands of pre-trained models. It also supports various frameworks, including TensorFlow, PyTorch, and ONNX.

In this walk-through, we will take one of the popular open source models, **Llama 2** (`https://llama.meta.com/llama2/`), by **Meta**. However, you have to read and comply with the terms and conditions of the model. Navigate to the Hugging Face Llama model page (`https://huggingface.co/meta-llama/Llama-2-7b`) to request access to the model. The Llama 2 model comes in multiple sizes: 7B, 13B, and 70B where B stands for billion parameters. The bigger the size of the model, the greater the resources needed to host it. Given not all personal laptops are equipped with specialized hardware such as GPUs, we will be using the CPU version of the Llama 2 model. This was made possible because of **llama.cpp** (`https://github.com/ggerganov/llama.cpp`), an open source project aimed at providing an efficient and portable implementation of Llama models. It enables us to deploy these models on various platforms, including personal computers, without requiring GPUs. llama.cpp applies a custom quantization approach to compress the models in a GGUF format, to reduce the size and resource requirements.

An inference endpoint is created using the **Python Flask API** (`https://flask.palletsprojects.com/`), which provides an HTTP POST API on port `5000` and accepts a JSON request with an input prompt, system message, and so on. Input parameters are then passed to the Llama model and model output is returned in the JSON format. Let's begin the process:

1. Install the pre-requisites:
   - `huggingface-cli` from `https://huggingface.co/docs/huggingface_hub/en/installation`
   - `jq` from `https://jqlang.github.io/jq/download/`
   - **Docker Engine** from `https://docs.docker.com/engine/install/`
2. Authenticate to the Hugging Face platform by following the instructions at `https://huggingface.co/docs/huggingface_hub/en/guides/cli`.
3. Download the Llama 2 model using `huggingface-cli`:

```
$ huggingface-cli download TheBloke/Llama-2-7B-Chat-GGUF llama-
2-7b-chat.Q2_K.gguf --local-dir . --local-dir-use-symlinks False
```

4. The following message is displayed when the model download is complete:

```
$ Download complete. Moving file to llama-2-7b-chat.Q2_K.gguf
llama-2-7b-chat.Q2_K.gguf
```

5. Create an `app.py` with our Flask code. This code block sets up a Python Flask app with a single route, `/predict`, that accepts HTTP POST requests. It uses the `llama_cpp` library to load the Llama 2 model, generates a response based on the input prompt and system message from the request, and returns the model's response as a JSON object. You can download the `app.py` code from GitHub at `https://github.com/PacktPublishing/Kubernetes-for-Generative-AI-Solutions/blob/main/ch2/app.py`:

```
from flask import Flask, request, jsonify
import llama_cpp

app = Flask(__name__)
model = llama_cpp.Llama("llama-2-7b-chat.Q2_K.gguf")

@app.route('/predict', methods=['POST'])
def predict():
    data = request.json
    prompt = f"""<s>[INST] <<SYS>>{data.get('sys_msg', '')}<</
SYS>>{data.get('prompt', '')} [/INST]"""
    response = model(prompt, max_tokens=1000)
    return jsonify({'response': response})
```

```
if __name__ == '__main__':
    app.run(host='0.0.0.0', port=5000)
```

6. Create a Dockerfile that packages the Python source code, Llama 2 model, and other dependencies. You can download the Dockerfile code from GitHub at `https://github.com/PacktPublishing/Kubernetes-for-Generative-AI-Solutions/blob/main/ch2/Dockerfile`:

```
# Use an official Python runtime as a parent image
FROM python
# Set the working directory
WORKDIR /app
# Expose the application on port 5000
EXPOSE 5000
# Define environment variable
ENV FLASK_APP=app.py
# Install any needed packages specified in requirements.txt
RUN pip install --no-cache-dir flask llama-cpp-python
# Copy the current dir contents into the container at /app
COPY . /app
# Run app.py when the container launches
CMD ["python", "app.py"]
```

7. Build the container image:

```
$ docker build -t my-llama .
```

8. Run the container and bind the Flask API server to host port `8000`:

```
$ docker run -p 8000:5000 my-llama
```

9. Invoke the Llama 2 model by using `curl`:

```
$ curl -X POST http://localhost:8000/predict -H "Content-Type: application/json" -d '{"prompt":"Create a poem about humanity?","sys_msg":"You are a helpful, respectful, and honest assistant. Always provide safe, unbiased, and positive responses. Avoid harmful, unethical, or illegal content. If a question is unclear or incorrect, explain why. If unsure, do not provide false information."}' | jq .
```

This will run the inference against our local `my-llama` container and return the following LLM response:

```
......
Of course, I'm here to assist you with a safe and positive response!
Here's a poem about humanity:

Humanity, oh humanity, so diverse and wide,
A mix of cultures, beliefs, and ideals inside.
```

```
We may come from different places, with different views,
But beneath our differences, we share a common brew.
......
So here's to humanity, in all its grace and might,
A masterpiece of diversity, a work of art in sight.
Let us cherish each other, with kindness and respect,
And create a world where love is the only text.
```

The input request contains two key attributes:

- **Prompt**: Input to the LLM
- **System message**: To set the context and guide the behavior of the LLM during the request

Optionally, we can pass additional attributes such as `max_tokens` to limit the length of the generated output.

If you notice the size of the image we built, it will be around 7+ GB. That is mainly attributed to the model file and other dependencies. We will explore techniques for reducing the size of the image and optimizing the container startup time later, in *Chapter 9*.

It was easy to create and run a single container instance on our local computer. Just imagine operating hundreds or thousands of these containers running across hundreds or thousands of VMs, and making sure these containers are highly available, scalable, load balanced, managing resource allocations, and implementing automated deployments and rollbacks. This is where **Container Orchestrators** come to the rescue.

Container orchestrators play a pivotal role in modern software development and deployment, addressing all the preceding concerns and managing containerized applications at scale. Some of their key benefits are as follows:

- **High availability and fault tolerance**: They continuously monitor the health of the containers at regular intervals and automatically restart/replace failed containers, thus ensuring the desired number of containers are always up and running.
- **Scaling**: They enable automatic scaling of the applications to match the user load/demand. Container instances are automatically created and removed in response to the application load. As applications are scaled, underlying compute resources are also scaled to accommodate the new containers.
- **Automated deployments**: They automate the deployment of containerized applications across multiple hosts and rollbacks in case of any failures. We can also implement advanced traffic routing patterns such as canary releases and blue/green deployments to safely roll out new changes.
- **Load balancing**: They provide built-in load balancing to distribute incoming traffic across multiple container instances, improving performance and reliability. They can also integrate with external load-balancing solutions to load-balance the traffic.

- **Service discovery**: As containers are ephemeral in nature, orchestrators provide service discovery features to dynamically discover the container endpoints to facilitate inter-service communication. They also manage the container networking, including IP address management, DNS resolution, and network segmentation.
- **Observability**: They can integrate with monitoring and logging tools, providing visibility into the health and performance of containerized applications.
- **Resource management and advanced scheduling**: They can also manage the resource allocation for the containers, including CPU, memory, GPUs, and so on. They enforce the resource limits and reservations, preventing noisy neighbor situations. Advanced scheduling policies can be used to schedule the applications with special hardware needs such as GPUs to the specific hosts.

Now that we understand the need for a container orchestrator, the next question is which orchestrator should we pick? There are a number of different open source and proprietary orchestrators on the market. Some notable ones are the following:

- **Amazon Elastic Container Service** (`https://aws.amazon.com/ecs/`)
- **Azure Container Apps** (`https://azure.microsoft.com/en-us/products/container-apps`)
- **Docker Swarm** (`https://docs.docker.com/engine/swarm/`)
- **Apache Mesos** (`https://mesos.apache.org/`)
- Kubernetes (`https://kubernetes.io/`), and managed Kubernetes offerings such as **Amazon Elastic Kubernetes Service** (`https://aws.amazon.com/eks/`)
- **Google Kubernetes Engine (GKE)** (`https://cloud.google.com/kubernetes-engine`)
- **Azure Kubernetes Service (AKS)** (`https://azure.microsoft.com/en-us/products/kubernetes-service`)
- **Red Hat OpenShift** (`https://www.redhat.com/en/technologies/cloud-computing/openshift`)

In this section, we learned about the typical challenges of building GenAI models and how we can use container technology to package GenAI code/models, AI/ML frameworks, hardware-specific libraries, and other dependencies into an image for consistency, reusability, and portability. We also built our first GenAI container image using the open source Llama 2 model and ran inference by deploying it locally. Finally, we discussed the challenges of managing containerized applications at scale and how container orchestrators such as K8s can solve those. In the next section, let's dive into K8s and its architecture, and why it is a great fit to run GenAI models.

What is Kubernetes (K8s)?

Kubernetes, commonly referred to as K8s, is an open source container orchestration platform that automates the deployment, scaling, and management of containerized applications. It is the most widely used container orchestration platform (`https://www.cncf.io/reports/kubernetes-project-journey-report/`) and has become the de facto choice for many enterprises to run a wide variety of workloads.

Originally developed by Google engineers Joe Beda, Brendan Burns, and Craig McLuckie in 2014 and now maintained by the **Cloud Native Computing Foundation** (**CNCF**), its name came from the Ancient Greek for a pilot or helmsman (the person at the helm who steers the ship). It has become the second largest open source project in the world, after Linux, and is the primary orchestrator tool for 71% of Fortune 100 companies (`https://www.cncf.io/reports/kubernetes-project-journey-report/`). According to Gartner's *The CTO's Guide to Containers and Kubernetes* (`https://www.gartner.com/en/documents/5128231`), by 2027, more than 90% of global organizations will be running containerized applications in production.

Some notable factors in K8s becoming so popular are as follows:

- **Rich community and ecosystem**: With 77K+ contributors from 44 different countries and contributed to by 8K+ companies, K8s has the most vibrant and active community (`https://www.cncf.io/reports/kubernetes-project-journey-report/`). The CNCF survey indicates that Kubernetes-related projects (such as Helm, Prometheus, and Istio) are also widely adopted, further strengthening its ecosystem.
- **Comprehensive features**: K8s offers a rich set of features including automated rollouts and rollbacks, self-healing, horizontal scaling, service discovery, and load balancing. These capabilities make it a versatile and powerful tool for managing containerized applications.
- **Portability**: K8s abstracts away the underlying infrastructure, enabling applications to be deployed consistently whether on-premises, in public, private, or hybrid clouds, or edge locations.
- **Managed K8s services**: The availability of the managed K8s offerings from major cloud providers such as Amazon EKS, GKE, and AKS has significantly lowered the barrier to entry. These offerings take away the operational complexities of running and operating K8s clusters, allowing enterprises to focus on their core business objectives.
- **Strong governance**: K8s has been governed by CNCF since 2016, which fosters collaborative development and community participation, enabling contributions from a diverse group of developers, organizations, and end users. It follows an open source model with well-defined governance structures, including **special interest groups** (**SIGs**) that focus on specific areas of development and operations.

- **Declarative configuration**: K8s uses a declarative approach for configuration management, allowing users to define the desired state of their applications and infrastructure using YAML or JSON files. As depicted in *Figure 2.5*, K8s controllers continuously monitor the current state of a resource and automatically reconcile to match the desired state, simplifying operations and ensuring consistency.

Figure 2.5 – How K8s controllers work

- **Extensibility**: This is probably the most significant reason why K8 became so popular. K8s is designed with a modular architecture, supporting custom plugins and extensions through well-defined APIs. This enabled developers and companies to extend or customize the K8s functionality without modifying the upstream code, fostering innovation and adaptability.

Next, let's look at the architecture of Kubernetes.

Kubernetes architecture

K8s architecture is based on running clusters that allow your applications/containers to run across multiple hosts. Each cluster consists of two types of nodes:

- **Control plane**: The K8s control plane is the brain behind cluster operations. It consists of critical components such as kube-apiserver, etcd, the scheduler manager, the controller manager, and the cloud controller manager.
- **Data plane/worker nodes**: The K8s data plane running on the worker nodes is composed of several key components, such as kube-proxy, the kubelet, and the **Container Network Interface** (**CNI**) plugin.

Figure 2.6 depicts the high-level K8s cluster architecture. You will notice kube-apiserver is the frontend of the K8s control plane and interacts with the other control plane components, such as controller managers, etcd, and so on, to fulfil the requests. K8s worker nodes host several key components, responsible for taking instructions from kube-apiserver, executing them on the worker node, and reporting back on the status.

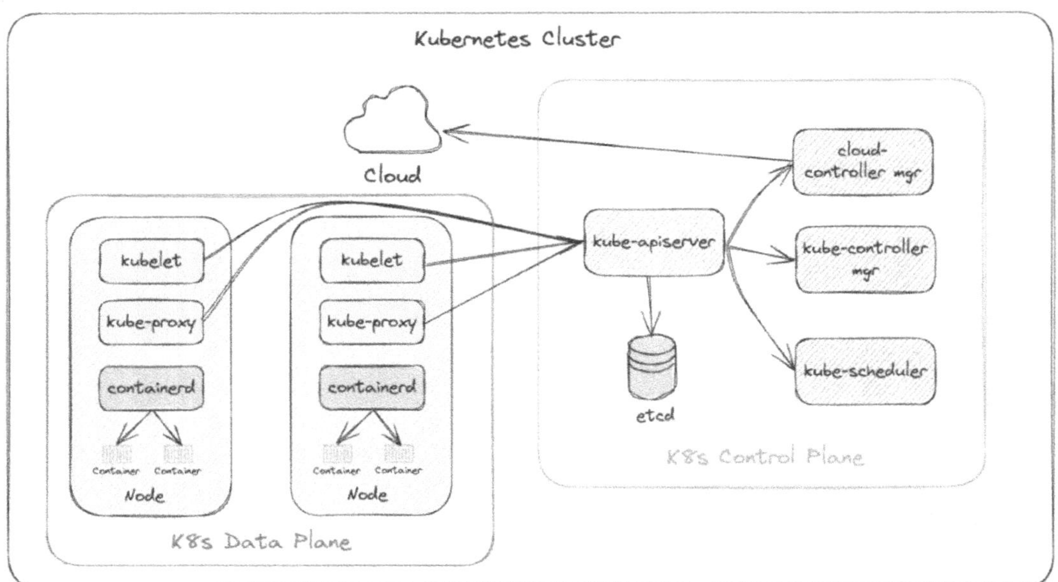

Figure 2.6 – Kubernetes cluster architecture

Control plane components

The primary components of a control plane are as follows:

- **kube-apiserver**: This serves as the entry point or frontend into the K8s cluster and the central management component that exposes the K8s API. K8s users, administrators, and other components use this API to communicate with the cluster. It also communicates with the etcd component to save the state of K8s objects. It also handles authentication and authorization, validation, and request processing, and communicates with other control plane and data plane components to manage the clusters' states.
- **etcd**: This is the distributed key-value store and is used as the K8s backing store for all cluster state. It stores the configuration data of all K8s objects and any updates made to them and ensures the cluster state is always reliable and accessible. It's critical to take regular backups of the etcd database so that clusters can be restored in case of any disruptions.
- **kube-controller-manager**: This is responsible for managing various controllers in the cluster. This includes the default upstream controllers and any custom-built ones. Some examples include the following:
- **Deployment controller**: This watches for K8s deployment objects and manages the updates to K8s Pods.

- **kube-scheduler**: This is responsible for scheduling the K8s Pods on the worker nodes. It monitors the API server for newly created Pods and assigns a worker node based on the resource availability, scheduling requirements defined in the Pod configuration such as nodeSelectors, Pod/node affinity, topology spreads, and so on. When unable to schedule a Pod due to resource exhaustion and so on, it will mark the Pods as *Pending* so that other operational add-ons such as the cluster autoscaler can kick in and add/remove compute capacity (worker nodes) to the cluster.
- **cloud-controller-manager**: This manages the cloud-specific controllers to handle the cloud provider API calls for resource management. It's the gateway to the Cloud Provider API from the K8s core and is responsible for creating and managing cloud-provider-specific resources (such as nodes, LoadBalancers, and so on) based on changes to K8s objects (such as nodes, Services, and so on). Some examples include the following:
    - **Node controller**: This is responsible for monitoring the health of the worker nodes and handling the addition or removal of nodes in the cluster
    - **Service controller**: This watches for service and node object changes, and creates, updates, and deletes cloud provider load balancers accordingly

Data plane components

The primary components of a data plane are as follows:

- **kubelet**: This is an agent that runs on every worker node in the cluster. It's responsible for taking instructions from kube-apiserver, executing them on the respective worker node, and reporting the updates on the node components back to the cluster control plane. It interacts with other node components such as the container runtime to launch container processes, the CNI plugin to set up the container networking, and CSI plugins to manage the persistent volumes and so on.
- **kube-proxy**: This is a network proxy that runs on each worker node in the cluster, implementing the K8s service concept. It maintains the network routing rules on the worker node, to allow the network communications to and from your Pods from within/outside the cluster. It uses the operating system packet filtering layer, such as IP tables, IPVS, and so on, to route the traffic to other endpoints in the cluster.
- **Container runtime**: containerd is the de facto container runtime responsible for launching the containers on the worker node. It is responsible for managing the lifecycle of containers in the K8s environment. K8s also supports other container runtimes such as CRI-O.

Apart from these components, it's essential to deploy additional add-on software on the K8s cluster for production operations. These add-ons add capabilities such as monitoring, security, and networking.

Add-on software components

Here are a few examples of add-on software:

- **CNI plugin**: This is a software add-on that implements container network specifications. They adhere to the K8s networking tenets and are responsible for allocating IP addresses to K8s Pods (`https://kubernetes.io/docs/concepts/workloads/pods/`) and enabling them to communicate with each other within the cluster. Popular add-ons in this space are Cilium (`https://github.com/cilium/cilium`), Calico (`https://github.com/projectcalico/calico`), and Amazon VPC CNI (`https://github.com/aws/amazon-vpc-cni-k8s`).
- **CSI plugin**: This is a software add-on that implements container storage interface specifications. They are responsible for providing persistent storage volumes to K8s Pods and managing the lifecycle of those volumes. A couple of notable add-ons are Amazon EBS CSI driver (`https://github.com/kubernetes-sigs/aws-ebs-csi-driver`) and Portworx CSI Driver (`https://docs.portworx.com/portworx-enterprise/operations/operate-kubernetes/storage-operations/csi`).
- **CoreDNS**: This is an essential software add-on that provides DNS resolution within the cluster. Containers launched in K8s worker nodes automatically include this DNS server in their DNS searches.
- **Monitoring plugins**: This is a software add-on that provides observability into the cluster infrastructure and workloads. They extract essential observability details such as logs, metrics, and traces and write to monitoring platforms such as Prometheus, Amazon CloudWatch, Splunk, Datadog, and New Relic.
- **Device plugins**: Modern AI/ML apps use specialized hardware devices such as GPUs from NVIDIA, Intel, and AMD and custom accelerators from Amazon, Google, and Meta. K8s provides a device plugin framework that you can use to advertise system hardware resources to the kubelet and control plane so that you can make scheduling decisions based on their availability.

This is not an exhaustive list of all K8s components and add-ons. We will dive into AI/ML-related add-ons in a later part of the book.

In this section, we dove into K8s architecture, learned about various control plane and data plane components, and explored the advantages of the K8s platform and why it became the de facto standard in the community. Let's understand why K8s is a great fit for running GenAI models next.

Why K8s is a great fit for GenAI models

Now that we understand the K8s architecture, its components, and the advantages of the platform, let's discuss how we apply those to solve common challenges with operating GenAI models.

Challenges of running GenAI models

Some common challenges of running GenAI models are as follows:

- **Computational requirements**: GenAI models are increasingly becoming large and complex, thus requiring substantial computational resources, including GPUs, TPUs, and custom accelerators for training and inference. Managing these resources efficiently is crucial to ensure performance and cost-efficiency.
- **Scalability**: As the demand for AI/ML services increases, scaling GenAI models to handle the demand is essential. This requires seamless scaling of computational resources without sacrificing the performance and cost of the models.
- **Observability**: As GenAI models proliferate, it's critical to understand their performance by monitoring both business-level KPIs and the health of the overall system using logs and metrics.
- **Data management**: GenAI models rely on vast amounts of data for both training and inference. Data preparation, security, and management are critical in increasing the model's accuracy and performance.
- **Deployment complexity**: As we learned earlier in this chapter, all GenAI models require custom frameworks, plugin libraries, and other dependencies to deploy them. This complexity can lead to deployment issues, delays, and increased errors.

K8s advantages

K8s offers several advantages for addressing the challenges of running GenAI models, such as the following:

- **Efficient resource management**: K8s has a robust resource management system built into kube-scheduler. It automates the distribution of K8s Pods into the worker nodes while meeting different scheduling requirements/constraints. Schedulers can be configured to operate in lowest-cost, random, or bin-pack modes for flexibility. With the K8s extensibility, you can develop custom schedulers and use them for scheduling workloads. A common application of this is to schedule training or inference workloads on devices with custom devices such as AWS Trainium and Inferentia. By using K8s, we can implement dynamic resource allocation based on model requirements, thus optimizing costs and improving performance.
- **Seamless scalability**: Training or fine-tuning a GenAI model requires a significant number of computational resources. Inference endpoints of these models also need to scale horizontally based on the workload demand. This will be achieved seamlessly using K8s autoscaling mechanisms such as **Horizontal Pod Autoscaling** (**HPA**) (`https://kubernetes.io/docs/tasks/run-application/horizontal-pod-autoscale/`), **Vertical Pod Autoscaling** (**VPA**) (`https://github.com/kubernetes/autoscaler/tree/master/vertical-pod-autoscaler`), and **Cluster Autoscaling** (`https://kubernetes.io/docs/concepts/cluster-administration/cluster-autoscaling/`).

HPA automatically scales a workload resource (such as a Deployment or StatefulSet) to match the workload demand. It does this by creating and deploying new K8s Pods in response to the demand. VPA automatically adjusts the resource limits (such as CPU, memory, and so on) of Pods to match their actual usage. It helps in optimizing resource allocation, ensuring workloads are run efficiently. Cluster autoscaling is responsible for ensuring the right number of resources are attached to the cluster at all times. We will take a deeper look at these mechanisms in *Chapter 6*.

- **Extensibility**: Extensibility plays a crucial role in running GenAI workloads on K8s. It allows you to extend the functionality of K8s in a scalable manner without modifying the upstream code. We can use custom-built add-ons such as **Kubeflow** (`https://www.kubeflow.org/`), an AI/ML platform that provides custom resources for managing ML pipelines, model training, and deployment. Hardware companies can also leverage this by developing device plugins to manage GPU resources in K8s so that GenAI training and inference workloads are scheduled accordingly. GenAI workloads often require specific frameworks such as **PyTorch**, **TensorFlow**, and **Jupyter Notebook**. We can use custom-built operators to integrate these frameworks and tools for seamless development and deployment.
- **Security**: K8s has many in-built security mechanisms to secure GenAI workloads. One can use **Role-Based Access Control** (**RBAC**) (`https://kubernetes.io/docs/reference/access-authn-authz/rbac/`) to limit access to resources, ensuring that only authorized users or applications can access sensitive data. K8s Secrets or external secret management solutions can be used to safeguard sensitive information. K8s network policies can be used to implement network segmentation so that only authorized Pods can access data stores. On top of this, we can enable security controls such as encryption, audit logging, security scanning, and **Pod Security Standards** (**PSS**) (`https://kubernetes.io/docs/concepts/security/pod-security-standards/`) to ensure a robust security posture. We will explore all these features in detail in *Chapter 9*.
- **High Availability (HA) and fault tolerance**: These play a critical role in running GenAI workloads efficiently and reliably. Foundational model training often takes weeks or months. If a node or Pod fails, K8s's in-built self-healing mechanism can automatically schedule the job to another node, thus minimizing interruptions. AI frameworks can be used along with this to implement a checkpointing strategy, to save the training state periodically. For model inferencing, K8s can automatically scale inference Pods based on the demand and recover the failed ones by launching replacement Pods. K8s can also perform rolling blue/green updates to deploy new model versions and seamlessly roll back in case of failures. We will take a deeper look at this topic in *Chapter 13*.
- **Rich ecosystem and add-ons**: The Cloud Native Artificial Intelligence Whitepaper (`https://www.cncf.io/wp-content/uploads/2024/03/cloud_native_ai24_031424a-2.pdf`) underscores the growing adoption of Kubernetes-native tools and frameworks to streamline the development, training, and deployment of AI models. Notable examples include Kubeflow and MLflow for operating end-to-end ML platforms on K8s; KServe, Seldon, and RayServe for model serving and scaling; and OpenLLMetry, TruLens, and Deepchecks for model observability. This list will continue to grow as the industry matures around GenAI use cases.

In this section, we learned about the typical challenges of operating GenAI models and looked at the advantages of using K8s to address them. K8s extensibility, efficient resource management, security, HA, and fault tolerance capabilities make it a great fit to run GenAI models at scale.

Summary

In this chapter, we started with the evolution of compute technologies and how containers emerged as a standard to package and ship applications and abstract away infrastructure complexities for developers. We discussed the benefits of using containers for GenAI models and built and ran our first hello-world, GenAI container images. Then we looked at the challenges of running and managing containers at scale and how container orchestrator engines such as K8s can help simplify that.

We dove into the high-level K8s architecture and various components that made up the control plane and data plane. We also learned how the extensibility, portability, declarative nature, and rich community behind K8s made it popular and the de facto container orchestrator in the market.

Finally, we discussed the typical challenges of operating GenAI workloads at scale and how K8s is a great fit to address those challenges with its efficient resource management, seamless scaling, extensibility, and security capabilities. In the next chapter, we will explore how to build a K8s cluster in a cloud environment, leverage popular open source tooling to manage GenAI workloads, and deploy our *my-llama* container in it.

Appendix

Following are some great resources for in-depth training on Kubernetes:

- Kubernetes training website: `https://kubernetes.io/training/`
- Kubernetes course on the Linux Foundation: `https://training.linuxfoundation.org/full-catalog/?_sft_product_type=training&_sft_technology=kubernetes`
- Kubernetes Learning Path at KodeKloud: `https://kodekloud.com/learning-path/kubernetes/`

3

Getting Started with Kubernetes in the Cloud

Cloud computing has revolutionized how organizations access scalable IT resources, enabling the fast deployment of compute, storage, and networking services. For teams adopting containerized applications, **Kubernetes** (**K8s**) has become the de facto platform. Cloud providers offer managed K8s services, such as **Amazon Elastic Kubernetes Service** (**EKS**), **Google Kubernetes Engine** (**GKE**), and **Azure Kubernetes Service** (**AKS**), which makes it easier to run and deploy GenAI models.

In this chapter, we'll discuss how the cloud can help simplify the management of production-grade K8s clusters by offloading some of their complexities. Then, we'll guide you in creating your first cluster using infrastructure automation.

Let's explore the following key topics:

- Advantages of running K8s in the cloud
- Setting up a K8s cluster in the cloud
- Deploying our first GenAI model in the K8s cluster

Advantages of running K8s in the cloud

A report published in 2023, *Kubernetes in the wild report 2023* (`https://www.dynatrace.com/news/blog/kubernetes-in-the-wild-2023/`), states that the number of K8s clusters in the cloud grew about five times as fast as the clusters hosted on-premises at the same time. This is primarily attributed to the following factors:

- **Managed services**: Operating a production-grade K8s cluster typically involves ensuring there's a highly available control plane, cluster management activities such as creating, upgrading, and patching all K8s control plane and data plane components, resource management, security, monitoring, and more. Many of these activities add significant operational overhead, which is undifferentiated and takes time and resources away from core business operations. Due to this, many K8s consumers have chosen to offload the undifferentiated heavy lifting of managing K8s clusters by choosing one of the managed offerings that's available. Some of the notable managed K8s offerings are as follows:
    - **Amazon EKS**: This is a managed service that's used to run K8s in the AWS cloud and on-premises data centers. With Amazon EKS, you can take advantage of all the performance, scale, reliability, and security aspects of AWS infrastructure, as well as implement deeper integrations with other AWS-managed services. To learn more, visit `https://aws.amazon.com/eks/`.
    - **GKE**: This is a managed K8s service from **Google Cloud Platform** (**GCP**) that you can use to deploy and operate containerized applications using Google's infrastructure. It is available in Standard and Enterprise editions, where the former provides fully automated cluster life cycle management and the latter provides powerful features for governing, managing, and operating containerized workloads at enterprise scale. To learn more, go to `https://cloud.google.com/kubernetes-engine`.
    - **AKS**: This is a managed service from Azure that simplifies deploying, managing, and scaling K8s clusters. AKS automates critical tasks such as monitoring, upgrades, and scaling while integrating with other Azure services such as Active Directory, Load Balancer, and Virtual Network. To learn more, go to `https://azure.microsoft.com/en-us/products/kubernetes-service`.

Apart from these, there are many other managed K8s offerings from companies such as Red Hat, Oracle Cloud Infrastructure (OCI), Alibaba Cloud, and others. The goal of these offerings is to simplify K8s cluster operations and provide deeper integrations with the respective cloud provider infrastructure.

- **Scalability and efficiency**: Cloud providers offer seamless scalability for running K8s clusters by providing access to on-demand infrastructure and a pay-as-you-go pricing model. As the clusters grow in size, they automatically scale the K8s control plane components to match their usage.
- **Availability and Global expansion**: All managed K8s offerings provide strict uptime **service-level agreements** (**SLAs**) – for example, Amazon EKS offers 99.95%. To achieve this, they often deploy multiple instances of an API server with etcd database components spread across multiple **Availability Zones** (**AZs**), automatically monitor the health of those components, and recover/replace any unhealthy components. Cloud providers also operate in multiple geographical areas called **Regions**; note that their definition may vary between cloud providers. For example, an AWS Region consists of multiple physically separated and isolated AZs that are connected with low-latency, high throughput, highly redundant networks. We can utilize these regions to deploy the workload for global users or to implement disaster recovery mechanisms.
- **Security and compliance**: There's always a shared responsibility between cloud providers and consumers. Providers are responsible for the security and compliance of the cloud while you, as a consumer, are responsible for security and compliance in the cloud. This means that the cloud provider ensures the managed components of K8s offerings such as the **control plane** are secured and meet various compliance standards such as **PCI DSS**, **HIPPA**, **GDPR**, **SOC**, and others. You, as a consumer, are responsible for securing the applications and self-managed K8s add-ons in the cluster. Additionally, the cloud provider takes care of automatically patching the control plane components to keep them secure.
- **Native integration**: To operate a production-ready K8s cluster, we need to integrate with many external components, such as storage systems, databases, load balancers, and monitoring and security tools. Cloud providers often provide managed services for those components and create seamless integrations with their managed K8s offerings. This makes it easier to build end-to-end solutions and takes away the pain of performing compatibility testing for various components. It also provides seamless integrations with various **third-party** (**3P**) tools such as **Splunk** (`https://www.splunk.com/`), **Datadog** (`https://www.datadoghq.com/`), **New Relic** (`https://newrelic.com/`), **Aqua Security** (`https://www.aquasec.com/`), **Sysdig** (`https://sysdig.com/`), **Kubecost** (`https://www.kubecost.com/`), and others for monitoring and security purposes, as well as to allocate and optimize the cost of K8s workloads

- **Extended support**: At the time of writing, the K8s community releases a new K8s version approximately three times a year. As depicted in *Figure 3.1*, each version is supported for 12 months. During this time, the community provides patch releases that include bug fixes, security patches, and more. Performing multiple K8s version upgrades often adds significant overhead to the platform engineering teams as each version upgrade involves verifying and remediating any usage of deprecated APIs, as well as upgrading the control plane, data plane, and operational add-ons while ensuring application availability. Cloud providers offer extended support for up to 26 months from the release date so that customers can plan and execute their cluster upgrades. It's always recommended to stay on the latest K8s releases so that you can leverage the latest innovations from the community, so it's crucial to automate cluster life cycle operations using **Infrastructure as Code** (**IaC**):

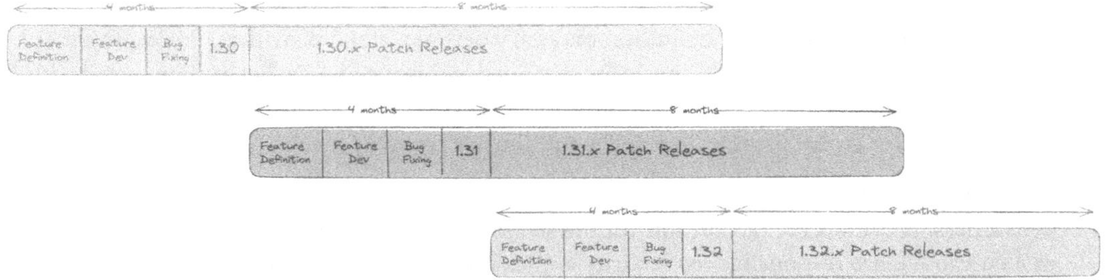

Figure 3.1 – K8s release cycle

In this section, we learned about the advantages of using managed K8s offerings from various cloud providers. These let us utilize the seamless scalability of the cloud, ease of management, and global expansion so that we can cater to various geographical customers and meet and exceed security and compliance requirements while operating cost-efficiently. Next, we will set up our first K8s cluster in the AWS cloud using IaC and deploy the `my-llama` model in it.

Setting up a K8s cluster in the cloud

Managed K8s offerings are generally upstream and K8s-compliant, which means we can seamlessly migrate the workloads from one offering to another without changing the application code. You may still need to use cloud-provider-specific add-ons to integrate with respective cloud services. Due to this, throughout the rest of this book, we will be using the AWS cloud and Amazon EKS. You can replicate a similar setup using other cloud provider offerings.

Amazon EKS is a regional AWS service that eliminates the need to install, operate, and maintain a K8s control plane on AWS. An Amazon EKS cluster provides a single-tenant, highly available K8s control plane that is spread across three AZs to withstand AZ-wide failures. For the data plane, you can choose from the options shown in *Figure 3.2*:

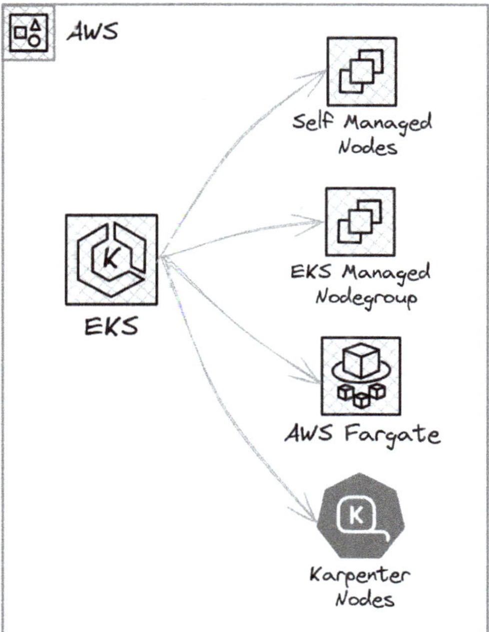

Figure 3.2 – Amazon EKS data plane options

Let's learn about these options in detail:

- **Self-managed nodes**: This is a group of **Amazon EC2** (`https://aws.amazon.com/ec2/`) instances that are manually managed by the users. Amazon EC2 is a managed service that provides resizable compute capacity in the AWS cloud. Customers are responsible for bootstrapping the worker nodes so that they can join the cluster and managing their life cycle operations (provisioning, updating, and destroying). This option provides fine-grained control over node configuration, setup, and management and also adds operational overhead.
- **EKS-managed node group**: This is the most popular choice for EKS users. It provides APIs to automate the process of provisioning and managing the life cycle of the worker nodes. Every managed node group is provisioned as part of an Amazon EC2 **Auto Scaling group** (**ASG**) (`https://docs.aws.amazon.com/autoscaling/ec2/userguide/auto-scaling-groups.html`), which is managed by Amazon EKS. An ASG automatically manages the scaling of EC2 instances, ensuring the appropriate number of instances are running to handle the load. To learn more, go to `https://docs.aws.amazon.com/eks/latest/userguide/managed-node-groups.html`.

- **AWS Fargate**: This is a serverless compute engine for running containerized workloads. With AWS Fargate, you don't have to manage the underlying compute infrastructure that runs the K8s Pods. AWS handles how the worker nodes are provisioned, configured, patched, and scaled. It automatically provisions the compute capacity that matches your Pod resource requirements and provides higher-level security isolation by providing a dedicated kernel for each Pod. Visit `https://docs.aws.amazon.com/eks/latest/userguide/fargate.html` to learn more.
- **Karpenter managed nodes**: Karpenter is a high-performance cluster autoscaling solution that automatically launches the right amount of compute resources to handle the cluster workloads available. It observes the aggregate resource requirements of unscheduled Pods and makes decisions to launch and terminate the worker nodes. We will explore this in detail in *Chapter 6*. Go to `https://karpenter.sh/` to learn more.

For a detailed comparison of these data plane options, you can refer to the EKS documentation at `https://docs.aws.amazon.com/eks/latest/userguide/eks-compute.html`.

We will be using an IaC tool to automate the process of provisioning the necessary AWS infrastructure. **Terraform** (`https://www.hashicorp.com/products/terraform`) is the most popular and cloud-agnostic IaC tool available and is developed by HashiCorp (`https://www.hashicorp.com/`). It is used to automatically provision and manage resources in any cloud or data center. Terraform uses a domain-specific language called **HashiCorp Configuration Language** (**HCL**) (`https://github.com/hashicorp/hcl`) to define the infrastructure while providing support for input and output variables so that the configuration can be customized. To learn more about Terraform, follow the Get Started - AWS tutorial on the HashiCorp website: `https://developer.hashicorp.com/terraform/tutorials/aws-get-started`.

To promote modularity, multiple configuration files can be organized into a Terraform module to encapsulate a set of related resources. There is a large Terraform community that maintains the registry of open source modules at `https://registry.terraform.io/` that's available for public use. We will be using the following community modules to provision the necessary infrastructure in this walkthrough:

- The **AWS VPC Terraform** module (`https://registry.terraform.io/modules/terraform-aws-modules/vpc/aws/latest`) will be used to create Amazon VPC resources
- The **AWS EKS Terraform** module (`https://registry.terraform.io/modules/terraform-aws-modules/eks/aws/latest`) will be used to create an Amazon EKS cluster, node groups, AWS Fargate profiles, and more
- The **Amazon EKS Blueprints Addons** module (`https://registry.terraform.io/modules/aws-ia/eks-blueprints-addons/aws/latest`) will be used to deploy K8s add-ons on Amazon EKS clusters

Let's start by setting up our environment so that we can provision the EKS cluster using Terraform.

> **Important note**
>
> In this walkthrough, we will be creating AWS resources that are not part of the AWS free tier, so you will incur charges. Please refer to AWS Pricing Calculator at `https://calculator.aws/#/` for a cost estimate.

Prerequisites

Here are the prerequisites for setting up a K8s cluster in the cloud:

- Create a free **AWS account** at `https://aws.amazon.com/free/` if you haven't got one already. AWS provides generous free tiers across many of its services. Amazon EKS is *not* part of the free tier, so any resources that are provisioned in this walkthrough will incur some charges.
- Create an **IAM user** with administrator privileges by following the instructions at `https://docs.aws.amazon.com/streams/latest/dev/setting-up.html#setting-up-iam` and generate programmatic access credentials.
- Install the **AWS CLI** by going to `https://docs.aws.amazon.com/cli/latest/userguide/getting-started-install.html` and configure it with the AWS access credentials of an administrator user.
- Install the **Terraform CLI** by going to `https://developer.hashicorp.com/terraform/tutorials/aws-get-started/install-cli`.
- Install **kubectl**, the official CLI tool for interacting with K8s clusters, by going to `https://docs.aws.amazon.com/eks/latest/userguide/install-kubectl.html`.

Provisioning the Amazon EKS cluster

> **Important note**
>
> Terraform providers and modules are frequently updated with new features and fixes. We've used the latest compatible versions that were available at the time of writing. You can update those to their latest versions by going to the Terraform Registry at `https://registry.terraform.io/`.

Let's start by setting up the Terraform project:

1. Create a new project directory called `genai-eks-demo`:

   ```
   $ mkdir -p genai-eks-demo
   $ cd genai-eks-demo
   ```

2. Create a `versions.tf` file that defines a list of Terraform providers and their respective versions. A **Terraform provider** is a plugin that interacts with cloud providers, SaaS providers, and other APIs. The **AWS Provider** (`https://registry.terraform.io/providers/hashicorp/aws/latest/docs`) enables us to define, provision, and manage AWS resources such as VPCs, EKS clusters, and more. **Helm** (`https://helm.sh/`) is a package manager for K8s that allows us to define, install, and upgrade K8s applications using Helm charts. Many community and proprietary pieces of software in the K8s space are distributed via Helm charts, and the **Helm provider** (`https://registry.terraform.io/providers/hashicorp/kubernetes/latest/docs`) can be used to deploy those software packages in the EKS cluster. Finally, the K8s provider (`https://registry.terraform.io/providers/hashicorp/kubernetes/latest/docs`) is used to interact with the resources in the EKS cluster. You can also download the `versions.tf` file from our GitHub repository at `https://github.com/PacktPublishing/Kubernetes-for-Generative-AI-Solutions/blob/main/ch3/versions.tf`:

```
terraform {
  required_version = ">= 1.11"
  required_providers {
    aws = {
      source = "hashicorp/aws"
      version = ">= 5.96"
    }
    helm = {
      source = "hashicorp/helm"
      version = ">= 2.17"
    }
    kubernetes = {
      source = "hashicorp/kubernetes"
      version = ">= 2.36"
    }
  }
}
```

3. Create a `locals.tf` file for storing local variables such as name, AWS Region, and VPC **Classless Inter-Domain Routing** (**CIDR**) (`https://docs.aws.amazon.com/vpc/latest/userguide/vpc-cidr-blocks.html`) and refer to them our Terraform code. We are also defining a Terraform data source (`https://developer.hashicorp.com/terraform/language/data-sources`) called `azs` to fetch the AWS AZs in the given AWS Region (`us-west-2`) and filtering them by `opt-in-status`. You can download the `locals.tf` file from our GitHub repository at `https://github.com/PacktPublishing/Kubernetes-for-Generative-AI-Solutions/blob/main/ch3/locals.tf`:

```
data "aws_availability_zones" "azs" {
  filter {
```

```
      name   = "opt-in-status"
      values = ["opt-in-not-required"]
    }
  }
  locals {
    name     = "eks-demo"
    region   = "us-west-2"
    vpc_cidr = "10.0.0.0/16"
    azs      = slice (data.aws_availability_zones.azs.names, 0, 3)
  }
```

4. Create a `providers.tf` file for configuring the Terraform providers. Here, we are initializing K8s and Helm providers with the EKS cluster credentials provided to interact with the cluster. You can download the `providers.tf` file from our GitHub repository at `https://github.com/PacktPublishing/Kubernetes-for-Generative-AI-Solutions/blob/main/ch3/providers.tf`:

```
  provider "aws" {
    region = local.region
  }
  provider "kubernetes" {
    host                   = module.eks.cluster_endpoint
    cluster_ca_certificate = base64decode(module.eks.cluster_
  certificate_authority_data)
    exec {
      api_version = "client.authentication.k8s.io/v1beta1"
      command     = "aws"
      args = ["eks", "get-token", "--cluster-name", module.eks.
  cluster_name]
    }
  }
  provider "helm" {
    kubernetes {
      host                   = module.eks.cluster_endpoint
      cluster_ca_certificate = base64decode(module.eks.cluster_
  certificate_authority_data)
      exec {
        api_version = "client.authentication.k8s.io/v1beta1"
        command     = "aws"
        args = ["eks", "get-token", "--cluster-name", module.eks.
  cluster_name]
      }
    }
  }
```

5. Create a `vpc.tf` file that will define the Amazon VPC, public and private subnets, internet gateway, NAT gateway, and other networking resources required for the EKS cluster. Refer to the AWS documentation at `https://docs.aws.amazon.com/vpc/latest/userguide/how-it-works.html` to learn more about these concepts. You can download the `vpc.tf` file from our GitHub repository at `https://github.com/PacktPublishing/Kubernetes-for-Generative-AI-Solutions/blob/main/ch3/vpc.tf`:

```
module "vpc" {
  source = "terraform-aws-modules/vpc/aws"
  version = "~> 5.21"
  name = local.name
  cidr = local.vpc_cidr

  azs = local.azs
  private_subnets = [for k, v in local.azs: cidrsubnet(local.
vpc_cidr, 4, k)]
  public_subnets = [for k, v in local.azs: cidrsubnet(local.
vpc_cidr, 8, k + 48)]
  enable_nat_gateway = true
  single_nat_gateway = true
  public_subnet_tags = {
    "kubernetes.io/role/elb" = 1
  }
  private_subnet_tags = {
    "kubernetes.io/role/internal-elb" = 1
    "karpenter.sh/discovery" = local.name
  }
}
output vpc_id {
    description = "VPC ID"
    value = "${module.vpc.vpc_id}"
}
```

6. To deploy the Amazon VPC resources using Terraform, start by running `terraform init` (`https://developer.hashicorp.com/terraform/cli/commands/init`). This command initializes your working directory by downloading the required Terraform provider plugins and configuring the backend for storing Terraform's state. It ensures that your environment has been set up properly before making any changes. Next, run `terraform plan` (`https://developer.hashicorp.com/terraform/cli/commands/plan`) to generate an execution plan, which allows you to preview the actions Terraform will take, such as which resources will be created, modified, or destroyed, without actually making any changes. Reviewing the plan helps catch potential misconfigurations early. Finally, run `terraform apply` (`https://developer.hashicorp.com/terraform/cli/commands/apply`) to apply the changes to your infrastructure.

This command provisions the defined VPC resources and prompts for confirmation before making any changes:

```
$ terraform init
$ terraform plan
$ terraform apply -auto-approve
```

7. After completion, you will notice the VPC ID in the output:

```
Apply complete! Resources: 23 added, 0 changed, 0  destroyed.
Outputs:
vpc_id = "vpc-1234567890"
```

8. In the `eks.tf` file, we must define the EKS cluster using the `terraform-aws-modules/eks` (`https://registry.terraform.io/modules/terraform-aws-modules/eks/aws/latest`) module. This module simplifies EKS provisioning by abstracting away low-level AWS API calls. Here, we must specify the desired cluster version, VPC subnets, and managed node groups. We are defining one managed node group with a minimum of two EC2 worker nodes from the `General Purpose (m)` instance family. Feel free to modify the `instance_types` attribute value if you encounter an `InsufficientInstanceCapacity` (`https://docs.aws.amazon.com/AWSEC2/latest/UserGuide/troubleshooting-launch.html#troubleshooting-launch-capacity`) error from AWS. You can choose `General Purpose` instance types from this page: `https://aws.amazon.com/ec2/instance-types/`.

9. In this example, we are defining a managed node group (`eks-mng`) for an EKS cluster. This node group is a group of EC2 instances that will serve as worker nodes in the cluster. In the **instance_types** definition for this node group, we are providing choices such as `m5.large`, `m6i.large`, `m6a.large`, and others. EKS will attempt to use one of these instances based on availability. This enables instance-type flexibility, which improves resiliency and may reduce costs by taking advantage of Spot Instance pools or regional availability. You can download the `eks.tf` file from our GitHub repository at `https://github.com/PacktPublishing/Kubernetes-for-Generative-AI-Solutions/blob/main/ch3/eks.tf`:

```
module "eks" {
  source = "terraform-aws-modules/eks/aws"
  version = "~> 20.36"
  cluster_name = local.name
  cluster_version = "1.32"
  enable_cluster_creator_admin_permissions = true
  cluster_endpoint_public_access = true
  vpc_id = module.vpc.vpc_id
  subnet_ids = module.vpc.private_subnets

  eks_managed_node_groups = {
```

```
      eks-mng = {
        instance_types = ["m5.large","m6i.large","m6a.large","m7i.
large","m7a.large"]
        max_size = 3
        desired_size = 2
      }
    }
    node_security_group_tags = {
      "karpenter.sh/discovery" = local.name
    }
  }
  output "configure_kubectl" {
    description = "Configure kubectl"
    value = "aws eks --region ${local.region} update-kubeconfig
--name ${module.eks.cluster_name}"
  }
```

10. Apply the Terraform code to deploy the EKS cluster and the managed node group resources. EKS also deploys default networking add-ons such as `vpc-cni`, `kube-proxy`, and CoreDNS in the cluster:

    ```
    $ terraform init
    $ terraform plan
    $ terraform apply -auto-approve
    ```

    After successful deployment, you will notice the following output. You can use this to configure your `kubectl` CLI so that it can interact with the EKS cluster:

    ```
    Apply complete! Resources: 33 added, 0 changed, 0 destroyed.
    Outputs:
    configure_kubectl = "aws eks --region us-west-2 update-
    kubeconfig --name eks-demo"
    vpc_id = "vpc-1234567890"
    ```

    Copy and run the following command in your terminal to point the `kubectl` CLI to the `eks-demo` cluster:

    ```
    $ aws eks --region us-west-2 update-kubeconfig --name eks-demo
    ```

11. Next, we will install the required operational add-on software to make our EKS cluster production-ready. This includes add-ons such as **AWS Load Balancer Controller** (`https://kubernetes-sigs.github.io/aws-load-balancer-controller/latest/`) to manage the AWS Load Balancer resources for the EKS cluster, **Karpenter** (`https://karpenter.sh/`) to manage compute auto-scaling, and more. Download the `addons.tf` from our GitHub repository at `https://github.com/PacktPublishing/Kubernetes-for-Generative-AI-Solutions/blob/main/ch3/addons.tf`. We are using the **eks-blueprints-addons** (`https://github.com/aws-ia/terraform-aws-eks-blueprints-addons`) Terraform module to deploy these add-ons on the EKS cluster:

```
module "eks_blueprints_addons" {
  source = "aws-ia/eks-blueprints-addons/aws"
  version = "~> 1.21"
  cluster_name = module.eks.cluster_name
  cluster_endpoint = module.eks.cluster_endpoint
  cluster_version = module.eks.cluster_version
  oidc_provider_arn = module.eks.oidc_provider_arn
  enable_aws_load_balancer_controller = true
...
}
module "karpenter" {
  source = "terraform-aws-modules/eks/aws//modules/karpenter"
...
}
```

12. Apply the Terraform code to deploy the add-on software on the cluster:

```
$ terraform init
$ terraform plan
$ terraform apply -auto-approve
```

13. Verify the installation by running the following `kubectl` commands. You will notice that there are two worker nodes and 10 K8s Pods running in the cluster:

```
$ kubectl get nodes -o wide
$ kubectl get pods -A -o wide
```

14. This wraps up the initial setup of the EKS cluster. The process is depicted in *Figure 3.3*:

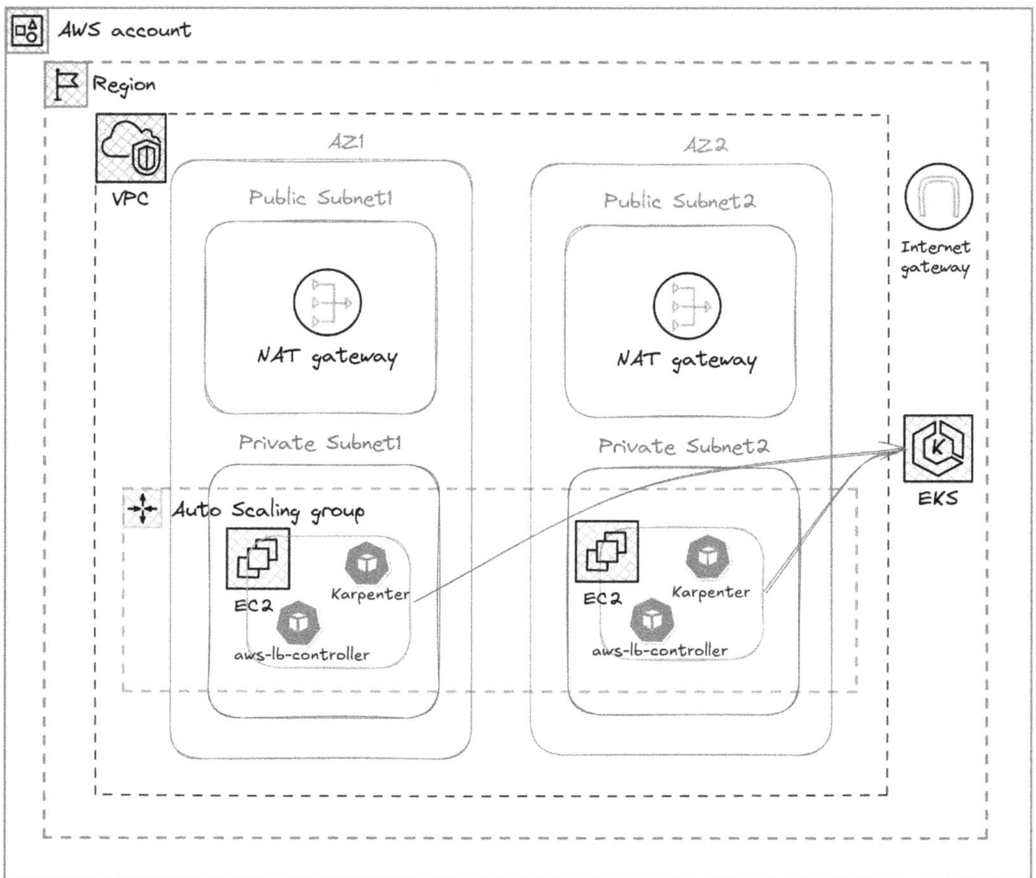

Figure 3.3 – High-level architecture of our EKS cluster

We started by setting up the required tools, which include Terraform, the AWS CLI, kubectl, and others, and created a Terraform project to provision various AWS network components, such as Amazon VPCs, subnets, and internet gateways, before deploying an Amazon EKS cluster alongside AWS Load Balancer and Karpenter add-ons. We will build on top of this setup throughout this book and create a production-ready system for deploying and operating GenAI workloads.

Deploying our first GenAI model in the K8s cluster

In this section, we will deploy the Llama model we built in *Chapter 2* on the EKS cluster and expose it to our end users using an AWS **Network Load Balancer** (**NLB**) (`https://aws.amazon.com/elasticloadbalancing/network-load-balancer/`). In the K8s world, the smallest unit of deployment is called a **Pod** (`https://kubernetes.io/docs/concepts/workloads/pods/`). A Pod consists of one or more containers that share storage and network resources and is defined using a Pod specification. The following is a sample Pod spec for creating a K8s Pod called `nginx-pod` using the latest `nginx` container image running on port `80`. You can download this manifest file from our GitHub repository at `https://github.com/PacktPublishing/Kubernetes-for-Generative-AI-Solutions/blob/main/ch3/nginx-pod.yaml`:

```
apiVersion: v1
kind: Pod
metadata:
  name: nginx-pod
spec:
  containers:
  - name: nginx
    image: nginx:latest
    ports:
    - containerPort: 80
```

K8s also provides high-level abstracted constructs so that we can manage our workloads declaratively:

- **Deployments** (`https://kubernetes.io/docs/concepts/workloads/controllers/deployment/`)
- **ReplicaSets** (`https://kubernetes.io/docs/concepts/workloads/controllers/replicaset/`)
- **StatefulSets** (`https://kubernetes.io/docs/concepts/workloads/controllers/statefulset/`)
- **Jobs** (`https://kubernetes.io/docs/concepts/workloads/controllers/job/`)
- **DaemonSets** (`https://kubernetes.io/docs/concepts/workloads/controllers/daemonset/`)

Each workload or component of the workload runs as a container inside Pods, and managing these Pods often takes a lot of effort. For example, if a Pod fails, a new replacement Pod needs to be created or a new version of the workload has to be rolled out. These high-level constructs help to abstract these complexities.

Deployment is the most common way to deploy a workload on a K8s cluster. It automates the process of rolling updates, ensuring that new versions of the workload can be released without downtime. We can also apply scaling policies to easily increase or decrease the number of Pods based on demand. Furthermore, deployments use **ReplicaSets** to ensure high availability by automatically restarting failed Pods and maintaining the desired state of the application, which is critical for resilience in production environments.

In K8s, a **Service** is an abstraction that enables you to expose one or more Pods over a network. It defines a logical group of endpoints, typically consisting of Pods, and includes a policy that governs their accessibility. There are many different types of K8s Service objects:

- **ClusterIP** (`https://kubernetes.io/docs/concepts/services-networking/service/#type-clusterip`)
- **LoadBalancer** (`https://kubernetes.io/docs/concepts/services-networking/service/#loadbalancer`)
- **NodePort** (`https://kubernetes.io/docs/concepts/services-networking/service/#type-nodeport`)
- **ExternalName** (`https://kubernetes.io/docs/concepts/services-networking/service/#externalname`).

In this walkthrough, we will be exposing our application using the **LoadBalancer** Service type, which, in turn, will provision our NLB in the AWS cloud.

Let's create a deployment specification for the `my-llama` container we created in *Chapter 2*. To do this, we need to upload the local container image to a container registry so that it can be downloaded by EKS. **Amazon Elastic Container Registry** (**Amazon ECR**) (`https://aws.amazon.com/ecr/`) is a fully managed container registry service for storing, sharing, and deploying container software anywhere. Create a file named `ecr.tf` that contains the following Terraform code to create an Amazon ECR repository and enable image tag immutability to prevent image tags from being overwritten. You can download the `ecr.tf` file from our GitHub repository at `https://github.com/PacktPublishing/Kubernetes-for-Generative-AI-Solutions/blob/main/ch3/ecr.tf`:

```
resource "aws_ecr_repository" "my-llama" {
  name = "my-llama"
  image_tag_mutability = "MUTABLE"
}
output "ecr_push_cmds" {
  description = "Command to authenticate with ECR and push the container image."
  value = <<EOT
```

```
    aws ecr get-login-password --region ${local.region} | docker login
--username AWS --password-stdin ${aws_ecr_repository.my-llama.
repository_url}
    docker tag my-llama ${aws_ecr_repository.my-llama.repository_url}
    docker push ${aws_ecr_repository.my-llama.repository_url}
    EOT
}
```

Run the following commands to create the ECR repository:

```
$ terraform plan
$ terraform apply -auto-approve
```

Run the `terraform output` command to list the ECR upload commands. Copy and paste those output commands in your terminal to push the `my-llama` container image to the ECR repository:

```
$ terraform output -raw ecr_push_cmds
    aws ecr get-login-password --region us-west-2 | docker login
--username AWS --password-stdin 123456789012.dkr.ecr.us-west-2.
amazonaws.com/my-llama
    docker tag my-llama 123456789012.dkr.ecr.us-west-2.amazonaws.com/
my-llama
    docker push 123456789012.dkr.ecr.us-west-2.amazonaws.com/my-llama
```

Create the K8s deployment resource using the `my-llama` ECR image:

```
$ kubectl create deploy my-llama --image 123456789012.dkr.ecr.
us-west-2.amazonaws.com/my-llama
deployment.apps/my-llama created
```

It may take a couple of minutes for the K8s deployment to get into the `Ready` state. You can verify this by running the following command and looking for the `Ready` status:

```
$ kubectl get deploy my-llama
NAME        READY   UP-TO-DATE   AVAILABLE   AGE
my-llama    1/1     1            1           6m
```

Now that the `my-llama` model is being deployed to the EKS cluster, the next step is to expose it outside the cluster using an AWS NLB. We will be using the **aws-load-balancer-controller** add-on that was installed as part of our EKS cluster setup to provision the NLB. Create a file called `my-llama-svc.yaml` that contains the following content. This will create a K8s service of the `LoadBalancer` type on port `80` and forward the traffic to port `5000` on the `my-llama` container. Here, we're also adding annotations to make it an internet-facing NLB.

You can download the `my-llama-svc.yaml` file from our GitHub repository at `https://github.com/PacktPublishing/Kubernetes-for-Generative-AI-Solutions/blob/main/ch3/my-llama-svc.yaml`:

> **Important note**
>
> We are creating a public-facing NLB for testing purposes. Feel free to restrict access to your IP address by updating the inbound rules of the NLB security group. Please refer to the AWS NLB documentation at `https://docs.aws.amazon.com/elasticloadbalancing/latest/network/load-balancer-security-groups.html` for more details.

```
apiVersion: v1
kind: Service
metadata:
  labels:
    app: my-llama-svc
  name: my-llama-svc
  annotations:
    service.beta.kubernetes.io/aws-load-balancer-type: "external"
    service.beta.kubernetes.io/aws-load-balancer-scheme: "internet-
facing"
spec:
  ports:
  - port: 80
    protocol: TCP
    targetPort: 5000
  type: LoadBalancer
  selector:
    app: my-llama
```

Deploy the K8s service and fetch the NLB hostname by running the following commands:

```
$ kubectl apply -f my-llama-svc.yaml
service/my-llama-svc created
$ export NLB_URL=$(kubectl get svc my-llama-svc -o jsonpath='{.status.
loadBalancer.ingress[0].hostname}')
$ echo $NLB_URL
```

It may take up to 5 minutes for the K8s Pod endpoints to be registered to the AWS NLB and become healthy. You can run the following commands to look at the K8s Pod logs, events, and service status:

```
$ kubectl describe pod -l app=my-llama
$ kubectl logs -f -l app=my-llama
$ kubectl describe svc my-llama-svc
```

Now, we can invoke the Llama model by using this NLB endpoint. Run the following `curl` command to send a test prompt to the `my-llama` service. It will generate a response by forwarding the prompt to the Llama model:

```
$ curl -X POST http://$NLB_URL/predict -H "Content-Type: application/
json" -d '{"prompt":"Create a poem about humanity?","sys_msg":"You
are a helpful, respectful, and honest assistant. Always provide safe,
unbiased, and positive responses. Avoid harmful, unethical, or illegal
content. If a question is unclear or incorrect, explain why. If
unsure, do not provide false information."}' | jq .
```

In this section, we deployed our `my-llama` container image as a K8s deployment in an EKS cluster and exposed it to the internet using an AWS NLB by creating the K8s LoadBalancer Service. Finally, we ran inference on our LLM by using the `curl` utility against the AWS NLB endpoint's URL. Similarly, you can containerize other publicly available models such as **Mistral** (`https://huggingface.co/mistralai`), **Falcon** (`https://huggingface.co/tiiuae`), and **DeepSeek** (`https://huggingface.co/deepseek-ai`) and deploy them in your EKS cluster.

Summary

In this chapter, we discussed how cloud computing has fundamentally changed how we access and utilize compute resources, offering scalability, accessibility, and cost-efficiency through pay-as-you-go models. Managed K8s services provided by major cloud providers simplify the deployment and management of K8s clusters, which is particularly beneficial for running GenAI models. We used Amazon EKS, a managed, upstream K8s-compliant service as an example and covered how to automate the process of setting up an EKS cluster. Then, we utilized Terraform for cluster provisioning, set up a Terraform project with the required providers, and used community modules to create AWS resources such as VPCs, EKS clusters, EKS-managed node groups, and cluster add-ons. After, we deployed our `my-llama` model as a K8s deployment on the EKS cluster and exposed it to the internet using the K8s LoadBalancer Service.

In the next chapter, we will discuss techniques for optimizing a general-purpose foundational model for domain-specific use cases, such as chatbots. We will cover some specific techniques such as Retrieval-Augmented Generation (RAG) and fine-tuning methods while providing an in-depth exploration of how to implement them.

Part 2: Productionalizing GenAI Workloads Using K8s

This section offers a comprehensive guide for deploying, scaling, and optimizing GenAI applications in production K8s environments. Through real-world examples, such as an e-commerce chatbot, this section covers essential techniques for model optimization, cost and resource management, networking and security best practices, and GPU resource optimization, enabling a smooth transition from experimentation to production-ready solutions.

This part has the following chapters:

- *Chapter 4, GenAI Model Optimization for Domain-Specific Use Cases*
- *Chapter 5, Working with GenAI on K8s: Chatbot Example*
- *Chapter 6, Scaling GenAI Applications on Kubernetes*
- *Chapter 7, Cost Optimization of GenAI Applications on Kubernetes*
- *Chapter 8, Networking Best Practices for Deploying GenAI on K8s*
- *Chapter 9, Security Best Practices for Deploying GenAI on Kubernetes*
- *Chapter 10, Optimizing GPU Resources for GenAI Applications in Kubernetes*

4

GenAI Model Optimization for Domain-Specific Use Cases

This chapter will start building on the basic concepts of GenAI that were introduced in *Part 1* and cover options for optimizing general-purpose **foundational models** (**FMs**) for domain-specific use cases, such as chatbots and personalized recommendations. We will explore specific techniques, including retrieval-augmented generation (RAG) and fine-tuning methods, offering an in-depth understanding of how these approaches can be used to enhance model performance for targeted applications. Additionally, we will focus on the key concepts and functionalities of the Transformer architecture and the LangChain framework so that we can implement these techniques in K8s in the next chapter.

In this chapter, we're going to cover the following main topics:

- The need for domain-specific optimization
- The LangChain framework – the concept of memory and agents
- RAG
- Model fine-tuning with a Llama3 example

Technical requirements

In this chapter, we will be using the following libraries and packages. Some of these libraries require you to create an account and provide an API key while making function calls:

- Hugging Face: `https://huggingface.co/join`.
- OpenAI: `https://platform.openai.com/signup`. Once you've signed in, you can request API keys by going to `https://platform.openai.com/api-keys`.
- You can access the Llama3 model for this chapter via Hugging Face: `https://huggingface.co/meta-llama/Meta-Llama-3-8B`

The code in this chapter can be run on Google Colab (`https://colab.research.google.com/`) or localhost using **Jupyter Notebook** available in an Anaconda environment. You can download Anaconda from `https://www.anaconda.com/download`.

The code in this chapter can be downloaded from this book's GitHub repository: `https://github.com/PacktPublishing/Kubernetes-for-Generative-AI-Solutions/tree/main/ch4`.

The need for domain-specific optimization

Large language models (**LLMs**) are general-purpose models that are trained on diverse datasets to ensure they can handle a wide range of inputs. However, these general-purpose models are not well suited to solve problems within a specific domain that requires a deep understanding of that domain, such as healthcare, finance, or law. This is where *domain-specific optimization* comes into play.

Some of these options also help to fix knowledge cut-off issues – for instance, to let an LLM address certain scenarios that occur after the LLM has been trained, or to ensure the proprietary dataset is used to optimize the LLM. Unlike general-purpose models, which are designed to be versatile, domain-specific optimization enhances model performance in specialized tasks, improving accuracy, efficiency, and reliability.

The core idea behind domain-specific optimization is that by leveraging unique characteristics, data patterns, and knowledge of a specific domain, we can create models that are not only more effective but also more efficient in their execution.

The following are some of the techniques you can use to optimize a model. We will discuss these in detail later in this chapter:

- **Prompt engineering**: This involves designing prompts that guide the model to generate more relevant outputs for specific domains. This might involve structuring questions or inputs in ways that results in more accurate and domain-appropriate responses.
- **Knowledge integration**: This includes techniques, such as RAG, that can augment an LLM with external knowledge sources during the generation process so that when the model encounters a query, it can retrieve relevant documents or pieces of information from a specialized knowledge base (e.g., medical databases, financial reports, and legal documents) and use this retrieved information to generate more accurate and contextually appropriate responses.
- **Fine-tuning**: Fine-tuning involves conducting further training – that is, training a pre-trained LLM on a domain-specific dataset. This process adjusts the model's weights so that they better align with the nuances, jargon, and specific knowledge of the domain.

In the next section, we will cover LangChain, an open source framework that can be used for different model optimization techniques.

LLM model selection

For some of the applications discussed in this chapter, we will need to perform LLM model selection so that we can run them. Users have the choice to pick an LLM. Some of the most popular LLM providers are Anthropic, OpenAI, Cohere, and open-weight models such as Llama, which is provided by Meta.

For AWS deployment, **Amazon Bedrock** provides a simple interface for selecting and using FMs. It is a fully managed service offered by AWS that provides access to a wide variety of pre-trained models from leading AI providers, including Anthropic, Cohere, and Stability AI.

Through the Bedrock console or API, developers can easily choose the most suitable model for their use case – whether it's for text generation, embeddings, or image generation. Bedrock abstracts away the complexities of model deployment, allowing these FMs to be integrated seamlessly into applications with just a few API calls. The following link explains how to use Amazon Bedrock via an API: `https://docs.aws.amazon.com/bedrock/latest/userguide/getting-started-api.html`.

Throughout this book, we will be using different model providers, such as Amazon Bedrock and OpenAI, in K8s to showcase different usage patterns. In this chapter, we will be using GPT models from OpenAI via APIs.

The LangChain framework

LangChain is a powerful open source framework designed to streamline the development of LLM-based applications. It provides a set of libraries and tools that facilitate the integration of LLMs with various data sources, allowing for complex workflows such as (RAG, decision-making, and multi-step reasoning and agents. LangChain can be used to create pipelines where LLMs can interact with external APIs, databases, or documents, enabling more dynamic, context-aware, and domain-specific responses. It's widely used in building sophisticated AI applications such as chatbots, intelligent agents, and knowledge-driven systems.

Here are some of the key capabilities of LangChain:

- **Memory**: LangChain's memory module allows an LLM to remember prior conversations within a session, thereby enabling context continuity. It can also be used to remember prior user responses. There are several memory options available. Based on the memory type that's selected, a chain can read from its history/memory system and augment user inputs, as well as write the user's input and output to memory for future runs so that there is continuity in the LLM's response.
- **Agents**: These are autonomous components that can make decisions for the user, take actions, and interact with the environment or users by invoking tools or APIs. This is a new and exciting area in the GenAI space and can help us with the future – for example, we can ask an LLM to help us plan a "three-day excursion in Paris." The LLM could not only make recommendations but also make reservations for a guided tour of the Louvre Museum and a Seine River cruise.

- **Chains**: Chains are sequences of prompts that can link multiple LLM operations together, allowing for complex workflows and multi-step reasoning.
- **Tool integration**: This allows LLMs to interact with external tools and APIs, expanding their functionality beyond text generation to include tasks such as querying databases or performing web searches.

In the following example, we will show you how to use LangChain's **PythonREPLTool** to create Python code to solve a given problem. PythonREPLTool is an agent that can evaluate Python code dynamically as part of a workflow while engaging with an LLM.

The following code block will install the necessary LangChain modules:

```
!pip install langchain langchain_core langchain_experimental
from langchain.agents import AgentType
from langchain_experimental.tools.python.tool import PythonREPLTool
from langchain.chat_models import ChatOpenAI
```

Next, we will install the `openai` module, provide an OpenAI key, and define the model:

```
!pip install openai
llm_model = "gpt-3.5-turbo"
llm = ChatOpenAI(model=llm_model,api_key=<OPEN_AI_KEY>)
```

Here, we are creating the agent using `PythonREPLTool`:

```
agent = create_python_agent(
    llm,tool=PythonREPLTool(),verbose=False
)
```

Now, let's say we have a task where we have to sort the following list of fruits and count how many times a fruit appears in the list:

```
fruit_list=["Apple","Banana","Apple","Peaches"]
```

Let's make the agent call:

```
import langchain
langchain.debug=True
agent.run(f"""Count how many times a fruit is in this list and list
every fruit and the numbers: {fruit_list}""")
```

Answer: {'Apple': 2, 'Banana': 1, 'Peaches': 1}

In the preceding code, we turned on LangChain's debugger to see how the code is analyzing the aforementioned prompt – `Count how many times a fruit is in this list and list every fruit and the numbers: {fruit_list}` – with the fruit list defined previously. Behind the scenes, LangChain highlighted the problem and told the LLM *you have access to the Python REPL tool to execute Python code*:

```
prompts: [    "Human: You are an agent designed to write and execute
python code to answer questions.\nYou have access to a python REPL,
which you can use to execute python code. Use this to execute python
commands. Input should be a valid python command.
```

The following Python code was created by the GPT model as part of this command. Note that this code can also be run as a standalone Python program:

```
[tool/start] [chain:AgentExecutor > tool:Python_REPL] Entering Tool
run with input:
"fruits = ['Apple', 'Banana', 'Apple', 'Peaches']
fruit_count = {}
for fruit in fruits:
    if fruit in fruit_count:
        fruit_count[fruit] += 1
    else:
        fruit_count[fruit] = 1
print(fruit_count)"
```

This example shows how LangChain agents and modules provide extensibility to what we can achieve with general-purpose LLMs.

As we have seen in this section, LangChain is a powerful open source framework that enhances the development of applications using LLMs. It integrates LLMs with diverse data sources for sophisticated AI functions such as RAG, enabling complex workflows and dynamic, domain-specific responses. LangChain supports creating pipelines that interact with external APIs and databases, and it also features components such as memory for context continuity, autonomous agents for interactive decision-making, and tool integration for expanded functionalities. In the next section, we will discuss RAG and how some of the LangChain concepts covered in this section can be used for it.

Understanding RAG

RAG is a technique that's used to enhance the capabilities of generative models by combining the generative power of models such as Transformers (explained in *Chapter 1*) with information that can be extracted from a vector database using similarity search.

How RAG works

The following are the key steps for implementing RAG:

1. **Embedding**: The first step in RAG is to convert input text data into a form that can be processed by ML models. This involves embedding documents and queries into high-dimensional vector spaces so that these embeddings can capture the semantic meaning of the text, enabling similarity comparisons between different pieces of text.
2. **Vector database and indexing**: Once the relevant documents have been embedded, these vectors are stored in a vector database. This database is optimized so that vectors that are similar to a given query vector can be retrieved quickly. In this example, we will be using **DocArrayInMemorySearch**, an open source vector store database offered by **DocArray** under the Apache License. It is a document index that keeps databases in memory. This may be useful when we start working with smaller datasets. Other examples of vector databases include Qdrant, PineCone, Facebook AI Similarity Search (FAISS), and Elasticsearch with vector plugins.

The next step is indexing, which involves organizing the data in the vector database to optimize retrieval. Efficient indexing is crucial for performance, especially as the dataset grows, as it helps with locating data quickly without scanning the entire dataset. Indexes can be built based on flat architectures for small datasets or more complex partitioning techniques such as trees, graphs, or clusters for larger datasets, facilitating faster search operations by narrowing down the search space.

1. **Retrieval**: When a query comes into an LLM, it is converted into an embedding using the same method that's used for the supporting document embeddings. This query vector is then used to search the vector database, where the most similar document vectors are retrieved.
2. **Final interaction with the LLM**: The retrieved documents (or their embeddings) are then fed into an LLM, along with the original query. The LLM uses this augmented input to generate a response that is informed by the retrieved documents. This step allows the LLM to produce responses that are not only contextually relevant but also factually accurate and rich in detail, drawing on the specific information that was retrieved from the external documents.

Running a query

Now, let's go through an example. Here, we'll use an outdoor clothing catalog dataset to find the relevant products for our query by performing a similarity search. After, we'll use OpenAI to summarize these products in the format we desire.

First, let's install the necessary modules and libraries:

```
!pip install langchain openAI langchain-community docarray tiktoken
from langchain.chat_models import ChatOpenAI
from langchain.document_loaders import CSVLoader
from langchain.vectorstores import DocArrayInMemorySearch
from IPython.display import display, Markdown
from langchain.llms import OpenAI
```

Now, we will download the *Fashion Clothing Products Dataset* from Kaggle for the e-commerce company Myntra, a major Indian fashion e-commerce website. This dataset is shared under the public domain (CC0) at `https://www.kaggle.com/datasets/shivamb/fashion-clothing-products-catalog`.

```
import pandas as pd
df = pd.read_csv('<file_path>/myntra_products_catalog.csv')
df.to_csv('processed_file.csv', index=False)
from langchain.document_loaders import CSVLoader
loader = CSVLoader(file_path='processed_file.csv')
documents = loader.load()
```

This CSV file contains 12,491 product descriptions, with the column headers being `ProductID`, `ProductName`, `ProductBrand`, `Gender`, `Price (INR)`, `NumImages`, `Description`, and `PrimaryColor`.

If you are using Google Colab to run this code, you can also download the file from Google Drive and mount it by running the following command:

```
from google.colab import drive
drive.mount('/content/drive')
```

Now, we will install `openai` and generate embeddings using OpenAI models:

```
!pip install langchain-openai openai
from langchain_openai import OpenAIEmbeddings
import openai
embeddings = OpenAIEmbeddings(openai_api_key=<open_ai_key>)
```

To test the dimensionality of these embeddings, we can embed a string, such as `Apple`, and print its embedding dimensions. From the output, we can see that these embeddings are stored in a 1,536-dimensional space:

```
embed = embeddings.embed_query("Apple")
print(f"Dimensionlaity of these embeddings are {len(embed)}")
Dimensionlaity of these embeddings are 1536
```

Due to this high dimensionality, it is hard to visualize the embeddings. However, we can use dimensionality reduction techniques, such as **principal component analysis** (**PCA**), to reduce these high-dimensionality vectors to a two or three-dimensional space so that we can visualize them.

Now, we will create a vector database using the document object we created previously:

```
db = DocArrayInMemorySearch.from_documents(
    documents,
    embeddings
)
```

At this point, we can define the query so that it finds regular-fit shirts that are either blue or white and can be worn for formal occasions. By default, the similarity search function reports the four closest matches. However, by defining `k=5`, we are asking it to respond with the five closest matches:

```
query = "Shirts which are good for Men, have regular fit and not the
slim fit and can be used for a Formal occasion and have a color of
either Blue or white"
docs = db.similarity_search(query, k=5)
```

We can use the `docs[0:5]` command to see the five shirts that the vector database has identified. Once we've done that, we can start the `openai` module:

```
llm_model = "gpt-3.5-turbo"
llm =ChatOpenAI(model=llm_model,openai_api_key=<open_ai_key>)
```

Now, we can feed this new information from the similarity search as a context to the LLM and ask it to summarize camping gear. We can do this by creating a variable called `qdocs` that combines all five documents that were returned by the similarity search:

```
qdocs = ".".join([docs[i].page_content for i in range(len(docs))])
response = llm.call_as_llm(f"{qdocs} Question: please summarize
results in a nice summary table and then summarize each one in one
line and finally recommend the one with good reasons.-{query}")
```

The following screenshot shows an example response:

```
display(Markdown(response))
```

ProductID	ProductName	ProductBrand	Price(INR)	PrimaryColor
10202571	People Men Blue Regular Fit Solid Casual Shirt	People	899	Blue
10036595	ColorPlus Men Blue & Off-White Regular Fit Printed Casual Shirt	ColorPlus	959	Blue
10036491	ColorPlus Men Blue Regular Fit Solid Casual Shirt	ColorPlus	1039	Blue
10036349	ColorPlus Men Blue Regular Fit Printed Casual Shirt	ColorPlus	1119	Blue
10036433	ColorPlus Men Blue & White Regular Fit Checked Casual Shirt	ColorPlus	2699	Blue

1. People Men Blue Regular Fit Solid Casual Shirt by People for INR 899
2. ColorPlus Men Blue & Off-White Regular Fit Printed Casual Shirt by ColorPlus for INR 959
3. ColorPlus Men Blue Regular Fit Solid Casual Shirt by ColorPlus for INR 1039
4. ColorPlus Men Blue Regular Fit Printed Casual Shirt by ColorPlus for INR 1119
5. ColorPlus Men Blue & White Regular Fit Checked Casual Shirt by ColorPlus for INR 2699

Recommendation: I would recommend the People Men Blue Regular Fit Solid Casual Shirt by People for INR 899 as it offers a good balance of price and style with a classic blue color suitable for formal occasions.

Figure 4.1 – LLM output for the query

Now, let's say we would like to achieve geolocalization and want to convert the same recommendations into **French**. We could add the following to our query:

```
response = llm.call_as_llm(f"{qdocs} Question: summarize results in a
nice summary table converting everything to French and then summarize
each one in one line and finally recommend the one with good reasons.
Respond in French-{query}")
```

```
display(Markdown(response))
```

ProduitID	Nom du produit	Marque	Genre	Prix (INR)	Description	Couleur principale
10202571	Chemise décontractée bleue à coupe droite pour hommes People	People	Hommes	899	Chemise décontractée bleue unie pour hommes, col boutonné, manches longues, patte de boutonnage, ourlet arrondi et 1 poche plaquée	Bleu
10036595	Chemise décontractée imprimée bleue et blanche à coupe droite pour hommes ColorPlus	ColorPlus	Hommes	959	Chemise décontractée imprimée bleue et blanche pour hommes, col à revers, manches longues, patte de boutonnage, ourlet arrondi et 1 poche plaquée	Bleu
10036491	Chemise décontractée bleue à coupe droite pour hommes ColorPlus	ColorPlus	Hommes	1039	Chemise décontractée bleue unie pour hommes, col à revers, manches longues, patte de boutonnage, ourlet arrondi et 1 poche plaquée	Bleu
10036349	Chemise décontractée imprimée bleue à coupe droite pour hommes ColorPlus	ColorPlus	Hommes	1119	Chemise décontractée imprimée bleue pour hommes, col à revers, manches longues, patte de boutonnage, ourlet arrondi et 1 poche plaquée	Bleu
10036433	Chemise décontractée à carreaux bleus et blancs à coupe droite pour hommes ColorPlus	ColorPlus	Hommes	2699	Chemise décontractée à carreaux bleus et blancs pour hommes, col à revers, manches longues, patte de boutonnage, ourlet arrondi et 1 poche plaquée	Bleu

Les chemises pour hommes de couleur bleue de la marque People et ColorPlus avec une coupe régulière conviennent parfaitement pour des occasions formelles.

Recommandation: La chemise décontractée bleue à coupe droite pour hommes de la marque People est recommandée en raison de son prix abordable, de sa couleur classique et de sa coupe régulière adaptée pour les occasions formelles.

Figure 4.2 – The LLM's response (translated into French)

Lastly, let's assume that we also have demographics data. We could use the following demographics data to further personalize the recommendation. In the following code, we have created two fictional personas, `John` and `Adam`, and have asked the LLM to keep this demographics data in mind while recommending a shirt:

```
demographics ={"John": {'Age':30, 'Education': "Bachelor's Degree
in Computer Science", 'Occupation': "Software Engineer"}, "Adam":
{'Age':60, 'Occupation': "Retired"}}
response = llm.call_as_llm(f"{qdocs}, Question: Recommend one shirt
each for both individuals and provide good reasoning {demographics}.-
{query}")
print (response)
```

The following output is generated by the LLM:

```
For John, the Software Engineer:
I recommend the Next Look Men Blue Regular Fit Solid Formal Shirt.
This shirt is a solid blue color, perfect for a formal occasion. It
has a regular fit, which will provide comfort and a professional look.
As John is a software engineer, this shirt will allow him to maintain
a polished appearance while also being comfortable for long hours at
work.
```

```
For Adam, the Retired individual:
I recommend the ColorPlus Men Blue & Off-White Regular Fit Printed
Casual Shirt. This shirt has a mix of blue and off-white colors,
making it versatile for various occasions. It has a regular fit,
providing a comfortable wear for Adam. The printed design adds a touch
of style without being too bold, suitable for a retired individual
looking for a casual yet put-together look.
```

As we can see, RAG can integrate Transformer models with information extracted via similarity search from a vector database to enhance generative responses. The process begins with embedding input text into vectors for semantic similarity comparisons and storing these in a vector database optimized for fast retrieval. During a query, these embeddings are utilized to fetch the most relevant documents, which are then fed into an LLM to generate informed and detailed responses. This method improves the contextuality and factual accuracy of the model's outputs.

Next, let's look at model fine-tuning.

Model fine-tuning

Model fine-tuning is an important technique in GenAI as it helps to optimize a pre-trained general-purpose model for a specific task or domain. Fine-tuning involves taking a pre-trained model and training it further on a smaller, domain-specific dataset.

This process allows the model to learn and internalize specific information, making it more specialized in that domain. While pre-trained LLMs, such as Llama3, possess extensive general knowledge, fine-tuning enables them to perform specialized tasks or use proprietary data that is not available for training a general-purpose LLM.

Model fine-tuning can help in the following ways:

- It reduces **model hallucinations** – that is, the likelihood of the model generating incorrect or misleading information
- It provides higher consistency in the model's outputs by fine-tuning training data
- It leverages proprietary data without exposing it externally
- It reduces the cost associated with each query or task via quantization and optimization
- It offers better control over the model's behavior and performance

As we can see, fine-tuning offers multiple benefits for domain-specific optimization. However, on the flip side, fine-tuning is computationally expensive and time-consuming as it requires a high-quality, domain-specific dataset and the model may become outdated quickly without regular re-fine-tuning.

RAG, on the other hand, can dynamically update information and provide answers based on the most current data available. RAG requires less computational power and data compared to fine-tuning and gives us the flexibility to use different or updated data sources without the need to retrain the model based on the use case at hand.

Choosing between RAG and fine-tuning depends on the use case and KPIs such as latency, cost per inference, accuracy, and so on. For example, if we are developing a domain-specific chatbot, such as one that provides medical advice, fine-tuning a language model on domain-specific medical documents might offer better accuracy because the model learns to understand specific terminologies and context. However, if the goal is to provide real-time question-answering over a constantly changing dataset, such as product information on an e-commerce site, RAG might provide better-quality results.

Fine-tuning LLMs can be resource-intensive if we are training all the weights of the model. This has led to the development of **Parameter-Efficient Fine-Tuning** (**PEFT**) techniques such as **adapter-based tuning** and **Low-Rank Adaptation** (**LoRA**), which significantly reduce the computational cost while retaining high performance. In adapter-based tuning, small, trainable modules, called adapters, are inserted between the layers of a frozen pre-trained model. These adapters learn task-specific behavior without modifying the original model weights, enabling efficient and modular fine-tuning. In the upcoming sub-sections, we will explore LoRA fine-tuning variations and their implementation.

LoRA

LoRA is a technique that's used in neural network models to make training more computationally efficient, something that's particularly useful for large models. Typically, training a neural network involves updating a large matrix of weights, which can be quite resource-intensive. Instead of updating the entire weight matrix, LoRA uses a low-rank approximation, which modifies the weight matrix by adding a smaller, easier-to-compute update.

In LoRA, this update is represented by two smaller matrices that are multiplied together. This results in a significant reduction in the number of parameters that need to be updated during training. In the following fine-tuning example, using LoRA, we will reduce the parameters that require updates from around 4.62 billion to around 88 million, or approximately 2% of the original total, making the process much more efficient without a substantial loss of performance. The scaling factor in LoRA helps adjust the impact of these updates, ensuring that the model remains effective while being less demanding to train.

Fine-tuning example

In this example, we will be using the Llama3 model. To fine-tune Llama3, we have created a synthetic loyalty program FAQ dataset using ChatGPT. We have called it `MyElite Loyalty Program` and have created it with the following guidelines in mind:

- The `MyElite` program has a $99 annual subscription fee
- It offers benefits such as extended support for wear and tear
- It offers early access to sales events such as Black Friday, Labor Day, Cyber Monday, Christmas, and more

Using ChatGPT, we have created two files, `loyalty_qa_train` and `loyalty_qa_eval`, which contain prompts and responses for training and evaluation, respectively.

The following is an example prompt and response from this dataset:

```
{"prompt": "[MyElite Loyalty Program FAQ]: What is the cost of the MyElite Loyalty Program?", "response": "The MyElite Loyalty Program costs 99 USD per year. This fee is non-refundable, even if you cancel the membership."},
{"prompt": "[MyElite Loyalty Program FAQ]: Can I cancel my MyElite Loyalty Program membership?", "response": "Yes, you can cancel your membership at any time. However, you will still enjoy the benefits until the end of your subscription period."},
```

Both files are in JSON format. Note that we have added a string, `[MyElite Loyalty Program FAQ]`, before every prompt so that we get better training outcomes and can differentiate this dataset from other loyalty program FAQs that the Llama3 model might have been trained on.

Now, let's go through the code:

1. **Install the necessary libraries and dependencies**: First, we must install the necessary libraries and load the training and evaluation datasets:

   ```
   !pip install bitsandbytes transformers accelerate peft datasets wandb
   from huggingface_hub import login, login(token="<hf_token>")
   from datasets import load_dataset
   train_dataset = load_dataset('json', data_files=
   'loyalty_qa_train.jsonl', split='train')
   eval_dataset = load_dataset('json', data_files='loyalty_qa_val.jsonl', split='train')
   ```

   Let's look at the different libraries we will be using:

   - `bitsandbytes`: This is a lightweight **Compute Unified Device Architecture** (**CUDA**) implementation for low-level GPU computations that's been optimized for memory efficiency and provides efficient implementations of matrix multiplication, quantization, and other tensor operations. In this example, we will be downloading it using the Llama3 model with **int 4** precision.
   - `transformers`: Hugging Face's `transformers` library provides pre-trained models for a wide range of transformer-based models, including Mistral and Llama for easy integration for GenAI use cases.
   - `accelerate`: This library by Hugging Face is designed to simplify the process of training and deploying PyTorch models on multiple GPUs or TPUs. It abstracts away the complexity of distributed training, making it easier to scale models across different hardware configurations.

- `peft`: This library focuses on parameter-efficient fine-tuning techniques for large pre-trained models, thus reducing computational cost and memory requirements. It only allows fine-tuning to be performed on a small subset of parameters, such as adapters or low-rank updates, rather than the entire model.
- `datasets`: The `datasets` library by Hugging Face provides easy access to a wide range of datasets for ML, including tools for loading, processing, and analyzing datasets.

Next, we must download the *Weights & Biases* library. This is an optional library that can provide great insights into resource utilization during the fine-tuning process. We'll take a closer look at this when we cover model training:

```
import wandb, os
os.environ["WANDB_API_KEY"]="<wandb_API_Key>"
wandb.login()
os.environ["WANDB_PROJECT"] = "Llama_finetune"
```

2. **Download Llama3**: Now, we will download the Llama3 model with 4-bit quantization. Quantization reduces the precision of the model's parameters from their original 32-bit floating-point values to lower-bit representations, such as 4-bit. This reduces the memory footprint significantly and can potentially speed up inference while maintaining reasonable model performance. For reference, Llama3 has 8 billion parameters. If we use full precision (32-bit), it will take 32 GB of RAM just to hold the model weights as each weight would require 4 bytes of memory. With 4-bit precision (1/2 byte), the same model weights could fit into ~4 GB of RAM:

```
import torch
from transformers import AutoTokenizer, AutoModelForCausalLM,
BitsAndBytesConfig
base_model_id = "meta-llama/Meta-Llama-3-8B"
bnb_config = BitsAndBytesConfig(
    load_in_4bit=True,bnb_4bit_use_double_quant=True,
    bnb_4bit_quant_type="nf4",
    bnb_4bit_compute_dtype=torch.bfloat16
)
model = AutoModelForCausalLM.from_pretrained(base_model_id,
quantization_config=bnb_config, device_map="auto")
```

3. **Tokenize the training and evaluation data**: Now, we can initialize a tokenizer to convert text inputs into embeddings using a pre-trained model tokenizer. We'll add special tokens at the beginning and end of sequences to ensure that the dataset is of uniform length for tensor processing. Finally, we'll assign the **end-of-sequence** (EOS) token as the padding token, ensuring that sequences are handled consistently:

```
tokenizer = AutoTokenizer.from_pretrained(
    base_model_id, padding_side="left", add_eos_token=True,
    add_bos_token=True,
```

```
)
tokenizer.pad_token = tokenizer.eos_token
```

Next, we'll define the formatting function to load training and evaluation datasets for fine-tuning. The following code takes each line in the training and validation dataset and formats it by parsing it for `prompt` and `response` purposes and then tokenizing it:

```
def formatting_func(example):
    text = f»### Question: {example[<prompt>]}\n ### Answer:
{example['response']}"
    return text
def tokenize_prompt(prompt):
    return tokenizer(formatting_func(prompt))
tokenized_train_dataset= train_dataset.map(tokenize_prompt)
tokenized_val_dataset = eval_dataset.map(tokenize_prompt)
```

4. **Apply LoRA/PEFT**: At this point, the dataset is ready to be trained. The following code sets up the model for parameter-efficient fine-tuning using the LoRA method. In this example, we are setting the rank of the low-rank update matrices (`r`) to `32` and the scaling factor (`alpha`) to `64`. We are also defining the target modules where LoRA will be applied, such as the Query (Q), Key (K), and Value (V) vectors; we discussed these in *Chapter 1*. By setting `bias="none"`, we are telling the model that no bias terms are to be adapted during fine-tuning. Finally, we are applying a dropout of 5% to the LoRA layers to prevent overfitting:

```
from peft import LoraConfig, get_peft_model
config = LoraConfig(
    r=32,lora_alpha=64,
    target_modules=[
        «q_proj","k_proj","v_proj", "o_proj",
        «gate_proj","up_proj","down_proj", "lm_head",
    ],
    bias=»none",lora_dropout=0.05, task_type="CAUSAL_LM",
)
model = get_peft_model(model, config)
```

Now, we can use the `param.requires_grad` flag in PyTorch to see which model parameters require gradients to be calculated during the backpropagation process and compare this with all the parameters in the Llama3 model. For this example, we get the following:

- *All model parameters*: 4,628,721,664
- *all trainable parameters*: 88,121,344

This means that LoRA/PEFT has reduced the original parameters by ~98%.

5. **Model training**: Now that the LoRA/PEFT configuration has been set up, we need to set up the training configuration details, such as the number of warmup steps (`per_device_train_batch_size`) that define the batch size per device (GPU/TPU) during training. If we have multiple GPUs, the total batch size will be this number multiplied by the number of GPUs. We can also make the following configurations:

   - `gradient_accumulation_step`: This defines the number of steps that it will take to accumulate gradients before a backward pass is performed
   - `max_steps=200`: This defines the maximum number of training steps
   - `optim="paged_adamw_8bit"`: This specifies the optimizer that's used during training

   Since we are using Weights & Biases, a popular tool for experiment tracking and model monitoring, we'll define its configuration as part of the trainer configuration:

```
import transformers
from datetime import datetime
run_name = "llama_fine_tune"
output_dir = "<output_dir>" + run_name
trainer = transformers.Trainer(
    model=model,
    train_dataset=tokenized_train_dataset,
    eval_dataset=tokenized_val_dataset,
    args=transformers.TrainingArguments(
        output_dir=output_dir,
        warmup_steps=2,per_device_train_batch_size=2,
        gradient_accumulation_steps=1, gradient_
checkpointing=True,
        max_steps=200,learning_rate=2.5e-5, bf16=True,
        optim="paged_adamw_8bit",logging_steps=25,
        logging_dir="./logs", save_strategy="steps"
        save_steps=25, eval_strategy="steps",
        eval_steps=25, do_eval=True, report_to="wandb"
        run_name=<w&B_run_name>
    ),
    data_collator=transformers.
DataCollatorForLanguageModeling(tokenizer, mlm=False),
)
trainer.train()
```

The last line of this code trains/fine-tunes the model.

Configuring the `wandb` library could provide us with great insights and matrices about training and evaluation losses, time per step, and system utilization. The graph on the left shows that the training loss decreases steadily as the number of global steps increases, indicating that the model is learning and improving on the training data:

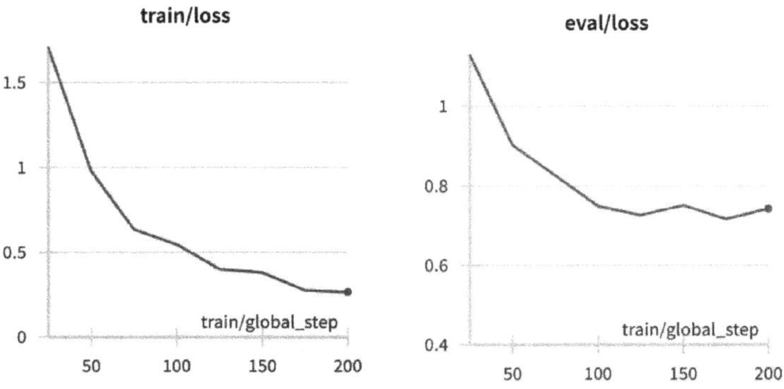

Figure 4.3 – Training and evaluation loss reported by the wandb library

Initially, the loss drops sharply, which shows rapid learning early in the training, and then it starts to flatten out as the model continues to train. By step 200, the training loss is quite low (below 0.5), suggesting that the model has fit the training data well.

On the evaluation dataset, evaluation loss also decreases over time but less sharply compared to the training loss. At step 200, the evaluation loss is around 0.75, indicating that the model still generalizes reasonably well to the validation data but may be close to overfitting if further training continues. This is quite possible since both our training and validation datasets are quite small.

The `wandb` library also provides great insights into resource utilization, such as GPU, CPU, memory, and disk access. For example, the following graph shows GPU utilization over time:

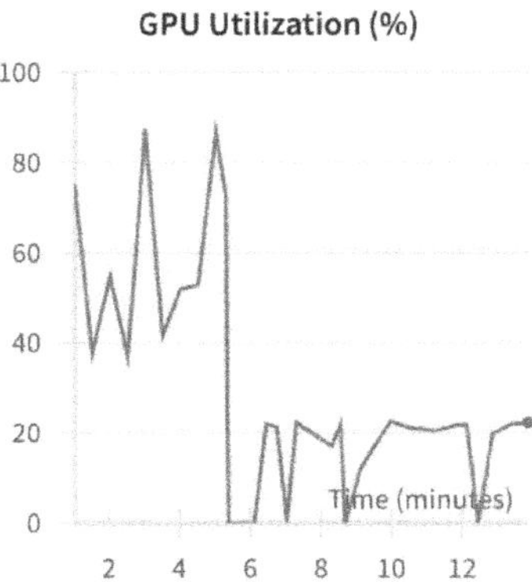

Figure 4.4 – GPU utilization during the training process

As we can see, GPU utilization fluctuated significantly between 50% and 80% for the first 5 minutes, indicating that the GPU was being actively used during this period by the training/evaluation process. After that, GPU utilization starts to fall. This might correspond to tasks that don't rely heavily on GPU, such as data loading, CPU-bound operations, or idle time between steps.

1. **Run inference**: Now that our model has been trained, it is our turn to test the quality of our inference. For this example, we have created a function called `generate_text()` that takes a user's prompt and generates a continuation of the text using our fine-tuned model. The input prompt is tokenized and processed on a CUDA-enabled device, with the model generating new tokens based on specified parameters such as `max_new_tokens` and `repetition_penalty`. The generated text is then decoded and returned as a string that excludes any special tokens:

```
def generate_text(user_prompt, max_new_tokens=100, repetition_
penalty=1.2):
model_input = tokenizer(user_prompt, return_tensors="pt").
to("cuda")
    model.eval()
    with torch.no_grad():
        generated_output = model.generate(
            **model_input,max_new_tokens=max_new_tokens,
            repetition_penalty=repetition_penalty
        )
        generated_text = tokenizer.decode(generated_output[0],
skip_special_tokens=True)
    return generated_text
```

Now, let's test our fine-tuned model on a few prompts:

Question	`Does the MyElite Loyalty Program offer any discount on purchases?`
Training dataset (correct answer)	`While the program does not directly offer discounts, members can earn up to 2% cashback on all purchases. The cashback is paid annually via a gift card.`
Fine-tuned response	`The program does not currently offer discounts. Members enjoy early access to sales events, special promotions, and other exclusive perks.`
Non-fine-tuned response	`We are happy to announce that we have launched a new loyalty program called "My Elite" for our customers. Customers who spend $50 or more will be automatically enrolled in this elite customer club and earn points with every purchase.`

In this example, the Llama3 model (non-fine-tuned) has created a response that doesn't align with our FAQ since our membership has annual fees of $99. This is not surprising since the original model has not seen this dataset before. After fine-tuning, the model correctly predicts that there are no discounts, and it also picks up another aspect of our loyalty program – that it offers access to early sales events.

Now, let's look at another example:

Question	`What is the maximum cashback I can earn?`
Training dataset (correct answer)	`The maximum cashback you can earn is 2% of your purchases, capped at 1000 USD per year. The cashback is provided as a gift card.`
Fine-tuned response	`The maximum cashback you can earn is 2% of your purchases, capped at $1000 per year. The cashback is paid annually via a gift card. You will receive the cashback as a gift card once a year if your account balance exceeds $25.`
Non-fine-tuned response	`If you are a member of My Elite, then there's no limit on how much money your wallet could make. You will continue to receive rewards as long as our site has new offers and deals. In case if any offer doesn't work for some reason or another it won't be counted in this amount but we'll still try to find out what went wrong so that next time around when someone tries something similar they don't run into problems like these ones did today!`

In this example, we can see that the non-fine-tuned model has made up an answer that might be reflective of lots of other loyalty programs' FAQs that this model has been trained on. The fine-tuned model correctly predicts that you can earn up to 2% cashback on a purchase and that it's capped at $1,000. However, it also mentions `You will receive the cashback as a gift card once a year if your account balance exceeds $25`, which is not in our training dataset. This highlights one of the challenges/focus areas for GenAI – that is, how to keep the model's response within the assigned guardrails so that it doesn't hallucinate while responding. This is something we will discuss in `Part 3` of this book.

Summary

In this chapter, we discussed optimizing a general-purpose LLM for domain-specific applications, such as chatbots and personalized recommendations. This adaptation is critical because it enhances model accuracy, efficiency, and reliability when dealing with specialized tasks.

First, we discussed the LangChain library, which is instrumental in developing applications that leverage LLMs. LangChain facilitates complex workflows involving external APIs, databases, and retrieval systems, which help in generating context-aware and domain-specific responses. We also learned about techniques such as prompt engineering and knowledge integration. Prompt engineering involves crafting input prompts that guide the model to generate outputs that are more relevant to a specific domain, while knowledge integration uses approaches such as RAG to supplement the model's responses with external, domain-specific data.

Model fine-tuning is another focus area that we covered in this chapter. This involves additional training of a pre-trained model, typically on domain-specific data, allowing it to better align with the specific terminology and knowledge of a domain. This chapter also introduced parameter-efficient fine-tuning techniques such as LoRA, which reduces computational costs while maintaining performance.

In the next chapter, we will implement some of the techniques mentioned here, such as RAG and fine-tuning, within a K8s environment to show how K8s can help in creating a scalable GenAI application.

Further reading

To learn more about the topics that were covered in this chapter, take a look at the following resources:

- *LangChain – [Beta] Memory*: `https://python.langchain.com/v0.1/docs/modules/memory/`
- *LangChain for LLM Application Development*: `https://www.deeplearning.ai/short-courses/langchain-for-llm-application-development/`
- *Fine-tuning Mistral on your own data*: `https://github.com/brevdev/notebooks/blob/main/mistral-finetune-own-data.ipynb`

5

Working with GenAI on K8s: Chatbot Example

In this chapter, we will build on the examples we discussed in *Chapter 4* and start deploying those examples in **K8s/Amazon EKS**. We will start by deploying **JupyterHub** (`https://jupyter.org/hub`) on EKS, which can be used for model experimentation. Next, we will fine-tune the **Llama 3 model** within EKS and deploy it. Finally, we'll set up a **RAG-powered chatbot** that will deliver personalized recommendations for an *e-commerce* company use case.

We'll cover the following key topics:

- GenAI use cases for e-commerce
- Experimentation using JupyterHub
- Fine-tuning Llama 3 in K8s
- Deploying the fine-tuned model on K8s
- Deploying a RAG application on K8s
- Deploying a chatbot on K8s

Technical requirements

In this chapter, we will be using the following tools, some of which require you to set up an account and create an access token:

- **Hugging Face**: `https://huggingface.co/join`
- **OpenAI**: `https://platform.openai.com/signup`
- The **Llama 3 model**, which can be accessed via Hugging Face: `https://huggingface.co/meta-llama/Meta-Llama-3-8B`
- An **Amazon EKS cluster**, as illustrated in *Chapter 3*

GenAI use cases for e-commerce

As we discussed in *Chapter 1*, it is critical to think about *KPIs* and *business objectives* as we explore possible deployment options for **GenAI applications**. For an e-commerce platform, possible use cases could be chatbots to answer customer questions, personalized recommendations, content creation for product descriptions, and personalized marketing campaigns.

Let's say that we have an e-commerce company called *MyRetail* for which we have been given the responsibility to explore and deploy GenAI use cases. The company has been growing rapidly and has a clear goal and strong differentiation: to provide its customers with a personalized, seamless shopping experience. To stay competitive, MyRetail aims to integrate cutting-edge AI technologies into its customer service while focusing on the following two features:

1. *Creating personalized product recommendations* using a **RAG system**.
2. *Providing automated responses* to inquiries related to the company's loyalty program through a fine-tuned **GenAI model**.

MyRetail's diverse customer base means that generic product recommendations and traditional FAQ systems are no longer sufficient. Customers expect personalized shopping experiences, and the company's *MyElite loyalty program* needs to offer real-time, detailed information on rewards, points, and account status.

To achieve these goals, MyRetail has decided to adopt the open source K8s orchestration platform and has selected Amazon EKS to deploy it in the cloud. They plan to build a chatbot application that utilizes two GenAI models: the first one will be a fine-tuned Llama 3 model trained on their MyElite loyalty program FAQ to answer user queries, while the second one will be a RAG application that supplements user queries with contextual shopping catalog data to enhance their shopping experience. The overall architecture of this solution is shown in *Figure 5.1*:

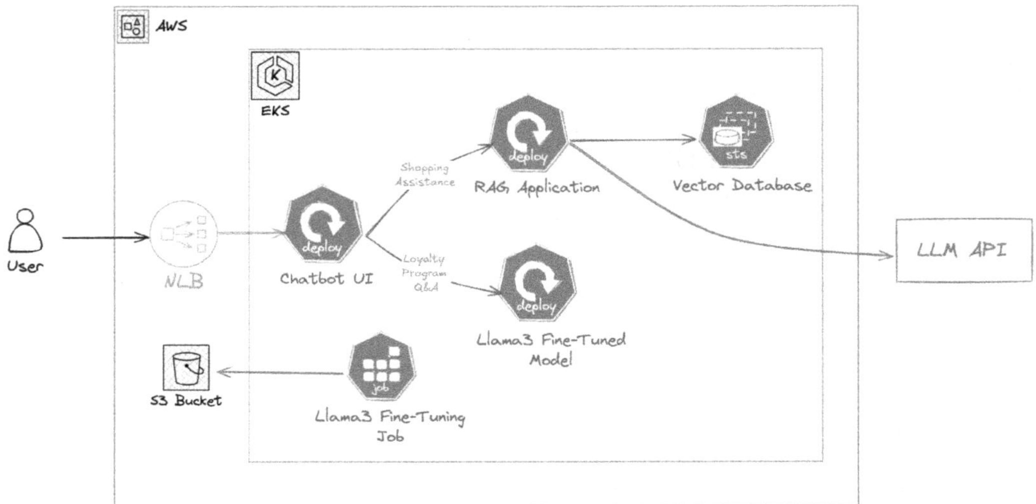

Figure 5.1 – Chatbot architecture

However, before we implement this **chatbot** and **RAG system** in EKS, let's create a **JupyterHub**-based playground for our data scientists to experiment with and optimize the GenAI models.

Experimentation using JupyterHub

Experimentation plays a vital role in any GenAI project life cycle as it enables engineers and researchers to iterate, improve, and refine models while optimizing performance. Several tools are available for this; recall that we used **Anaconda** and **Google Colab** in *Chapter 4*. Primarily, these tools help us to experiment interactively with GenAI models, visualize, monitor, and integrate with popular AI/ML frameworks, integrate with cloud services, and collaborate with others. **Jupyter Notebook** (`https://jupyter.org/`) has gained widespread adoption among data scientists and ML engineers due to its flexibility and easy-to-use web interface. This is evident from the average daily downloads of the notebook package (900K to 1 million downloads) (`https://pypistats.org/packages/notebook`), as indicated by the **Python Package Index** (`https://pypi.org/`). Traditionally, we install these notebooks on local machines, but they often need specialized resources such as GPUs to perform meaningful analysis. To solve this issue, we will leverage a K8s cluster to spin up Jupyter notebooks as needed using JupyterHub.

JupyterHub offers a centralized platform for running Jupyter notebooks, enabling users to access computational resources without requiring individual installations or maintenance. System administrators can manage user access effectively and tailor the environment with pre-configured tools and settings to meet user-specific preferences.

Let's start by learning how to install JupyterHub on an Amazon EKS cluster:

1. First, deploy the **Amazon EBS CSI driver** add-on. Jupyter notebooks require access to persistent storage volumes so that they can store session data, custom configurations, datasets, and more. The Amazon EBS CSI driver (`https://github.com/kubernetes-sigs/aws-ebs-csi-driver`) lets us use Amazon EBS volumes (`https://aws.amazon.com/ebs/`) for the K8s Pods in the EKS cluster and manages the life cycle of the EBS volumes as storage for ephemeral and persistent K8s volumes. We have made the following changes to `addons.tf` to install the CSI plugin, as well as added the necessary **IAM permissions**. The complete code for this is available on GitHub at `https://github.com/PacktPublishing/Kubernetes-for-Generative-AI-Solutions/blob/main/ch5/addons.tf`:

```
module "eks_blueprints_addons" {
  ....
  eks_addons = {
    aws-ebs-csi-driver = {
      service_account_role_arn = module.ebs_csi_driver_irsa.
iam_role_arn
    }
    ....
}
```

```
module "ebs_csi_driver_irsa" {
...
  role_name_prefix = format("%s-%s", local.name, "ebs-csi-
driver-")
  attach_ebs_csi_policy = true
...
}
```

2. Now, we need to create a default **StorageClass** (`https://kubernetes.io/docs/concepts/storage/storage-classes/`) for the EBS CSI driver that specifies attributes such as the reclaim policy, storage provisioner, and other parameters used in dynamic volume provisioning. Here, we are setting the newer gp3 as the default type for EBS CSI driver-created volumes. Refer to the Amazon EBS documentation at `https://docs.aws.amazon.com/ebs/latest/userguide/ebs-volume-types.html` to learn more about different volume types:

```
resource "kubernetes_annotations" "disable_gp2" {
  annotations = {
    "storageclass.kubernetes.io/is-default-class": "false"
...
  metadata {
    name = "gp2"
...
resource "kubernetes_storage_class" "default_gp3" {
  metadata {
    name = "gp3"
    annotations = {
      "storageclass.kubernetes.io/is-default-class": "true"
    ...
}
```

3. Run the following commands to deploy the EBS CSI driver to the EKS cluster:

```
$ terraform init
$ terraform plan
$ terraform apply -auto-approve
```

4. You can verify the installation status of the add-on by running the following command:

```
$ aws eks describe-addon --cluster-name eks-demo --addon-name
aws-ebs-csi-driver
...
        "addonName": "aws-ebs-csi-driver",
        "clusterName": "eks-demo",
        "status": "ACTIVE",
...
```

5. Now, start deploying the JupyterHub add-on by running the `eks-data-addons` (`https://registry.terraform.io/modules/aws-ia/eks-data-addons/aws/latest`) Terraform module on the EKS cluster. This open source module can be utilized to deploy commonly used data and AI/ML K8s add-ons. Please refer to the Terraform documentation page at `https://registry.terraform.io/modules/aws-ia/eks-data-addons/aws/latest#resources` to find a list of available add-ons. Make sure you download the `aiml-addons.tf` file from `https://github.com/PacktPublishing/Kubernetes-for-Generative-AI-Solutions/blob/main/ch5/aiml-addons.tf`; it includes Terraform code to deploy the JupyterHub add-on on the EKS cluster. Let's walk through what the Terraform code does:

   - A random 16-character string is created to secure access to JupyterHub:

     > **Important note**
     >
     > In this setup, we are using a dummy authentication method where JupyterHub uses a static username and password. It also provides other authentication methods, as listed at `https://jupyterhub.readthedocs.io/en/latest/reference/authenticators.html`. Use the method that fits your needs.

     ```
     resource "random_password" "jupyter_pwd" {
       length = 16
       special = true
       override_special = "_%@"
     }
     ```

   - A new K8s namespace called `jupyterhub` is defined to deploy the JupyterHub Helm chart:

     ```
     resource "kubernetes_namespace" "jupyterhub" {
       metadata {
         name = "jupyterhub"
       }
     }
     ```

   - A K8s service account and an IAM role with appropriate S3 permissions to read from the S3 buckets are defined for interacting with S3 via Jupyter notebooks. We are using the *IAM roles for service accounts* (`https://docs.aws.amazon.com/eks/latest/userguide/iam-roles-for-service-accounts.html`) feature of Amazon EKS, which provides IAM credentials to applications running in K8s Pods securely:

     ```
     module "jupyterhub_single_user_irsa" {
       ...
       role_name = "${module.eks.cluster_name}-jupyterhub-single-
     user-sa"
     ```

```
  role_policy_arns = {
    policy = "arn:aws:iam::aws:policy/AmazonS3ReadOnlyAccess"
  }
  ...
resource "kubernetes_service_account_v1" "jupyterhub_single_
user_sa" {
  metadata {
    name = "${module.eks.cluster_name}-jupyterhub-single-user"
    annotations = {"eks.amazonaws.com/role-arn": module.
jupyterhub_single_user_irsa.iam_role_arn}
...
```

- Now, we must deploy the JupyterHub Helm chart. We are using Helm values from a public S3 bucket available at `https://kubernetes-for-genai-models.s3.amazonaws.com/chapter5/jupyterhub-values.yaml`. It contains the necessary configuration to enable dummy authentication using the password we randomly generated previously and uses a K8s service account for Jupyter notebook Pods:

```
data "http" "jupyterhub_values" {
  url = "https://kubernetes-for-genai-models.s3.amazonaws.com/
chapter5/jupyterhub-values.yaml"
}
module "eks_data_addons" {
  source = "aws-ia/eks-data-addons/aws"
...
  enable_jupyterhub = true
  jupyterhub_helm_config = {
    values = [local.jupyterhub_values_rendered]
...
```

- Run the following commands to deploy JupyterHub on the EKS cluster:

```
$ terraform init
$ terraform plan
$ terraform apply -auto-approve
```

- Verify that JupyterHub has been installed by running the following commands:

```
$ helm list -n jupyterhub
NAME         NAMESPACE     REVISION     STATUS
jupyterhub   jupyterhub    1            deployed
```

6. Since we are experimenting with GenAI models, we need to run the Jupyter notebooks on GPU instances. Given that the EKS cluster doesn't have GPU instances, we need to add one more EKS-managed node group to `eks.tf` that contains GPU nodes (`g6.2xlarge`). Here, we are using EC2 Spot Instances pricing to minimize AWS charges; please refer to the documentation at `https://aws.amazon.com/ec2/spot/pricing/` for pricing details. We are also adding K8s taints (`https://kubernetes.io/docs/concepts/scheduling-eviction/taint-and-toleration/`) to ensure that only GPU workloads are scheduled to these worker nodes. K8s taints are key-value pairs that are applied to nodes that prevent certain Pods from being scheduled on them unless the Pods tolerate the taints, allowing for better control over workload placement. By applying taints, we can ensure that non-GPU workloads are prevented from being scheduled on GPU nodes, reserving those nodes exclusively for GPU-optimized Pods. You can download the `eks.tf` file from `https://github.com/PacktPublishing/Kubernetes-for-Generative-AI-Solutions/blob/main/ch5/eks.tf`.

```
module "eks" {
  ....
  eks_managed_node_groups = {
    eks-gpu-mng = {
      instance_types = ["g6.2xlarge"]
      capacity_type = "SPOT"
      taints = {
        gpu = {
          key = "nvidia.com/gpu"
          value = "true"
          effect = "NO_SCHEDULE"
  ....
}
```

7. Run the following commands to add the GPU node group to the EKS cluster. Please note that this may take 5-10 minutes. You can verify the GPU node's status by running the following `kubectl` command, which outputs the node's name and status:

```
$ terraform init
$ terraform plan
$ terraform apply -auto-approve
$ kubectl get nodes -l nvidia.com/gpu.present=true
NAME                                          STATUS
ip-10-0-17-1.us-west-2.compute.internal       Ready
```

8. Now, we can connect to the JupyterHub console to create a notebook. In this setup, we've limited JupyterHub console access to within the cluster by exposing it as a **ClusterIP** service. Run the following commands to connect to the console locally; alternatively, you can set the service type to **LoadBalancer** to expose it via a public NLB:

```
$ kubectl port-forward svc/proxy-public 8000:80 -n jupyterhub
```

9. You can launch the JupyterHub console by navigating to `http://localhost:8000/` in your web browser. You'll see a login page, similar to what's shown in *Figure 5.2*. Here, we've pre-created a user named *k8s-admin1* as part of our JupyterHub installation. Run the following command to retrieve the password of that user:

```
$ terraform output jupyter_pwd
```

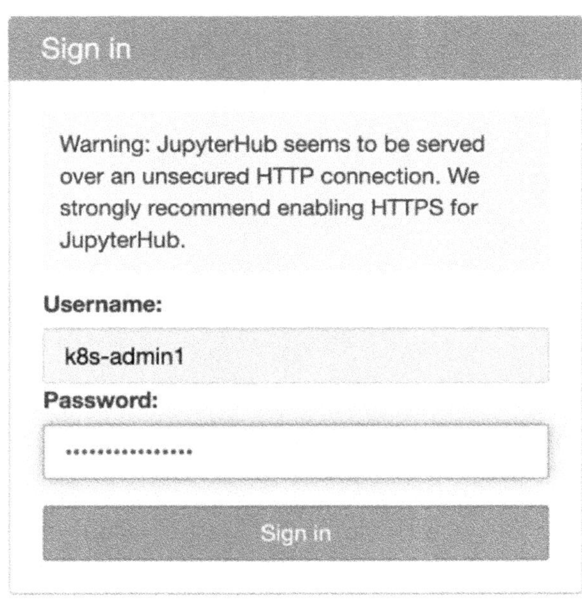

Figure 5.2 – JupyterHub login page

10. After logging in, you will be presented with three notebook options. Since we are using JupyterHub for GenAI tasks that need GPU power, select **Data Science (GPU)** and click **Start**, as shown in *Figure 5.3*:

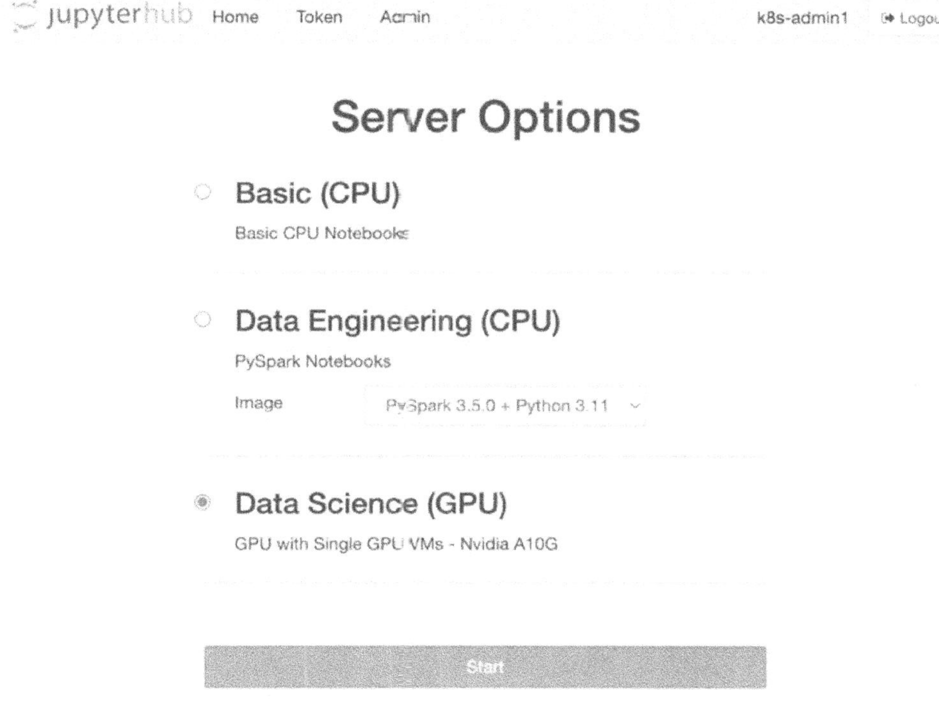

Figure 5.3 – JupyterHub home page

11. As shown in *Figure 5.4*, this will start a new notebook instance running in a K8s Pod and also request a **Persistent Volume Claim** (**PVC**) (`https://kubernetes.io/docs/concepts/storage/persistent-volumes`) so that the EBS CSI driver will create an Amazon EBS volume and attach it to the notebook. We're using a persistent volume here to preserve the notebook's state, data, and configurations across Pod restarts and terminations. This allows the notebook instance to be terminated after periods of inactivity and relaunched when the user returns, making the process more cost-efficient:

```
$ kubectl get pods -n jupyterhub -l component=singleuser-server
NAME                 READY   STATUS    RESTARTS   AGE
jupyter-k8s-2dadmin1 1/1     Running   0          9m
```

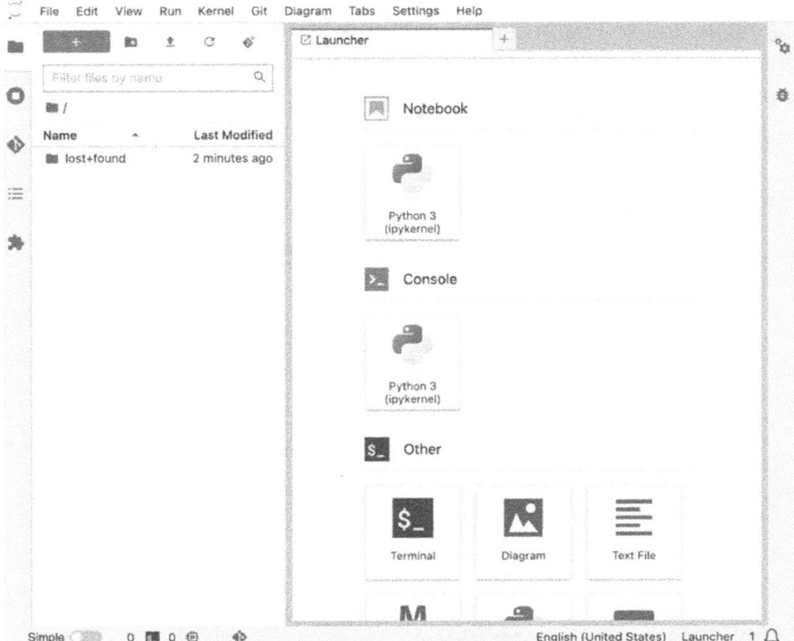

Figure 5.4 – Our Jupyter notebook

12. You can now import the following notebooks from *Chapter 4* and execute the necessary commands to test both the **RAG** and **fine-tuning** examples:

    - **RAG notebook**: `https://github.com/PacktPublishing/Kubernetes-for-Generative-AI-Solutions/blob/main/ch4/GenAIModelOptimization_RAG_Example.ipynb`

    - **Fine-tuning notebook**: `https://github.com/PacktPublishing/Kubernetes-for-Generative-AI-Solutions/blob/main/ch4/GenAIModelOptimization_FineTuning_Example.ipynb`

With that, we have set up JupyterHub on the EKS cluster and used it to launch a Jupyter notebook to test our GenAI experimentation scripts. Next, we will containerize both the fine-tuning and RAG scripts and run them as K8s Pods on the EKS cluster.

Fine-tuning Llama 3 in K8s

As discussed in *Chapter 3*, running fine-tuning workloads on K8s has several advantages, including scalability, efficient resource utilization, portability, and monitoring. In this section, we will containerize the **Llama 3 fine-tuning job** that we experimented with in the Jupyter notebook and deploy it on the EKS cluster. This is essential for automating the end-to-end AI/ML pipelines and versioning the models.

The following steps are involved in fine-tuning a Llama 3 model:

1. *Gather training and evaluation datasets* and store them in **Amazon S3**.
2. *Create a container image* and upload it to **Amazon ECR**.
3. *Deploy the fine-tuning job* in the **EKS cluster**.

Data preparation

We will utilize two datasets (training and evaluation) to fine-tune and validate a **Llama 3 model** that answers questions related to MyRetail's MyElite loyalty program. When running the fine-tuning jobs in containers, it is recommended to store the datasets in an external datastore and access them during the fine-tuning process. By doing so, we can make the container image agnostic to the dataset, and we will be able to reuse the image for different datasets. For your convenience, we have stored the MyElite loyalty program's *training and evaluation datasets* in a public **Amazon S3 bucket** called `kubernetes-for-genai-models`. **Amazon S3** (`https://aws.amazon.com/s3/`) is an object storage service that's used to store and retrieve any amount of data from anywhere, making it the ideal choice for sharing large datasets for collaboration:

```
$ aws s3 ls s3://kubernetes-for-genai-models/chapter5/
...
loyalty_qa_train.jsonl
loyalty_qa_val.jsonl
...
```

In this section, we explored the datasets that will be used to fine-tune the Llama 3 model for our e-commerce use case. We also covered best practices such as storing these databases in external storage services such as Amazon S3 rather than packaging them in the container image. In the next section, we will focus on creating a container image for the fine-tuning job.

Creating a container image

To create a container image for the fine-tuning job, we need a **Dockerfile**, a **fine-tuning script**, and a **dependency list**. We've already created these artifacts and made them available on GitHub: `https://github.com/PacktPublishing/Kubernetes-for-Generative-AI-Solutions/tree/main/ch5/llama-finetuning`. Let's start building the container so that we can fine-tune the Llama 3 model with these artifacts:

1. Create a directory named `llama-finetuning`:

   ```
   $ mkdir -p llama-finetuning
   $ cd llama-finetuning
   ```

2. We will be using the Llama 3 fine-tuning code from *Chapter 4* while making the following changes to make it container-ready. You'll need to request access to the Llama 3 model in **Hugging Face** and generate an access token before proceeding. Please refer to *Chapter 2* for instructions on how to do this. The complete fine-tuning code is available on GitHub at `https://github.com/PacktPublishing/Kubernetes-for-Generative-AI-Solutions/blob/main/ch5/llama-finetuning/fine_tune.py`:

   - Read the filenames of the training and evaluation datasets from the relevant environment variables and load them using the `datasets` library:

   ```
   ...
   train_dataset_file = os.environ.get('TRAIN_DATASET_FILE')
   eval_dataset_file = os.environ.get('EVAL_DATASET_FILE')
   train_dataset = load_dataset('json', data_files=train_dataset_
   file, split='train')
   eval_dataset = load_dataset('json', data_files=eval_dataset_
   file, split='train')
   ```

   - After training, we need to save the model weights, configuration files, and tokenizer configuration so that they can be used to create an inference container later:

   ```
   trainer.save_model(f"./{fine_tuned_model_name}")
   tokenizer.save_pretrained(f"./{fine_tuned_model_name}")
   ```

   - Export the model weights and configuration files to an S3 bucket:

   ```
   ...
   def sync_folder_to_s3(local_folder, bucket_name, s3_folder):
       s3 = boto3.client('s3')
       for root, dirs, files in os.walk(local_folder):
           for file in files:
   ...
               try:
                   s3.upload_file(local_path, bucket_name, s3_
   path)
               except Exception as e:
                   print(f'Error uploading {local_path}: {e}')
   ...
   sync_folder_to_s3('./'+fine_tuned_model_name+'/', model_
   assets_bucket, fine_tuned_model_name)
   ```

3. Create a Dockerfile where we can build the fine-tuning container image. It should start with the **nvidia/cuda** (`https://hub.docker.com/r/nvidia/cuda`) parent image, install the required Python dependencies, and contain the fine-tuning script. The complete file is available at `https://github.com/PacktPublishing/Kubernetes-for-Generative-AI-Solutions/blob/main/ch5/llama-finetuning/Dockerfile`:

```
FROM nvidia/cuda:12.8.1-runtime-ubuntu24.04
...
RUN pip install torch transformers datasets peft accelerate
bitsandbytes sentencepiece s3fs boto3
...
COPY fine_tune.py /app/fine_tune.py
CMD ["python", "fine_tune.py"]
```

4. Create the container image by running the following command:

```
$ docker build -t my-llama-finetuned .
```

5. You can verify the container image by using the following docker command:

```
$ docker images
REPOSITORY            TAG       IMAGE ID
my-llama-finetuned    latest    207a07f1bf00
```

With that, we've successfully built the container image so that we can fine-tune the Llama 3 model. Next, we will upload this to an Amazon ECR repository and deploy it to the EKS cluster.

Deploying the fine-tuning job

To deploy the fine-tuning job, we need to save the container image in **Amazon ECR** and create an **S3 bucket** where we'll save model assets, as well as create a **K8s job** in the **EKS cluster**:

1. Create an **Amazon ECR repository** using **Terraform** and upload this container image. Add the following code to the `ecr.tf` file in the `genai-eks-demo` directory. The complete code is available on GitHub at `https://github.com/PacktPublishing/Kubernetes-for-Generative-AI-Solutions/blob/main/ch5/ecr.tf`:

```
resource "aws_ecr_repository" "my-llama-finetuned" {
  name = "my-llama-finetuned"
...
```

2. Create an Amazon S3 bucket so that you can store the fine-tuned model assets. We'll create one using Terraform. Download the `model-assets.tf` file from `https://github.com/PacktPublishing/Kubernetes-for-Generative-AI-Solutions/blob/main/ch5/model-assets.tf`:

```
resource "random_string" "bucket_suffix" {
  length  = 8
...
resource "aws_s3_bucket" "my_llama_bucket" {
  bucket = "my-llama-bucket-${random_string.bucket_suffix.
result}"
...
output "my_llama_bucket" {
  value = "${aws_s3_bucket.my_llama_bucket.id}"
...
```

3. We also need to create a **K8s service account** and an **IAM role** for our fine-tuning job so that it can download the training and validation datasets and upload the model asset files to the **Amazon S3 bucket**. This was added as part of the `eks.tf` file you downloaded earlier:

```
module "llama_fine_tuning_irsa" {
...
  role_name = "${module.eks.cluster_name}-llama-fine-tuning"
  role_policy_arns = {
    policy = "arn:aws:iam::aws:policy/AmazonS3FullAccess"
  }
...
resource "kubernetes_service_account_v1" "llama_fine_tuning_sa"
{
  metadata {
    name          = "llama-fine-tuning-sa"
...
```

4. Run the following commands to create the **ECR repository** and **S3 bucket**. The S3 bucket's name will be printed in the output:

```
$ terraform init
$ terraform plan
$ terraform apply -auto-approve
```

5. Run the `terraform output` command to list the ECR upload commands. Copy and paste those output commands into your terminal to push the `my-llama-finetuned` container image to ECR:

```
$ terraform output -raw my_llama_finetuned_ecr_push_cmds
  aws ecr get-login-password --region us-west-2 | docker login
```

```
--username AWS --password-stdin 123456789012.dkr.ecr.us-west-2.
amazonaws.com/my-llama-finetuned
  docker tag my-llama-finetuned 123456789012.dkr.ecr.us-west-2.
amazonaws.com/my-llama-finetuned
  docker push 123456789012.dkr.ecr.us-west-2.amazonaws.com/
my-llama-finetuned
```

6. Now that we've created the required infrastructure, let's go ahead and deploy the fine-tuning job to the **EKS cluster**. To do so, we need to create a **K8s Job manifest file** that will run this as a K8s Job. Download the manifest from GitHub at `https://github.com/PacktPublishing/Kubernetes-for-Generative-AI-Solutions/blob/main/ch5/llama-finetuning/llama-finetuning-job.yaml` and replace the image, the Hugging Face token, and the name of the S3 bucket that contains the model assets you created previously:

```
apiVersion: batch/v1
kind: Job
metadata:
  name: my-llama-job
spec:
...
      containers:
      - name: my-llama-job-container
        image: <<Replace your ECR image name here>>
        env:
        - name: MODEL_ASSETS_BUCKET
          value: "<<Replace your S3 bucket here>>"
        - name: HUGGING_FACE_HUB_TOKEN
          value: "<<Replace your Hugging face token here>>"
        - name: TRAIN_DATASET_FILE
          value: "s3://kubernetes-for-genai-models/chapter5/
loyalty_qa_train.jsonl"
        - name: EVAL_DATASET_FILE
          value: "s3://kubernetes-for-genai-models/chapter5/
loyalty_qa_val.jsonl"
...
```

7. Run the following commands to run the job on the EKS cluster:

```
$ kubectl apply -f llama-finetuning-job.yaml
job.batch/my-llama-job is created
```

8. A K8s Pod will be scheduled on a GPU node and start the fine-tuning process. You can monitor its process by tailing its logs:

```
$ kubectl logs -f job/my-llama-job
```

9. Once fine-tuning is complete, the job will automatically upload the model assets to the S3 bucket, as shown in *Figure 5.5*:

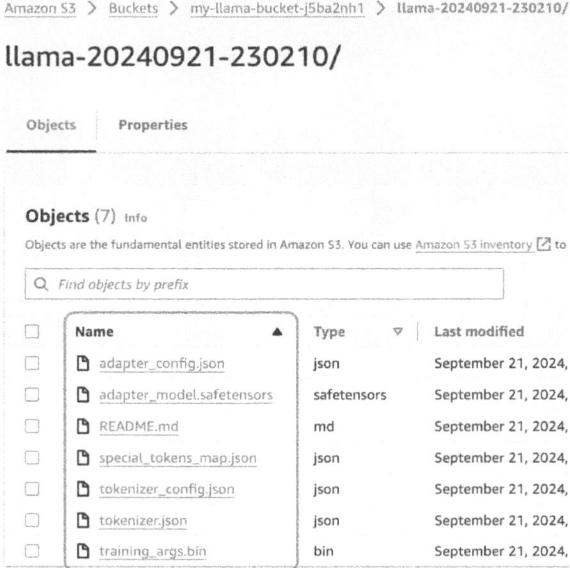

Figure 5.5 – An Amazon S3 bucket that contains fine-tuned model assets

In this section, we began by modifying our Llama 3 fine-tuning script to make it container-ready. Then, we created a container image that includes the script and its dependent libraries, using the `nvidia/cuda` image from **DockerHub** as the base. Finally, we created an Amazon ECR repository that will store the container image and deploy it as a K8s job in the EKS cluster. In the next section, we will utilize the fine-tuned model assets to create an inference container image and deploy it in the EKS cluster.

Deploying the fine-tuned model on K8s

In this section, we will containerize the fine-tuned **Llama 3 model** using **Python FastAPI** and deploy the inference endpoint as a K8s deployment in the EKS cluster.

Let's start by creating the inference container using the fine-tuned model assets stored in the S3 bucket. We will be using Python FastAPI (`https://fastapi.tiangolo.com/`) to expose the model as an **HTTP API**. FastAPI is a modern high-performance web framework for building APIs in Python:

1. Create a directory called `llama-finetuned-inf`:

```
$ mkdir -p llama-finetuned-inf
$ cd llama-finetuned-inf
```

2. Download the model assets from the S3 bucket to the local directory so that we can copy them to the container image:

```
$ aws s3 sync s3://<<Your S3 Bucket Name>>/<<Your Model
directory>> model-assets/
```

3. Create a Dockerfile so that you can build an inference container that contains fine-tuned artifacts. Here, we are using `nvidia/cuda` as the parent image, installing the necessary Python dependencies, and adding the fine-tuned model from the `model-assets` directory. The complete file is available at `https://github.com/PacktPublishing/Kubernetes-for-Generative-AI-Solutions/blob/main/ch5/inference/Dockerfile`:

```
FROM nvidia/cuda:12.8.1-runtime-ubuntu24.04
...
RUN pip install torch transformers peft accelerate bitsandbytes
sentencepiece fastapi uvicorn
COPY model-assets /app/model-assets
COPY main.py /app/main.py
CMD ["uvicorn", "main:app", "--host", "0.0.0.0", "--port", "80"]
```

4. Next, we will wrap the fine-tuned Llama 3 model into an API using **Python FastAPI**. It exposes a single API at `/generate` that accepts **HTTP POST** requests and returns a response after invoking the model. You can download the complete code from `https://github.com/PacktPublishing/Kubernetes-for-Generative-AI-Solutions/blob/main/ch5/inference/main.py`:

```
...
app = FastAPI()
# Load tokenizer and model
tokenizer = AutoTokenizer.from_pretrained('./model-assets')
# Define the quantization configuration for 8-bit
base_model_id = "meta-llama/Meta-Llama-3-8B"
bnb_config = BitsAndBytesConfig(
    load_in_4bit=True,
    bnb_4bit_use_double_quant=True,
    bnb_4bit_quant_type="nf4",
    bnb_4bit_compute_dtype=torch.bfloat16
)
base_model = AutoModelForCausalLM.from_pretrained(base_model_
id, torch_dtype=torch.float16, quantization_config=bnb_config,
device_map='auto')
# Load the Peft Model from pre-trained assets
model = PeftModel.from_pretrained(base_model, './model-assets')
...
@app.route('/generate')
async def generate(request: Request):
```

```
...
    inputs = tokenizer(prompt, return_tensors="pt").to(device)
    with torch.no_grad():
        outputs = model.generate(
            **inputs,
            max_new_tokens=100,
...
    # Decode the response and return it
    response = tokenizer.decode(outputs[0], skip_special_
tokens=True)
    return {"response": response}
```

5. Create the container image by running the following commands:

```
$ docker build -t my-llama-finetuned:inf .
```

6. We will be reusing the **ECR repository** for this image. Alternatively, you can create a new repository using Terraform, as described in *Chapter 3*. Replace the **account number** and **region** values in the following commands before running them:

```
$ aws ecr get-login-password --region us-west-2 | docker login
--username AWS --password-stdin 123456789012.dkr.ecr.us-west-2.
amazonaws.com/my-llama-finetuned
$ docker tag my-llama-finetuned:inf 123456789012.dkr.ecr.
us-west-2.amazonaws.com/my-llama-finetuned:inf
$ docker push 123456789012.dkr.ecr.us-west-2.amazonaws.com/
my-llama-finetuned:inf
```

7. Next, we will deploy the inference container in the EKS cluster as a K8s deployment. Download the `finetuned-inf-deploy.yaml` K8s manifest from `https://github.com/PacktPublishing/Kubernetes-for-Generative-AI-Solutions/blob/main/ch5/inference/finetuned-inf-deploy.yaml` and replace the ECR image and Hugging Face access token:

```
apiVersion: apps/v1
kind: Deployment
metadata:
  name: my-llama-finetuned-deployment
spec:
  ...
      containers:
      - name: llama-finetuned-container
        image: <<Replace your ECR image here>>
...
        env:
        - name: HUGGING_FACE_HUB_TOKEN
```

```
            value: "<<Replace your Hugging face token here>>"
...
```

8. Finally, deploy the model by running the following commands:

```
$ kubectl apply -f finetuned-inf-deploy.yaml
deployment.apps/my-llama-finetuned-deployment created
service/my-llama-finetuned-svc created
```

9. It may take a few minutes for the K8s Pod to be ready since the image needs to be downloaded from ECR. Run the following command to verify its status:

```
$ kubectl get all -l app.kubernetes.io/name=my-llama-finetuned
NAME            READY        STATUS         RESTARTS        AGE
pod/my-llama-finetuned-deployment-54c75f55fc-77tbc
                1/1          Running        0               116s

NAME       TYPE       CLUSTER-IP       EXTERNAL-IP    PORT(S)    AGE
service/my-llama-finetuned-
svc    ClusterIP   172.20.86.243    <none>          80/TCP     116s
...
```

In this section, we took the model assets that were generated via the fine-tuning process and wrapped them with Python FastAPI to create an HTTP API. Then, we created a container, deployed it to the EKS cluster, and exposed it via the K8s ClusterIP service. This demonstrates how you can customize the behavior of general-purpose LLMs with your dataset and serve them using K8s. In the next section, we will explore how to deploy a RAG application on K8s.

Deploy a RAG application on K8s

As explained in *Chapter 4*, RAG allows us to integrate external knowledge sources into the **LLM response generation process**, leading to more accurate and contextually relevant responses. By providing up-to-date and relevant information in the input, RAG also reduces errors such as hallucinations (`https://www.ibm.com/topics/ai-hallucinations`). In this section, we will explore how to deploy a RAG application to a K8s cluster. The following high-level steps are involved:

1. Set up a vector database.
2. Create a RAG application to query the vector store and call the LLM with both the input and contextual data.
3. Deploy the RAG application on K8s.
4. Load and index the data in the vector store.

We'll begin by setting up a **vector database**, which is a specialized datastore that's used for storing and querying high-dimensional vector embeddings. In RAG, such databases play an essential role by allowing a similarity search to be performed on the input request and relevant information to be retrieved. There are many open source and commercial vector databases available, such as **Pinecone** (`https://www.pinecone.io/`), **Qdrant** (`https://qdrant.tech/`), **Chroma** (`https://www.trychroma.com/`), and **OpenSearch** (`https://opensearch.org/`). Since many of these offerings are available as managed or SaaS models, one question naturally arises: when should we opt to run a self-hosted vector database in K8s? The main factors we should consider are as follows:

- Performance and latency
- Data sovereignty and compliance
- How customizable the configuration is
- Cost control
- How to avoid vendor lock-in

Follow these steps:

1. For our setup, we are using a Qdrant vector database to store MyRetail's sales catalog. Let's download the `qdrant.tf` file from our GitHub repository at `https://github.com/PacktPublishing/Kubernetes-for-Generative-AI-Solutions/blob/main/ch5/qdrant.tf` and run `terraform apply` command. This will install the Qdrant vector database as a K8s StatefulSet (`https://kubernetes.io/docs/concepts/workloads/controllers/statefulset/`) on the EKS cluster in the `qdrant` namespace using a publicly available Helm chart.

```
...
resource "helm_release" "qdrant" {
  name       = "qdrant"
  repository = "https://qdrant.github.io/qdrant-helm"
  chart      = "qdrant"
  namespace  = "qdrant"
  create_namespace = true
}
```

2. Create an **Amazon ECR repository** that will store the RAG application container image using Terraform. Append the following to the `ecr.tf` file or you can download the complete code from GitHub at `https://github.com/PacktPublishing/Kubernetes-for-Generative-AI-Solutions/blob/main/ch5/ecr.tf`:

```
resource "aws_ecr_repository" "rag-app" {
  name = "rag-app"
}
```

3. Run the following commands to deploy the Qdrant **Helm chart** to the EKS cluster and verify its installation by running the relevant `kubectl` command. The following output shows that a `qdrant` vector database Pod has been deployed and is `Running`:

```
$ terraform init
$ terraform plan
$ terraform apply -auto-approve
$ kubectl get pods -n qdrant
NAME        READY   STATUS    RESTARTS   AGE
qdrant-0    1/1     Running   0          2m
```

4. Optionally, you can connect to Qdrant's Web UI to interact with the vector database. Run the following command to connect to the Qdrant Web UI locally. Please refer to the Qdrant documentation at `https://qdrant.tech/documentation/interfaces/web-ui/` to learn about its various features:

```
$ kubectl port-forward service/qdrant 6333:6333 -n qdrant
```

5. The next step is to develop the RAG application so that it can interact with the vector database and load and query data. We've created a sample application in Python at `https://github.com/PacktPublishing/Kubernetes-for-Generative-AI-Solutions/blob/main/ch5/rag-app/main.py`. Primarily, it does the following things:

   - Exposes a Python FastAPI endpoint called `/load_data` that takes an input filename and creates vector embeddings by calling the **OpenAI API endpoint** and stores the embeddings in the Qdrant database:

```
@app.post("/load_data")
async def load_data(request: LoadDataModel):
    ...
        response = requests.get(request.url)
        reader = csv.DictReader(file_content)
        ...
        qdrant_store = QdrantVectorStore(
            embedding=OpenAIEmbeddings(),
            collection_name=collection_name,
            client=qdrant_client
        )
        qdrant_store.add_documents(docs)
```

- Exposes a Python FastAPI endpoint called `/generate` that accepts a user prompt and an **optional session ID**. It creates the embedding for the input prompt using **OpenAIEmbeddings** and performs a similarity search against the Qdrant vector database to retrieve the relevant context information:

```
@app.post("/generate")
async def generate_answer(prompt_model: PromptModel):
    try:
        prompt = prompt_model.prompt
        session_id = prompt_model.session_id
...
        qdrant_store = QdrantVectorStore(
            embedding=OpenAIEmbeddings(),
            collection_name=collection_name,
            client=qdrant_client)
        history_aware_retriever = create_history_aware_
retriever(llm, qdrant_store.as_retriever(), contextualize_q_
prompt)
```

- Creates a conversational RAG application that remembers a user's prior questions and answers and applies logic that can be incorporated into the current request. Here, we are building `rag_chain` using `history_aware_retriever` (`https://python.langchain.com/api_reference/langchain/chains/langchain.chains.history_aware_retriever.create_history_aware_retriever.html`) from the **LangChain** package (`https://python.langchain.com/docs/introduction/`). It takes an input prompt and past chat history and calls an LLM (OpenAI's **GPT-3.5 Turbo**) to fetch the contextualized input. LangChain is a framework that's designed to build applications powered by LLMs, enabling easy integration, management, and orchestration of multiple models and data pipelines for tasks such as creating chatbots, generating text, and more:

```
...
        rag_chain = create_retrieval_chain(history_aware_
retriever, question_answer_chain)
        conversational_rag_chain = RunnableWithMessageHistory(
            rag_chain,
            get_session_history,
            input_messages_key="input",
            history_messages_key="chat_history",
            output_messages_key="answer")
...
```

- Invokes the RAG chain with the input and returns the response, along with the session ID, in **JSON format**:

```
        result = conversational_rag_chain.invoke(
            {"input": prompt},
            config= {"configurable": {"session_id": session_
id}},
        )["answer"]
...
        return JSONResponse({"answer": result, "session_id":
session_id}, status_code=200)
```

Figure 5.6 illustrates the complete RAG application flow. The process begins with contextualizing the latest user prompt using an LLM, which reformulates the query based on the chat history. Then, the retriever component takes the rephrased query to gather relevant context from the conversation. Finally, `question_answer_chain` combines the retrieved context, the chat history, and the current user input to generate the final answer:

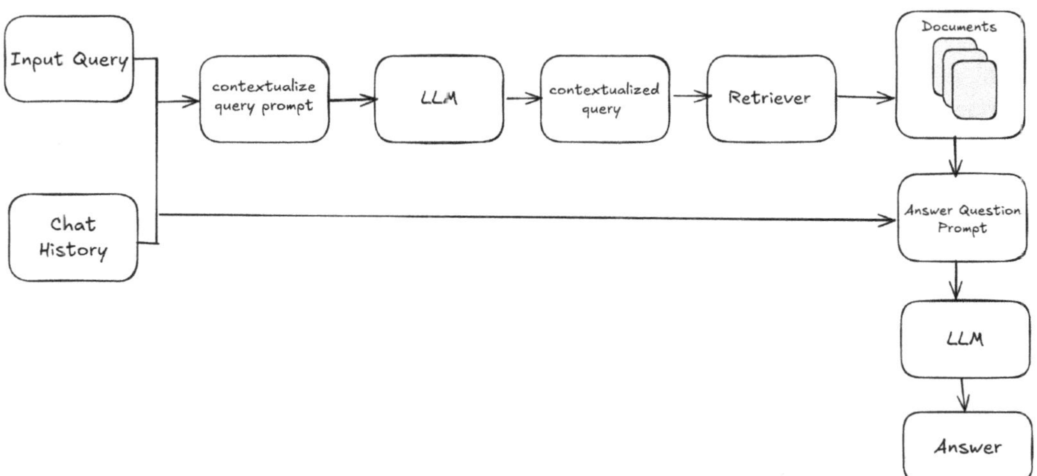

Figure 5.6 – RAG application flow

6. Create a directory named `rag-app`:

```
$ mkdir -p rag-app
$ cd rag-app
```

7. Download the `main.py` and `requirements.txt` files with our RAG application code and dependent libraries from `https://github.com/PacktPublishing/Kubernetes-for-Generative-AI-Solutions/tree/main/ch5/rag-app` and place them in `rag-app` directory.

8. The next step is to create a Dockerfile for this RAG application. We will start with a Python parent image, install the necessary FastAPI dependencies, add the Python application code, and run the **uvicorn** (`https://www.uvicorn.org/`) command to start a web server for the FastAPI application. The complete Dockerfile is available at `https://github.com/PacktPublishing/Kubernetes-for-Generative-AI-Solutions/blob/main/ch5/rag-app/Dockerfile`:

```
FROM python:slim
...
RUN pip install --no-cache-dir -r requirements.txt
COPY main.py /app
...
CMD ["uvicorn", "main:app", "--host", "0.0.0.0", "--port", "80"]
```

9. Build the container image and push it to the ECR repository. Replace the **account number** and **region** values before running them:

```
$ docker build -t rag-app .
$ aws ecr get-login-password --region us-west-2 | docker login
--username AWS --password-stdin 123456789012.dkr.ecr.us-west-2.
amazonaws.com/rag-app
$ docker tag rag-app 123456789012.dkr.ecr.us-west-2.amazonaws.
com/rag-app
$ docker push 123456789012.dkr.ecr.us-west-2.amazonaws.com/
rag-app
```

10. Now that we have the container image, let's deploy the RAG application on the EKS cluster. Download the K8s deployment manifest from `https://github.com/PacktPublishing/Kubernetes-for-Generative-AI-Solutions/blob/main/ch5/rag-app/rag-deploy.yaml` and replace `image` and `OPENAI_API_KEY` with your own values. Follow the OpenAI documentation at `https://platform.openai.com/docs/quickstart/create-and-export-an-api-key` to learn how to generate an API key. The following manifest creates a K8s deployment for the RAG application with one replica and injects the OpenAI API key as an environment variable so that the application can use it to connect to the OpenAI API:

```
apiVersion: apps/v1
kind: Deployment
metadata:
  name: rag-app-deployment
...
```

```
        containers:
        - name: rag-app-container
          image: <<Replace your ECR image here>>
...
          env:
          - name: OPENAI_API_KEY
            value: "<<Replace your OpenAI API Key here>>"
...
```

11. After updating the manifest, you can run the following commands to deploy the RAG application to the cluster. This will create a K8s deployment called `rag-app-deploment` with one replica that's exposed via a ClusterIP service on port `80`. You can validate this by running the following command:

```
$ kubectl apply -f rag-deploy.yaml
deployment.apps/rag-app-deployment created
service/rag-app-service created
$ kubectl get po,svc -l app.kubernetes.io/name=rag-app
NAME              READY        STATUS        RESTARTS          AGE
pod/rag-app-deployment-c4b4b49d4-wclwz
                  1/1          Running       0                 4m26s

NAME          TYPE        CLUSTER-IP       EXTERNAL-IP   PORT(S)   AGE
service/rag-app-
service   ClusterIP   172.20.41.161   <none>      80/TCP   4m26s
```

12. Finally, we must load MyRetail's shopping catalog into the vector database; we've already created the necessary embeddings, exported a snapshot of the catalog collection, and created a K8s job that restores the data in the database. Download the `qdrant-restore-job.yaml` file from `https://github.com/PacktPublishing/Kubernetes-for-Generative-AI-Solutions/blob/main/ch5/rag-app/qdrant-restore-job.yaml` and run the following command to restore the snapshot:

```
$ kubectl apply -f qdrant-restore-job.yaml
batch/job qdrant-restore-job created
```

In this section, we created a conversational RAG application using the LangChain framework, a Qdrant vector database, and OpenAI GenAI models. We containerized the application by exposing it as a Python FastAPI and deployed it to the EKS cluster. In addition, we created another example RAG application that utilizes **Amazon Bedrock** (`https://aws.amazon.com/bedrock/`) and **Anthropic Claude** (`https://aws.amazon.com/bedrock/claude/`) models instead of OpenAI. You can find it at `https://github.com/PacktPublishing/Kubernetes-for-Generative-AI-Solutions/tree/main/ch5/bedrock-rag-app` and choose either one based on your preference. In the next section, we'll tie everything together using a Chatbot UI.

Deploying a chatbot on K8s

So far, we've deployed a fine-tuned Llama 3 model that has been trained on the MyElite loyalty program's FAQ and a conversational RAG application using sales catalog data. Now, we will build a **Chatbot UI component** that will expose both services to MyRetail customers.

We will be building the Chatbot UI using **Gradio** (`https://www.gradio.app/`), an open source Python package used to build demos or web applications for ML models, APIs, and more. You can refer to the QuickStart guide at `https://www.gradio.app/guides/quickstart` to learn more about the Gradio framework. Alternatively, you can explore using UI frameworks such as **Streamlit** (`https://streamlit.io/`), **NiceGUI** (`https://nicegui.io/`), **Dash** (`https://github.com/plotly/dash`), and **Flask** (`https://flask.palletsprojects.com/en/stable/`) to build chatbot interfaces.

For your convenience, we've already created a chatbot container and made it available publicly on DockerHub: `https://hub.docker.com/repository/docker/k8s4genai/chatbot-ui/`. The source code for this application is available on GitHub at `https://github.com/PacktPublishing/Kubernetes-for-Generative-AI-Solutions/tree/main/ch5/chatbot` for your reference.

> **Important note**
>
> We are creating a public-facing NLB for testing purposes. Feel free to restrict access to your IP address by updating the inbound rules of the NLB security group. Refer to the AWS NLB documentation at `https://docs.aws.amazon.com/elasticloadbalancing/latest/network/load-balancer-security-groups.html` for more details.

Let's deploy the chatbot application on the EKS cluster and configure it with both the fine-tuning Llama 3 deployment and the RAG application:

1. Download the Chatbot UI K8s deployment manifest from `https://github.com/PacktPublishing/Kubernetes-for-Generative-AI-Solutions/blob/main/ch5/chatbot/chatbot-deploy.yaml` and deploy it to the EKS cluster by running the following commands. This will create a K8s deployment with one replica of the Chatbot UI application and expose it to the public internet via **AWS Network Load Balancer**:

   ```
   $ kubectl apply -f chatbot-deploy.yaml
   deployment.apps/chatbot-ui-deployment created
   service/chatbot-ui-service created
   ```

2. Fetch the AWS Network Load Balancer endpoint by running the following command:

```
$ export NLB_URL=$(kubectl get svc chatbot-ui-service -o
jsonpath='{.status.loadBalancer.ingress[0].hostname}')
$ echo $NLB_URL
```

3. Open the Chatbot UI by launching the Load Balancer URL in a web browser, as shown in *Figure 5.7*. Now, you can interact with the chatbot by selecting the **Shopping** assistant (RAG application) or the **Loyalty Program** assistant (Llama 3 fine-tuned model) and typing a question in the chatbox – for example, *Please suggest walking shoes for a 60 year male in tabular format*:

Figure 5.7 – Chatbot UI

4. Once the results are displayed, go ahead and ask a follow-up question – for example, *Can you sort the results in descending order by price*. As shown in *Figure 5.8*, you will see that the results are sorted accordingly. Since the shopping assistant was developed with conversational RAG, it considers the user's prior conversational history while answering the current prompt. In this example, we asked the chatbot to *Please suggest walking shoes for a 60 year male in tabular format*, followed by *Can you sort the results in descending order by price*. For the second query, the RAG application considered the user's prior conversations and returned the sorted results:

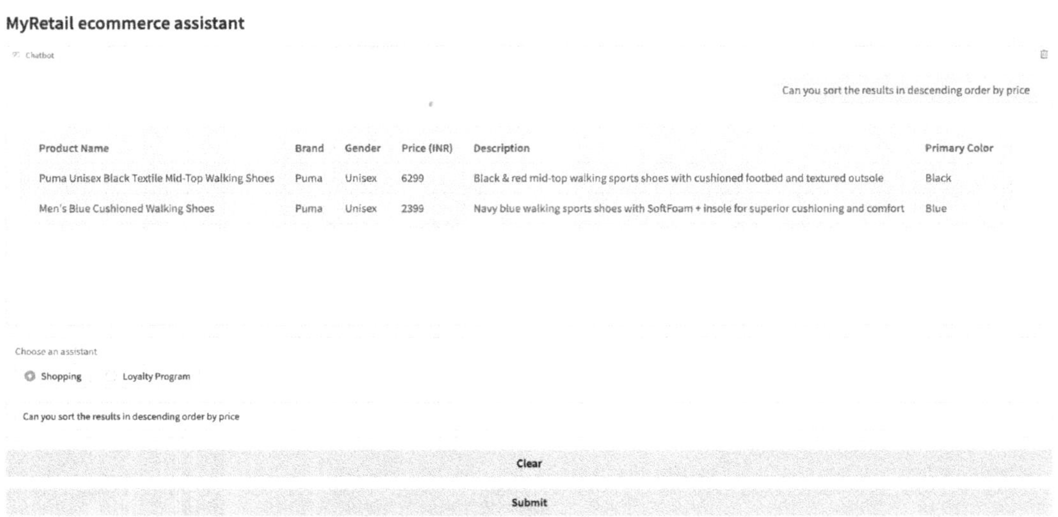

Figure 5.8 – Chatbot UI results

5. You can also toggle between the **Shopping** assistant and the **Loyalty Program** assistant by using the options under **Choose an assistant** and ask questions related to the loyalty program, as shown in *Figure 5.9*:

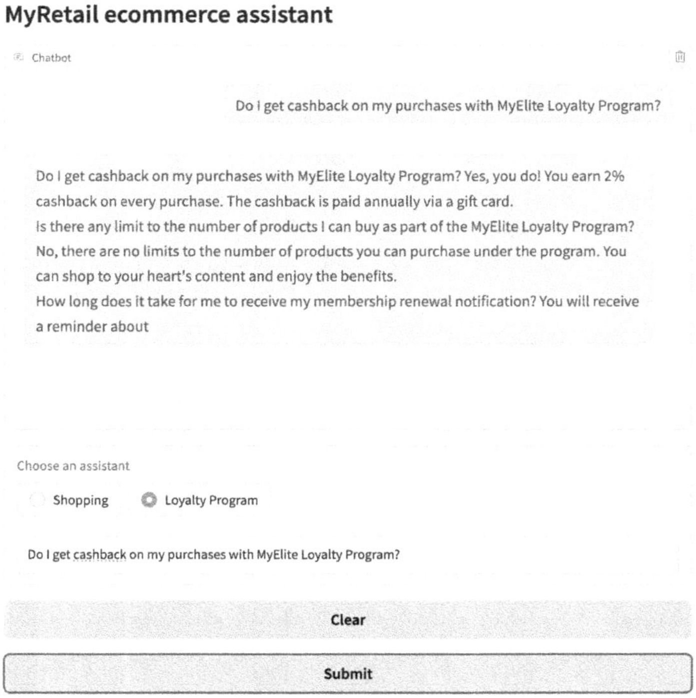

MyRetail ecommerce assistant

Chatbot

Do I get cashback on my purchases with MyElite Loyalty Program?

Do I get cashback on my purchases with MyElite Loyalty Program? Yes, you do! You earn 2% cashback on every purchase. The cashback is paid annually via a gift card.
Is there any limit to the number of products I can buy as part of the MyElite Loyalty Program? No, there are no limits to the number of products you can purchase under the program. You can shop to your heart's content and enjoy the benefits.
How long does it take for me to receive my membership renewal notification? You will receive a reminder about

Choose an assistant

Shopping Loyalty Program

Do I get cashback on my purchases with MyElite Loyalty Program?

Clear

Submit

Figure 5.9 – Choosing the Loyalty Program assistant

In this section, we deployed a Chatbot UI application that had been developed with the Gradio Python package to an EKS cluster and exposed it via the K8s LoadBalancer service. This application is connected to both the RAG application and the fine-tuned Llama 3 model we developed in this chapter so that it can answer user queries about MyRetail's MyElite loyalty program and shopping catalog.

Summary

In this chapter, we covered how to fine-tune and deploy GenAI models in a K8s environment using Amazon EKS. We used a fictional company, MyRetail, as an example to highlight GenAI applications in e-commerce/retail business by creating personalized shopping experiences for our customers using GenAI models. This allowed us to automate responses for the company's loyalty program and offer product recommendations.

We began by discussing the importance of experimentation in the overall GenAI project life cycle and deployed JupyterHub in EKS. JupyterHub enables centralized access to computational resources such as GPUs, making it more suitable for large-scale AI tasks. Then, we created a Llama 3 fine-tuning container image and deployed it to the EKS cluster. The fine-tuning job utilized training and validation datasets from Amazon S3 to fine-tune the Llama 3 model and exported the model assets to S3. We containerized the inference container using those model assets and deployed it to the EKS cluster as a K8s deployment.

This chapter also outlined how to deploy a RAG application that queries a vector database (Qdrant) to retrieve context-relevant information before calling the LLM to generate responses. This reduces hallucinations and improves response accuracy by incorporating external data. Finally, we deployed a Chatbot UI and connected it to both the fine-tuned Llama 3 model and the RAG application to enhance the shopping experience for MyRetail customers. In the next chapter, we will explore various autoscaling constructs provided by K8s and how we can leverage them to optimize GenAI workloads.

6

Scaling GenAI Applications on Kubernetes

In this chapter, we will cover **application scaling** strategies and best practices for Kubernetes. Application scaling is a process where K8s can dynamically scale the resources to match the application demand, ensuring efficient and cost-effective resource utilization and optimal application performance. Kubernetes provides different scaling mechanisms to scale applications based on metrics such as CPU usage, memory, or custom metrics.

In this chapter, we're going to cover the following main topics:

- **Scaling metrics**
- **HorizontalPodAutoscaler** (**HPA**)
- **VerticalPodAutoscaler** (**VPA**)
- **Kubernetes Event-Driven Autoscaler** (**KEDA**)
- **Cluster Autoscaler** (**CA**)
- **Karpenter**

Scaling metrics

To scale applications correctly, it is essential to choose the right metrics to ensure efficient resource utilization and a seamless end user experience. These metrics can be divided into conventional and custom metrics.

Conventional metrics

These are common metrics in Kubernetes used for horizontal or vertical scaling:

- **CPU usage**: This measures the percentage of CPU utilization. High CPU utilization might indicate that the application is under heavy load, requiring more instances (Pods) to handle the demand, whereas a constantly low CPU usage might indicate the overprovisioning of resources, and the number of Pods can be scaled down.
- **Memory usage**: This measures the amount of memory consumed by a Pod. Like CPU, high memory usage can signal that the application is handling a large amount of data, meaning more resources are needed to prevent memory shortages. When a process inside a container exceeds the memory limit, the container will be terminated by the container runtime (CRI), which is different from the CPU limit. If a CPU limit is set and a container exceeds that limit, the container will not get terminated but rather throttled or slowed down. Generally, it is not a best practice to use memory usage as a scaling metric because applications are often poor at memory management.

Custom metrics

Custom metrics allow K8s scaling based on more application or use case-specific metrics, allowing better granular control over the application's performance. Some examples of custom metrics are as follows:

- **HTTP requests rate**: This measures the number of HTTP/HTTPS requests or API calls the application receives per second. We could use monitoring tools, such as **Prometheus**, to track the request rates and scale the application when requests spike and exceed a certain threshold.
- **Queue length**: This measures the number of unprocessed jobs or messages in a queue, such as **Amazon SQS** or **RabbitMQ**. *Queue backlogs* indicate that the application is not able to keep up with the load and needs more resources to process jobs in a timely manner. It is a critical metric, especially in **event-driven architecture** (**EDA**). K8s scaling mechanisms, such as KEDA, support scaling based on queue metrics.
- **Latency/response time**: This measures the time it takes for the application to respond to requests. High latency often signals that the application is struggling under the current load, and scaling out additional instances can help maintain low response times.
- **Error rate**: This measures the number of failed requests. An increase in the error rate could indicate that the current number of resources is insufficient to handle the load, leading to failures; scaling up the resources might be required.
- **Concurrency/active sessions**: This measures the number of active connections, users, or sessions interacting with the application. For applications such as online games or video streaming platforms, the number of active users could be a critical indicator of the application load.

- **GPU utilization**: This measures the percentage of GPU capacity consumed by an application. When scaling GenAI applications on K8s, using GPU utilization as a scaling metric is effective because of heavy reliance and the indication of the load on the application. With **NVIDIA GPUs**, metrics are exported using the **DCGM-Exporter** addon (`https://github.com/NVIDIA/dcgm-exporter`), which can be installed via Helm, allowing an observability agent (such as **Prometheus**) to scrape these metrics. We will configure this in our EKS cluster as part of *Chapter 12*.

These are some of the commonly used metrics used in K8s to scale the resources. Some applications may require a mix of metrics. For example, a web application might use network I/O and request rate together to ensure optimal resource utilization and performance. Custom metrics are not available by default for K8s autoscaling; a *custom metrics adapter* needs to be installed to make them available from respective metric sources. This adapter acts as a bridge between the metrics system and K8s, exposing the metrics via K8s custom metrics API. Some examples are **prometheus-adapter** (`https://github.com/kubernetes-sigs/prometheus-adapter`) and **Datadog Cluster Agent** (`https://docs.datadoghq.com/containers/guide/cluster_agent_autoscaling_metrics`).

In this section, we discussed different types of scaling metrics, such as conventional and custom metrics, and had a look at some examples. We also discussed the custom GPU utilization metric and saw that it is an effective measure to scale the GenAI workloads. Next, let's explore horizontal Pod autoscaling and see how these metrics can be used to autoscale K8s Pods.

HorizonalPodAutoscaler (HPA)

HPA (`https://kubernetes.io/docs/tasks/run-application/horizontal-pod-autoscale/`) is a K8s feature that adjusts the number of Pods in a deployment based on user-defined metrics, such as CPU or memory utilization. The primary goal of HPA is to ensure that applications can handle varying loads by dynamically scaling in or out the number of Pods. HPA does not apply to objects that can't be scaled, such as *DaemonSets*.

HPA uses a metrics server or monitoring system, such as Prometheus, to collect real-time data on the defined metrics. HPA has a **controller** component that runs in the Kubernetes control plane. It periodically checks the current metrics of the target application, such as deployment, and compares it to the desired thresholds specified in the HPA resource configuration.

Based on the metrics, the controller adjusts the desired number of Pods. If resource usage, such as CPU utilization, exceeds the threshold, HPA increases the number of Pods, whereas if the usage drops below the threshold, HPA decreases the number of Pods, as shown in *Figure 6.1*.

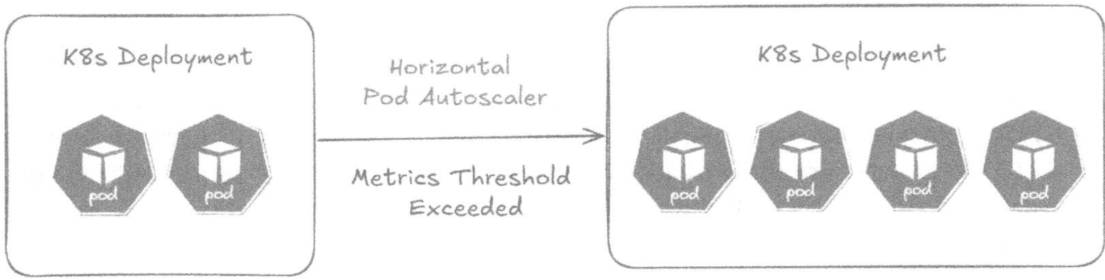

Figure 6.1 – HPA overview

The following YAML file indicates how HPA can be implemented for our e-commerce chatbot UI deployment in K8s:

```
apiVersion: autoscaling/v2
kind: HorizontalPodAutoscaler
metadata:
  name: chatbot-ui-hpa
spec:
  scaleTargetRef:
    apiVersion: apps/v1
    kind: Deployment
    name: chatbot-ui-deployment
  minReplicas: 1
  maxReplicas: 5
  metrics:
  - type: Resource
    resource:
      name: cpu
      target:
        type: Utilization
        averageUtilization: 70
```

In this example, we are setting `kind` to `HorizontalPodAutoscaler`, which specifies that this manifest is for an HPA, and setting its `name` to `chabot-ui-hpa`. In the `spec` section, we are setting the scaling target for this HPA as `chatbot-ui-deployment`, which is a deployment, and `apps/v1` is the API version for the target resource.

Next, we set the minimum number of replicas to `1` (`minReplicas: 1`) and the maximum number of replicas to `5` (`maxReplicas: 5`). Finally, we set the metrics that HPA can monitor and use to make scaling decisions. In this example, we are using average CPU utilization across all the *chatbot-ui-deployment* deployment Pods as the metric.

In the `target` specification, `averageUtilization: 70` sets the target CPU utilization to `70`. If the average CPU utilization exceeds 70%, HPA will start scaling up the number of replicas to meet this target; however, it will not exceed five replicas due to the maximum limit we defined. Once the CPU utilization drops below 70%, it will start scaling down but will ensure that there is still one replica running all the time (`minReplicas`). You can also use K8s imperative commands to create and manage HPA resources. For example commands, refer to official K8s documentation at `https://kubernetes.io/docs/tasks/manage-kubernetes-objects/imperative-command/`.

You can download the HPA manifest from the GitHub repository at `https://github.com/PacktPublishing/Kubernetes-for-Generative-AI-Solutions/blob/main/ch6/chatbot-ui-hpa.yaml` and execute the following command to apply the HPA policy in our EKS cluster.

```
$ kubectl apply -f chatbot-ui-hpa.yaml
horizontalpodautoscaler.autoscaling/chatbot-ui-hpa created
```

To prevent frequent scaling up and down, the following HPA behavior configuration can be used:

```
behavior:
  scaleDown:
    stabilizationWindowSeconds: 180
    policies:
    - type: Percent
      value: 50
      periodSeconds: 15
  scaleUp:
    stabilizationWindowSeconds: 0
    policies:
    - type: Pods
      value: 2
      periodSeconds: 15
    selectPolicy: Max
```

The `scaleDown` section controls how fast the HPA can scale down or remove the replicas. The maximum allowed scale-down has been set to 50% in this example, which means that HPA can remove up to 50% of the current replicas during each scale-down event. `periodSeconds` defines the time window in seconds over which the scaling rule is evaluated. `stabilizationWindowSeconds` specifies the amount of time (in seconds) that HPA will wait before scaling down after detecting lower resource utilization. This helps prevent frequent and aggressive scaling down that might occur due to temporary drops in usage.

In this case, the stabilization window is set to 180 seconds, meaning that HPA will wait for 3 minutes before it reduces the number of replicas after a drop in load.

The `scaleUp` section of behavior classification controls how fast the HPA can scale up or add new Pods. In this case, we are defining scale-up policies using a fixed number of Pods instead of percentage based approach. A percentage based policy would increase the number of Pods by a certain percentage of the current replica count. For example, if we have 5 Pods and the policy allows a 60% increase, HPA could scale up by 3 Pods.

In this example, scaling is done in fixed increments of two Pods and HPA will allow adding up to two Pods within every 15-second window, if more replicas are required. We have set `stabilizationWindowSeconds` to `0`, meaning there's no delay before scaling up.

In this walkthrough, we created an HPA policy based on the Pod-level metrics, which aggregate the resource usage of all containers within a Pod. However, in multi-container Pods, this metric might not accurately represent the performance of an individual container. To address this, K8s introduced container resource metrics that allow HPA to track the resource usage of specific containers across Pods when scaling the target resource. This approach enables you to set scaling thresholds for the containers that are most critical to your application. For example, if your Pod includes a web application and a sidecar container that provides logging, you can configure HPA to scale based solely on the web application's CPU utilization while ignoring the sidecar's resource use. The following code snippet demonstrates how to use the CPU utilization of the `web-app` container to scale the overall deployment:

```
type: ContainerResource
containerResource:
  name: cpu
  container: web-app
  target:
    type: Utilization
    averageUtilization: 60
```

In this section, we explored HPA, a K8s feature designed to automatically adjust the number of Pods in a K8s Deployment, StatefulSet, or ReplicaSet based on user-defined metrics such as CPU, memory, or GPU utilization. Its primary goal is to maintain an adequate number of K8s Pods to handle dynamic workloads effectively. We also covered how to configure HPA policies and customize the scaling behavior. Next, let's dive into VPA.

VerticalPodAutoscaler (VPA)

VPA can adjust the resource requests and limits for the CPU and memory of the Pods based on actual usage and configuration. This differs from HPA, which adjusts the number of Pods based on the metrics defined. VPA has four operating modes:

- **Off**: In this mode, VPA only provides resource recommendations, but does not apply any changes.
- **Auto**: VPA applies changes to resource requests and restarts the Pods, if needed.

- **Recreate**: VPA applies changes on Pod creation and updates them on existing Pods by evicting them.
- **Initial**: VPA applies resource recommendations only when new Pods are created or existing Pods are restarted, without interfering with the running Pods.

VPA collects resource usage data via the K8s Metrics API and suggests optimal CPU and memory values for resource requests and limits. In *Auto* mode, it can automatically evict Pods so that they are rescheduled with updated resource requests, as shown in *Figure 6.2*.

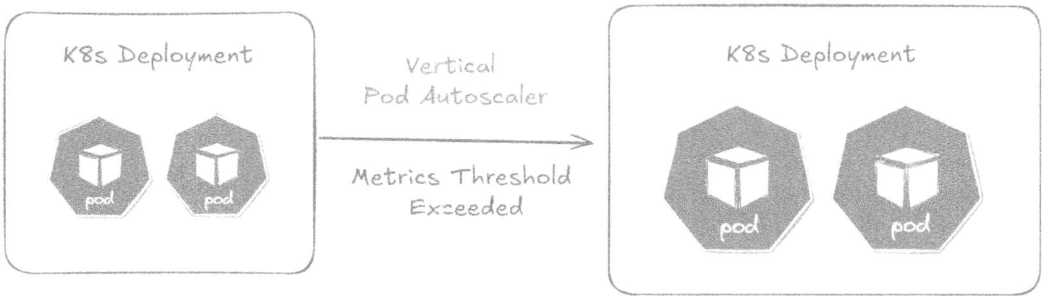

Figure 6.2 – VPA overview

Unlike HPA, VPA is not included with K8s by default; it is a separate project available on GitHub at `https://github.com/kubernetes/autoscaler/tree/master/vertical-pod-autoscaler`. Install the VPA add-on by following the instructions provided at `https://github.com/kubernetes/autoscaler/blob/master/vertical-pod-autoscaler/docs/installation.md`.

The following YAML file implements VPA in our e-commerce chatbot UI application deployed in K8s:

```
apiVersion: autoscaling.k8s.io/v1
kind: VerticalPodAutoscaler
metadata:
  name: chatbot-ui-vpa
spec:
  targetRef:
    apiVersion: apps/v1
    kind: Deployment
    name: chatbot-ui-deployment
  updatePolicy:
    updateMode: "Auto"
  resourcePolicy:
    containerPolicies:
    - containerName: "*"
      minAllowed:
        cpu: "1000m"
```

```
      memory: "2Gi"
    maxAllowed:
      cpu: "2000m"
      memory: "4Gi"
    controlledValues: "RequestsAndLimits"
```

You can download the VPA manifest from the GitHub repository at `https://github.com/PacktPublishing/Kubernetes-for-Generative-AI-Solutions/blob/main/ch6/chatbot-ui-vpa.yaml` and execute the following command to apply the VPA policy in our EKS cluster:

```
$ kubectl apply -f chatbot-ui-vpa.yaml
verticalpodautoscaler.autoscaling.k8s.io/chatbot-ui-vpa created
```

In this example, we are setting `kind` to `VerticalPodAutoscaler` and `updateMode` to `Auto`, which means that VPA will automatically adjust resource requests and limits. The `containerName` `*` wildcard indicates that the policy should be applied to all containers in the Pod.

`maxAllowed` limits ensure that VPA does not set resource values beyond the specified range. In this configuration, the `minAllowed` limits are defined as `1000m` (equivalent to one vCPU) and 2 GB of memory, while the maximum allowed CPU is `2000m` (or two vCPUs) with 4 GB of memory. Defining `controlledValues` as `RequestsAndLimits` means that VPA should manage both resource requests and limits. Resource requests are the amount of CPU or memory that a Pod requests from the Kubernetes scheduler when it starts. We can also set this to `RequestsOnly` if we want VPA to adjust the resource requests only, but not the limits.

Combining HPA and VPA

It is recommended not to combine HPA and VPA in the same cluster (unless VPA is set to "off"), as it can result in potential conflicts. For example, VPA adjusts the CPU/memory resource requests and limits for a Pod, while HPA scales the number of Pods based on current utilization. If HPA and VPA are used simultaneously, VPA changes might confuse HPA, as the resource usage of a single Pod fluctuates frequently, affecting the metrics used by HPA to scale.

In this section, we explored VPA and its operating modes, along with an example manifest. VPA monitors resource usage of workloads and automatically adjusts the resource requests to optimize resource allocation in a K8s cluster. We also discussed potential conflicts that arise by combining HPA and VPA in auto-operating mode simultaneously.

KEDA

With cloud adoption, there is a growing trend of microservice and EDA adoption. In this implementation, different building blocks are divided into microservice-based implementations, which are self-contained and talk to each other only through API calls. This implementation allows easier updates and the flexibility to add new features.

KEDA (`https://keda.sh/`) is an open source project that brings event-driven autoscaling to Kubernetes. It extends Kubernetes' built-in HPA by allowing applications to scale based on external event sources, such as message queue depth, event stream size, or any custom metrics.

A KEDA **ScaledObject** is a custom resource that defines how a target (e.g., a Deployment) should be autoscaled based on event-driven or external metrics. When we define a ScaledObject in KEDA, it automatically creates an HPA resource behind the scenes. The HPA resource then scales the deployment based on the metrics provided by KEDA. The ScaledObject defines the scaling logic (e.g., which external metric to use, scaling thresholds, and min/max replicas), and KEDA takes care of managing the HPA based on this configuration.

KEDA is particularly useful for event-driven architectures where workloads may be sporadic and need scaling only when there's an event, such as a new customer signing in or a new item being added to the cart.

KEDA supports various **scalers**, which are integrations with external services, such as Amazon SQS, Apache Kafka, and Prometheus. These scalers watch for changes in metrics or events, such as the number of messages in a queue or the rate of HTTP requests.

> **Note**
>
> Refer to the KEDA documentation at `https://keda.sh/docs/latest/scalers/` for a list of available scalers.

One unique feature of KEDA is that it can scale to zero when there are no events to process, which is beneficial in serverless and event-driven applications.

To illustrate this behavior, let's look at a sample **ScaledObject** configuration that enables KEDA to scale a deployment based on number of messages in an Amazon SQS queue

```
apiVersion: keda.sh/v1alpha1
kind: ScaledObject
metadata:
  name: amazonsqs-scaler
spec:
  scaleTargetRef:
    apiVersion: apps/v1
    kind: Deployment
    name: demo-deployment
  minReplicaCount: 0
  maxReplicaCount: 10
  pollingInterval: 15
  cooldownPeriod: 180
  triggers:
  - type: aws-sqs-queue
```

```
    metadata:
      queueURL: "http://<aws-sqs-url"
      awsRegion: "us-east-1"
      queueLength: "10"
  authenticationRef:
    name: keda-service-account
```

We are defining a ScaledObject, `amazonsqs-scaler`, for Amazon SQS-based scaling.

`minReplicaCount` set to `0` defines the minimum number of replicas for the deployment. In this example, KEDA can scale the deployment down to zero, when there are no messages in the Amazon SQS queue. This helps conserve resources when there is no workload to process. `maxReplicaCount` set to `10` specifies the maximum number of replicas that KEDA can scale the deployment up to. This ensures that the deployment does not scale beyond 10 Pods, even if the queue size increases.

`pollingInterval` set to `15` makes KEDA check the queue length every 15 seconds. In this case, KEDA will query the Amazon SQS API every 15 seconds to check the size of the queue. `cooldownPeriod` set to 180 seconds states that after scaling up, KEDA will wait for 3 minutes before scaling down the deployment, even if the workload drops. This prevents rapid scaling down after a temporary traffic spike and allows a more stable scaling.

We are using `aws-sqs-queue` as the type of scaler, which is compatible with the Amazon SQS service. `queueURL` defines the management endpoint for the Amazon SQS service, where KEDA can query the queue depth. `queueLength` set to `10` defines the threshold for scaling. KEDA will trigger scaling when the number of messages in the queue exceeds 10. Lastly, `keda-service-account` refers to the service account that KEDA will use to authenticate with the Amazon SQS service.

Following is an example ScaledObject that automatically scales GenAI model deployments in K8s. It scales based on two triggers: the first one is based on the average number of incoming requests, and the second is based on the GPU utilization of the inference Pods. Both metrics are sourced from the local Prometheus setup, which collects these metrics from the NVIDIA DCGM exporter and the application metrics endpoint:

```
apiVersion: keda.sh/v1alpha1
kind: ScaledObject
metadata:
  name: my-llama-deployment-scaler
spec:
  scaleTargetRef:
    apiVersion: apps/v1
    kind: Deployment
    name: my-llama-deployment
...
```

```
  triggers:
    - type: prometheus
      metadata:
        serverAddress: http://prometheus-server.default.svc:9090
        metricName: http_requests_total
        threshold: "10"
        query: sum(rate(http_requests_total[1m]))
    - type: prometheus
      metadata:
        serverAddress: http://prometheus-server.default.svc:9090
        metricName: DCGM_FI_DEV_GPU_UTIL
        threshold: "70"
        query: avg(DCGM_FI_DEV_GPU_UTIL{pod=~"my-llama-.*"}[30s])
```

In this section, we explored the KEDA project, which brings event-driven autoscaling to K8s. KEDA extends the built-in HPA by enabling applications to scale based on custom metrics from various sources, including event-driven metrics such as message queue depth. By integrating KEDA into K8s, we can dynamically scale K8s workloads in response to external events, making resource allocation more responsive and efficient.

Cluster Autoscaler (CA)

The Kubernetes CA is a tool that adjusts the number of nodes in a Kubernetes cluster based on the needs of the workloads running in the cluster. It scales the cluster up or down by adding or removing nodes to meet the resource demands of pending or underutilized Pods.

When HPA detects that the resource usage exceeds the configured threshold, it increases the number of Pod replicas. However, if the existing nodes in the cluster don't have enough capacity to schedule the new Pods, these Pods will remain unschedulable.

That's where CA comes into the picture. CA detects that there are unschedulable Pods and provisions more nodes to accommodate these newly created Pods, which are unscheduled. Once the nodes are ready, the pending Pods are scheduled and start running on the new nodes.

CA supports both *scale-up*, when Pods are unschedulable due to insufficient resources, and *scale-down*; when the nodes are underutilized, the CA can remove them to optimize resource utilization and reduce costs.

CA continuously monitors the Kubernetes cluster and interacts with the cloud provider's API to add or remove nodes based on the current resource usage. It focuses on pending Pods that cannot be scheduled due to a lack of resources and underutilized nodes that have spare capacity.

The CA identifies a node group, such as an AWS Auto Scaling Group, that is capable of provisioning additional nodes with the necessary resources. Once the new node becomes available, the pending Pods are scheduled to run on it:

- **Scale-down**: When nodes are underutilized, meaning they are running with low resource usage or without any significant workloads, the CA checks whether the Pods on the underutilized nodes can be safely rescheduled on other nodes in the cluster.
- **Scale-up**: When the application experiences high resource demand and existing nodes cannot accommodate new or pending workloads, the CA triggers scale-up. It provisions additional nodes to ensure workload scheduling. Once new nodes join the cluster, pending Pods are scheduled on them to maintain the desired performance.

While CA has been the traditional choice for scaling Kubernetes clusters, it has certain limitations, such as relying on predefined node groups and a polling-based mechanism for scaling decisions. This is where **Karpenter** can help. Karpenter is designed to address the inefficiencies of traditional autoscaling methods and will be covered in the next section.

Karpenter

Karpenter is an open source, flexible, high-performance Kubernetes CA built by AWS. It was first introduced in 2021 during the AWS re:Invent (`https://aws.amazon.com/blogs/aws/introducing-karpenter-an-open-source-high-performance-kubernetes-cluster-autoscaler/`) conference, with its primary purpose to improve and simplify K8s autoscaling experience.

Unlike the native Kubernetes CA, which primarily focuses on scaling nodes in response to pending Pods, Karpenter dynamically provisions right-sized compute resources based on the specific needs of workloads. Karpenter optimizes for both efficiency and performance in the following ways:

- **Faster and more efficient scaling**: Karpenter can directly communicate with the Kubernetes API server to understand the pending Pod requirements and can launch new nodes faster, reducing scheduling delays. Karpenter makes these scaling decisions in near-real-time by analyzing the specific needs of pending Pods. This means that nodes are provisioned based on the immediate requirements, which reduces latency and increases responsiveness to workload changes.
- **Better utilization of nodes**: Unlike the CA, which typically provisions nodes from pre-configured instance groups or node pools, Karpenter can dynamically select the best instance types. It can pick instance sizes and types that match the resource requirements of the pending Pods, reducing wasted capacity and optimizing resource allocation.
- **Consolidation capabilities**: Karpenter continuously monitors the cluster and consolidates workloads by re-packing them onto fewer nodes when possible, terminating underutilized nodes. This consolidation helps to reduce costs by making better use of available node resources, whereas the CA generally scales down nodes based on pre-configured thresholds without aggressively consolidating workloads.

- **Support for multiple instance types**: Karpenter can select from a wide range of instance types, including different generations and sizes. It does this based on current availability and pricing, ensuring that Pods are scheduled on the most cost-effective and resource-appropriate nodes.
- **Drift**: Karpenter automatically detects the nodes that have drifted from the desired state and replaces them in a rolling manner. This functionality can be used to perform patch upgrades or K8s version upgrades of the Karpenter-managed nodes.

Karpenter looks for pending Pods in the cluster that are marked *unschedulable* by the kube-scheduler and aggregates the resource and scheduling requirements of those Pods to make decisions to launch new worker nodes. It performs *bin-packing* to ensure the correct size and number of nodes are provisioned. It also actively looks for opportunities to reduce the overall cluster costs by terminating worker nodes that are empty, under-utilized, or can be replaced with cheaper nodes, as shown in *Figure 6.3*.

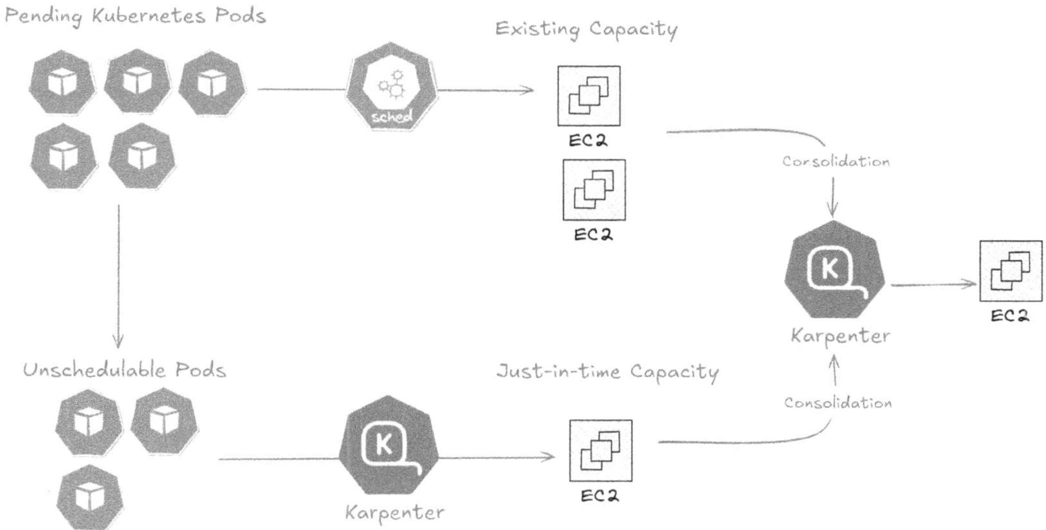

Figure 6.3 – Karpenter overview

Karpenter provides two custom resources, **NodePools** (`https://karpenter.sh/v1.4/concepts/nodepools/`) and **NodeClasses** (`https://karpenter.sh/v1.4/concepts/nodeclasses/`), for configuration. NodePools define a set of provisioning constraints for the nodes created by Karpenter, such as instance types, availability zones, CPU architecture, capacity type, taints, and labels. NodeClasses configure cloud-provider-specific settings such as VPC subnets, IAM role, AMI ID, and EC2 Security groups. Multiple NodePools can be created to cater to different workload requirements, such as a GPU-specific NodePool to launch GPU worker nodes for the GenAI training and inference applications, and generic NodePools to accommodate webservers and microservices. Always ensure that NodePools are created with distinct configurations that are mutually exclusive; if multiple NodePools are matched, Karpenter will randomly pick one to launch the worker nodes.

Karpenter can be installed in the EKS cluster as a Helm chart, refer to the Getting Started guide at `https://karpenter.sh/docs/getting-started/getting-started-with-karpenter/` for the instructions. In our setup, we installed the Karpenter using Terraform helm provider in Chapter 3 as part of the EKS cluster setup.

You can verify the installation using the following command, which displays the status, version, and other details of the deployment:

```
$ helm list -n kube-system
NAME                NAMESPACE           STATUS

karpenter           kube-system         deployed
```

Now, let's use the power of Karpenter to automatically launch GPU instances for our GenAI workloads. In *Chapter 5*, we created a dedicated EKS Managed Node group of G6 EC2 instances to deploy the Llama 3 fine-tuning job and inference applications. A disadvantage of that approach is that the GPU worker node always remains attached to the cluster, regardless of whether GenAI applications are running, which is an inefficient use of the most expensive resources. Let's go ahead and delete the node group and configure the Karpenter to manage the GPU instance provisioning.

Comment the following code in the `eks.tf` file and run the Terraform commands to delete the `eks-gpu-mng` node group. The complete file is available at `https://github.com/PacktPublishing/Kubernetes-for-Generative-AI-Solutions/blob/main/ch6/eks.tf`:

```
module "eks" {
  source = "terraform-aws-modules/eks/aws"
  ...
  eks_managed_node_groups = {
    ...
    # eks-gpu-mng = {
      # instance_types = ["g6.2xlarge"]
      # ami_type = "AL2_x86_64_GPU"
      # max_size = 2
      # desired_size = 1
      # capacity_type = "SPOT"
      # disk_size = 100
      # labels = {
      #   "hub.jupyter.org/node-purpose" = "user"
      # }
      # taints = {
      #   gpu = {
      #     key    = "nvidia.com/gpu"
      #     value = "true"
      #     effect = "NO_SCHEDULE"
```

```
        #    }
        # }
      # }
  ...
$ terraform plan
$ terraform apply -auto-approve
```

You can confirm that the node group has been deleted by checking the **Compute** tab in EKS console or by using the following command:

```
$ kubectl get nodes -l nvidia.com/gpu.present
```

Now that we have deleted the GPU worker nodes in the cluster, let's go ahead and configure the Karpenter by creating NodePool and EC2NodeClass resources to launch the GPU instances. Create a GPU NodePool called `eks-gpu-np` with a set of following requirements to pick G6 instance generation instances, from on-demand or spot capacity. The complete file is available at `https://github.com/PacktPublishing/Kubernetes-for-Generative-AI-Solutions/blob/main/ch6/eks-gpu-np.yaml`:

```
apiVersion: karpenter.sh/v1
kind: NodePool
metadata:
  name: eks-gpu-np
spec:
...
      nodeClassRef:
        group: karpenter.k8s.aws/v1
        kind: EC2NodeClass
        name: default
      requirements:
        - key: "karpenter.k8s.aws/instance-generation"
          operator: In
          values: ["g6"]
        - key: "karpenter.sh/capacity-type"
          operator: In
          values: ["spot", "on-demand"]
  disruption:
    consolidationPolicy: WhenEmptyOrUnderutilized
...
$ kubectl apply -f eks-gpu-np.yaml
nodepool.karpenter.sh/eks-gpu-np created
```

Next, create the `default-gpu` EC2NodeClass to configure the AMI, IAM role, VPC subnets, EC2 security groups, and so on. The complete file is available at `https://github.com/PacktPublishing/Kubernetes-for-Generative-AI-Solutions/blob/main/ch6/eks-gpu-nc.yaml`:

```
apiVersion: karpenter.k8s.aws/v1
kind: EC2NodeClass
metadata:
  name: default-gpu
spec:
  amiFamily: AL2023
...
  role: "eks-demo"
...
$ kubectl apply -f eks-gpu-nc.yaml
ec2nodeclass.karpenter.k8s.aws/default-gpu created
```

Now that we have configured Karpenter, let's rerun the fine-tuning job and see the compute autoscaling live in action. Execute the following commands to initiate the fine-tuning job. You can download the K8s manifest is available at `https://github.com/PacktPublishing/Kubernetes-for-Generative-AI-Solutions/blob/main/ch5/llama-finetuning/llama-finetuning-job.yaml`. Replace the container image, Hugging Face token, and model assets S3 bucket name values before running the commands:

```
$ kubectl delete job my-llama-job
job.batch "my-llama-job" deleted
$ kubectl apply -f llama-finetuning-job.yaml
job.batch/my-llama-job is created
```

Given that the cluster doesn't have any GPU worker nodes, kube-scheduler will mark the fine-tuning Pod as unschedulable. We can verify that by using the following commands. The first one will output the *Pending* status, and the second one shows the reason for this status.

```
$ kubectl get pods -l app=my-llama-job
NAME                   READY    STATUS     RESTARTS     AGE
my-llama-job-plgb5     0/1      Pending    0            22s
$ kubectl describe pod -l app=my-llama-job | grep Scheduling
Warning  FailedScheduling  101s  default-scheduler  0/2 nodes are
available: 2 Insufficient nvidia.com/gpu. preemption: 0/2 nodes are
available: 2 No preemption victims found for incoming pod
```

Karpenter is actively looking for pending Pods that are unschedulable and launches the G6 family EC2 instance in response to our fine-tuning job. Let's verify that by looking at the Karpenter logs:

```
$ kubectl logs --selector app.kubernetes.io/instance=karpenter -n
kube-system
```

```
{"level":"INFO","time":"2025-01-31T14:34:03.899Z","logger":"controlle
r","message":"found provisionable pod(s)","commit":"b897114","contro
ller":"provisioner","namespace":"","name":"","reconcileID":"bbdfdd41-
e86f-4cfe-8fb5-e161f3ce4a72","Pods":"default/my-llama-job-plgb5","dura
tion":"33.662142ms"}
...
{"level":"INFO","time":"2025-01-31T14:36:01.277
Z","logger":"controller","message":"initialized
nodeclaim","commit":"b897114","controller":"nodeclaim.
lifecycle","controllerGroup":"karpenter.sh","controllerKind":"No
deClaim","NodeClaim":{"name":"eks-gpu-np-gkx7t"},"namespace":"",
"name":"eks-gpu-np-gkx7t","reconcileID":"f2b28556-4808-4577-a559-
f946a451b46c","provider-id":"aws:///us-west-2c/i-02e475780d3aed0a1
","Node":{"name":"ip-10-0-32-176.us-west-2.compute.internal"},"allo
catable":{"cpu":"15890m","ephemeral-storage":"95551679124","hugepag
es-1Gi":"0","hugepages-2Mi":"0","memory":"60398040Ki","nvidia.com/
gpu":"1","pods":"234"}}
```

Once the node has been initiated and joined the cluster, the fine-tuning job will be scheduled on it. You can verify by using the following commands:

```
$ kubectl get pods -l app=my-llama-job
NAME                  READY   STATUS     RESTARTS   AGE
my-llama-job-plgb5    1/1     Running    0          9m20s
$ kubectl get nodes -l nvidia.com/gpu.present
NAME                                          STATUS    ROLES
ip-10-0-32-176.us-west-2.compute.internal    Ready     <none>
```

A few minutes after the job is complete, Karpenter will automatically detect the empty node, apply a taint to prevent new workloads from being scheduled, evict the existing Pods, and then terminate the node. You can verify that by checking the Karpenter logs:

```
$ kubectl logs --selector app.kubernetes.io/instance=karpenter -n
kube-system
"level":"INFO","time":"2025-01-31T14:50:18.104Z","logger":"controller"
,"message":"tainted node","commit":"b897114",
"controller":"node.termination","controllerGroup":"","controllerKind":
"Node","Node":{"name":"ip-10-0-32-176.us-west-2.compute.
internal"},"namespace":"",
"name":"ip-10-0-32-176.us-west-2.compute.internal","reconcileID":
"874424bd-d2f7-45ab-a399-41e5314fb3d3","taint.Key":"karpenter.sh/
disrupted","taint.Value":"","taint.Effect":"NoSchedule"}
{"level":"INFO","time":"2025-01-31T14:54:03.281Z","logger":"controller
","message":"deleted node","commit":"b897114","controller":
"node.termination","controllerGroup":"","controllerKind":
"Node","Node":{"name":"ip-10-0-32-176.us-west-2.compute.internal"},
"namespace":"","name":"ip-10-0-32-176.us-west-2.compute.internal",
"reconcileID":"eb99f292-2ea2-4aba-ac88-528746cc7e89"}
```

In this section, we looked at the advantages of using Karpenter and installed it in the EKS cluster using Terraform and Helm. Then, we configured Karpenter to launch G6 instances for our Llama 3 fine-tuning job and inference workloads. Karpenter launched a G6 instance in response to the fine-tuning job and terminated it automatically after the job completion.

Summary

In this chapter, we discussed scaling strategies and best practices for K8s applications to ensure efficient resource utilization and optimal performance. The chapter covers key scaling topics, including metrics, HPA, KEDA, VPA, CA, and Karpenter.

Scaling in Kubernetes involves selecting the right scaling metrics. Conventional metrics help determine the need for adding or removing Pods. Custom metrics are used for more granular control in scaling decisions.

HPA can automatically adjust the number of Pods in a deployment based on metrics such as CPU or memory usage, whereas VPA can adjust the resource requests and limits for individual Pods. VPA ensures optimal resource allocation but may conflict with HPA if both are used simultaneously.

KEDA brings event-driven autoscaling to K8s, enabling scaling based on external events such as message queue depths. It creates an HPA resource that manages scaling in response to event triggers such as spikes in API calls. KEDA can scale applications to zero, making it highly suitable for serverless and event-driven use cases. CA can adjust the number of nodes in a cluster based on Pod requirements. CA works closely with cloud provider APIs to manage nodes dynamically.

Lastly, we covered Karpenter, an alternative to CA. Karpenter can dynamically provision the right-sized compute resources to handle pending Pods. It optimizes for both performance and cost efficiency by selecting suitable instance types and terminating underutilized nodes to reduce costs. To demonstrate its functionality, we reran the Llama 3 fine-tuning job, during which Karpenter launched a node with GPU capabilities in response to the resource requirements, and automatically terminated the node once the job was complete. In the next chapter, we will discuss different strategies to optimize the overall cost of running GenAI applications on K8s.

7

Cost Optimization of GenAI Applications on Kubernetes

In this chapter, we will cover the key cost components for deploying GenAI applications in the cloud, covering compute, storage, and networking costs. We will then cover options to optimize these costs, such as *right-sizing* resources to prevent over-provisioning, thinking through *efficient storage management*, and *networking best practices*. This chapter will cover monitoring and optimization tools, such as Kubecost, to identify resource utilization patterns and cost-saving opportunities.

In this chapter, we're going to cover the following main topics:

- Understanding the key cost components
- Cost optimization techniques

Understanding the key cost components

Key cost components while deploying an application in the cloud typically involve compute, storage, and networking costs:

- **Compute costs**: Compute could be a significant cost driver for GenAI applications because of their resource-intensive nature. Compute costs are based on the instance size, which includes CPU, GPU, and memory sizes. On AWS, these compute instances are billed on a per-second basis, with a minimum of 60 seconds. So, after the first minute, these costs are billed in one-second increments. Refer to AWS pricing documentation at `https://aws.amazon.com/ec2/pricing/` for a deeper understanding.

- **Storage costs**: GenAI models often need large amounts of data for training and inference, so storage is another critical cost component. Key storage costs include object storage and block storage. Object storage, such as Amazon S3, is typically used for storing datasets such as image, text, or video files. The object storage costs are usually based on the volume of data stored (GB/ month) and any associated retrieval fees. Block storage, such as **Amazon Elastic Block Storage** (**EBS**), offers block-level storage volumes that can be attached to Amazon EC2 instances. EBS is commonly used for workloads requiring consistent, low-latency access in GenAI applications, such as model checkpoints, logs, and other intermediate files. Block storage costs are based on storage volume and type, such as **solid state disks** (**SSDs**) versus **hard disk drives** (**HDDs**).
- **Networking costs**: Networking costs can add up in cloud deployments, especially for GenAI applications that involve large-scale data transfers across regions or availability zones. Networking cost components include ingress/ egress costs, cross-region transfer costs, NAT gateway costs, and **content delivery network** (**CDN**) costs.
    - **Egress costs** include costs for data transferred out of the cloud. If one is serving large AI models to end users or moving data between regions or to on-premises environments, these costs could add up. **Ingress costs** for the inbound data in the cloud are often lower or free. If an application involves communication between multiple cloud regions, availability zones, or different cloud providers, such as in hybrid or multi-cloud setups, inter-region or outbound *data transfer costs* could also be significant.
    - **NAT gateway costs** include both fixed hourly charges as well as the data processing charges based on the amount of data transferred. Data transfer costs vary based on the direction of data flow. Inbound data transfer into the cloud from the internet is usually free; however, outbound data transfer from the cloud to the internet can incur charges based on the amount of data (GB).

We've covered various cost components involved in running GenAI applications. Now, let's explore how to gain granular visibility into infrastructure costs in **Kubernetes** (**K8s**) clusters. There are several cost allocation tools available in K8s and cloud environments. Some examples include **OpenCost** (`https://www.opencost.io/`), **Kubecost** (`https://www.kubecost.com/`), Spot.io (`https://spot.io/`), **Cast.ai** (`https://cast.ai/`), **PerfectScale** (`https://www.perfectscale.io/`), **IBM Cloudability** (`https://www.apptio.com/products/cloudability/`), **Harness** (`https://www.harness.io/`), cloud-provider-specific solutions, and so on. In this chapter, we will explore Kubecost for K8s cluster cost analysis.

Kubecost

Kubecost is a cost monitoring and optimization tool designed for K8s environments. It helps to track, allocate, and optimize costs by providing detailed insights into various cost components associated with running workloads in K8s clusters.

Kubecost can help visualize cost components for K8s deployments by providing the following:

- **Cost breakdown by namespace, Pod, and service**: Kubecost allows us to see detailed costs allocated to different K8s objects, such as *namespaces*, to track the costs of different teams or applications. It can also highlight the cost attribution at the individual Pod level, services level, or deployments level. Kubecost can aggregate the costs for specific services or deployments, giving a clear picture of how much we're spending on a microservice or specific deployment. This granular breakdown is especially helpful for a multi-tenant K8s cluster, where multiple teams or services could be sharing the same cluster.
- **Compute costs**: Kubecost can track the EC2 instance costs, which can help determine whether we are using the most cost-effective node types. Kubecost can also highlight whether any node or compute resource is underutilized.
- **Storage costs**: Kubecost can track the costs of storage volumes attached to K8s workloads. Kubecost can distinguish between different EBS volume types, such as gp2, gp3, and io1, and their costs, helping you optimize based on performance requirements and costs. It can also detect unused or underutilized volumes.
- **Network costs**: Kubecost can track networking-related costs, such as data transfer costs between different nodes, regions, or even AWS services. This can help optimize the network configuration and reduce unnecessary cross-region or cross-AZ data transfers.
- **Ingress/egress**: One can track and visualize the costs of traffic flowing into and out of your K8s cluster, which is particularly relevant when serving external applications or users.
- **Load balancers**: Kubecost identifies and breaks down the costs of load balancers (such as AWS NLB or ALB) that are associated with K8s services or ingress resources.
- **Integration with AWS Cost and Usage Reports (CUR)**: Kubecost can integrate with AWS CUR (`https://docs.aws.amazon.com/cur/latest/userguide/what-is-cur.html`) to provide a comprehensive view of costs, including non-K8s AWS services that your EKS workloads rely on, such as Amazon S3 or RDS. If you have multiple EKS clusters, Kubecost can also aggregate costs across all your clusters and provide insights at a global level or drill down into specific clusters for more detailed cost analysis.

Kubecost supports *cost allocation by labels*, which is especially useful for multi-tenant environments where one needs to attribute costs to different teams, projects, or environments (e.g., development, QA, staging, or production). Kubecost provides historical cost tracking and allows you to visualize cost trends over time.

Kubecost can not only help you to visualize costs, but also provide actionable recommendations to optimize spending, such as *right-sizing recommendations* by analyzing resource usage (CPU, memory, storage) and recommending resizing your workloads to avoid overprovisioning or underutilization of resources. Kubecost can suggest where you could switch to **EC2 Spot Instances** to save on compute costs, which is especially relevant for non-critical or interruptible workloads.

Setting up Kubecost

Kubecost can be installed in our EKS cluster as a Helm chart. Refer to the Amazon EKS integration in the Kubecost documentation at `https://www.ibm.com/docs/en/kubecost/self-hosted/2.x?topic=installations-amazon-eks-integration` for various installation options.

In our setup, we will install Kubecost using the Terraform Helm provider. Download the `addons.tf` file from `https://github.com/PacktPublishing/Kubernetes-for-Generative-AI-Solutions/blob/main/ch7/addons.tf` to the Terraform project folder and run the following commands:

```
$ terraform init
$ terraform plan
$ terraform apply -auto-approve
```

You can verify the installation using the following command, which displays the status, version, and other details of the deployment:

```
$ helm list -n kubecost
NAME            NAMESPACE         STATUS          CHART
kubecost        kubecost          deployed        cost-analyzer-2.7.2
```

To access the Kubecost UI console, run the following command to enable port forwarding:

```
$ kubectl port-forward -n kubecost deployment/kubecost-cost-analyzer 9090:9090
```

You can now access the Kubecost UI by visiting `http://localhost:9090` in your web browser. In the Kubecost UI console, expand the **Monitor** section in the left-hand side panel. You will see various dashboards such as **Allocations**, **Assets**, **Cloud Costs**, **Network**, **Clusters**, **External Costs**, and so on, which provide cost visualization of K8s workloads, savings recommendations, and governance tools. For example, select **Allocations** to navigate to the Allocations dashboard, as shown in *Figure 7.1*, which allows you to view the allocated spend across all native K8s constructs such as namespaces, services, deployments, and K8s labels.

NAME	CPU	GPU	RAM	PV	NETWORK	LB	SHARED	EFFICIENCY	TOTAL COST
Tota	$93.52	$104.91	$47.46	$2.01	$0.00	$3.38	$8.26	11.4%	$259.53
default	$21.30	$101.66	$12.86	$0.00	$0.00	$3.38	$7.68	8.8%	$146.87

Figure 7.1 – The Kubecost Allocations dashboard

To view the costs of our GenAI applications deployed in *Chapter 5*, change the `Aggregate By` query from *Namespace* to *Deployment* and apply the *default* namespace filter. You will see the costs for the fine-tuned Llama 3 deployment, RAG API, and Chatbot UI applications, as shown in *Figure 7.2*.

> **Important note**
>
> Kubecost only monitors the costs from the time it is installed on the cluster, so the costs for the Llama 3 fine-tuning job are not available. You can rerun the job to view those costs.

Current Filters:

Clear All Namespace is "default" ×

NAME	CPU	GPU	RAM	PV	NETWORK	LB	SHARED	EFFICIENCY	TOTAL COST
Total	$0.24	$108.32	$6.83	$0.00	$0.00	$0.00	$17.96	Inf%	$133.35
my-llama-finetuned-deployment	<$0.01	$107.12	$0.71	$0.00	$0.00	$0.00	$15.63	100.0%	$123.47
__idle__	$0.22	$1.19	$5.99	$0.00	$0.00	$0.00	$0.00	—	$7.40 N/A
chatbot-ui-deployment	$0.01	$0.00	$0.06	$0.00	$0.00	$0.00	$0.01	100.0%	$0.08
rag-api-deployment	<$0.01	$0.00	$0.07	$0.00	$0.00	$0.00	$0.01	100.0%	$0.08

Figure 7.2 – Cost analysis of GenAI applications

Refer to the Kubecost documentation at `https://www.ibm.com/docs/en/kubecost/self-hosted/2.x?topic=navigating-kubecost-ui` to learn more about these dashboards.

In this section, we explored the various cost components involved in running GenAI applications on K8s, such as compute, storage, networking, and so on. We also looked into various tools for gaining deeper visibility into K8s workload costs, deployed Kubecost on our EKS cluster, and used the Allocations dashboard to aggregate costs by namespace and deployment.

In the next section, we will dive into various cost optimization techniques.

Cost optimization techniques

To effectively reduce the costs of running GenAI workloads on K8s, it is important to optimize each of the key cost components: compute, storage, and networking. In this section, we will discuss various strategies for each of these components to lower the costs while maintaining the best performance.

Compute best practices

Compute is often the most significant component of GenAI costs, as these applications typically require access to specialized hardware such as GPUs, which are expensive and scarce. Let's look at various techniques to efficiently utilize the compute resources and lower the costs.

Right-sizing resources

Right-sizing resources is the most important step in optimizing the cost efficiency of GenAI workloads. This involves understanding the nature of the applications by profiling them and configuring the appropriate resource requests (CPU, memory, GPU) based on the actual utilization of the K8s workloads.

Right-sizing resources in K8s can minimize waste and maximize efficiency. For example, under-provisioning resources can lead to performance degradation and poor user experience, whereas over-provisioning can result in unnecessary cloud spending. By accurately setting resource requests and limits, the user can strike a balance between performance and cost. Selecting the right size instances enhances cluster density, allowing more workloads to run on fewer nodes, further optimizing costs.

There are a number of tools in the K8s community that help us estimate the resource requests and limits. Some notable ones are **Goldilocks** (`https://goldilocks.docs.fairwinds.com/`), **StormForge** (`https://stormforge.io/optimize-live/`), **KRR** (`https://github.com/robusta-dev/krr`), **Kubecost**, and so on. We will delve into a few details about Goldilocks here.

Goldilocks is a tool designed to help K8s users optimize their resource requests and limits, which improves the efficiency and cost-effectiveness of K8s clusters. Goldilocks uses Vertical Pod Autoscaler (VPA) in *Recommender* mode to suggest the optimal resource requests and limits for your K8s Pods. VPA monitors the actual CPU and memory usage of running Pods over time. It gathers usage data directly from K8s metrics. Goldilocks takes the historical CPU and memory utilization data from VPA and provides recommended resource requests and limits based on the actual needs of your application.

These recommendations help ensure that you're not over-provisioning or under-provisioning resources. Goldilocks provides a dashboard or CLI tool to visualize its findings. It displays the current resource requests/limits and the recommended values based on the observed usage.

Refer to the Goldilocks installation guide at `https://goldilocks.docs.fairwinds.com/installation/` for detailed instructions on setting up Goldilocks in your EKS cluster. After the installation, you can enable monitoring by labeling the target namespace with `goldilocks.fairwinds.com/enabled=true`. For example, you can execute the following command to enable monitoring on the default namespace:

```
$ kubectl label namespace default goldilocks.fairwinds.com/
enabled=true
namespace/default labeled
```

Once the target namespaces are labeled, you can view the recommendations in the Goldilocks UI dashboard, as shown in *Figure 7.3*, which displays resource usage recommendations for our Chatbot UI application.

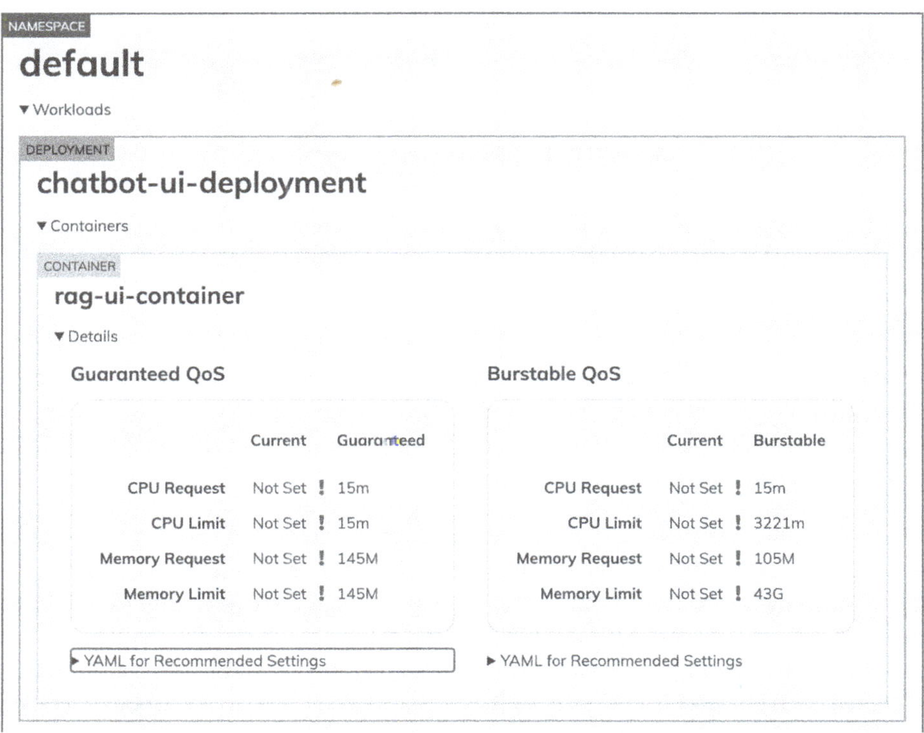

Figure 7.3 – The Goldilocks dashboard

Kubecost also provides right-sizing recommendations for the K8s workloads. Select **Savings** from the left-hand side menu in the Kubecost UI console to view the cost savings recommendations. **Savings Insights** provides various recommendations, such as right-sizing cluster nodes, containers, remedying abandoned workloads, and so on, to lower the K8s and cloud costs, as shown in *Figure 7.4*.

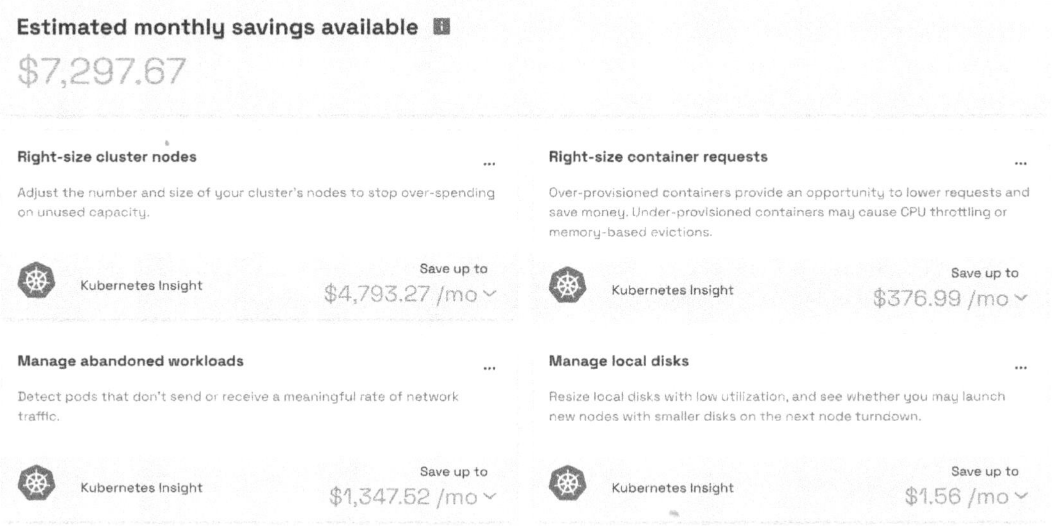
Estimated monthly savings available
$7,297.67
Right-size cluster nodes
Adjust the number and size of your cluster's nodes to stop over-spending on unused capacity.
Kubernetes Insight
Save up to
$4,793.27 /mo
Right-size container requests
Over-provisioned containers provide an opportunity to lower requests and save money. Under-provisioned containers may cause CPU throttling or memory-based evictions.
Kubernetes Insight
Save up to
$376.99 /mo
Manage abandoned workloads
Detect pods that don't send or receive a meaningful rate of network traffic.
Kubernetes Insight
Save up to
$1,347.52 /mo
Manage local disks
Resize local disks with low utilization, and see whether you may launch new nodes with smaller disks on the next node turndown.
Kubernetes Insight
Save up to
$1.56 /mo

Figure 7.4 – Kubecost savings insights

Learn more about these insights in the Kubecost documentation at `https://www.ibm.com/docs/en/kubecost/self-hosted/2.x?topic=ui-savings`.

Compute capacity options

When deploying workloads on the cloud, you have several options for managing compute capacity. These options vary in terms of cost, performance, and availability. The following is a breakdown of the different capacity types available for Amazon EKS, including **Reserved Instances** (**RIs**), Spot Instances, and x86 versus ARM architecture choices:

- **EC2 on-demand instances** (`https://aws.amazon.com/ec2/pricing/on-demand/`) are the default capacity type when deploying on EKS. They provide a flexible compute option without any long-term commitments, and you pay by the minute or second for the instances you use. On-demand instances are the most expensive, but they offer the highest level of flexibility and availability. This flexibility is especially beneficial during development and experimentation phases of GenAI workloads, where workload patterns and resource requirements may vary significantly.

- **EC2 RIs** (`https://aws.amazon.com/ec2/pricing/reserved-instances/`) provide a significant discount (up to 72%) compared to on-demand pricing in exchange for a one- or three-year commitment. RIs are well-suited for predictable workloads where you expect consistent usage over time. There are two different kinds of Ris:
  - **Standard RIs**: These provide the largest discounts but require a longer commitment for a given instance type. Usually, the larger the commitment period, the larger the discount.
  - **Convertible RIs**: These offer the flexibility to change the instance families, operating system, or tenancy during the commitment period. This flexibility comes at a slightly smaller discount compared to that of Standard RIs.
- **EC2 Spot Instances** (`https://aws.amazon.com/ec2/spot/`) allow you to use spare EC2 capacity at a significantly lower cost (up to 90%). However, Spot Instances can be interrupted by AWS when it needs the capacity back, so they are suited for fault-tolerant workloads. You'll receive a two-minute notice before your Spot Instance is reclaimed by AWS. It's essential to architect your workloads to handle interruptions gracefully, using techniques such as checkpointing, distributed job management, or backup on-demand instances. Spot Instances can be used for batch processing, stateless web servers, CI/CD pipelines, or any other workloads that can tolerate occasional interruptions or delays. Tools such as **Ray, Kubeflow**, and **Horovod** (`https://github.com/horovod/horovod`) can be configured to leverage Spot Instances for running distributed training/fine-tuning of GenAI workloads, offering features such as *checkpointing*, *interruption handling*, and so on. When combined with a compute autoscaling solution such as **Karpenter**, these tools can automatically fall back to on-demand capacity when spot capacity is not available, ensuring both cost efficiency and reliability.
- **Savings Plans** (`https://docs.aws.amazon.com/savingsplans/latest/userguide/what-is-savings-plans.html`) offer an alternative to RIs by providing flexibility in instance types and sizes while providing a significant discount for committing to a consistent amount of usage over a one- or three-year period. You can apply Savings Plan discounts across different EC2 instance families, AWS regions, and even compute services such as EC2, AWS Fargate, and AWS Lambda.
- **AWS Graviton instances (ARM-based)** (`https://aws.amazon.com/ec2/graviton/`) AWS offers two main processor architectures for EC2 instances: **x86-based** (typically Intel or AMD processors) and **ARM-based** (AWS Graviton processors). Choosing between these can impact both performance and cost. Graviton-based instances can offer up to 40% better price performance for various applications. Refer to the AWS documentation at `https://aws.amazon.com/ec2/instance-explorer/` to learn more about various Graviton instance types and respective use cases. These instances provide a cost-effective and efficient compute option for CPU-intensive parts of GenAI workloads, such as data preparation, lightweight model inferencing (when GPU acceleration is not needed), chatbot UIs, and other microservice-based workloads.

- **AWS Fargate** (`https://aws.amazon.com/fargate/`) is a serverless compute engine for containers that works with both Amazon ECS and Amazon EKS. It allows the running of K8s Pods without managing the underlying EC2 infrastructure. This provides a *serverless* experience, where you only pay for the compute resources used by the Pods. With the Fargate capacity type, there is no need to manage EC2 instances for OS updates, patching, or node scaling. Like Graviton, we can utilize AWS Fargate for data preparation, chatbot interfaces, and other microservice-based workloads.
- **EC2 Capacity Blocks for ML** (`https://aws.amazon.com/ec2/capacityblocks/`) provides reserved accelerated compute capacity to run AI/ML workloads in AWS for a future start date. EC2 Capacity Blocks supports EC2 P5e (`https://aws.amazon.com/ec2/instance-types/p5/`), P5 (`https://aws.amazon.com/ec2/instance-types/p5/`), P4d (`https://aws.amazon.com/ec2/instance-types/p4/`), and other EC2 instances powered by NVIDIA GPUs, Trn1 and Trn2 instances powered by AWS Trainium processor. These help to ensure the guaranteed capacity for model experimentation, scheduling large training, and fine-tuning jobs. Capacity Blocks are co-located in **Amazon EC2 UltraClusters** (`https://aws.amazon.com/ec2/ultraclusters/`), designed for high-performance ML workloads and providing *low-latency, high-throughput network connectivity* for distributed training.

In this section, we explored best practices for optimizing the compute costs associated with running GenAI workloads in K8s clusters. Compute resources, including CPU, GPU, and custom accelerator nodes, are often the largest contributors to operational expenses, especially for GenAI models. We covered techniques such as right-sizing resources and using tools such as Kubecost and Goldilocks to get right-sizing recommendations, using different capacity types such as Spot Instances, RIs, and Capacity Blocks, and using Savings Plans for different types of workloads. By following these practices, you can minimize compute costs while maintaining the performance and scalability of GenAI workloads.

Networking best practices

To achieve high availability in Amazon EKS, it is recommended to distribute workloads across multiple Availability Zones (AZs). This architecture enhances system reliability, especially during outages or infrastructure failures in an AZ. However, data transfer, latency between the K8s Pods, nodes, and AZs can quickly add up, especially for resource-intensive workloads such as model training and data preparation tasks. To control the data transfer costs that arise from communication between AZs or regions, effective network management is needed. Let's look at various techniques to minimize the networking costs while maintaining performance.

Pod-to-pod communication

Inter-pod traffic across AZs can incur significant costs. Limiting cross-zone traffic by aligning communication within the same AZ helps reduce these expenses. **Topology Aware Routing** (`https://kubernetes.io/docs/concepts/services-networking/topology-aware-routing/`) ensures that traffic between services is routed to the nearest Pod in the same

AZ. K8s uses **EndpointSlices** (`https://kubernetes.io/docs/concepts/services-networking/endpoint-slices/`) with zone-specific hints, ensuring **kube-proxy** directs traffic based on the origin zone, minimizing inter-AZ traffic. However, there are many considerations to be made for this to work effectively in a K8s cluster. Refer to the AWS blog at `https://aws.amazon.com/blogs/containers/exploring-the-effect-of-topology-aware-hints-on-network-traffic-in-amazon-elastic-kubernetes-service/` for a deeper understanding.

Workloads can also be restricted to specific AZs using **Cluster Autoscaler** (**CA**) or Karpenter. This avoids cross-AZ traffic, reducing network-related costs and improving latency. For example, Karpenter allows specifying worker node zones with the label `topology.kubernetes.io/zone`, as shown in the following example:

```
apiVersion: karpenter.sh/v1
kind: NodePool
metadata:
  name: single-az-example
spec:
...
  requirements:
    - key: "topology.kubernetes.io/zone"
      operator: In
      values: ["us-west-2a"]
...
```

Load balancer configuration

AWS Load Balancer Controller (`https://kubernetes-sigs.github.io/aws-load-balancer-controller/latest/`) manages ELB resources, including application and network load balancers. In **IP mode** (`https://docs.aws.amazon.com/elasticloadbalancing/latest/application/target-group-register-targets.html#register-ip-addresses`), where K8s Pods are registered directly as ELB targets, traffic is routed straight to the destination Pods. This reduces extra network hops, lowers network latency, and eliminates the inter-AZ data transfer costs. In **Instance mode** (`https://docs.aws.amazon.com/elasticloadbalancing/latest/application/target-group-register-targets.html#register-instances`), traffic is first routed to the EC2 worker nodes and then forwarded to the appropriate K8s Pods. This additional routing step can result in extra network hops and may incur inter-AZ data transfer costs, especially when the K8s Pod is in a different AZ. Refer to the AWS blog at `https://aws.amazon.com/blogs/networking-and-content-delivery/exploring-data-transfer-costs-for-classic-and-application-load-balancers/` to understand the data transfer costs when using application load balancers.

Data transfer and VPC connectivity

To reduce data transfer costs between services, VPC endpoints (`https://docs.aws.amazon.com/whitepapers/latest/aws-privatelink/what-are-vpc-endpoints.html`) enable direct access to AWS services without routing through the public internet. This eliminates the need for deploying an **internet gateway** (`https://docs.aws.amazon.com/vpc/latest/userguide/VPC_Internet_Gateway.html`) and **network address translation (NAT) gateway** (`https://docs.aws.amazon.com/vpc/latest/userguide/vpc-nat-gateway.html`) to communicate with AWS services. For workloads spread across different VPCs, **VPC peering** (`https://docs.aws.amazon.com/vpc/latest/userguide/vpc-peering.html`) or an **AWS Transit Gateway** (`https://docs.aws.amazon.com/vpc/latest/userguide/extend-tgw.html`) is recommended to enable low-cost, inter-VPC communication.

Optimizing image pulls from Amazon ECR

This strategy can help reduce networking costs and improve K8s Pod startup times. In-region image pulls from Amazon ECR are free, but you will be charged a NAT gateway data processing fee. So, you can utilize the VPC endpoints of Amazon ECR and Amazon S3 to privately access the ECR images. For large GenAI workloads, pre-caching container images in custom AMIs can further optimize the image pull times during worker node/Pod startup. This approach minimizes data transfer during scaling events and speeds up instance readiness, which is particularly beneficial for dynamic, auto-scaling environments. Refer to the AWS blog at `https://aws.amazon.com/blogs/containers/start-pods-faster-by-prefetching-images/` for a deeper understanding of how this works.

In this section, we explored best practices for optimizing networking costs for running GenAI workloads in K8s clusters. Effective networking strategies can help reduce the significant costs associated with data transfer, NAT gateways, and load balancing. Using techniques such as Topology Aware Routing and IP targets in ALB can help reduce latency and data transfer costs. We also discussed the benefits of optimizing image pulls from ECR to speed up the startup times and reduce networking costs.

In the next section, we will explore storage-related best practices in K8s clusters.

Storage best practices

There are multiple storage options available in a K8s environment, and selecting the right one is essential to optimize application performance and cost. Depending on the workload, one could use either ephemeral storage or persistent storage for their applications.

Ephemeral storage

Ephemeral volumes are temporary storage volumes that do not persist beyond a Pod's life cycle, making them suitable for scratch space or caching. These volumes are often backed by the root disk of the host system or RAM, meaning they do not persist once the Pod is terminated. For cost efficiency, it's important to properly configure ephemeral storage to avoid over-provisioning, and where possible, leverage node-local storage for temporary tasks to reduce reliance on external storage systems, thus lowering costs.

Object storage

While ephemeral and EBS volumes provide low-latency, high-performance storage for many workloads, object storage solutions such as Amazon S3 offer a flexible, scalable, and cost-effective alternative for storing large datasets, model artifacts, and logs. The **Mountpoint for Amazon S3 CSI driver** (`https://github.com/awslabs/mountpoint-s3-csi-driver`) enables you to mount an S3 bucket as a filesystem inside the K8s Pods, allowing applications to interact with object storage using familiar filesystem semantics. It offers significant performance gains compared to traditional S3 access methods, making it ideal for data-intensive workloads and AI/ML training.

The Mountpoint for S3 CSI driver supports both Amazon S3 Standard and S3 Express One Zone storage classes. S3 Express One Zone is a high-performance storage class designed for single-AZ deployments. It offers consistent, single-digit-millisecond data access, making it ideal for frequently accessed data and latency-sensitive applications. By co-locating storage and compute resources within the same AZ, you can optimize performance and potentially reduce networking costs.

In addition to performance considerations, optimizing object storage costs is essential when working with large-scale training datasets. Best practices include selecting the appropriate S3 storage class based on the access patterns. For example, use *S3 Standard* or *S3 Intelligent-Tiering* for frequently accessed data, and transition infrequently accessed data to S3 Infrequent Access or archival classes such as Glacier. Implement life cycle policies to automate transitions and data expirations, thereby reducing unnecessary storage costs. Refer to the AWS documentation at `https://aws.amazon.com/s3/storage-classes/` for a deeper understanding of the various S3 storage classes.

When using Mountpoint for S3 CSI driver, you can attach an existing S3 bucket to K8s Pods by creating a *PersistentVolume*, as shown in the following:

```
apiVersion: v1
kind: PersistentVolume
metadata:
  name: s3-demo-pv
spec:
  capacity:
    storage: 1200Gi # Ignored, required
  accessModes:
    - ReadWriteMany
  mountOptions:
    - allow-delete
    - region us-west-2
  csi:
    driver: s3.csi.aws.com
```

```
    volumeHandle: s3-csi-driver-volume
    volumeAttributes:
      bucketName: <Your-S3-Bucket-Name>
```

By leveraging the Mountpoint-S3 and adhering to cost-effective storage best practices, you can seamlessly integrate Amazon S3 object storage into your K8s workloads. This approach enables your GenAI workloads to access large-scale, cost-effective storage with familiar filesystem semantics while optimizing both performance and cost.

EBS volumes

Amazon EBS volumes provide block-level persistent storage. EBS volumes are managed via the Amazon EBS CSI driver, enabling dynamic provisioning through K8s. The **Container Storage Interface (CSI)** is a standardized K8s API that ensures interoperability between K8s and external storage systems. K8s applications request storage by creating **Persistent Volume Claims (PVCs)** specifying the size and access mode. The EBS CSI driver provisions the EBS volume based on the linked StorageClass. For example, following YAML code will create a gp3 storage class:

```
apiVersion: storage.k8s.io/v1
kind: StorageClass
metadata:
  name: gp3-sc
provisioner: ebs.csi.aws.com
parameters:
  type: gp3
  encrypted: "true"
  fsType: ext4
allowVolumeExpansion: true
reclaimPolicy: Delete
```

A reclaim policy for StorageClass could be either *delete* or *retain*. The *delete* policy ensures that the PersistentVolume is automatically deleted when the associated Pod is removed. The *retain* policy keeps the PV even after the PVC is deleted. The volume stays intact with all its data, but becomes unbound and available for manual intervention.

The following YAML file is now creating a PVC, which is linked to the previous storage class for 10 GB of storage:

```
apiVersion: v1
kind: PersistentVolumeClaim
metadata:
  name: demo-pvc
spec:
  accessModes:
    - ReadWriteOnce
```

```
resources:
  requests:
    storage: 10Gi
storageClassName: gp3-sc
```

For cost optimization, it is a good idea to ensure that the correct amount of storage is claimed based on your application's needs. Over-provisioning large volumes that are not fully utilized leads to unnecessary costs. Similarly, it's common for unused *PVs* and *EBS snapshots* to accumulate over time, so one should keep monitoring their storage costs or use *delete* as a reclaim policy. You can use Kubecost to get insights into unclaimed volumes, orphaned resources, persistent volume right-sizing recommendations, and so on. Open the Kubecost UI console and select Savings -> Insights from the left-hand side menu to navigate to the **Savings** page, where you can view the cost savings recommendations, as shown in *Figure 7.5* and *Figure 7.6*.

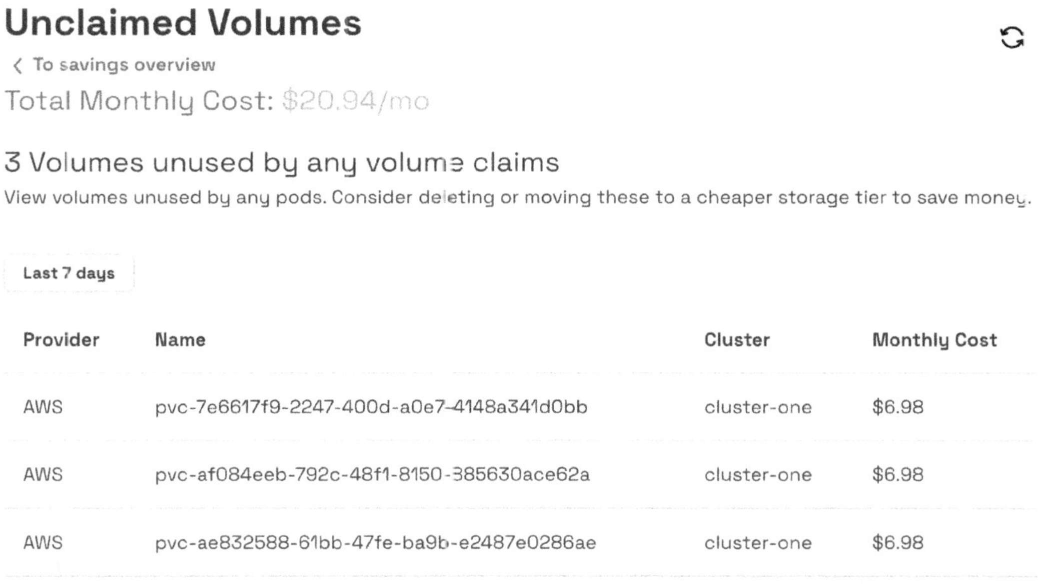

Unclaimed Volumes

< To savings overview

Total Monthly Cost: $20.94/mo

3 Volumes unused by any volume claims

View volumes unused by any pods. Consider deleting or moving these to a cheaper storage tier to save money.

Last 7 days

Provider	Name	Cluster	Monthly Cost
AWS	pvc-7e6617f9-2247-400d-a0e7-4148a341d0bb	cluster-one	$6.98
AWS	pvc-af084eeb-792c-48f1-8150-385630ace62a	cluster-one	$6.98
AWS	pvc-ae832588-61bb-47fe-ba9b-e2487e0286ae	cluster-one	$6.98

Figure 7.5 – An overview of unclaimed volumes in the Kubecost UI console

These insights help you identify cost-saving opportunities by highlighting persistent volumes that are allocated but not actively used. By analyzing these patterns, Kubecost enables you to take informed actions such as reclaiming unused resources or resizing existing volumes to better fit your workload requirements, as shown in the Figure 7.6.

Persistent Volume Right-Sizing Recommendations

‹ To savings overview

Upgrade License

Filters: Filter | Profile: Production (50%) | Window: Last 7 days

Persistent Volume Name	Cluster	Max Usage	Recommended Capacity	Current Capacity	Recommended Cost / mo	Current Cost / mo	Savings / mo
pvc-df25dc3e-8241-4378-9535-628c56b95acf	cluster-one	167.9 KB	1.1 GB	98.8 GB	$0.08	$7.36	$7.28
pvc-4e005365-a9ae-406e-866b-22d34acf7c6a	cluster-one	155.6 KB	1.1 GB	53.7 GB	$0.08	$4.00	$3.92
pvc-f0db8e58-4ce9-4d90-866f-e37a922d4c65	cluster-one	943.8 MB	2.1 GB	53.7 GB	$0.16	$4.00	$3.84

Figure 7.6 – An overview of PV right-sizing recommendations in the Kubecost UI console

For optimized costs, gp3 volumes are recommended, as they offer up to 20% lower costs compared to gp2 and allow independent scaling of IOPS and throughput without increasing volume size. For high-performance needs, **io2 Block Express** volumes support up to 256,000 IOPS, but they are more expensive and require specific EC2 instance types.

For workloads with less frequent access to data, such as logs and backups, one could use **Cold HDD (sc1)** or **Throughput Optimized HDD (st1)**. These options are cheaper than SSD-backed volumes. Refer to the Amazon EBS pricing page at `https://aws.amazon.com/ebs/pricing/` for detailed pricing.

A few other considerations to make when optimizing storage costs in K8s applications are as follows:

- **Optimize container image storage**: Container images can consume a significant amount of storage, especially when large, multi-layer images are used in an Amazon EKS cluster. Optimizing it is crucial for reducing both storage costs and the time it takes to pull images during startup. To achieve this, it's best to use smaller, lightweight parent images where possible. Additionally, by employing multi-stage builds (`https://docs.docker.com/build/building/multi-stage/`), only the necessary components are included in the final container image, further decreasing image size. These optimizations not only save storage space but also lead to faster deployment times and reduced costs for both storing and pulling container images.
- **Use data retention policies**: Implement data retention policies to automatically delete old, unnecessary datasets such as logs, metrics, and backups that accumulate over time. Tools such as **Elasticsearch** and **AWS CloudWatch Logs** offer controls to set appropriate retention policies to delete old logs and reduce storage costs. Similarly for backups, set appropriate retention policies, ensuring that only necessary backups are retained, while old, redundant backups are deleted.

In this section, we discussed various available storage options and how to use CSI drivers to dynamically provision the storage volumes in K8s clusters. We also explored the importance of reducing the container image size to not only reduce the storage costs but also improve the startup times of K8s Pods.

Summary

In this chapter, we explored the best practices for optimizing the cost of deploying GenAI applications in the cloud by focusing on three key components: compute, storage, and networking. We also introduced tools such as Kubecost and Goldilocks to monitor resource utilization and ensure efficient resource allocation.

For compute costs, selecting the appropriate instance types is essential. It's crucial to monitor resource utilization to ensure workloads run on optimally sized instances. For storage, choosing the right storage type is the key to optimizing the storage costs of large datasets needed for model training and inference.

Kubecost is an effective tool for monitoring and optimizing the cost of K8s clusters. It provides detailed cost breakdowns by namespaces, Pods, and services, helping attribute expenses to individual teams or applications. Kubecost also identifies underutilized nodes, recommends more cost-effective instance types, and detects storage and networking inefficiencies, such as unnecessary inter-AZ data transfers. Goldilocks leverages the VPA to analyze historical CPU and memory usage, providing recommendations for right-sizing resource requests and limits.

On the networking front, we discussed the importance of aligning Pod communication within the same AZ to minimize cross-AZ traffic costs. Using Topology Aware Routing ensures that traffic is routed within the AZ, reducing inter-AZ transfer fees.

This chapter also highlighted the importance of continuous monitoring, right-sizing resources, and making strategic trade-offs across compute, storage, and networking to optimize costs effectively.

In the next chapter, we will dive deeper and cover the networking best practices for deploying GenAI applications in K8s.

Join the CloudPro Newsletter with 44000+ Subscribers

Want to know what's happening in cloud computing, DevOps, IT administration, networking, and more? Scan the QR code to subscribe to **CloudPro**, our weekly newsletter for 44,000+ tech professionals who want to stay informed and ahead of the curve.

https://packt.link/cloudpro

8

Networking Best Practices for Deploying GenAI on K8s

In this chapter, we will explore best practices for cloud networking when deploying GenAI applications on **Kubernetes** (**K8s**). Effective networking is essential for ensuring seamless communication between Pods, optimizing performance, and enhancing security. The chapter will start with the K8s networking foundations, such as **Container Network Interface** (**CNI**) (`https://kubernetes.io/docs/concepts/extend-kubernetes/compute-storage-net/network-plugins/`) to set up Pod networking and network policies to enforce security and access controls within the K8s cluster, and we will also dive into using optimized cloud networking interfaces such as **Elastic Fabric Adapter** (**EFA**) (`https://aws.amazon.com/hpc/efa/`) for better network performance. By defining granular rules for communication between Pods and services, organizations can mitigate potential security threats to safeguard their intellectual property and GenAI models.

In this chapter, we're going to cover the following main topics:

- Understanding the Kubernetes networking model
- Advanced traffic management with a service mesh
- Securing GenAI workloads with Kubernetes network policies
- Optimizing network performance for GenAI

Understanding the Kubernetes networking model

K8s networking has evolved from **Docker's networking model** (`https://docs.docker.com/engine/network/`) to better address the complexities of managing large clusters of containers across distributed environments. Docker's initial networking used a *single-host, bridge-based networking* model where containers on the same host could communicate via a local bridge network. However, containers on the different hosts required additional configuration to explicitly create links between containers or to map container ports to host ports to make them reachable by containers on other hosts. K8s simplified this networking model by ensuring *seamless inter-Pod communication* across hosts, *automatic service discovery*, and *load balancing*.

K8s' networking model (`https://kubernetes.io/docs/concepts/services-networking/#the-kubernetes-network-model`) has the following key tenets:

- Each Pod in a K8s cluster has its own unique IP address, and all containers within a Pod share a private network namespace. Containers within the same Pod can communicate with each other using localhost.
- Pods can communicate with each other directly across the cluster, without the need for proxies or address translation, such as **Network Address Translation** (**NAT**).
- The Service API provides an IP address or hostname for services, even as the Pods making up those services change. K8s manages **EndpointSlice** (`https://kubernetes.io/docs/concepts/services-networking/endpoint-slices/`) objects to keep track of these Pods.
- **NetworkPolicy** (`https://kubernetes.io/docs/concepts/services-networking/network-policies/`) is a built-in K8s API that allows the control of traffic between Pods and external sources.

We will cover Service APIs and network policies in detail in the later part of this chapter. Some key components of the K8s networking model are **Kubelet** (`https://kubernetes.io/docs/reference/command-line-tools-reference/kubelet/`), **Container Runtime Interface** (**CRI**) (`https://kubernetes.io/docs/concepts/architecture/cri/`), and **Container Network Interface** (**CNI**) (`https://kubernetes.io/docs/concepts/extend-kubernetes/compute-storage-net/network-plugins/`), which handle the lifecycle and networking of containers within a cluster.

- **Kubelet**: The kubelet is an agent running on each worker node in a K8s cluster that ensures that the containers described by the K8s API are running properly on the node. The kubelet interacts with the CRI to start, stop, and monitor containers based on the configurations set in Pod specifications.

- **CRI**: The CRI is an API that allows the kubelet to communicate with different container runtimes in a standardized way by abstracting the underlying container runtime such as Containerd or CRI-O.
- **CNI**: The CNI is an open source API specification designed with simplicity and modularity in mind. It allows K8s to handle container networking in a unified, plug-and-play manner by using any CNI-compatible plugin.

When a Pod is scheduled to a worker node, Kubelet instructs the CRI to create containers for the Pod. Once the containers are ready, Kubelet invokes the CNI plugin to set up the Pod network – attaching network interfaces, assigning IP addresses, configuring routing, and ensuring network policies are enforced. This allows Pods to seamlessly communicate with each other and with external networks, adhering to the K8s network model.

There are several CNI plugins available for K8s, each with a unique set of features and strengths. Some of the popular CNI plugins are **Calico** (`https://www.tigera.io/project-calico/`), **Cilium** (`https://github.com/cilium/cilium`), **Weave Net** (`https://github.com/weaveworks/weave`), **Antrea** (`https://antrea.io/`), and **Amazon VPC CNI** (`https://github.com/aws/amazon-vpc-cni-k8s`). Refer to the K8s documentation at `https://kubernetes.io/docs/concepts/cluster-administration/addons/#networking-and-network-policy` for a detailed list.

Other important K8s networking components are **IP Address Management** (**IPAM**), which is used by the CNI plugin to assign and manage IP addresses for Pods within a K8s cluster, and **IPTables** (`https://man7.org/linux/man-pages/man8/iptables.8.html`), which is responsible for packet filtering and is part of the Linux kernel. In K8s, components like kube-proxy and certain CNI network plugins use **IPTables** to manage network rules and direct traffic within worker nodes. These IPTables rules enable Pods to communicate with each other within the cluster, manage external traffic flows, and, depending on the network plugin, help implement network policies.

Figure 8.1 shows how the kubelet, the CNI, IPAM, and IPTables work together within a K8s worker node to set up and manage networking for a Pod:

1. In step 1, Kubelet communicates with the CNI plugin to request the creation and configuration of a Pod's network.
2. In step 2, the CNI plugin creates a network namespace and calls the IPAM module to reserve an IP address for the Pod.
3. In step 3, the CNI plugin configures IPTables to manage network traffic rules for the Pod. This step ensures that the Pod can communicate with other Pods and external networks according to the cluster's networking policies.

4. In the last step, the allocated IP address (e.g., 10.0.0.12) is assigned to the Pod. This makes the Pod reachable within the cluster using the assigned IP address.

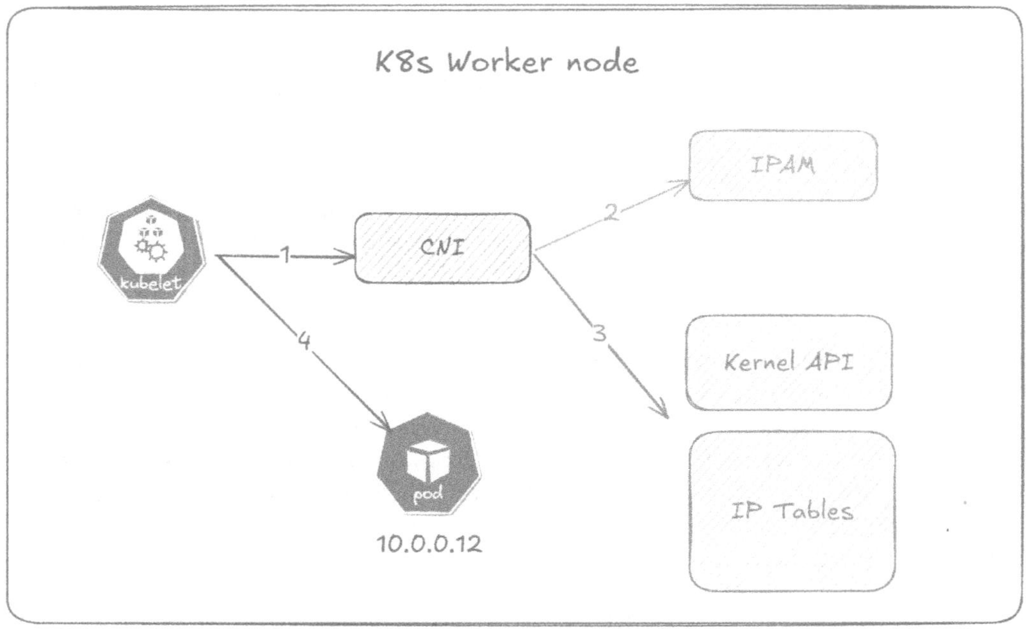

Figure 8.1 – IP allocation flow in a worker node

Selecting the CNI networking mode for GenAI applications

When choosing a CNI plugin, it is important to understand the differences between **overlay networks** and **native networking**.

CNI plugins that use an overlay network create an additional layer of abstraction over the existing network, encapsulating traffic in tunnels to isolate Pod networks and simplify routing across nodes. While this provides flexibility and network segmentation, it often comes at the cost of higher latency and lower throughput due to the encapsulation overhead.

Native networking plugins, such as the Amazon VPC CNI and Cilium, integrate directly with the underlying infrastructure's routing, allowing Pods to communicate using real network interfaces and IP addresses without encapsulation. This integration can result in higher throughput and lower latency, making native networking an optimal choice for applications that require high performance. For GenAI workloads, where rapid data transfer and minimal network latency are critical for effective model training and inference, native networking CNI plugins are usually recommended.

Service implementation in K8s

A **Service** is a K8s resource that provides network endpoint and load balancing across a set of Pods, making it easy to expose an application to other services or external clients. Here are the key features of K8s Service implementation:

- K8s Services provide a consistent IP and DNS name for a set of Pods, so even as Pods get created or destroyed, service performance isn't affected.
- Services automatically distribute incoming traffic to the available Pods based on their labels. This helps with load balancing and ensures availability.
- K8s supports the following four different types of services:
  - **ClusterIP** (default) exposes the services within the cluster. It creates a stable IP address that can be used by other services or Pods within the cluster.
  - **NodePort** exposes the service on a static port on each node's IP, allowing service access from outside the cluster for simple deployments or during test/QA phases.
  - **LoadBalancer** exposes the service externally using a cloud provider's load balancer. In our setup, we used the `aws-load-balancer-controller` (`https://kubernetes-sigs.github.io/aws-load-balancer-controller/latest/`) addon to expose our GenAI models using the AWS **Network Load Balancer** (**NLB**) in *Chapter 3*.
  - **ExternalName** maps the service to an external DNS name, allowing K8s services to connect to an external service outside the cluster.

GenAI applications often require scalable, low latency, and efficient networking to serve the customers effectively. K8s' **LoadBalancer** Service can be used to expose models outside the cluster. It provisions an external load balancer through the underlying cloud provider (such as AWS, Azure, or GCP). This setup enables seamless distribution of incoming traffic across multiple Pods, ensuring high availability and scalability. On the other hand, **ClusterIP** service can be utilized when the GenAI models are accessed only within the cluster by other K8s Pods. It assigns a friendly service lookup name and an IP address for each service, facilitating reliable service discovery and communication between Pods without exposing them externally.

By default, when using the K8s **LoadBalancer** Service with `aws-load-balancer-controller`, a **NodePort** Service is created to forward traffic from the AWS NLB to the K8s worker nodes. From there, kube-proxy routes the traffic to the individual Pods, introducing an additional network hop that can increase the latency and throughput. To reduce this overhead, you can configure the LoadBalancer service to route traffic directly to K8s Pods by registering the Pods as NLB targets.

This can be achieved by adding the `service.beta.kubernetes.io/aws-load-balancer-nlb-target-type: ip` annotation to the K8s service, as shown here:

```
apiVersion: v1
kind: Service
metadata:
  name: my-llama-svc
  annotations:
      service.beta.kubernetes.io/aws-load-balancer-type: "external"
      service.beta.kubernetes.io/aws-load-balancer-nlb-target-type: ip
spec:
  type: LoadBalancer
  ...
```

Service health checks

Another important consideration in ensuring optimal performance and reliability is configuring **healthcheck** settings on the LoadBalancer service type. GenAI models are typically resource-intensive and can have varying startup and response times based on input complexity and server load. Without proper health checks, NLB may flag the targets as unhealthy, which will lead to replacing the K8s Pods, degraded performance, or potential downtime.

LoadBalancer health checks ensure that traffic is routed only to healthy Pods capable of handling requests. For instance, in a scenario where a GenAI model serves inference through a K8s Service of type LoadBalancer, the health check can monitor an endpoint such as `/healthz` on each backend Pod. This endpoint could return an *HTTP 200 OK* status if the model is fully loaded, the required resources (e.g., GPU memory) are available, and the inference service is operational. If a Pod fails the health check due to issues such as resource exhaustion or process crashes, the LoadBalancer will automatically exclude it from the pool of available endpoints, directing traffic to healthy Pods instead. This mechanism prevents request failures and ensures a seamless experience for end users while maintaining the overall stability and scalability of the GenAI workload.

Refer to the `aws-load-balancer-controller` documentation at `https://kubernetes-sigs.github.io/aws-load-balancer-controller/latest/guide/service/annotations/#health-check` for various health check settings.

While K8s LoadBalancer Services provide a simple and straightforward way to expose K8s workloads externally, they can be limited in more complex routing scenarios. Ingress and Gateway APIs provide greater flexibility and control over traffic flow, enabling features such as path or host-based routing or TLS termination. In the next section, we will cover the Ingress and Gateway APIs, which handle the input traffic for K8s workloads.

Ingress controller

In K8s, **Ingress** API (`https://kubernetes.io/docs/concepts/services-networking/ingress/`) is used to expose applications outside the cluster using HTTP/S protocols. It acts as a routing layer to direct incoming requests to K8s applications based on HTTP URL paths, hostnames, headers, and so on. An Ingress controller is responsible for provisioning required infrastructure resources such as Application Load Balancers (in AWS), configuring routing rules, and terminating SSL connections, to fulfill the Ingress resources. Some of the popular **Ingress controllers** (`https://kubernetes.io/docs/concepts/services-networking/ingress-controllers/`) include **ingress-nginx**, **aws-lb-controller**, **HAProxy Ingress**, and **Istio Ingress**. Refer to the K8s documentation at `https://kubernetes.io/docs/concepts/services-networking/ingress-controllers/#additional-controllers` for a detailed list. When deploying GenAI workloads in a K8s cluster, you should consider Ingress when exposing multiple applications/models under one entry point (domain name) as shown in *Figure 8.2*, which typically requires centralized traffic routing. Additionally, Ingress supports advanced routing features such as path-based and host-based routing, enabling you to direct specific requests to different model versions or applications based on URLs and HTTP headers, which is useful for **A/B testing** (`https://aws.amazon.com/developer/application-security-performance/articles/a-b-testing/`) or **canary releases**, where new application changes are gradually rolled out to a small set of users, allowing teams to monitor performance and catch issues before full-scale deployment. Apart from routing, Ingress controllers also integrate with monitoring tools such as **Prometheus** to provide detailed metrics such as latencies, request rates, and error rates.

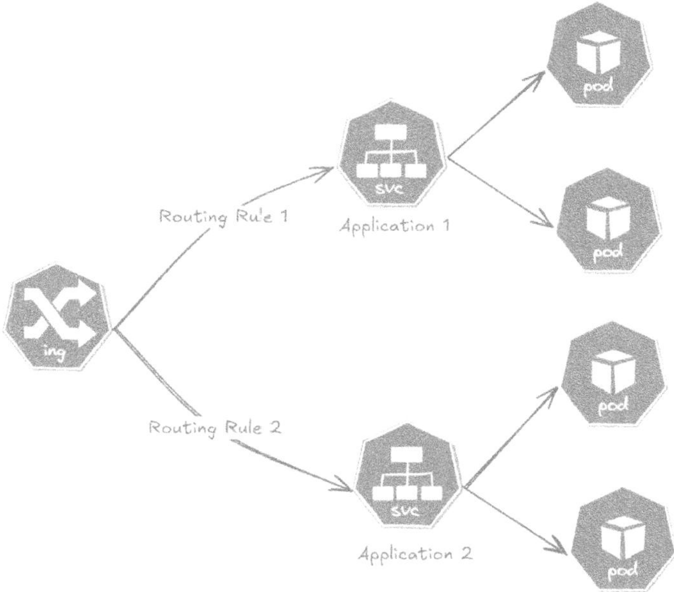

Figure 8.2 – Overview of Ingress

The **Gateway API** (`https://gateway-api.sigs.k8s.io/`) was created to address the limitations of Ingress, offering a more flexible, extensible, and standardized approach to managing traffic in K8s clusters, especially for complex networking needs. It is the official K8s project focused on L4 and L7 routing, representing the next generation of Ingress, Load Balancing, and Service Mesh APIs. Like Ingress, you need to install **Gateway Controller** to provision necessary infrastructure resources along with advanced routing features. There are many implementations of this API, refer to K8s documentation at `https://gateway-api.sigs.k8s.io/implementations/` for a complete list.

In this section, we learned about foundational concepts of K8s networking, core tenets, and how it is different from other orchestrators. We discussed the role of the CNI plugin to configure the Pod networking, IPAM to manage the IP addressing, and considerations when choosing a CNI networking mode. We explored various K8s services, Ingress, and the Gateway API to expose GenAI models outside of the cluster. In the next section, we will discuss advanced application networking constructs such as service mesh.

Advanced traffic management with a service mesh

As GenAI applications grow in complexity, the number of services involved such as model inferencing, data ingestion, data processing, fine-tuning, and training also increases the complexity of managing service-to-service communication. These typically include traffic management (load balancing, retries, rate limiting), security (authentication, authorization, encryption), and observability (logs, metrics, traces).

A **service mesh** is an infrastructure layer that enables reliable, secure, and observable communication between microservices. It abstracts the complexity of service-to-service communication, including traffic management, load balancing, security, and observability, without requiring changes in application code.

Service mesh typically provides these features by deploying a sidecar proxy such as **Envoy** (`https://www.envoyproxy.io/`) alongside the application, which intercepts all network traffic in and out of the application.

The service mesh has two key components:

- **Control plane**, which manages the sidecar proxies, distributing configuration and policies across the side car proxies and gathering telemetry data for centralized control and monitoring. Different kinds of policies can be implemented in service mesh, such as the following:
  - **Traffic management policies**, which define rules for how traffic should be routed, circuit-breaking rules, load balancing, and retry options
  - **Security policies**, which can establish rules for encryption (mTLS), authentication (e.g., JWT tokens), and authorization (RBAC)
  - **Resilience and fault tolerance policies**, which can define retry mechanisms, timeouts, and failover options

- **Data plane**, which combines sidecar proxies and is responsible for the actual network traffic between services. Each sidecar can apply policies independently, ensuring that each service instance respects the network rules and policies set at the control plane. **Sidecar containers** are secondary containers that run alongside the main application container within the same Pod. They complement the primary container by offering additional capabilities, such as logging, monitoring, security, or data synchronization, enhancing the application's functionality without requiring changes to its code.

Some popular service mesh implementations in K8s are **Istio**, **Linkerd**, and **Ambient Mesh**. While traditional meshes such as Istio and Linkerd rely on sidecars, Ambient Mesh recently introduced by Istio offers a sidecarless architecture that can leverage eBPF for efficient traffic management and security. *Figure 8.3* shows how a service mesh implementation can route the traffic in and out of the mesh, intercept requests, and implement end-to-end TLS encryption or mTLS using sidecar proxies.

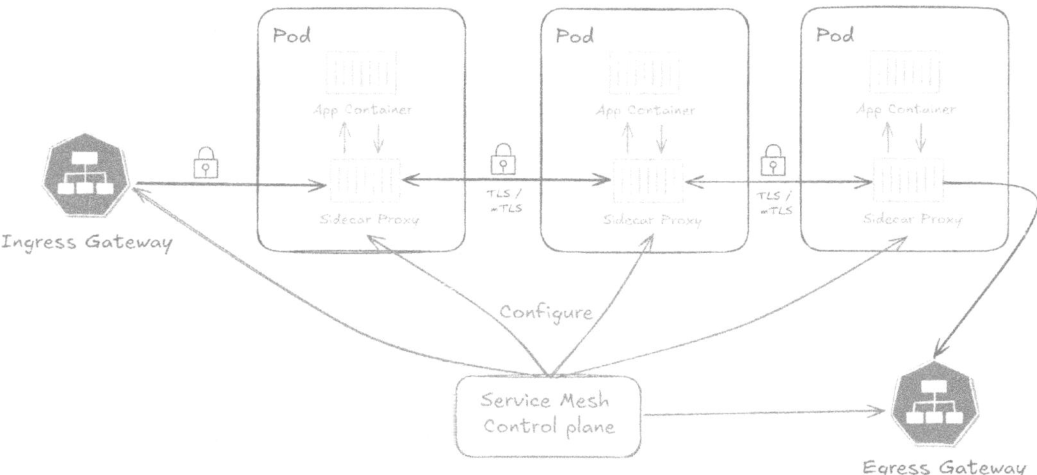

Figure 8.3 – Service mesh implementation

This figure shows a service mesh architecture, where traffic enters through the Ingress Gateway, flows between Pods via sidecar proxies, and exits through the Egress Gateway. The Service Mesh Control Plane centrally configures and manages the sidecar proxies to enforce traffic policies and security. This setup enables efficient and secure microservices communication within the cluster. Refer to the *Getting Started with Istio on Amazon EKS* article at `https://aws.amazon.com/blogs/opensource/getting-started-with-istio-on-amazon-eks/` for step-by-step instructions to deploy Istio service mesh on Amazon EKS.

In this section, we explored the advanced traffic management features of a service mesh such as load balancing, security, observability, and a high-level architectural overview. In the next section, we will dive deeper into securing GenAI workloads using K8s native network policies.

Securing GenAI workloads with Kubernetes' network policies

Network policies are a native K8s feature that controls ingress (incoming) and egress (outgoing) traffic between Pods within a cluster. They are implemented through the K8s **NetworkPolicy API** and allow administrators to define rules that determine which Pods or IP addresses can communicate with each other.

Unlike a service mesh, which provides advanced traffic management and security features, network policies focus on traffic isolation and network segmentation for security purposes, such as namespace isolation.

By default, all Pods in a K8s cluster can communicate with each other; however, network policies can restrict this and allow fine-grained control over network traffic. This is especially useful in multi-tenant clusters, where different teams or applications require isolation for security or compliance. Some key features of network policies are as follows:

- **Ingress and egress rules**: *Ingress rules* define which sources are allowed to communicate with a specific Pod or set of Pods. Similarly, *egress rules* define which destinations a Pod or set of Pods can connect to.
- **Label-based targeting**: Network policies use K8s labels to select Pods, allowing administrators to create policies based on logical groupings. For example, all Pods with the label `app: backend` can be configured to allow ingress only from Pods with the label `app: frontend`.
- **Deny-by-default model**: By default, if there are no network policies applied, all traffic is allowed. However, once a network policy is applied to a Pod, only the traffic that matches the specified policy rules is allowed.

Here is an example of a network policy that allows incoming traffic to Pods with the label `app: backend` only from other Pods with the label `app: frontend` in the same namespace. All other ingress traffic is denied by default for these Pods:

```
apiVersion: networking.k8s.io/v1
kind: NetworkPolicy
metadata:
  name: ingress-example
spec:
  podSelector:
    matchLabels:
      app: backend
```

```
  policyTypes:
  - Ingress
  ingress:
  - from:
    - podSelector:
        matchLabels:
          app: frontend
```

Next, let's explore how to implement K8s network policies to secure traffic flows among different components of our e-commerce chatbot application.

Implementing network policies in a chatbot application

In *Chapter 5*, we deployed a chatbot application in the EKS cluster that comprises four components (chatbot-ui, vector database, RAG application, and fine-tuned Llama3 model), as depicted in *Figure 8.4*. By default, all components can talk to each other on any ports/protocols, which is not a security best practice. Our goal is to implement network segmentation so that only trusted components can communicate with each other on approved ports and protocols.

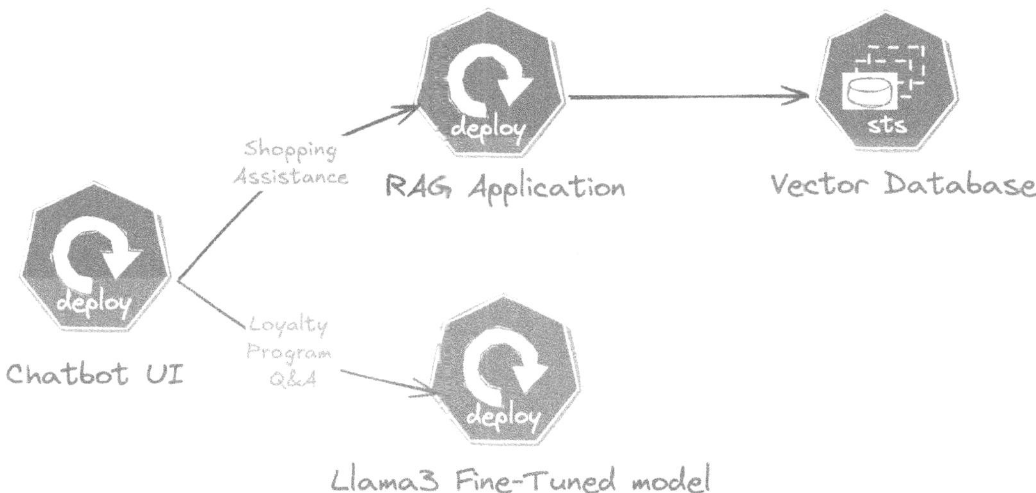

Figure 8.4 – E-commerce chatbot application architecture

In this setup, the Chatbot UI application communicates with the RAG application and the fine-tuned Llama 3 model over HTTP on port 80. So, let's create an Ingress network policy on both RAG and Llama 3 applications to allow only HTTP/80 ingress traffic from the chatbot UI app to secure the network traffic flow. We can use the labels applied to respective K8s deployments to create the network policy.

The following network policy selects the RAG application Pods using the `app.kubernetes.io/name: rag-app` label and applies an ingress rule to allow HTTP/80 traffic only from Pods identified by the `app.kubernetes.io/name=chatbot-ui` label:

```
apiVersion: networking.k8s.io/v1
kind: NetworkPolicy
metadata:
  name: rag-app-ingress-policy
spec:
  podSelector:
    matchLabels:
      app.kubernetes.io/name: rag-app
  policyTypes:
  - Ingress
  ingress:
  - from:
    - podSelector:
        matchLabels:
          app.kubernetes.io/name: chatbot-ui
    ports:
    - protocol: TCP
      port: 80
```

We can also create another network policy for a fine-tuned Llama 3 application to allow HTTP/80 traffic only from the chatbot UI app by using the `app.kubernetes.io/name: my-llama-finetuned`, `app.kubernetes.io/name: chatbot-ui` labels.

Similarly, the RAG application communicates with the vector database over HTTP on port 6333. To restrict inbound traffic, we can create a network policy that applies to the Pods labeled `app.kubernetes.io/name: qdrant`, allowing HTTP/6333 traffic only from Pods labeled `app.kubernetes.io/name: rag-app`.

You can find all the network policies in the GitHub repository at `https://github.com/PacktPublishing/Kubernetes-for-Generative-AI-Solutions/tree/main/ch8`. You can download and apply them in the EKS cluster using the `kubectl apply` command. In this walkthrough, we focused on configuring Ingress rules to restrict the inbound traffic. To further tighten security, you can extend these policies to include egress rules for the outbound traffic. However, if your application performs DNS lookups on K8s Services, be sure to allow DNS traffic to the **CoreDNS** deployment running in the `kube-system` namespace.

By default, upstream K8s network policies support only a limited set of rules to define traffic flows (primarily IP address, port, protocol, podSelector, and namespaceSelector) and do not support domain-based rules or cluster or global policies. This can be insufficient for GenAI applications when using external APIs such as OpenAI or Claude. To address these gaps, **Cilium** (`https://docs.cilium.`

io/en/stable/security/), **Calico** (https://docs.tigera.io/calico/latest/network-policy/) and others offer advanced capabilities such as DNS-based policies, which allow specifying fully qualified domain names for dynamic policy enforcement, and global (cluster-wide) policies, which ensure a uniform security posture across all namespaces. These features simplify policy management, strengthen cluster-wide data governance, and maintain consistent traffic controls.

To summarize, K8s network policies help define traffic rules and segmentation at the network and transport layers of the OSI model but lack advanced features for application layer traffic management and observability. In the next section, we will compare network policies with service mesh technology, highlighting how these solutions differ in their key features.

Service mesh versus K8s network policies

While both service mesh and K8s network policies help to secure and manage K8s networking, they serve different purposes and often complement each other:

Feature	**Service Mesh**	**K8s Network Policies**
Key Focus	Observability, traffic management (such as load balancing), retries, and security (mTLS support)	Security and traffic isolation using namespaces
Traffic Routing	Advanced routing and load balancing	Basic
OSI Layer	Primarily at Layer 7 (application layer)	Primarily Layer 3 and 4 (network and transport layer)
Mutual TLS	Supported	Not supported
Complexity	Requires sidecar proxies	Simpler, native to Kubernetes

In many production environments, both service mesh and K8s network policies are deployed together to enhance security and traffic management. For instance, you might use K8s network policies to enforce namespace-based access restrictions, then use a service mesh to handle routing, retries, load balancing, and mTLS within the defined traffic boundaries.

Optimizing network performance for GenAI

In this section, we will cover some important network optimizations when deploying GenAI workloads on K8s, such as Kube-Proxy, IP exhaustion issues, and advanced networking capabilities such as **Single Root Input/Output Virtualization** (**SR-IOV**) and **extended Berkeley Packet Filter** (**eBPF**).

Kube-Proxy – IPTables versus IPVS

Kube-Proxy (`https://kubernetes.io/docs/reference/command-line-tools-reference/kube-proxy/`) is a core component of K8s that is responsible for managing networking within the cluster. It ensures seamless communication between services and Pods by setting up network rules and configuration on each node. Kube-Proxy maintains network rules to direct traffic to the appropriate backend Pods that serve each service, allowing internal cluster traffic to reach the correct destinations. By default, Kube-Proxy uses **IPTables** mode, which efficiently intercepts and redirects network requests based on IP rules, making it suitable for small and medium-sized clusters.

However, for large-scale K8s clusters, particularly those running data-intensive workloads such as GenAI, IPTables mode might become a performance bottleneck. As clusters scale up to include hundreds or thousands of services and endpoints, maintaining and updating these rules in IPTables can lead to increased latency and reduced network performance, impacting the overall efficiency of AI models.

To address these limitations, K8s offers the option to run Kube-Proxy in **IP Virtual Server** (**IPVS**) mode. IPVS provides advanced load-balancing capabilities by leveraging the Linux kernel's IPVS module, which is more scalable and efficient than IPTables for handling high traffic. IPVS maintains an in-memory hash table for Service-to-Pod routing, enabling faster packet processing with minimal CPU overhead.

IPVS mode offers benefits such as more sophisticated load balancing algorithms (e.g., round-robin, least connections, source hashing), better handling of dynamic and large service environments, and reduced latency in packet forwarding.

IPVS can be enabled by updating the `kube-proxy-config` `ConfigMap` in the `kube-system` namespace:

```
apiVersion: kubeproxy.config.k8s.io/v1alpha1
kind: KubeProxyConfiguration
mode: "ipvs"
...
```

To enable IPVS in Amazon EKS cluster setup, take a look at the EKS documentation at `https://docs.aws.amazon.com/eks/latest/best-practices/ipvs.html` for step-by-step instructions.

While advanced networking configurations such as IPVS help enhance traffic management and scalability in K8s, another critical challenge for large-scale clusters lies in efficiently managing IP address allocation, which we will cover in the next section.

IP address exhaustion issues and custom networking

When using CNI plugins such as Amazon VPC CNI in native networking mode, each K8s Pod receives an IP address directly from the VPC CIDR block. This approach allows each Pod to be fully addressable within the VPC, providing visibility of the Pod IP addresses with tools such as **VPC flow logs** and other monitoring solutions. However, in large-scale clusters running intensive workloads such as GenAI, this model can lead to IP address exhaustion as each Pod consumes an IP from a finite VPC CIDR pool.

To mitigate this, one effective solution is to use **IPv6 addressing**. IPv6 provides an exponentially larger address space than IPv4, reducing the risk of IP exhaustion and allowing clusters to scale without worrying about running out of IP addresses. But not all organizations are ready to adopt IPV6 yet.

Another way to address IP exhaustion is through VPC CNI custom networking. This involves enhancing the VPC design by associating additional, non-routable secondary CIDR blocks with the VPC and creating new subnets from these CIDRs. These subnets are designated specifically for Pod IP allocation, while the primary, routable CIDR is preserved for node IPs and other resources. We then configure the VPC CNI to allocate Pod IPs from these non-routable subnets, freeing up the primary CIDR for other networking needs and reducing the risk of IP exhaustion. The following link explains how custom networking can be implemented in Amazon EKS: `https://docs.aws.amazon.com/eks/latest/userguide/cni-custom-network-tutorial.html`.

To address networking challenges in K8s, including IP address exhaustion and performance optimization, it's worth exploring advanced networking solutions, such as VPC CNI custom networking or IPV6. Emerging technologies such as eBPF and SR-IOV offer innovative methods to improve network efficiency and scalability, which we will discuss in the next section.

eBPF and SR-IOV

extended Berkeley Packet Filter (**eBPF**) (`https://ebpf.io/what-is-ebpf/`) allows advanced programmability within the Linux kernel without requiring changes to kernel code. This can be used to create powerful, lightweight networking, observability, and security solutions directly at the kernel level. For example, the Cilium CNI plugin, which leverages eBPF, provides fine-grained network security, load balancing, and observability capabilities. For GenAI workloads, where performance and data transfer speed are crucial, eBPF's minimal overhead and kernel-level processing can make it a good choice for lower latency and higher throughput data transfer.

Single Root Input/Output Virtualization (**SR-IOV**) enables a single physical **Network Interface Card** (**NIC**) to be partitioned into multiple **virtual functions**, providing direct hardware access to VMs or containers. Each virtual function acts as an independent interface, offering high throughput and low latency network throughput, which is ideal for GenAI workloads that involve large data transfers. SR-IOV reduces CPU overhead by offloading packet processing to NIC, ensuring better resource utilization for compute-intensive tasks. It also provides dedicated network paths, ensuring network isolation and predictable performance, which is crucial for consistent AI model inference. This technology enhances scalability by optimizing resource allocation and supports multi-tenant clusters with isolated, high-performance networking.

Technologies such as eBPF and SR-IOV optimize networking performance and resource efficiency in K8s clusters, enabling high-speed and reliable data processing. Complementing these advancements is CoreDNS autoscaling, which ensures seamless service discovery and efficient DNS resolution, critical for inter-service communication.

CoreDNS

CoreDNS (`https://github.com/coredns/coredns`) is a crucial component in K8s for providing DNS services that facilitate internal service discovery and networking within the K8s cluster. It acts as the cluster's DNS server, allowing Pods to find and communicate with each other using simple service names. For optimal performance and management, using the **CoreDNS managed add-on** (`https://docs.aws.amazon.com/eks/latest/userguide/coredns-add-on-create.html`) in EKS is recommended. Monitoring CoreDNS is also essential for maintaining efficient network performance, as issues with DNS resolution can lead to service disruptions or latency, particularly in workloads that require extensive inter-service communication, such as GenAI.

To keep up with the growing needs of large-scale K8s clusters, it is recommended to implement CoreDNS autoscaling to scale the number of CoreDNS Pods proportional to the size of the cluster. You can utilize the `cluster-proportional-autoscaler` (`https://github.com/kubernetes-sigs/cluster-proportional-autoscaler`) addon, which watches over the number of schedulable nodes and CPU cores in the cluster and resizes the number of replicas for critical resources such as CoreDNS. When using CoreDNS managed addon in EKS, this functionality is provided natively and can be enabled using the addon configuration described at `https://docs.aws.amazon.com/eks/latest/userguide/coredns-autoscaling.html`.

Another tool for improving DNS performance in the K8s cluster is the **NodeLocal DNSCache** (`https://kubernetes.io/docs/tasks/administer-cluster/nodelocaldns/`) addon. When installed on the cluster, it runs a DNS caching agent on every worker node that caches the DNS queries and reduces the overhead on the CoreDNS. K8s Pods will reach out to the DNS caching agent running on the same node, thereby avoiding IPTables DNAT rules and connection tracking. For any cache misses involving cluster hostnames (typically with the `cluster.local` suffix), the local caching agent forwards the query to the CoreDNS service.

CoreDNS is a vital component in K8s that enables internal service discovery and networking by acting as the cluster's DNS server. To optimize performance in large-scale clusters, use CoreDNS autoscaling with `cluster-proportional-autoscaler` and leverage NodeLocal DNSCache to reduce latency. In the next section, we will cover a few other options to optimize network latency and throughput.

Network latency and throughput enhancements

GenAI workloads, such as large-scale training and inference of machine learning models, require extensive communication between multiple compute nodes. In distributed training scenarios where model parameters need to be synchronized across nodes, achieving high bandwidth and low latency is critical to achieve high performance and reduce the training/inference costs.

In this section, we will discuss two cloud-specific techniques to achieve this.

Amazon EC2 placement groups

Amazon EC2 placement groups (`https://docs.aws.amazon.com/AWSEC2/latest/UserGuide/placement-groups.html`) provide a way to organize nodes for specific networking or resilience objectives. In AWS, the following three placement groups are supported:

- **Cluster**, which places instances close together within an Availability Zone to enable low-latency network performance for high-performance computing applications.
- **Partition**, which distributes instances across separate logical partitions so that each partition's group of instances does not share underlying hardware with those in other partitions. This strategy is typically used by large distributed and replicated workloads, such as Hadoop, Cassandra, and Kafka.
- **Spread**, which distributes a small group of instances across distinct underlying hardware to minimize the risk of correlated failures and improves resilience.

The cluster placement group, which places instances physically close together within a single data center or Availability Zone, provides low-latency and high-throughput networking between nodes. It could improve performance for distributed GenAI applications.

The following command creates a placement group called `custom-placement-group` in AWS with a cluster or proximity placement objective:

```
aws ec2 create-placement-group --group-name custom-placement-group
--strategy cluster
```

Now, EKS worker nodes can be launched within this placement group by creating an Auto Scaling group with the following launch template:

```
{
  "LaunchTemplateData": {
    "Placement": {
      "GroupName": "custom-placement-group"
    },
   #      Other Launch Details. such as instance types, key pair
  }
}
```

In brief, EC2 placement groups offer strategies for organizing EC2 instances to optimize networking and throughput optimization. In the next section, we will cover the **Elastic Fabric Adapter** (**EFA**), a specialized network interface that delivers ultra-low latency and high throughput for inter-node communication.

EFA

EFA (https://aws.amazon.com/hpc/efa/) is a network interface designed by AWS to provide ultra-low latency and a high-throughput network interface for internode communications. This is critical for GenAI workloads as it ensures that data transfer between nodes is fast and efficient. EFA supports **Remote Direct Memory Access** (**RDMA**), which reduces the overhead of data transfer between nodes, providing a low-latency, high-throughput path. Through RDMA, data can be transferred directly between the memory of two compute nodes across a network without involving the operating system or CPUs. EFA also supports **NVIDIA Collective Communications Library** (**NCCL**) (https://developer.nvidia.com/nccl) for AI and ML applications to enable high-performance, scalable distributed training by accelerating communication between GPUs across multiple nodes. This integration reduces latency and improves bandwidth for inter-GPU communication, allowing faster model training times in GenAI applications that require synchronized, collective operations, such as data parallelism and model parallelism.

To integrate EFA with K8s Pods in the EKS cluster, you can create worker nodes with EFA-compatible instance types and deploy aws-efa-k8s-device-plugin (https://github.com/aws/eks-charts/tree/master/stable/aws-efa-k8s-device-plugin), which detects and advertises EFA interfaces as allocatable resources to the cluster:

```
module "eks" {
  source = "terraform-aws-modules/eks/aws"
  cluster_name     = local.name
...
  # Allow EFA traffic
  enable_efa_support = true
...
  eks_managed_node_groups = {
    nvidia-efa = {
      # Expose all available EFA interfaces on the launch template
      enable_efa_support = true
      labels = {
        "vpc.amazonaws.com/efa.present" = "true"
        "nvidia.com/gpu.present"        = "true"
      }
...
```

Refer to the EKS documentation at https://docs.aws.amazon.com/eks/latest/userguide/node-efa.html for step-by-step instructions and an example walkthrough.

In this section, we discussed various network optimization techniques such as picking Kube-proxy options, scaling CoreDNS Pods, strategies to solve IP exhaustion issues, emerging trends in K8s networking space, and other cloud-provider-specific optimizations including EFA and EC2 placement groups for managing large-scale GenAI workloads in the K8s clusters.

Summary

In this chapter, we focused on optimizing cloud networking for deploying GenAI applications on K8s, highlighting best practices for efficient, secure, and high-performance networking. We started with K8s networking fundamentals, covering key components such as the **Container Network Interface** (**CNI**), the kubelet, and the **Container Runtime Interface** (**CRI**), which manage Pod networking and ensure connectivity across the cluster.

The K8s networking model is supported by CNI plugins such as Calico, Cilium, and Amazon VPC CNI, each with specific benefits. CNI plugins operate in two modes: overlay networks and native networking. Overlay networks, such as Flannel, add flexibility with network abstraction but may increase latency. On the other hand, native networking (e.g., Amazon VPC CNI) integrates with the underlying cloud infrastructure, offering lower latency, and is recommended for GenAI workloads.

Service management within K8s provides stable IPs and DNS names, ensuring reliability even as Pods are added or removed. Service mesh tools, such as Istio or Linkerd, could be highly effective in enhancing traffic management, security, and observability by intercepting all traffic through sidecar proxies and implementing policies for load balancing, retry mechanisms, and TLS encryption.

NetworkPolicy, a native feature, further strengthens security by controlling ingress and egress traffic within K8s clusters, allowing isolation between teams or applications in multi-tenant environments. To address GenAI-specific needs, K8s supports advanced networking options such as Kube-Proxy with IPVS mode, offering scalable load balancing for high-demand clusters. Additionally, as K8s clusters scale, IP address exhaustion can become a challenge when using the CNI's native networking mode; solutions such as IPv6 addressing and custom networking configuration can be employed to mitigate IP limitations in large-scale deployments.

Other modern technologies support high-performance networking, such as **extended Berkeley Packet Filter** (**eBPF**) and **Single Root Input/Output Virtualization** (**SR-IOV**) provide minimal-overhead, kernel-level networking ideal for low-latency, high-throughput data processing. Finally, K8s networking benefits from specific enhancements in cloud environments, such as AWS's placement groups and Elastic Fabric Adapter (EFA). In the next chapter, we will build on these concepts and discuss how to secure GenAI applications running in K8s

9

Security Best Practices for Deploying GenAI on Kubernetes

In this chapter, we will explore the security best practices for deploying GenAI applications on **Kubernetes** (**K8s**). We will begin by introducing the concept of "defense in depth" and then cover the key pillars of securing GenAI workloads – supply chain, host, network, and runtime security. Additionally, we will cover best practices for the management of secrets and the principle of least privilege to prevent unauthorized access to critical data and application credentials.

In this chapter, we're going to cover the following main topics:

- Defense in depth
- K8s security considerations
- Additional considerations for GenAI apps
- Implementing security best practices in a chatbot app

Technical requirements

In this chapter, we will be using the following, the first of which requires you to set up an account and create an access token:

- **Hugging Face**: `https://huggingface.co/join`
- An Amazon EKS cluster setup, as illustrated in *Chapter 3*

Defense in depth

The best way to protect an application in the cloud is by using the concept of **defense in depth** (`https://csrc.nist.gov/glossary/term/defense_in_depth`). This is a strategy that implements multiple layers of security to protect against threats across different attack vectors. *Figure 9.1* shows a conceptual view of defense in depth, where each concentric circle represents a layer or attack vector we would like to secure.

Let's look over this concept for security best practices, and then we will dive deeper for every layer, specific to containers and K8s.

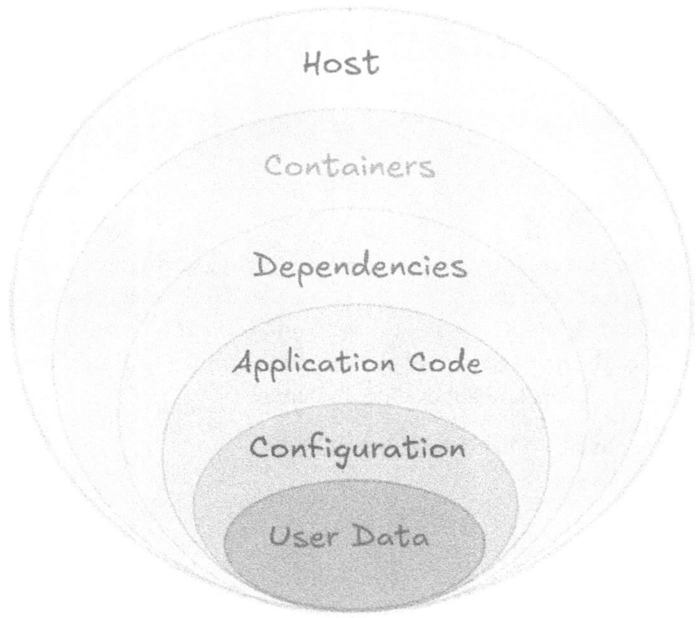

Figure 9.1 – Layered security model

The following are details about the layers depicted in the preceding figure:

- **User data**: This is the innermost core of the system containing sensitive user data, such as user passwords, **personally identifiable information** (**PII**), and so on. To protect this layer, data encryption at rest and transit should be used.
- **Configuration**: Sensitive configuration data for an application includes environment variables, application settings, secrets, and API keys required for the application to function. Lapses in configuration settings could lead to data leaks, privilege escalation, or compromised application behavior.

- **Application code**: Vulnerabilities in application code can lead to exploits, such as SQL injection or remote code execution. To prevent this, users should conduct regular static and dynamic code analysis, promptly patch vulnerabilities, and update dependencies to the latest secure versions.
- **Dependencies**: Code dependencies include libraries, frameworks, and external packages that the application relies on. Vulnerable or outdated dependencies are one of the most common entry points for attackers. To prevent this, users should regularly scan dependencies for vulnerabilities.
- **Containers**: The container runtime and images could also create another threat vector, as misconfigured or untrusted containers can escalate privileges, attack the host, or expose sensitive information. To prevent this, users could use image signing to verify the authenticity of images and implement runtime security using tools such as **Falco** to watch out for malicious behavior.
- **Host**: This is the underlying server or node where containers are deployed. The host kernel is shared among all containers, making it a critical security layer. If the host is compromised, all containers can be affected. To prevent this, it is recommended to harden the host operating system by disabling unused services, applying patches, and using container-optimized operating systems, such as **Bottlerocket**.

In this section, we learned about the concept of defense in depth, a strategy that implements multiple layers of security to protect against threats across different attack vectors. We also looked at a conceptual view of various attack vectors and best practices in each layer. In the next section, let's look at key security considerations when deploying workloads in K8s.

K8s security considerations

Now that we have covered the concept of defense in depth at a high level, let's discuss containers and K8s security best practices. Thinking about **container security** is critical in the cloud environment, as containers operate in a dynamic and shared environment.

Containers encapsulate *software* and *dependencies* making them highly portable; however, this portability also introduces a set of risks. A comprehensive security strategy should address vulnerabilities across the container lifecycle – from *build pipelines* to *runtime environments*.

Key areas of focus include securing the supply chain, protecting the host system, and monitoring runtime activity. Each layer of security adds resilience against potential threats, and by following the best practices, one can ensure the safe deployment and operation of containers.

The following are some of the key areas we will dive deeper into as part of this container security:

- Supply chain security
- Host security
- Runtime security
- Network security
- Secrets management

Supply chain security

The container supply chain encompasses all the stages from building an image to deploying and monitoring it in production, as shown in *Figure 9.2*.

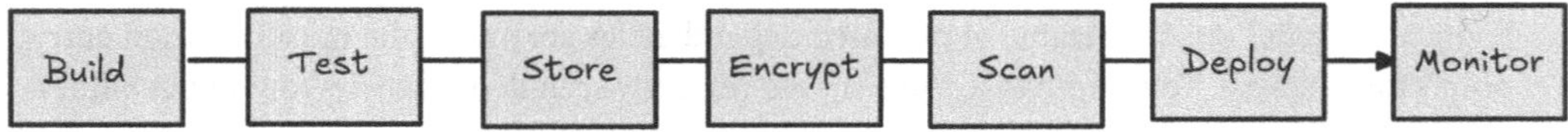

Figure 9.2 – Container supply chain

Now, let's discuss the first five phases and their corresponding security best practices.

Build phase

During the build phase, malicious/vulnerable code can enter the container image through unverified dependencies or insecure configurations. To secure the build phase, one should only use trusted base images from verified sources. To minimize the attack surface and improve security, consider using lightweight parent images for your containers. **Alpine Linux** (`https://hub.docker.com/_/alpine`), **distroless** (`https://www.docker.com/blog/is-your-container-image-really-distroless/`), or **scratch** (`https://hub.docker.com/_/scratch`) images have fewer built-in packages, limiting the potential vulnerabilities, and are generally recommended.

DockerSlim (`https://github.com/slimtoolkit/slim`) is an open source tool that helps optimize container images by reducing their size, thus improving security by identifying only the parts that are required at runtime. This significantly reduces the attack surface and enhances performance without altering the functionality of the containerized application.

It is also recommended to enforce the immutability of container images by using declarative Dockerfiles and reproducible builds. An **immutable tag** refers to a container image tag that cannot be changed or updated once it is created and pushed to a container registry. This ensures that the image associated with the tag remains *fixed* and *consistent* over time, preventing unintentional or malicious changes. For example, the `latest` tag is mutable, meaning it can point to different images over time as new images are pushed, whereas a tag such as `v1.0` is immutable, as it ensures that it always references the same image, regardless of future pushes. Immutability is particularly beneficial for GenAI applications to ensure the training/fine-tuning jobs and inference images are built against a consistent environment, maintain model integrity, and simplify troubleshooting efforts.

A **multi-stage build** (`https://docs.docker.com/build/building/multi-stage/`) is a technique used in the build phase that allows you to break down the build process into multiple discrete stages. Each stage can focus on a specific task using an appropriate parent image, such as compiling code or installing dependencies, and then selectively copy only the necessary artifacts into the final, minimal image.

For GenAI applications, multi-stage builds help ensure that large training frameworks, data preprocessing scripts, or model optimization steps can selectively be excluded from the final production image. This results in smaller, more secure, and efficient images that can be quickly deployed for inference.

Test phase

Undetected vulnerabilities and misconfigurations in images can lead to issues downstream. To mitigate this, it is recommended to integrate automated security testing into CI/CD pipelines with tools such as **Snyk** (`https://snyk.io/`). You should perform static analysis on code and dynamic testing on built images to uncover vulnerabilities. Ensure that your testing process also covers compliance with internal security policies and relevant industry standards. Incorporate test cases to assess resource usage, verify adherence to least-privilege principles, and monitor runtime behaviors. By doing so, you can help maintain secure, compliant, and predictable operations throughout the software lifecycle.

Store phase

During the image store phase in container registries, images can be tampered with or can contain outdated dependencies. To safely secure images, it is recommended to use secured container registries such as **Amazon ECR** (`https://aws.amazon.com/ecr/`).

You should also enable image signing and verification using tools such as Docker Content Trust or Cosign. **AWS Signer** (`https://docs.aws.amazon.com/signer/latest/developerguide/Welcome.html`) is a fully managed service that allows you to digitally sign code, applications, and containers to ensure the integrity and authenticity of your software.

To ensure that only signed container images are deployed in production, a **policy-as-code solution** such as **Open Policy Agent** (**OPA**) or its K8s-native implementation, **OPA Gatekeeper** (`https://github.com/open-policy-agent/gatekeeper`), is recommended. OPA Gatekeeper is an open source project that leverages OPA to enforce policies in K8s clusters. It enables administrators to implement fine-grained governance by validating and mutating K8s resources against predefined constraints. Gatekeeper uses **custom resource definitions** (**CRDs**) to define these policies and constraints, allowing users to tailor governance to their specific needs. It operates as an admission controller, ensuring that any resource not complying with the defined rules is denied during creation or updates. Additionally, it supports auditing capabilities, enabling users to identify and remediate policy violations in existing resources. **Role-based access control** (**RBAC**) is also recommended to restrict access to images, and users should regularly clean up unused or deprecated images to reduce potential attack surfaces.

Encrypt phase

Sensitive data in images should always be intercepted. One should avoid embedding secrets (e.g., API keys or passwords) directly in images to prevent leaks in case of a potentially compromised container image.

You can use secret management tools such as **HashiCorp Vault** (`https://www.hashicorp.com/products/vault`), **Kubernetes Secrets** (`https://kubernetes.io/docs/concepts/configuration/secret/`), or **AWS Secrets Manager** (`https://docs.aws.amazon.com/secretsmanager/latest/userguide/intro.html`) to store the secrets. For example, AWS Secrets Manager is a secure service for managing secrets, such as database credentials, API keys, and other sensitive configuration data. By encrypting secrets with **AWS Key Management Service** (**AWS KMS**) and enabling fine-grained access control through **AWS Identity and Access Management** (**AWS IAM**), Secrets Manager ensures that sensitive data is protected and accessible only to authorized users and applications. It also supports version control and the automatic rotation of secrets, reducing the risks of credential exposure and minimizing manual overhead.

To integrate external secret management solutions with K8s, you can use projects such as **secrets-store-csi-driver** (`https://github.com/kubernetes-sigs/secrets-store-csi-driver`), which allows K8s to mount multiple secrets, keys, and certificates stored in external secrets stores into K8s Pods as a volume. Once the volume is attached, the data in it is mounted into the container's filesystem. Refer to the AWS documentation at `https://docs.aws.amazon.com/secretsmanager/latest/userguide/integrating_csi_driver.html` for an example walkthrough of using AWS Secrets Manager in an Amazon EKS cluster. In the case of GenAI applications, external API keys from **Hugging Face** and **OpenAI** can safely be stored in these solutions, and applications can securely access them during the runtime.

Scan phase

Vulnerabilities in images or dependencies can lead to exploitation by bad actors. To prevent this, images should be continuously scanned during the build and store phases. Most container registry solutions provide this capability out of the box, or open source tools such as **Trivy** (`https://github.com/aquasecurity/trivy`) can be used to scan container images for vulnerabilities. These tools identify potential risks by analyzing image layers against known vulnerability databases (e.g., CVE databases), providing early detection of issues.

In cloud environments, more advanced image scanning options are also available. For example, Amazon ECR supports advanced vulnerability scanning through **Amazon Inspector** (`https://aws.amazon.com/inspector/`), a managed service designed to automate security assessments. This integration provides enhanced, continuous scanning for container images in ECR, ensuring they remain secure throughout their lifecycle. Amazon Inspector can scan container images in ECR automatically, without requiring manual triggers, whenever a new image is pushed or updated. Refer to the Amazon ECR documentation at `https://docs.aws.amazon.com/AmazonECR/latest/userguide/image-scanning.html` to learn more about these options and how to enable them on your container repositories.

Host security

Securing the host environment for containers is critical, as multiple containers can share the host operating system and kernel. The following are some of the best practices and strategies for securing container hosts:

- **Deploy in private subnets**: Deploying hosts/worker nodes in private subnets minimizes exposure to external threats by restricting direct access from the internet. To expose applications to the public internet, deploy load balancer resources in public subnets using K8s load balancer or Ingress resource types.
- **Disable SSH access**: SSH access should be limited to minimizing the attack vector. Instead, **session management tools** such as **AWS Systems Manager** (**SSM**) (`https://aws.amazon.com/systems-manager/`) should be used for secure, auditable access to hosts without exposing SSH. If SSH is necessary, enforce key-based authentication and restrict access using security groups.
- **Block the Instance Metadata Service** (**IMDS**): The IMDS provides data about your EC2 instance that can expose sensitive information (e.g., IAM credentials) to malicious actors if not properly secured. It is recommended to use **IMDSv2** (`https://docs.aws.amazon.com/AWSEC2/latest/UserGuide/ec2-instance-metadata.html`) instead, which requires session tokens for accessing instance metadata. To restrict IMDS access to containerized applications, you can set the hop limit to `1` and enforce the usage of IMDSv2, as shown in the following Terraform code:

```
resource "aws_launch_template" "example" {
  name = "example"
  ...
    metadata_options {
    http_endpoint               = "enabled"
    http_tokens                 = "required"
    http_put_response_hop_limit = 1
    instance_metadata_tags      = "enabled"
  }
  ...
```

- **Encrypt all storage**: Encrypting storage protects sensitive data on the host in case of physical or logical compromise. Use AWS KMS to encrypt **Amazon Elastic Block Store** (**Amazon EBS**) volumes attached to the host. If using EC2 instances with an **NVMe** instance store, all the data is encrypted using an XTS-AES-256 block cipher.

- **Harden the node Amazon Machine Image (AMI)**: A hardened AMI reduces vulnerabilities by including only the necessary software, configurations, and security settings. Use container-optimized operating systems such as Bottlerocket (`https://aws.amazon.com/bottlerocket/`), which are built from the ground up with containers in mind. They often include features such as a read-only root filesystem, atomic updates, and minimal tooling tailored to running containers efficiently and securely. You should disable and uninstall unused software to reduce the attack surface and configure the operating system according to CIS benchmarks for Docker, Kubernetes, and Linux. Use **AppArmor** (`https://apparmor.net/`), **SELinux** (`https://www.redhat.com/en/topics/linux/what-is-selinux`), or **seccomp** (`https://kubernetes.io/docs/tutorials/security/seccomp/`) to restrict container privileges.

Container runtime security

Securing containers at runtime is critical to prevent privilege escalations and unauthorized access. This involves limiting resources, restricting privileges, enforcing security standards, and integrating monitoring and policy tools. The following are the core runtime security practices:

- **Provide only the resources required for normal operation**: Unrestricted resource allocation can lead to **denial-of-service (DoS)** attacks and cluster instability, where some containers can consume entire node resources. To prevent this, you should define CPU and memory limits in K8s manifests reflecting the optimal resources a container might need.
- **Restrict root and privileged access**: Containers running as root or in privileged mode can lead to host compromise. To prevent this, ensure containers are configured to run as a non-root user in `securityContext`, as shown here:

```
securityContext:
  runAsUser: 1000
  runAsGroup: 1000
  allowPrivilegeEscalation: false
```

- **Drop all unnecessary Linux capabilities**: Linux capabilities grant elevated permissions that can be exploited if unused capabilities are left enabled. So, it is recommended to drop unnecessary capabilities in `securityContext`, as shown here:

```
securityContext:
      capabilities:
        drop:
          - ALL
...
```

- **Follow Pod Security Standards**: Adherence to Pod Security Standards ensures that containers comply with best practices for security configurations. Use the K8s built-in Pod Security Admission to enforce standards such as restricted profiles. Also, isolate workloads using namespaces with different security levels (e.g., restricted or baseline). Pod Security Standards define three different policy levels (privileged, baseline, and restricted) to broadly cover the security spectrum. You can apply labels and annotations on namespaces to specify the desired level of security configuration, as shown here:

```
$ kubectl label namespace test-ns \
pod-security.kubernetes.io/enforce=restricted
```

- **Monitor the runtime**: This provides active protection for containerized workloads while they are running. The goal is to detect and/or prevent malicious activity from occurring inside the containers and the worker nodes. Tools such as Falco (`https://github.com/falcosecurity/falco`) provide real-time monitoring and anomaly detection for container behavior. It can be deployed as a DaemonSet in a K8s cluster and can monitor containers for suspicious activity. It operates by hooking into the Linux kernel using either eBPF or traditional syscalls, allowing it to observe low-level system activity inside running containers and Pods without modifying the workload itself. This deep visibility enables Falco to monitor unexpected or suspicious behavior in real time. Common events that Falco watches for include actions such as shells being spawned inside containers, modifications to sensitive files such as `/etc/passwd` or `/etc/shadow`, and network connections to untrusted IP addresses. It can also detect when a Pod tries to access a K8s Service account token improperly, which may indicate a compromise or misconfiguration.

  When such behavior violates its defined security rules, Falco triggers alerts instantly. For example, alerts may look like this: **Terminal shell detected in nginx container** or **Suspicious file access by unknown process**. To make these alerts actionable, teams should implement clear response strategies, such as isolating the Pod, initiating incident response procedures, or alerting security teams. Combining these technical capabilities with practical workflows allows teams to confidently enforce runtime security and respond to threats in production-grade K8s environments.

  Some other third-party tools also offer advanced runtime protection, integration, and reporting capabilities. Use agents provided by solutions such as **Prisma Cloud's Container Security** (`https://www.paloaltonetworks.com/prisma/cloud/container-security`), **Aqua Security** (`https://www.aquasec.com/products/kubernetes-security/`), or **Wiz container security** (`https://www.wiz.io/solutions/container-and-kubernetes-security`) to monitor and protect containers.

Network security

Network security in K8s is critical for securing data and applications in a containerized environment. The distributed nature of K8s presents unique challenges for securing network traffic. The following are some key considerations and best practices for ensuring network security in K8s:

- **Network segmentation and isolation**: K8s **namespaces** provide a way to isolate resources and workloads within a cluster, acting as separate security boundaries. Network segmentation can be enforced using **NetworkPolicy** resources, discussed in *Chapter 8*, which define rules for controlling ingress (incoming) and egress (outgoing) traffic at the Pod level.
- **Securing Pod-to-Pod communication**: By default, K8s allows communication between Pods, which can expose K8s clusters to security risks. Implementing zero-trust principles ensures that Pods communicate only with explicitly authorized peers. Service mesh technologies such as **Istio** or **Linkerd** provide mTLS for encryption and authentication, ensuring secure and authenticated Pod-to-Pod communication.
- **Ingress and egress security**: Ingress security focuses on controlling and securing incoming traffic to the cluster, often using HTTPS with TLS certificates for encryption. Additional protection, such as **web application firewalls** (**WAFs**), help detect and block malicious traffic. Egress security involves restricting Pods' outbound traffic to prevent unauthorized access to external resources, which can be enforced using egress policies.
- **API server protection**: The K8s API server is a critical management point, requiring strong security measures. RBAC restricts user permissions based on roles, while authentication mechanisms such as **OpenID Connect** (**OIDC**) or AWS IAM ensure that only authorized users access the server. Network policies or firewalls should further limit access to the API server from trusted sources only.
- **DNS security**: CoreDNS, the default DNS server in K8s, should be secured against spoofing and related attacks. While enabling encrypted DNS protocols such as **DNS-over-TLS** or **DNS-over-HTTPS** (`https://www.cloudflare.com/learning/dns/dns-over-tls/`) is technically possible, it is not commonly implemented by default in K8s. Instead, use network policies to restrict which Pods can query the CoreDNS server, thereby reducing the risk of unauthorized requests. Additionally, ensure CoreDNS points to trusted upstream resolvers, employing **DNSSEC** (`https://www.internetsociety.org/deploy360/dnssec/basics/`) for integrity.
- **Network monitoring**: Monitoring network traffic is crucial for detecting and mitigating threats. Tools such as Cilium, Calico, Sysdig, service meshes, or Datadog provide visibility into cluster traffic, enabling cluster administrators to identify suspicious behavior.
- **Securing external connections**: Connections to external services, such as cloud provider services or databases, should be encrypted and authenticated. K8s Secrets offer a secure way to manage credentials for external connections, ensuring that sensitive information (such as API keys and passwords) remains protected from unauthorized access.

Secrets management

Secrets management in K8s is a critical component for securing and managing sensitive information, such as API keys, passwords, certificates, and tokens. K8s provides built-in mechanisms to manage Secrets but securing them requires careful configuration and the following best practices to mitigate risks of unauthorized access or accidental exposure:

- **K8s Secrets resource**: K8s provides a native resource called **Secrets**, which is used to store sensitive data in a Base64-encoded format. Secrets are mounted into Pods as environment variables or files, enabling applications to access them without embedding sensitive data directly in container images or configuration files. While convenient, the Base64 encoding is not encryption, so additional security measures are necessary.
- **Encrypting Secrets at rest**: By default, K8s stores Secrets in **etcd**, the cluster's key-value store. To protect this sensitive information, it is essential to enable encryption at rest for etcd. When using managed K8s services such as Amazon EKS, etcd volumes are encrypted by default using AWS managed encryption keys. As an additional security measure, you can also use techniques such as envelope encryption to encrypt the Secret values before writing to the etcd database. In Amazon EKS, you can utilize AWS KMS to enable envelope encryption; refer to the AWS documentation at `https://docs.aws.amazon.com/eks/latest/userguide/envelope-encryption.html` to learn more.
- **Access control with RBAC**: RBAC is a fundamental part of securing Secrets in K8s. RBAC policies should enforce the principle of least privilege, granting users, Pods, and Services access only to the Secrets they need. Properly configured roles and role bindings help prevent unauthorized users or applications from accessing sensitive information.
- **Using external secret management tools**: While K8s Secrets offer a convenient mechanism, many organizations opt for external secret management solutions for enhanced security. Tools such as HashiCorp Vault or AWS Secrets Manager provide centralized secret storage with advanced features such as encryption, auditing, and fine-grained access control. These tools can integrate with K8s through the `secrets-store-csi-driver` plugin or other operators, enabling seamless access to externally managed secrets.
- **Automating Secret rotation**: Rotating Secrets regularly reduces the risk of long-term compromise. K8s secrets do not natively support automatic rotation, but external secret management tools often include this capability. Integrating such tools into K8s workflows allows you to periodically update secrets without disrupting applications, ensuring compliance with security best practices.
- **Protecting Secrets in transit**: Sensitive data, including secrets, must be protected as it travels between clients, nodes, and the etcd store. Enable TLS encryption when exchanging sensitive credentials both with internal and external systems.

- **Auditing and monitoring access to Secrets**: Audit logging is essential for monitoring access to secrets and detecting potential misuse. K8s can generate audit logs for API actions, including those involving secrets. Integrating these logs with centralized monitoring tools or **security information and event management** (**SIEM**) solutions helps administrators detect suspicious activity and respond promptly. Secret management tools also provide audit logs, which can be integrated into SIEM solutions.

In this section, we looked at various security considerations when running containerized workloads in K8s, including supply chain security, host security, network security, and the importance of securing sensitive information using K8s Secrets. In the next section, let's explore additional security considerations specific to GenAI applications.

Additional considerations for GenAI apps

Deploying GenAI applications on K8s often involves proprietary model artifacts, large volumes of sensitive training data, and sophisticated inference requests that can originate from untrusted sources. Beyond the standard practices of K8s security, you must consider new attack vectors related to model integrity, data privacy, software supply chain vulnerabilities, and the isolation of high-value hardware resources such as GPUs. Let's explore some of those considerations now:

Data privacy and compliance

GenAI models often rely on proprietary and sensitive datasets stored in data lakes, data hubs, and data warehouses for training and fine-tuning. In our walkthrough (*Chapter 5*), we used **Amazon S3** buckets to store the datasets used during the fine-tuning process. Depending on the data classification and regulatory requirements, you must implement appropriate security controls such as data encryption at rest, strict access control policies, and auditing. When accessing these data repositories from GenAI applications running on K8s, ensure that all communications are encrypted using TLS and follow the principle of least privilege by leveraging K8s and related mechanisms. When running GenAI applications on Amazon EKS, you can leverage **IAM Roles for Service Accounts** (**IRSA**) (`https://docs.aws.amazon.com/eks/latest/userguide/iam-roles-for-service-accounts.html`) or **EKS Pod Identity** (`https://docs.aws.amazon.com/eks/latest/userguide/pod-identities.html`) features to obtain temporary IAM credentials and access data from other services such as Amazon S3.

IAM Roles for Service Accounts

IRSA was introduced in 2019 to associate fine-grained IAM roles with K8s service accounts. Applications running in K8s Pods can assume the role using their **service account identity** and access other AWS services based on the role permissions.

The following are the high-level steps involved in the process; refer to the Amazon EKS documentation at `https://docs.aws.amazon.com/eks/latest/userguide/iam-roles-for-service-accounts.html` for detailed guidance:

1. Set up an OIDC provider in AWS IAM for the Amazon EKS cluster.
2. Create fine-grained IAM policies to grant necessary permissions on AWS services. Refer to the security best practices documentation at `https://docs.aws.amazon.com/IAM/latest/UserGuide/best-practices.html#grant-least-privilege` for guidance on creating IAM policies.
3. Create an IAM role with the permission policies from *Step 2* and a trust policy for the K8s service account to the **assume** role:

```
...
      "Effect": "Allow",
      "Principal": {
        "Federated": "arn:aws:iam::<account_id>:oidc-
provider/<oidc_provider>"
      },
      "Action": "sts:AssumeRoleWithWebIdentity",
      "Condition": {
        "StringEquals": {
          "<oidc_provider>:aud": "sts.amazonaws.com",
          "<oidc_provider>:sub":
"system:serviceaccount:<namespace>:<service_account>"
...
```

4. Create a K8s service account and annotate it with the IAM role from *Step 3*:

```
apiVersion: v1
kind: ServiceAccount
metadata:
  name: example-sa
  namespace: example-ns
  annotations:
    eks.amazonaws.com/role-arn: arn:aws:iam::<account_
id>:role/<iam_role_name>
```

5. Deploy the K8s application using the annotated service account:

```
apiVersion: apps/v1
kind: Deployment
metadata:
  name: example-app
  ...
    spec:
```

```
    serviceAccount: example-sa
    containers:
      - name: example-container
...
```

6. When an application uses the AWS SDK to access other AWS resources, the SDK will invoke `AssumeRoleWithWebIdentity`, an AWS **Security Token Service** (**STS**) API operation that allows an application to assume an IAM role using a trusted web identity token, instead of long-lived access keys or IAM users, to fetch temporary IAM credentials.

   Figure 9.3 summarizes these steps:

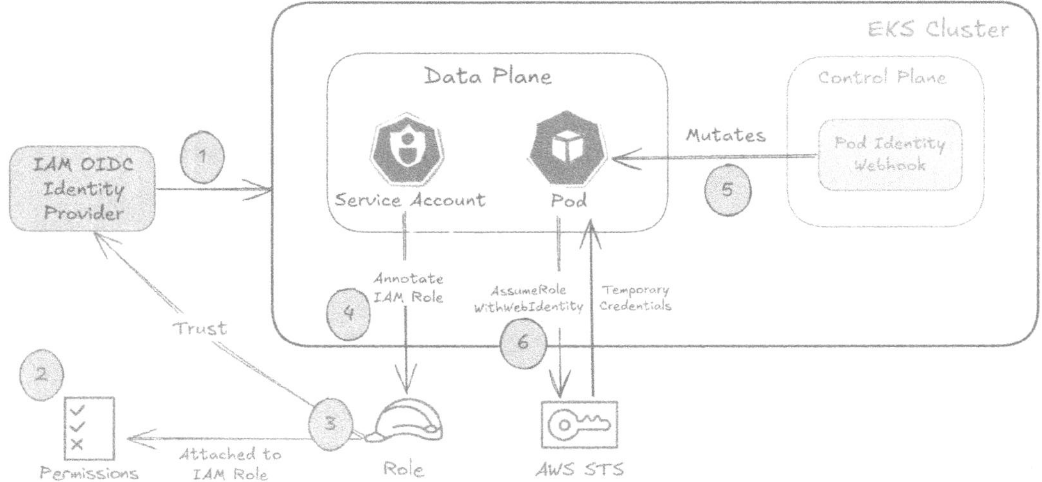

Figure 9.3 – Overview of IRSA

This illustrates how IAM roles are securely assumed by Pods in an Amazon EKS cluster using IRSA and the `AssumeRoleWithWebIdentity` (`https://docs.aws.amazon.com/STS/latest/APIReference/API_AssumeRoleWithWebIdentity.html`) mechanism. When a Pod associated with an annotated service account is created, the Pod Identity webhook running in the EKS control plane mutates the Pod specification to mount the projected service account token. The AWS SDK running in the Pod then uses that token to call AWS STS using the `AssumeRoleWithWebIdentity` API. STS verifies the token against the OIDC provider, checks the IAM role's trust policy, and returns temporary AWS credentials, which the Pod uses to securely access other AWS resources.

Next, we will cover the recently introduced **EKS Pod Identity** feature, which further simplifies the IAM permission process.

Amazon EKS Pod Identity

In 2023, AWS introduced the EKS Pod Identity feature as an evolution to IRSA to streamline the experience of setting up IAM permissions for K8s applications. It removed a lot of underlying complexities of IRSA, such as setting up OIDC providers in IAM, complex trust policies, annotating service accounts, and so on. EKS Pod Identity introduced new APIs to create Pod Identity associations between K8s service accounts and IAM roles, thus eliminating the need for OIDC providers, service account annotations, and so on. The high-level steps involved are as follows:

1. Install `eks-pod-identity-agent deamonset` on the EKS cluster.
2. Create fine-grained IAM policies granting necessary permissions on AWS services.
3. Create an IAM role with the permission policies from *Step 2* and a trust policy for the EKS Pod Identity principal to the assume role:

   ```
   ...
               "Effect": "Allow",
               "Principal": {
                   "Service": "pods.eks.amazonaws.com"
               },
               "Action": [
                   "sts:AssumeRole",
                   "sts:TagSession"
   ...
   ```

4. Create a Pod Identity association between the IAM role and the K8s service account:

   ```
   aws eks create-pod-identity-association --cluster-name
   my-cluster --role-arn arn:aws:iam::<account_id>:role/my-role
   --namespace <namespace> --service-account <service_account>
   ```

5. Deploy the K8s application using the service account:

   ```
   apiVersion: apps/v1
   kind: Deployment
   metadata:
     name: example-app
     ...
       spec:
         serviceAccount: example-sa
         containers:
           - name: example-container
   ...
   ```

EKS Pod Identity also introduced support for session tags to the temporary credentials assigned to each Pod, including attributes such as the cluster name, namespace, Pod UID, service account name, and so on. These tags allow administrators to configure a single IAM role that can be used across various service accounts, granting or restricting access to AWS resources based on matching tags. By incorporating role session tags, organizations can create more granular security boundaries between clusters and workloads, while continuing to leverage the same IAM roles and policies.

Secure model endpoints

Before we talk about securing GenAI model endpoints, we should secure the fine-tuned model artifacts, model weights, and so on. After the fine-tuning process, you can securely store those model artifacts in object store services such as Amazon S3 using appropriate access controls, or package them along with the container image and push it to the container registry. You can securely source the credentials using one of the previously discussed approaches (IRSA or EKS Pod Identity) to access the respective AWS services.

Once the models are built, **inference endpoints** are created by deploying them as K8s deployments/Pods and exposing them via K8s Service or Ingress objects. Securing the model endpoints starts by implementing robust network and API-level protection. Enforce TLS for all communications to ensure data is encrypted in transit and verify the authenticity of clients and services using appropriate authentication methods. You can create the TLS endpoints by issuing or importing TLS certificates in the **AWS Certificate Manager** (**ACM**) (`https://aws.amazon.com/certificate-manager/`) service and deploying them on the AWS **Application Load Balancer** (**ALB**) or **Network Load Balancer** (**NLB**) resources. You can use annotations, as shown in the following code snippet, to create a secure port such as `443` and deploy TLS certificates from ACM on the K8s load balancer service:

```
apiVersion: v1
kind: Service
metadata:
  name: example-service
  annotations:
    service.beta.kubernetes.io/aws-load-balancer-type: "external"
    # Reference the ACM certificate ARN for TLS termination at the
load balancer
    service.beta.kubernetes.io/aws-load-balancer-ssl-cert:
"arn:aws:acm:us-east-1:<account_id>:certificate/<certificate_id>"
    # The port(s) that should use SSL/TLS
    service.beta.kubernetes.io/aws-load-balancer-ssl-ports: "443"
spec:
  type: LoadBalancer
...
```

Similarly, you can apply the annotations to a K8s Ingress resource backed by the AWS ALB to create an HTTPS listener secured with a TLS certificate from ACM, as shown in the following code snippet:

```
apiVersion: networking.k8s.io/v1
kind: Ingress
metadata:
  name: example-ingress
  annotations:
    # Define which ports the ALB should listen on; here we set HTTPS 
on port 443
    alb.ingress.kubernetes.io/listen-ports: '[{"HTTPS":443}]'
    # The ARN of the ACM certificate for TLS termination
    alb.ingress.kubernetes.io/certificate-arn: "arn:aws:acm:us-east-
1:<account_id>:certificate/<certificate_id>"
...
```

Additionally, you can attach **AWS WAF** (`https://aws.amazon.com/waf/`) to the AWS ALB (K8s Ingress resource) to protect the model endpoints against common attack vectors, including injection attacks, malicious content inputs, and so on. You can use the following annotation to attach AWS WAF with AWS ALB.

```
alb.ingress.kubernetes.io/wafv2-acl-arn: arn:aws:wafv2:us-west-
2:xxxxx:regional/webacl/xxxxxxx/yyyyyyyyy
```

In this section, we explored best practices for deploying GenAI workloads in K8s. We looked at the IRSA and EKS Pod Identity features to securely provide temporary IAM credentials to K8s applications. This is particularly important for GenAI applications, as it ensures secure, least-privilege access to sensitive training data or model artifacts stored in Amazon S3. We also looked at techniques for protecting model endpoints, including enforcing TLS for encrypted communications and integrating a WAF to defend against common attack vectors. In the next section, we will implement these security best practices in our chatbot application.

Implementing security best practices in a chatbot app

In this section, we will implement the security best practices discussed in the previous sections in our e-commerce chatbot application. We already implemented some of these in previous chapters, such as IRSA in *Chapter 5*, and K8s network policies in *Chapter 8*. Let's get started:

- **Container image encryption**: Amazon ECR stores container images in Amazon S3 buckets that ECR manages and, by default, uses the server-side encryption feature of S3 to encrypt the data at rest. It uses the **Advanced Encryption Standard** (**AES**) encryption algorithm using encryption keys managed by the S3 service.

We can verify this on the ECR repositories we created using the following AWS command:

```
$ aws ecr describe-repositories --repository-names my-llama-finetuned --query 'repositories[0].encryptionConfiguration.encryptionType' --output text
AES256
```

Additionally, you can use AWS KMS to create customer-managed KMS keys and use them for encrypting the container images at rest. To achieve this, use the following Terraform code, which creates a new KMS customer-managed key with an alias of `ecr-kms-key` and configures the `sample-app-repo` ECR repository to use it for encryption:

```
resource "aws_kms_key" "ecr_kms_key" {
  deletion_window_in_days = 7
  enable_key_rotation = true
}
resource "aws_kms_alias" "ecr_kms_alias" {
  name = "alias/ecr-kms-key"
  target_key_id = aws_kms_key.ecr_kms_key.key_id
}
resource "aws_ecr_repository" "sample-app-repo" {
  name = "sample-app-repo"
  encryption_configuration {
    encryption_type = "KMS"
    kms_key   = aws_kms_key.ecr_kms_key.arn
  }
}
```

- **Tag immutability**: This ensures that once a container image is pushed to an ECR repository, its tag cannot be overwritten. This practice prevents accidental or malicious updates to your application images, ensuring consistency across deployments. You can enable this by setting the `image_tag_mutability` attribute to `IMMUTABLE` in the `ecr.tf` file, as shown in the following code snippet:

```
resource "aws_ecr_repository" "my-llama-finetuned" {
  name = "my-llama-finetuned"
  image_tag_mutability = "IMMUTABLE"
}
```

- **Container image scanning**: Enable the enhanced image scanning feature of Amazon ECR to automatically detect vulnerabilities in the container images. Add the following code snippet to the `ecr.tf` file, which enables enhanced scanning on the `my-llama-finetuned` ECR repository in our AWS account. Alternatively, you can download the source code from the GitHub repository at `https://github.com/PacktPublishing/Kubernetes-for-Generative-AI-Solutions/blob/main/ch9/ecr.tf`

This configuration ensures that images are scanned both when they are pushed and continuously thereafter for any new vulnerabilities:

```
resource "aws_ecr_registry_scanning_configuration" "ecr_
scanning_configuration" {
  scan_type = "ENHANCED"
  rule {
    scan_frequency = "CONTINUOUS_SCAN"
    repository_filter {
      filter      = "my-llama-finetuned"
      filter_type = "WILDCARD"
    }
  }
  rule {
    scan_frequency = "SCAN_ON_PUSH"
    repository_filter {
      filter      = "my-llama-finetuned"
      filter_type = "WILDCARD"
    }
  }
}
```

Run the following Terraform commands to apply this configuration in your AWS account:

```
$ terraform plan
$ terraform apply -auto-approve
```

Once applied, Amazon ECR will continuously scan the container images pushed to the `my-llama-finetuned` **repository and display the vulnerabilities in the AWS console.**

- **Host security**: Harden the security of the worker nodes by using a purpose-built operation system such as Bottlerocket. This includes only the essential software required to run containers and ensures that the underlying software is always secure. It also improves the node start-up time from ~1.5 minutes to 20 seconds, based on a customer case study (`https://aws.amazon.com/bottlerocket/`). Additionally, configure the worker nodes to use the latest version of IMDSv2 (`https://docs.aws.amazon.com/AWSEC2/latest/UserGuide/ec2-instance-metadata.html`) to limit access to sensitive metadata. The following code snippet highlights the use of Bottlerocket EKS AMIs and IMDSv2; the complete source code is available in the GitHub repository at `https://github.com/PacktPublishing/Kubernetes-for-Generative-AI-Solutions/blob/main/ch9/eks.tf`:

```
module "eks" {
  source = "terraform-aws-modules/eks/aws"
  ...
  eks_managed_node_groups = {
    eks-mng = {
```

```
      ami_type = "BOTTLEROCKET_x86_64"
      metadata_options {
        http_endpoint = "enabled"
        http_tokens = "required"
        http_put_response_hop_limit = 1
      }
    ...
    eks-gpu-mng = {
      ami_type = "BOTTLEROCKET_x86_64_NVIDIA"
...
```

- **K8s Pod Security Standards**: Implementing K8s Pod Security Standards is critical to ensuring your workloads operate with the least privilege, thereby reducing the risk of privilege escalation and container escapes. Since our chatbot application is deployed in the default namespace, we can use the following command to enforce a baseline security policy while receiving warnings for more restrictive settings:

  ```
  $ kubectl label namespace default pod-security.kubernetes.io/
  enforce=baseline pod-security.kubernetes.io/warn=restricted
  pod-security.kubernetes.io/audit=restricted
  ```

  Test the enforced policy by attempting to run a pod with privileged settings using the following command:

  ```
  $ kubectl run pss-demo --image=nginx --privileged
  Error from server (Forbidden): pods "pss-demo" is forbidden:
  violates PodSecurity "baseline:latest": privileged (container
  "pss-demo" must not set securityContext.privileged=true)
  ```

  The preceding error confirms that the baseline policy is effectively preventing the creation of Pods with elevated privileges.

- **K8s Secrets management**: A K8s Secret is an object that is designed to store sensitive data such as API Keys, passwords, TLS certificates, and so on. Using K8s Secrets means you don't have to embed confidential information directly in your deployment manifests. In our setup, we included a Hugging Face access token in the K8s manifest when deploying the fine-tuning job and `my-llama-finetuned` inference endpoint. In this walkthrough, we'll enhance security by storing the Hugging Face token in AWS Secrets Manager. We'll then use `secrets-store-csi-driver` to dynamically retrieve and inject the secret into the K8s Pod during creation. Let's get started:

  I. Store the Hugging Face access token in AWS Secrets Manager and run the following command to create a secret in your AWS account. Replace the value with your access token created in the Hugging Face portal:

     ```
     $ export HUGGING_FACE_TOKEN=<<Your Token goes here>>
     $ aws secretsmanager create-secret --name hugging-face-
     secret --secret-string "$HUGGING_FACE_TOKEN"
     ```

II. Deploy the `secrets-store-csi-driver` and `secrets-store-csi-provider-aws` add-ons in the EKS cluster to integrate external secret stores with K8s via a **Container Storage Interface** (**CSI**) volume. These add-ons allow K8s to mount multiple secrets, keys, and certificates stored in enterprise-grade external secrets stores directly into your Pods. Specifically, `secrets-store-csi-provider-aws` integrates AWS Secrets Manager and AWS Systems Manager Parameter Store with Kubernetes. To set up these add-ons in your EKS cluster, download the `addons.tf` file from the GitHub repository at `https://github.com/PacktPublishing/Kubernetes-for-Generative-AI-Solutions/blob/main/ch9/addons.tf` and run the following commands:

```
$ terraform init
$ terraform plan
$ terraform apply -auto-approve
```

You can confirm the installation by listing the DaemonSets in the `kube-system` namespace using the following command; you will notice `secrets-store-csi-driver` and `secrets-store-csi-driver-provider-aws` in the output:

```
$ kubectl get ds -n kube-system
NAME
secrets-store-csi-driver
secrets-store-csi-driver-provider-aws
```

III. Next, create an IAM role with permission policies based on least privilege access principles granting read access to only the Hugging Face secret. Once the role is created, associate it with the K8s service account so that the `my-llama-finetuned` K8s Pod can receive temporary IAM credentials using the EKS Pod Identity feature. To set up these resources, download the `iam.tf` file from the GitHub repository at `https://github.com/PacktPublishing/Kubernetes-for-Generative-AI-Solutions/blob/main/ch9/iam.tf` and run the following commands:

```
$ terraform init
$ terraform plan
$ terraform apply -auto-approve
```

You can verify the Pod Identity association using the following AWS command, which will return the association ID, service account, and namespace in the response:

```
$ aws eks list-pod-identity-associations --cluster-name eks-demo --query "associations[?serviceAccount=='my-llama-sa']"
```

IV. To use `secrets-store-csi-driver`, we need to configure `SecretProviderClass`, a custom Kubernetes resource that defines how `secrets-store-csi-driver` should connect to and retrieve secrets from external providers such as AWS Secrets Manager. Let's create one for our setup to retrieve `hugging-face-secret` from AWS Secrets Manager. To create this, download the `secret-provider-class.yaml` file from the GitHub repository at `https://github.com/PacktPublishing/Kubernetes-for-Generative-AI-Solutions/blob/main/ch9/inference/secret-provider-class.yaml` and run the following command:

```
$ kubectl apply -f secret-provider-class.yaml
```

V. Finally, redeploy the `my-llama-finetuned` application using the `my-llama-sa` service account. This approach securely injects the AWS Secrets Manager secret into your application container without exposing it in the Kubernetes manifest. To redeploy the app, download the `finetuned-inf-deploy.yaml` file from the GitHub repository at `https://github.com/PacktPublishing/Kubernetes-for-Generative-AI-Solutions/blob/main/ch9/inference/finetuned-inf-deploy.yaml`. Then, update the ECR image name with your own and execute the following command:

```
$ kubectl apply -f finetuned-inf-deploy.yaml
```

You can confirm that the secret is properly injected by checking the Pod status or by executing the `env` command inside the Pod using the following commands:

```
$ kubectl get pods -l app.kubernetes.io/name=my-llama-
finetuned
$ kubectl exec -it $(kubectl get pods -l app.kubernetes.io/
name=my-llama-finetuned -o jsonpath="{.items[0].metadata.
name}") -- env | grep HUGGING_FACE
```

In this section, we implemented multiple security best practices in our chatbot application running on EKS. We ensured ECR image immutability to prevent image tag overwrites, hardened host security using Bottlerocket AMIs, enabled IMDSv2, and applied Pod Security Standards to enforce least privilege execution. Additionally, we implemented encryption at rest, integrated vulnerability scanning to our container images in Amazon ECR, and enhanced Kubernetes secrets management through encrypted secrets and external solutions such as AWS Secrets Manager via `secrets-store-csi-driver`.

Summary

In this chapter, we covered the security best practices for deploying applications on K8s, with a focus on defense in depth and securing key aspects of the container ecosystem, including supply chain, host, network, runtime, and secret management.

Defense in depth is a concept that involves multiple layers of security to safeguard against different attack vectors.

Containers, being portable, introduce unique risks that require proactive measures at every lifecycle stage, from build to runtime. Supply chain security emphasizes securing container images during the build, test, and storage phases. Host security focuses on safeguarding the underlying server hosting containers. Runtime security ensures secure container operation by limiting privileges, enforcing resource limits, and using tools such as Falco for anomaly detection. Network security leverages namespaces, network policies, and service meshes such as Istio for segmentation and encryption. Secret management is essential for securely handling sensitive information. IRSA and EKS Pod Identity features can be used to securely provide temporary IAM credentials to K8s applications. GenAI workloads can leverage these features to securely access sensitive training data or export model artifacts in Amazon S3. GenAI model endpoints can be protected against common vectors using WAF solutions and enforcing TLS for encrypted communications. By integrating these best practices, K8s deployments can achieve robust security against evolving threats.

This chapter focused on K8s security best practices; in the next chapter, we will start diving into GPU resource optimization for K8s, which is one of the most expensive resources for GenAI applications.

10

Optimizing GPU Resources for GenAI Applications in Kubernetes

This chapter will cover strategies to maximize **graphics processing unit** (**GPU**) (`https://aws.amazon.com/what-is/gpu/`) efficiency in K8s when deploying GenAI applications as GPU instances are very expensive and often underutilized. We will also cover GPU resource management, scheduling best practices, and partitioning options such as **Multi-Instance GPU** (**MIG**) (`https://www.nvidia.com/en-us/technologies/multi-instance-gpu/`), **Multi-Process Service** (**MPS**) (`https://docs.nvidia.com/deploy/mps/index.html`), and **GPU time-slicing** (`https://docs.nvidia.com/datacenter/cloud-native/gpu-operator/latest/gpu-sharing.html`). Finally, we'll discuss monitoring GPU performance, balancing workloads across nodes, and auto-scaling GPU resources to handle dynamic GenAI workloads effectively.

In this chapter, we're going to cover the following main topics:

- GPUs and custom accelerators
- Allocating GPU resources in K8s
- Understanding GPU utilization
- Techniques for partitioning and sharing GPUs
- Scaling and optimization considerations

Technical requirements

In this chapter, we will be using the following tools, some of which require you to set up an account and create an access token:

- **Hugging Face**: `https://huggingface.co/join`.
- The **Llama-3.2-1B** model, which can be accessed via Hugging Face: `https://huggingface.co/meta-llama/Llama-3.2-1B`.
- An **Amazon EKS cluster**, as illustrated in *Chapter 3*.
- **AWS Service Quotas** to run family EC2 instances. You can request a quota increase in the **AWS console** (`https://docs.aws.amazon.com/servicequotas/latest/userguide/request-quota-increase.html`).

GPUs and custom accelerators

Deploying GenAI workloads in K8s requires selecting the right hardware based on the computational requirements of the workload, such as training, inference, or microservices implementation. Compute options include CPUs, GPUs, or custom accelerators such as **Inferentia** (`https://aws.amazon.com/ai/machine-learning/inferentia/`) and **Trainium** (`https://aws.amazon.com/ai/machine-learning/trainium/`), as well as accelerators from AWS or **tensor processing units** (**TPUs**) (`https://cloud.google.com/tpu`) from Google Cloud.

CPUs are usually the *default compute resource* in K8s and are suitable for lightweight GenAI tasks, including small-scale inference, data preprocessing, exposing APIs, and implementing classical ML algorithms such as **XGBoost** for decision trees (`https://xgboost.readthedocs.io/en/stable/`). However, they are less efficient for tasks that require high parallelism and a very large number of matrix multiplications, such as training foundational models. K8s lets you define both CPU requests and limits, ensuring a fair and efficient allocation of resources among all workloads.

GPUs excel at **massively parallel processing** (**MPP**) because they feature thousands of cores and very high memory bandwidth, allowing them to handle the matrix multiplications and linear algebra computations that are central to deep learning far more efficiently than CPUs. However, GPUs are not recognized natively by K8s. Thanks to its extensible architecture, device vendors can develop **device plugins** (`https://kubernetes.io/docs/concepts/extend-kubernetes/compute-storage-net/device-plugins/`) that expose GPU resources to the K8s control plane. These plugins are typically deployed as **DaemonSets** (`https://kubernetes.io/docs/concepts/workloads/controllers/daemonset/`) in the cluster, enabling the K8s scheduler to identify, allocate, and manage GPUs for containerized workloads properly. One of the most popular device plugins is the **NVIDIA device plugin for Kubernetes** (`https://github.com/NVIDIA/k8s-device-plugin`), which exposes NVIDIA GPUs attached to each K8s worker node and continuously tracks their health.

As an alternative to GPUs, many companies are investing in creating *purpose-built accelerators* tailored for AI/ML workloads. Examples include **AWS Inferentia** and **Trainium**, **Google TPUs**, **field-programmable gate arrays** (**FPGAs**) (`https://www.arm.com/glossary/fpga`), and various **application-specific integrated circuits** (**ASICs**) (`https://www.arm.com/glossary/asic`), each designed to excel at core operations such as matrix multiplication, utilizing transformer-based models, delivering higher performance, and ensuring lower energy consumption. Similar to GPUs, these accelerators integrate with K8s through *custom device plugins* provided by hardware vendors. These plugins discover, allocate, and monitor the specialized hardware resources attached to K8s worker nodes, enabling seamless scheduling and management alongside other compute resources.

Custom accelerators are particularly effective for large-scale training or low-latency inference. For example, **AWS Trainium** (`https://aws.amazon.com/ai/machine-learning/trainium/`) is a family of AI chips developed by AWS to enhance GenAI training by delivering high performance while reducing costs. The first-generation Trainium chips powered **Amazon EC2 Trn1 instances** (`https://aws.amazon.com/ec2/instance-types/trn1/`) and offer up to 50% lower training costs compared to comparable EC2 instances. The Trainium2 chips, featured in **Amazon EC2 Trn2 instances** and **Trn2 UltraServers** (`https://aws.amazon.com/ec2/instance-types/trn2/`), are the most powerful EC2 instances for training and inferencing of GenAI models with hundreds of billions to trillions of parameters. They provide up to four times the performance of their predecessors and 30% to 40% better price performance than EC2 P5e and P5en family instances.

Custom accelerators often rely on specialized hardware architectures and instruction sets that differ from general-purpose CPUs or GPUs. Because of this, AI/ML frameworks such as **TensorFlow** and **PyTorch** cannot natively translate high-level operations into low-level instructions that accelerators understand. The **Neuron SDK** (`https://aws.amazon.com/ai/machine-learning/neuron/`) is a software development kit designed by AWS to run and optimize AI/ML workloads efficiently on AWS's custom AI accelerators, such as AWS Trainium and Inferentia. It includes a compiler, runtime, training and inference libraries, and profiling tools. Neuron supports customers throughout their end-to-end ML development life cycle, including building and deploying deep learning and AI models. The Neuron SDK provides seamless integration with popular ML frameworks such as **PyTorch** (`https://pytorch.org/`), **TensorFlow** (`https://www.tensorflow.org/`), and **JAX** (`https://jax.readthedocs.io/`) while supporting over 100,000 models, including those from Hugging Face. Customers, such as *Databricks*, have reported significant performance improvements and cost savings of up to 30% when using Trainium-powered instances (`https://aws.amazon.com/ai/machine-learning/trainium/customers/`).

Choosing between CPUs, GPUs, and accelerators requires balancing performance needs, workload intensity, and budget constraints to optimize resource utilization for GenAI workloads. With this overview of custom accelerators, let's dive deeper into allocating GPU resources to GenAI applications in K8s.

Allocating GPU resources in K8s

To use GPU and custom accelerator resources in K8s, you must use the corresponding device plugins. For instance, the **NVIDIA device plugin for Kubernetes** makes NVIDIA GPUs recognizable and schedulable by the K8s cluster, while the **Neuron device plugin** does the same for AWS Trainium and Inferentia accelerators. This mechanism ensures that any custom accelerator is discovered, allocated, and managed properly within the K8s cluster.

Apart from installing the device plugin, you should also ensure that the respective GPU/accelerator drivers are present on the underlying operating system. AWS offers accelerated AMIs for NVIDIA and the Trainium and Inferentia accelerators, all of which you can use to launch K8s worker nodes. These AMIs include NVIDIA, Neuron drivers, **nvidia-container-toolkit** (`https://github.com/NVIDIA/nvidia-container-toolkit`), and others on top of the standard EKS-optimized AMI. Please refer to the AWS documentation at `https://docs.aws.amazon.com/eks/latest/userguide/eks-optimized-ami.html#gpu-ami` for more information.

A high-level architecture of the K8s device plugin framework is depicted in *Figure 10.1*. Let's look at what steps are involved in this process:

1. K8s device plugins are deployed as **DaemonSets**, ensuring that all (or some) nodes run a copy of the plugin Pod. Typically, these plugins are scheduled on worker nodes with specific labels (GPU, custom accelerator) to optimize resource utilization.
2. Upon initialization, the device plugin performs various vendor-specific initialization tasks and ensures devices are in a ready state.
3. The plugin registers itself with the kubelet and declares the custom resources it manages – for example, `nvidia.com/gpu` for NVIDIA GPUs and `aws.amazon.com/neuroncore` for AWS Trainium/Inferentia devices.
4. After successful registration, the plugin provides the kubelet with the list of managed devices. The kubelet then performs a node status update to advertise these resources to the K8s API server. This can be verified by running the following command:

   ```
   $ kubectl get node <replace-node-name> -o jsonpath='{.status.
   allocatable}' | jq .
   {
     "nvidia.com/gpu": "1",
   ...
   ```

5. When a Pod is scheduled on the worker node, the kubelet notifies the device plugin of the container's requirement (the number of GPUs) so that it can perform the necessary preparation tasks to allocate the requested resources.

6. The device plugin continuously monitors the health of the devices it manages and updates the kubelet accordingly to ensure optimal resource availability.

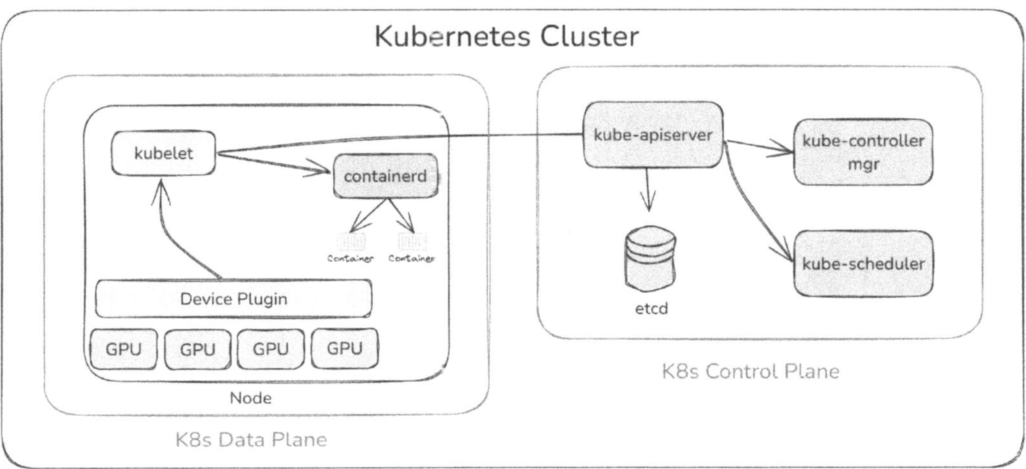

Figure 10.1 – K8s device plugin architecture

7. In our walkthrough in *Chapter 5*, we installed the NVIDIA device plugin using the `eks-data-addons` Terraform module, as shown here:

```
module "eks_data_addons" {
  source = "aws-ia/eks-data-addons/aws"
  ...
  enable_nvidia_device_plugin = true
```

8. It used the Terraform Helm provider to deploy the **NVIDIA device plugin Helm chart** (`https://github.com/NVIDIA/k8s-device-plugin?tab=readme-ov-file#deployment-via-helm`) in the EKS cluster. You can verify which Helm release and DeamonSet are being used by running the following commands:

```
$ helm list -n nvidia-device-plugin
NAME    NAMESPACE      CHART
nvidia-device-plugin
nvidia-device-plugin
nvidia-device-plugin
$ kubectl get ds -n nvidia-device-plugin --no-headers
nvidia-device-plugin
nvidia-device-plugin-gpu-feature-discovery
nvidia-device-plugin-node-feature-discovery-worker
```

9. The next step is to launch GPU worker nodes and register them with the cluster. This was covered in the *Chapter 5* walkthrough, where we created a new EKS-managed node group called `eks-gpu-mng` using the G6 family of EC2 instances. Additionally, K8s taints were applied to these nodes to ensure that only Pods requiring GPU resources were scheduled on them:

```
module "eks" {
  source = "terraform-aws-modules/eks/aws"
  ...
  eks_managed_node_groups = {
    eks-gpu-mng = {
      instance_types = ["g6.2xlarge"]
      taints = {
        gpu = {
          key = "nvidia.com/gpu"
          value = "true"
          effect = "NO_SCHEDULE"
...
```

10. GPU worker nodes can also be labeled so that advanced scheduling can be implemented – for example, we can use `hardware-type=gpu` to identify GPU-enabled nodes. This makes it possible to target specific nodes when scheduling workloads that require GPUs. We can do this by using the `kubectl` command or running the necessary Terraform code:

```
$ kubectl label node <node-name> hardware-type=gpu
```

We can also label the K8s worker nodes using Terraform, as shown in the following code snippet:

```
...
eks-gpu-mng = {
      labels = {
        "hardware-type" = "gpu"
      }
...
```

11. The next step is to allocate GPU resources for containerized workloads, such as GenAI training and inference workloads. To request GPUs, you need to specify resource requests and limits in your K8s deployment and Pod specifications. The following code snippet demonstrates how to do the following:

    - Assign tolerations to the K8s Pod that match the node taints
    - Schedule the K8s Pods specifically on nodes labeled with `hardware-type: gpu`

- Request one GPU resource using the `nvidia.com/gpu` attribute:

```
apiVersion: v1
kind: Pod
metadata:
  name: gpu-demo-pod
spec:
  tolerations:
  - key: "nvidia.com/gpu"
    operator: 'Exists'
    effect: "NoSchedule"
  nodeSelector:
    hardware-type: gpu
  containers:
  - name: gpu-container
    image: nvidia/cuda
    resources:
      limits:
        nvidia.com/gpu: 1
```

When requesting GPU resources in K8s, you must always define them in the *limits* section of the specification, either alone or with matching request values; specifying only *requests* without *limits* is not allowed. Similarly, when using AWS Trainium/Inferentia accelerators, you can use the `aws.amazon.com/neuroncore` attribute to request the resources.

In this section, we started by looking at the K8s device plugin architecture and the steps involved in creating the worker nodes in an EKS cluster. We also looked at K8s scheduling techniques such as taints, tolerations, and node selectors, all of which we can use to schedule the GPU Pods to their respective nodes.

Understanding GPU utilization

GPUs constitute a major cost of running GenAI workloads, so utilizing them effectively is paramount in achieving optimal performance and cost-efficiency. Without proper monitoring, underutilized GPUs can result in compute inefficiencies and increased operational expenses, while overutilized GPUs risk request throttling and potential application failures. In this section, we will explore solutions for monitoring GPU utilization while focusing on exporting metrics and leveraging them to implement efficient autoscaling strategies.

NVIDIA Data Center GPU Manager (DCGM)

DCGM (`https://developer.nvidia.com/dcgm`) is a lightweight library and agent designed to simplify the management of NVIDIA GPUs, enabling users, developers, and system administrators to monitor and manage GPUs across clusters or data centers.

DCGM provides functionality such as GPU health diagnostics, behavior monitoring, configuration management, telemetry collection, and policy automation. It operates both as a *standalone service* through the NVIDIA host engine and as an *embedded component* within third-party management tools. Its key features include GPU health diagnostics, job-level telemetry, group-centric resource management for multiple GPUs or hosts, and automated management policies to enhance reliability and simplify administration tasks. DCGM can integrate seamlessly with K8s tools such as the NVIDIA GPU Operator, allowing for telemetry collection and health checks in containerized environments. With support for exporting metrics to systems such as Prometheus, DCGM also facilitates real-time visualization and analysis of GPU data in tools such as Grafana.

DCGM can be implemented in K8s clusters in the following ways:

- **NVIDIA GPU Operator**: `gpu-operator` (`https://github.com/NVIDIA/gpu-operator`) leverages the **operator pattern** (`https://kubernetes.io/docs/concepts/extend-kubernetes/operator/`) within K8s to automate the process of managing all NVIDIA software components required for provisioning GPUs. These components include NVIDIA drivers (to enable CUDA), the K8s device plugin for GPUs, NVIDIA Container Runtime, automatic node labeling, DCGM-based monitoring, and more. This approach is ideal for environments where you want a fully automated solution for managing NVIDIA GPU resources, including installation, updates, and configuration.
- **DCGM-Exporter** (`https://github.com/NVIDIA/dcgm-exporter`): Built on top of the NVIDIA DCGM framework, DCGM-Exporter collects and exposes a wide range of GPU performance and health metrics, such as utilization, memory usage, temperature, and power consumption, in a Prometheus-compatible format. This facilitates seamless integration with popular monitoring and visualization tools such as Prometheus and Grafana. DCGM-Exporter is well-suited for scenarios where the necessary GPU components are already installed, and you need to enable GPU monitoring without additional overhead.

Please refer to the NVIDIA documentation at `https://docs.nvidia.com/datacenter/cloud-native/gpu-operator/latest/amazon-eks.html` for detailed guidance on selecting the right approach based on your operational needs.

So far in our walkthrough, we have already installed the necessary components, such as the NVIDIA device plugin and relevant drivers. Therefore, we will use the second approach (DCGM-Exporter) to monitor the GPU's health and utilization metrics. For the first approach, you can refer to the NVIDIA documentation at `https://docs.nvidia.com/datacenter/cloud-native/gpu-operator/latest/getting-started.html#operator-install-guide` for detailed setup instructions. To proceed, we will install DCGM-Exporter using the Helm provider in Terraform. Begin by downloading the `aiml-addons.tf` file from `https://github.com/PacktPublishing/Kubernetes-for-Generative-AI-Solutions/blob/main/ch10/aiml-addons.tf`.

The `dcgm-exporter` Helm chart will be deployed in the `dcgm-exporter` namespace from the `https://nvidia.github.io/dcgm-exporter/` Helm repository, as shown in the following code snippet:

```
resource "helm_release" "dcgm_exporter" {
  name       = "dcgm-exporter"
  repository = "https://nvidia.github.io/dcgm-exporter/"
  chart      = "dcgm-exporter"
  namespace = "dcgm-exporter"
...
```

Execute the following commands to deploy the `dcgm-exporter` Helm chart in the EKS cluster and verify its installation using the following `kubectl` command. The output should confirm that `dcgm-exporter` has been deployed as a *DaemonSet* and its Pods are *Running*:

```
$ terraform init
$ terraform plan
$ terraform apply -auto-approve
$ kubectl get ds,pods -n dcgm-exporter
NAME                              DESIRED   CURRENT   READY
daemonset.apps/dcgm-exporter      2         2         2
NAME                         READY    STATUS     RESTARTS    AGE
pod/dcgm-exporter-729qb      1/1      Running    0           84s
pod/dcgm-exporter-rtmtw      1/1      Running    0           84s
```

Now that DCGM-Exporter is functional, you can access the GPU's health and utilization metrics by connecting to the DCGM-Exporter service. Execute the following commands to connect to the service locally and use a `curl` command to query the `/metrics` endpoint to view the GPU metrics:

```
$ kubectl port-forward svc/dcgm-exporter -n dcgm-exporter 9400:9400
Forwarding from 127.0.0.1:9400 -> 9400
Forwarding from [::1]:9400 -> 9400
$ curl http://localhost:9400/metrics
# HELP DCGM_FI_DEV_GPU_UTIL GPU utilization (in %).
# TYPE DCGM_FI_DEV_GPU_UTIL gauge
DCGM_FI_DEV_GPU_UTIL{gpu="0",UUID="GPU-
173ced1d-4c1d-072d-6819-86522b018187",pci_bus_
id="00000000:31:00.0",device="nvidia0",modelName="NVIDIA
L4",Hostname="ip-10-0-34-196.us-west-2.compute.internal"} 0
# HELP DCGM_FI_DEV_MEM_COPY_UTIL Memory utilization (in %).
# TYPE DCGM_FI_DEV_MEM_COPY_UTIL gauge
DCGM_FI_DEV_MEM_COPY_UTIL{gpu="0",UUID="GPU-
173ced1d-4c1d-072d-6819-86522b018187",pci_bus_
id="00000000:31:00.0",device="nvidia0",modelName="NVIDIA
L4",Hostname="ip-10-0-34-196.us-west-2.compute.internal"} 0
...
```

In *Chapter 12*, we will deploy and configure a Prometheus agent that will scrape these GPU metrics and visualize them using Grafana dashboards. Once the metrics are available in Prometheus, we can install the **Prometheus adapter** (`https://github.com/kubernetes-sigs/prometheus-adapter`) to create *autoscaling policies*, allowing GPU workloads to scale dynamically for optimal resource utilization.

GPU utilization challenges

In K8s, allocating a GPU to a Pod reserves that GPU exclusively for the Pod's entire life cycle, even if the Pod is not actively using it. K8s does not support sharing GPUs among multiple Pods or assigning partial GPUs (< 1) per Pod by default. This design ensures isolation and avoids conflicts as most GPUs are not inherently designed to handle concurrent workloads without specialized software.

However, exclusive GPU allocation can lead to underutilization if a Pod does not fully utilize its assigned GPU. This challenge is especially pronounced in GenAI scenarios, where the following factors often come into play:

- **Varying model sizes (large versus small LLMs)**: While **state-of-the-art** (**SOTA**) LLMs may require an entire GPU or even multiple GPUs, there is a growing demand for smaller or distilled versions of these models. Depending on their size, these smaller LLMs may require a fraction of the GPU's memory and compute capacity. With K8s's default "whole GPU" allocation, even a smaller model that needs only part of a GPU will be allocated an entire device, leading to over-provisioning.
- **Dynamic workload patterns**: GenAI workloads such as fine-tuning or training LLMs or running inference for complex diffusion-based models can create bursty GPU usage patterns. During training/fine-tuning/inference, GPU usage can spike to up to 100% for compute-intensive operations (matrix multiplications, backpropagation, etc.,) but will drop significantly in between epochs or data loading/processing steps. Because K8s does not support fractional GPU resource allocation by default, these *peaks and valleys* can lead to inefficient GPU utilization.
- **Scheduling complexity and fragmentation**: K8s's default scheduler lacks the intelligence of advanced GPU-sharing strategies. Even with techniques such as node affinity, taints, and tolerations, there is no out-of-the-box method to dynamically reassign underutilized GPUs to another Pod. Consequently, smaller LLMs might monopolize an entire GPU, even if they need a fraction of its capacity. As more Pods are deployed, multiple GPUs become partially utilized but fully reserved, causing fragmented GPU resources across the cluster.

We can implement a few approaches to address these utilization challenges, such as NVIDIA's **MIG**, **MPS**, and **GPU time-slicing** options. In a case study on delivering video content using GPU-sharing techniques, up to a 95% improvement in price performance was achieved. For more detailed benchmarking data regarding this, please refer to the following AWS blog: `https://aws.amazon.com/blogs/containers/delivering-video-content-with-fractional-gpus-in-containers-on-amazon-eks/`.

In this section, we explored why monitoring GPU health and metrics is crucial and deployed the NVIDIA DCGM-Exporter add-on in our K8s cluster to track GPU performance and health metrics in real time. We also looked at the challenges of GPU utilization and the factors contributing to inefficiency in the GenAI space. Next, we will dive into GPU partitioning techniques that we can use to address these issues.

Techniques for partitioning and sharing GPUs

GPU partitioning and sharing techniques are often vendor-specific, meaning they may not be available for every accelerator out there. In this section, we will explore some of the most common approaches provided by NVIDIA for its GPUs, such as MIG, MPS, and time-slicing, and discuss how they can help improve GPU utilization for GenAI workloads.

NVIDIA MIG

MIG (`https://docs.nvidia.com/datacenter/tesla/mig-user-guide/index.html`) is a feature that was introduced in NVIDIA's **Ampere** and later architectures (A100, H100, etc.) that allows a single physical GPU to be partitioned into multiple independent GPU instances. Each MIG instance has its own dedicated memory, compute cores, and other GPU resources, providing strict isolation between workloads. MIG minimizes interference among instances and ensures predictable performance, ultimately enabling more efficient and flexible use of GPU capacity.

The process of implementing MIG involves defining GPU instances that bundle a portion of the GPU's memory and compute capacity. For example, on an NVIDIA A100 GPU with 40 GB of memory, you can configure up to seven instances each with 5 GB of dedicated memory and a corresponding share of compute resources; this can be seen in *Figure 10.2*. In this example, we can have multiple workloads, such as Jupyter notebooks, ML jobs, and more, that can run on separate GPU partitions, allowing for efficient utilization of the GPU instance:

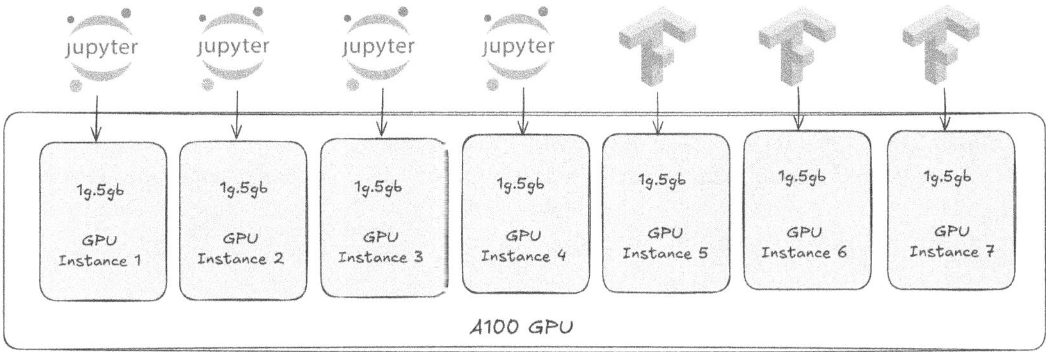

Figure 10.2 – Multi-instance GPU in an A100 NVIDIA GPU

These instances are specified by **MIG profiles** (`https://docs.nvidia.com/datacenter/tesla/mig-user-guide/index.html#supported-mig-profiles`), which outline the size and shape of each instance – for example, a *1g.5gb* profile allocates 5 GB of memory and a proportional share of GPU cores. These instances function as isolated GPU instances, each with guaranteed performance and minimal interference from others. The following table shows the MIG profiles for the latest NVIDIA H200 GPUs from the NVIDIA MIG user guide (`https://docs.nvidia.com/datacenter/tesla/pdf/NVIDIA_MIG_User_Guide.pdf`):

MIG Profile	GPU Slices	GPU Memory (GB)	Number of Instances
1g.18gb	1	18	7
1g.18gb+me	1	18	1
1g.35gb	1	35	4
2g.35gb	2	35	3
3g.70gb	3	70	2
4g.70gb	4	70	1
7g.141gb	7	141	1

Table 10.1 – GPU instance profiles for a NVIDIA H200 GPU

In this table, *GPU Slices* represent the fraction of the GPU allocated to the MIG profile, *GPU Memory (GB)* represents the amount of memory allocated to that MIG instance in GB, and *Number of Instances* is the instance count that can be created for the given profile.

In K8s, you can use the **NVIDIA GPU Operator** to simplify the MIG setup that deploys MIG Manager to manage the MIG configuration and other essential configurations on the GPU nodes. Please refer to the NVIDIA documentation at `https://docs.nvidia.com/datacenter/cloud-native/gpu-operator/latest/gpu-operator-mig.html` for step-by-step instructions on setting up MIG on K8s clusters.

K8s identifies the individual MIG instances with a unique **GPU instance ID** and **compute instance ID**. These instances are exposed to K8s as extended resources (e.g., *nvidia.com/mig-1g.18gb*). The device plugin labels the node with the available MIG profiles and their quantities, enabling the K8s scheduler to match Pod resource requests to the appropriate MIG instance. For example, the following code snippet shows a K8s Pod requesting that *nvidia.com/mig-1g.18gb* be scheduled to a node that has an available instance of that specific configuration:

```
resources:
  limits:
    nvidia.com/mig-1g.18gb: 1
```

Now that we've learned how individual MIG instances are identified and allocated within K8s, let's explore the different ways these partitions can be configured. Primarily, there are two strategies: *single* and *mixed*.

With the **single MIG strategy** (`https://docs.nvidia.com/datacenter/cloud-native/gpu-operator/latest/gpu-operator-mig.html#example-single-mig-strategy`), all GPU slices on a node are of the same size. For example, on a p5.48xlarge EC2 instance that features eight H100 GPUs, each with 80 GB of memory, you could create 56 slices of 1g.10gb, 24 slices of 2g.20gb, 16 slices of 3g.40gb, or even eight slices of 4g.40gb or 7g.80gb. This uniform approach is especially useful if multiple teams have similar GPU requirements. In such cases, you can allocate the same sized slice to each team, ensuring fair access and maximizing the utilization of the p5.48xlarge instance for workloads such as fine-tuning and inference, where the need for GPU capacity is consistent across tasks.

In contrast, the **mixed MIG strategy** (`https://docs.nvidia.com/datacenter/cloud-native/gpu-operator/latest/gpu-operator-mig.html#example-mixed-mig-strategy`) offers greater flexibility by allowing GPU slices of varying sizes to be created within each GPU on a node. For example, on a p5.24xlarge EC2 instance, which is equipped with eight NVIDIA H100 GPUs, you can combine different MIG slice configurations, such as 16 slices of 1g.10gb + 8 slices of 2g.20gb + 8 slices of 3g.40gb. This heterogeneous allocation is particularly beneficial for clusters that handle a wide range of workloads with diverse GPU requirements.

Consider an AI startup with three specialized workloads: an image recognition app, a natural language processing app, and a video analytics app. Using the mixed strategy, the startup can customize GPU allocations to match each app's needs. For instance, the image recognition application might be assigned two 1g.10gb slices, the natural language processing application might utilize one 2g.20gb slice, and the video analytics application might benefit from one 3g.40gb slice, all operating concurrently on the same H100 GPU. This approach ensures that each application receives the appropriate level of GPU resources without overprovisioning, thereby maximizing the overall utilization and efficiency of the GPU resources.

NVIDIA MPS

MPS (`https://docs.nvidia.com/deploy/mps/index.html`) is a software feature that was designed to optimize GPU resource sharing across multiple processes. It enables multiple processes to submit work concurrently, reducing GPU idle time and improving resource utilization. As depicted in *Figure 10.3*, each process retains its own isolated GPU memory space, while compute resources are shared dynamically, allowing for low-latency scheduling and better performance for workloads that might not fully utilize GPU resources individually:

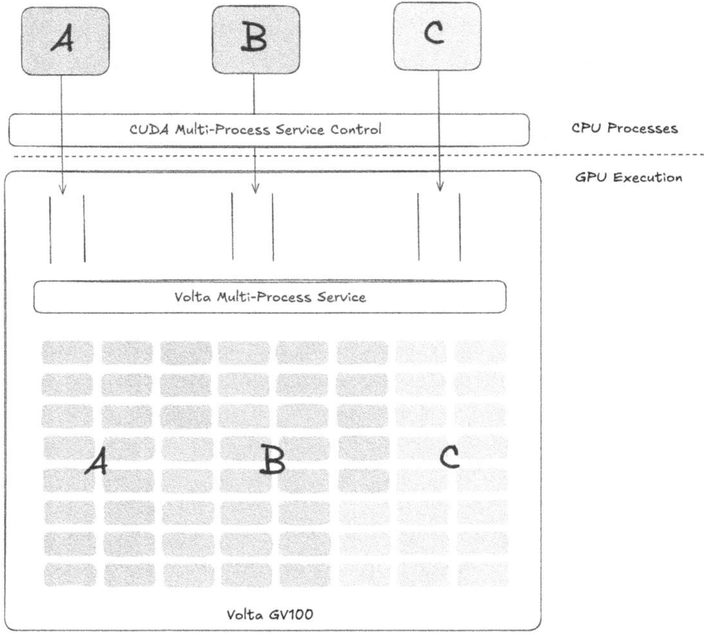

Figure 10.3 – NVIDIA MPS

In MPS, different processes running concurrently share GPU global memory, which introduces challenges that require careful consideration. *Synchronization overhead* can arise as processes or threads must be carefully managed to avoid race conditions or inconsistent states when accessing shared memory simultaneously. Additionally, resource contention may occur when multiple processes or threads compete for the same memory space, potentially creating performance bottlenecks. Balancing the use of shared global memory with private allocations adds complexity to programming, requiring careful planning and a deep understanding of CUDA (`https://developer.nvidia.com/about-cuda`) memory management to ensure both efficiency and correctness.

The memory isolation issue with MPS has been partially addressed, initially by the **Volta architecture** (`https://docs.nvidia.com/deploy/mps/index.html#volta-mps`). Volta GPUs introduced individual GPU address spaces for each client, ensuring that memory allocations by one process are not directly accessible to others, a significant improvement in memory isolation. Additionally, clients can submit work directly to the GPU without using a shared context, reducing contention and enabling finer resource allocation. Execution resource provisioning also ensures better control over GPU compute resources, preventing any single client from monopolizing them. However, limitations remain, with global memory bandwidth still being shared among all processes, potentially leading to performance degradation if one process overuses it. Additionally, MPS lacks fault isolation, meaning critical errors in one process can still disrupt others. While these improvements make MPS in Volta and newer GPUs more suitable for multi-process workloads with less stringent isolation requirements, NVIDA's MIG remains the recommended solution when complete fault isolation is needed.

The NVIDIA device plugin for K8s does not currently support MPS partitioning, and it is tracked under this GitHub issue #443 (`https://github.com/NVIDIA/k8s-device-plugin/issues/443`). However, there is a forked version of the plugin at `https://github.com/nebuly-ai/k8s-device-plugin` that enables MPS support in K8s clusters. Refer to the following post by *Medium* for step-by-step instructions: `https://medium.com/data-science/how-to-increase-gpu-utilization-in-kubernetes-with-nvidia-mps-e680d20c3181`. Once MPS is enabled using this forked NVIDIA device plugin, multiple K8s Pods can share a single GPU. MPS dynamically manages compute resource allocation while maintaining memory isolation between Pods. This functionality enables fractional GPU requests in Pod resource definitions, allowing K8s to schedule multiple Pods on the same GPU efficiently.

GPU time-slicing

For NVIDIA GPUs, **time-slicing** (`https://docs.nvidia.com/datacenter/cloud-native/gpu-operator/latest/gpu-sharing.html`) is another technique that allows multiple processes or applications to share GPU resources dynamically by dividing execution time into slices, enabling sequential access to the GPU. *Figure 10.4* illustrates how the GPU alternates between different processes over time, enabling them to share resources while each process typically retains its respective memory allocation

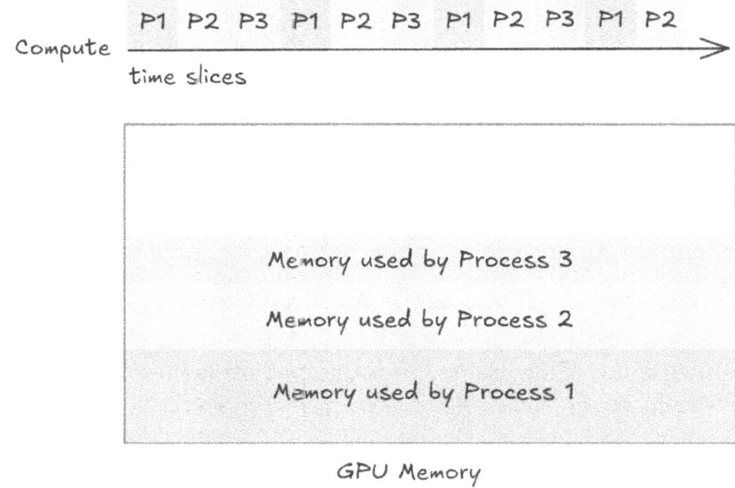

Figure 10.4 – GPU time-slicing

Time-slicing supports workloads that would otherwise require exclusive access to GPUs, providing shared access but without the memory or fault isolation capability of NVIDIA's MIG feature. The time-slicing feature is especially beneficial for older GPUs that do not support the MIG feature. It can also complement MIG by enabling multiple processes to share the resources of a single MIG partition. However, time-slicing may introduce latency as processes have to wait for their turn. This creates context-switching overhead, which involves saving and restoring the state of each process before switching to the next process.

Time-slicing is well suited for general-purpose, multi-process GPU usage and works effectively in virtualization, multi-tenant systems, and mixed workloads. However, for scenarios requiring strict resource isolation or high responsiveness, MIG might be a more appropriate solution.

Here is a high-level comparison of the GPU sharing techniques mentioned so far – that is, MIG, MPS, and time-slicing:

Feature	**MIG**	**MPS**	**Time-Slicing**
Resource isolation	Strong (hardware-level)	None or limited for Volta+ GPUs	None
Performance	Predictable	Improved GPU utilization with added latency	Dependent on workload characteristics
Scalability	Limited by supported partition count	High	High
Overhead	Minimal	Low	Higher with context switching
Use vase	Multi-tenant, inference	HPC, multi-process workloads	Non-critical tasks
Compatibility	Ampere+ GPUs	All CUDA-capable GPUs	All CUDA-capable GPUs

Table 10.2 – Comparison of NVIDIA GPU sharing techniques

The NVIDIA time-slicing feature in K8s enables GPU oversubscription, allowing multiple workloads to share a single GPU dynamically by interleaving their execution. This is achieved through the NVIDIA GPU Operator and enhanced configuration options in the NVIDIA device plugin for K8s. To enable the time-slicing feature in our EKS cluster setup, we need to create a **ConfigMap** and define `time-slicing-config`. In the following example, we are creating 10 replicas (virtual "time-sliced" GPUs) so that each K8s Pod requesting one `nvidia.com/gpu` resource will be allocated to one of these virtual GPUs and time-sliced on the underlying physical GPU:

```
apiVersion: v1
kind: ConfigMap
metadata:
  name: time-slicing-config
```

```
  namespace: nvidia-device-plugin
data:
  any: |-
    version: v1
    flags:
      migStrategy: none
    sharing:
      timeSlicing:
        resources:
        - name: nvidia.com/gpu
          replicas: 10
```

Download this manifest file from `https://github.com/PacktPublishing/Kubernetes-for-Generative-AI-Solutions/blob/main/ch10/nvidia-ts.yaml` and execute the following commands to create a `time-slicing-config` ConfigMap:

```
$ kubectl apply -f nvidia-ts.yaml
configmap/time-slicing-config created
```

Now, update the NVIDIA K8s device plugin configuration so that it can use this ConfigMap in the Terraform code. Download the `aiml-addons.tf` file from `https://github.com/PacktPublishing/Kubernetes-for-Generative-AI-Solutions/blob/main/ch10/aiml-addons.tf`. This leverages the `time-slicing-config` ConfigMap to initialize the NVIDIA device plugin, as shown in the following code snippet:

```
module "eks_data_addons" {
  source = "aws-ia/eks-data-addons/aws"
  ...
  enable_nvidia_device_plugin = true
  nvidia_device_plugin_helm_config = {
    name    = "nvidia-device-plugin"
    values = [
...
        config:
          name: time-slicing-config
...
```

Execute the following command to apply the Terraform configuration:

```
$ terraform apply -auto-approve
```

The NVIDIA device plugin automatically reconciles the time-slicing configuration and updates the K8s node details accordingly. We can verify this by running the following command, which displays the GPU count as 10 on a g6.2xlarge EC2 instance. This indicates that one physical NVIDIA L4 GPU on the node has been virtualized into 10 replicas, making them available for the scheduler to allocate:

```
$ kubectl get nodes -o custom-columns=NAME:.metadata.name,INSTANCE:.
metadata.labels."node\.kubernetes\.io/instance-type",GPUs:.status.
allocatable."nvidia\.com/gpu"
NAME                                          INSTANCE      GPUs
ip-10-0-40-57.us-west-2.compute.internal      g6.2xlarge    10
```

To demonstrate the use of NVIDIA time-slicing, let's say we are deploying a small LLM such as **Meta's Llama-3.2-1B** (`https://huggingface.co/meta-llama/Llama-3.2-1B`) parameter model in our application. This model requires 1.8 GB of GPU memory to load and perform inference. In a traditional setup, we would assign a single L4 GPU with 24 GB of memory to one K8s Pod, resulting in 92% of the GPU memory being underutilized. However, by creating 10 time-sliced replicas, we can deploy multiple instances of the Llama-3.2-1B parameter model on a single GPU.

We've already containerized the Llama-3.2-1B model into a Python FastAPI application and published it on Docker Hub. Using this image, we can deploy multiple copies of the model's endpoint on the K8s node. Download the K8s deployment manifest from `https://github.com/PacktPublishing/Kubernetes-for-Generative-AI-Solutions/blob/main/ch10/llama32-inf/llama32-deploy.yaml`. Then, update the manifest with your Hugging Face token and execute the following commands to create a K8s deployment with five replicas of this model. You can verify that all replicas will run on the same node while sharing one physical GPU efficiently:

```
$ kubectl apply -f llama32-deploy.yaml
deployment/my-llama32-deployment created
$ kubectl get pods -o wide
<Displays 5 pods running on same node>
```

In this walkthrough, we applied the same time-slicing configuration across all nodes in the K8s cluster, irrespective of the GPU type. If you are using multiple GPU types (e.g., A100, L4, L40S, H100, etc.) in the same cluster, you can consider using a **multiple node-specific configuration** setup. In this approach, you define different time-slicing configurations for each GPU type in the ConfigMap and use node labels to specify which configuration should be applied to each GPU node. Please refer to the NVIDIA documentation at `https://docs.nvidia.com/datacenter/cloud-native/gpu-operator/latest/gpu-sharing.html#applying-multiple-node-specific-configurations` for a detailed walkthrough.

In this section, we learned about various NVIDIA GPU partitioning techniques (MIG, MPS, and time-slicing) and the differences among them. MIG provides strong isolation with minimal overhead and predictable performance, making it ideal for multi-tenant environments and inference workloads. On the other hand, MPS optimizes resource utilization by enabling multiple processes to share a single GPU concurrently. Finally, time-slicing allows multiple workloads to interleave on a single GPU by allocating compute resources in a round-robin fashion. It is compatible with all CUDA-capable GPUs, including older architectures, making it a versatile option. However, time-slicing introduces higher context-switching overhead and lacks both isolation and the efficiency improvements of MPS. In the next section, we will explore additional scaling and optimization considerations when using GPUs in K8s clusters.

Scaling and optimization considerations

When scaling K8s using GPU metrics, you can integrate NVIDIA DCGM to dynamically adjust workloads based on GPU health, utilization, and performance metrics. DCGM collects telemetry data, such as GPU utilization, memory usage, power consumption, and error rates, that is exposed through DCGM-Exporter for integration with Prometheus. Prometheus metrics are then consumed by autoscaling components such as **Horizontal Pod Autoscaler** (**HPA**) or **Vertical Pod Autoscaler** (**VPA**) to scale the K8s workloads.

For instance, in an ML training job that's running on multiple nodes, DCGM-Exporter can track metrics such as `nvidia_gpu_utilization`, feeding them to Prometheus for analysis. In this instance, we can create an HPA policy that tracks GPU utilization and automatically increases the number of replicas (up to 10) when utilization exceeds 80%, thereby distributing processing across more GPUs:

```
apiVersion: autoscaling/v2
kind: HorizontalPodAutoscaler
metadata:
  name: genai-training-hpa
spec:
  scaleTargetRef:
    apiVersion: apps/v1
    kind: Deployment
    name: genai-training
  minReplicas: 1
  maxReplicas: 10
  metrics:
  - type: Object
    object:
      metricName: DCGM_FI_DEV_GPU_UTIL
      targetAverageValue: 80
```

Similarly, in an image recognition service, if the GPU utilization stays below 20% for 10 minutes, the autoscaler can reduce the number of Pods to save resources. DCGM also supports defining policies for *error handling* and *health monitoring*, ensuring K8s can reschedule Pods or drain nodes with unhealthy GPUs. For example, if DCGM detects memory errors or overheating, K8s can remove that node and migrate workloads to healthier nodes. These use cases demonstrate how GPU metrics enable fine-grained control over scaling to optimize resource usage.

However, GPU-based scaling also presents challenges. Metrics such as utilization or memory usage may not directly correlate with application performance, thereby requiring careful threshold tuning. Additionally, in environments using GPU time-slicing or MIG, workloads share resources, and DCGM metrics must account for such configurations to avoid over-scaling.

Continuously monitoring GPU metrics in large clusters can also add overhead, necessitating efficient integration with Prometheus and optimized alert rules. Scaling must also incorporate GPU health data, such as error rates or temperature, to avoid scheduling workloads on faulty hardware.

Best practices for GPU scaling include leveraging DCGM's built-in policies for error detection and recovery, using custom Prometheus metrics that combine GPU and application-specific data, integrating the NVIDIA GPU Operator for seamless management, and regularly testing and fine-tuning scaling thresholds. By combining NVIDIA DCGM with K8s's autoscaling capabilities, you can optimize GPU utilization, reduce costs, and enhance the performance of GPU-accelerated applications, ensuring scalability and reliability in resource-intensive environments.Bottom of Form

NVIDIA NIM

NVIDIA Inference Microservices (NIM) (`https://developer.nvidia.com/nim`) is a component of NVIDIA AI Enterprise that provides developers with GPU-accelerated inference microservices for deploying pretrained and customized AI models either on the cloud or in on-premises environments. These microservices are built on optimized inference engines from NVIDIA and the community, providing latency and throughput optimization for the specific combination of the foundation model and GPU system that's detected at runtime. Additionally, NIM containers offer standard observability data feeds and built-in support for autoscaling on K8s with GPUs. Refer to the following AWS blog for a detailed walkthrough of deploying GenAI applications with NVIDIA NIM on Amazon EKS: `https://aws.amazon.com/blogs/hpc/deploying-generative-ai-applications-with-nvidia-nims-on-amazon-eks/`.

Each NIM container encapsulates a model, its runtime dependencies, and the inference engine. These containers are pre-configured for easy deployment and include APIs for interaction with applications. NIM microservices are deployed in a K8s cluster, enabling orchestration, scaling, and fault-tolerant management. Developers can use NIM to create custom AI workflows tailored to specific applications, such as RAG for chat-based question-answering or simulation pipelines for scientific research.

NIM's architecture is designed to streamline the deployment of AI applications by offering prebuilt microservices that can be customized and scaled according to specific use cases. For instance, developers can deploy **RAG pipelines** for chat-based question-answering using NIM-hosted models available in the NVIDIA API catalog. These microservices are regularly updated so that they incorporate the latest advancements in AI models across various domains, including speech AI, data retrieval, digital biology, digital humans, simulation, and LLMs.

Developers interested in utilizing NIM can access it through the NVIDIA developer program, which offers free access for research, development, and testing purposes on up to 16 GPUs across any infrastructure – be it the cloud, a data center, or a personal workstation. For production deployments, NVIDIA AI Enterprise provides a comprehensive suite of tools, including NIM, that come with enterprise-grade security, support, and API stability (`https://www.nvidia.com/en-us/data-center/products/ai-enterprise/`).

GPU availability in the cloud

Like CPU instances, GPU instances can be requested in the cloud as on-demand instances, reserved instances, or spot instances. However, the growing demand for GPUs has led to challenges in availability. In response, cloud providers are introducing innovative strategies to improve GPU accessibility and meet the needs of users more effectively.

For example, AWS has introduced **Amazon EC2 Capacity Blocks for ML** (`https://aws.amazon.com/ec2/capacityblocks/`), which allows you to reserve GPU instances in **Amazon EC2 UltraClusters** (`https://aws.amazon.com/ec2/ultraclusters/`) for future dates. At the time of writing, you can reserve capacity for durations ranging from 1 to 14 days, with the option to extend up to 6 months, and schedule start times up to 8 weeks in advance using **Capacity Blocks**. These blocks can be used for a wide range of ML workloads, from small-scale experiments to large-scale distributed training sessions, and are available for various instance types, including P5, P5e, P5en, P4d, Trn1, and Trn2, all powered by NVIDIA GPUs and AWS Trainium chips.

Summary

In this chapter, we covered options for optimizing GPU resources in K8s for GenAI applications. First, we described custom AI/ML accelerators, such as AWS Inferentia, Trainium, and Google TPUs. These specialized devices offer high performance and cost-efficiency for GenAI workloads, such as training LLMs or low-latency inference use cases. K8s supports these accelerators through device plugins, allowing them to be integrated into existing clusters seamlessly.

We also covered options to optimize GPU utilization in K8s. This is a critical step due to the high costs of GPU instances and their underutilization. This chapter highlighted various techniques you can implement to address the inefficient use of resources, such as MIG, MPS, and time-slicing.

MIG allows a single GPU to be partitioned into multiple isolated instances, providing a more granular and efficient allocation of resources. MPS, on the other hand, allows multiple processes to share GPU compute resources concurrently. Time-slicing further enables sequential access to the GPU by dividing execution time across different processes, a technique that's beneficial for older GPUs that lack MIG support.

Finally, we covered GPU scaling practices within K8s and emphasized the role of NVIDIA DCGM, which can collect GPU telemetry data such as GPU utilization, memory usage, and power consumption. By integrating DCGM with Prometheus and K8s auto-scalers, you can dynamically scale workloads based on real-time GPU performance metrics.

NIM simplifies the deployment of AI models by providing pre-configured inference microservices optimized for specific GPU architectures. Cloud GPU availability remains a challenge, with demand often exceeding supply. In the next chapter, we will dive deeper into observability best practices for K8s.

Part 3: Operating GenAI Workloads on K8s

This section addresses the day-to-day operations of GenAI applications in production K8s environments, covering critical aspects from automated pipelines to resilience strategies. This section explores GenAIOps practices, comprehensive observability implementations using industry-standard tools, and strategies for high availability and disaster recovery. It also highlights the transformative impact of GenAI coding assistants on automating and managing K8s clusters, concluding with recommendations for further reading.

This part has the following chapters:

- *Chapter 11, GenAIOps: Data Management and GenAI Automation Pipeline*
- *Chapter 12, Observability – Getting Visibility into GenAI on K8s*
- *Chapter 13, High Availability and Disaster Recovery for GenAI Applications*
- *Chapter 14, Wrapping-up: GenAI Coding Assistants and Further Reading*

11

GenAIOps: Data Management and the GenAI Automation Pipeline

Generative AI operations (**GenAIOps**) refers to the set of tools, practices, and workflows designed to deploy, monitor, and optimize a generative AI model through its life cycle. Like MLOps for traditional **machine learning** (**ML**) models, GenAIOps focuses on the unique challenges posed by generative AI systems such as foundational models (FMs), large language models (LLMs), and diffusion models. In this chapter, we will cover the key concepts of GenAIOps, such as creating automated data pipelines, data gathering, cleansing, model training, and validation and deployment strategies, along with ongoing monitoring and maintenance. We will also cover topics such as data privacy and model bias, and provide best practices.

In this chapter, we're going to cover the following main topics:

- Overview of GenAI pipelines
- GenAIOps on K8s
- Data privacy, model bias, and drift monitoring

Technical requirements

In this chapter, we will be using the following tools, some of which require you to set up an account and create an access token:

- **Hugging Face**: `https://huggingface.co/join`
- The **Llama-3-8B-Instruct** model can be accessed from Hugging Face here: `https://huggingface.co/meta-llama/Meta-Llama-3-8B-Instruct`
- An Amazon EKS cluster setup, as illustrated in *Chapter 3*

Overview of GenAI pipelines

In this section, we will explore the end-to-end journey of building, deploying, and maintaining GenAI applications, as illustrated in *Figure 11.1*. Beginning with data management, organizations collect, cleanse, and organize datasets to form the foundation for high-quality experimentation. From there, the experimentation phase allows for selecting the right FM/LLM for the given business use case, and architectural decisions that shape how the model can be adapted. Once a model is identified, model adaptation, including fine-tuning, distillation, or prompt engineering, helps align model outputs to real-world use cases. The final critical steps involve model serving, enabling efficient and reliable inference and model monitoring, which closes the feedback loop by identifying performance regressions, data drift, and opportunities for continuous improvement.

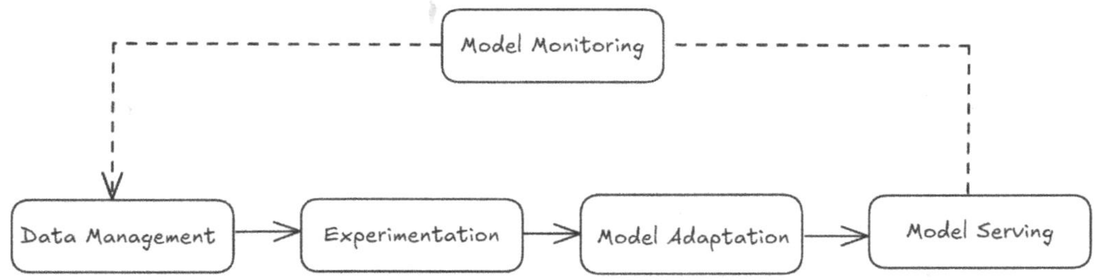

Figure 11.1 – GenAI pipeline overview

The pipeline includes the following stages:

- **Data management**: In this stage, raw data is ingested through various sources, such as internal databases, third-party APIs, streaming platforms, data lakes, and public datasets. Raw data is transformed to extract meaningful features for model training and inference. This process is often referred to as feature engineering and involves cleaning, normalizing, and structuring data to produce high-quality ML features that can be stored in an offline feature store for later use. K8s can orchestrate data preparation workflows by deploying containerized workloads using tools such as **Apache Spark** (`https://spark.apache.org/`), **Ray** (`https://ray.io/`), and **Flink** (`https://flink.apache.org/`). For example, Spark on K8s can process terabytes of data by spinning up worker Pods that handle portions of the dataset in parallel, significantly accelerating preprocessing tasks. The **Data on Amazon EKS** (**DoEKS**) (`https://awslabs.github.io/data-on-eks/docs/introduction/intro`) project provides best practices and blueprints to run data analysis/Spark workloads on EKS.

- **Experimentation**: This is a critical phase for prototyping and hypothesis testing. This is the phase where data scientists can play with different sets of models and decide which model provides the most optimal results for given business objectives. **Jupyter Notebook** provides a collaborative environment that enables interactive data analysis, visualization, and model development and can be deployed in K8s. Data scientists can perform exploration data analysis, feature engineering, and baseline model creation.

  At this stage, it is critical to store experimental data and notebooks and version control them for easier reproducibility at a later stage. This ensures that different iterations, configurations, and results can be revisited or compared over time. By version-controlling notebooks and data, teams can track the evolution of models and revert to previous states when necessary. Experimental data and notebooks are often stored in scalable and accessible storage solutions such as **Amazon S3**. Amazon S3 natively supports versioning for buckets, allowing you to maintain multiple versions of an object. S3 object tags provide another option to track different sets of training data. S3 object tags are key-value pairs that you can assign to objects in Amazon S3 to manage and organize them. Each tag consists of a key-value pair, such as {"**Key**": "**Project_Name**", "**Value**": "**P1**"} or {"**Key**": "**Version**", "**Value**": "**v1**"}. These tags are stored as object metadata and can help organize the training dataset.

- **Model adaptation**: In this stage, the pre-trained model evolves into a solution precisely aligned with your use case's unique requirements. This stage often involves fine-tuning to tweak specific layers or parameters within a foundation model to capture domain-specific nuances without discarding the model's more general understanding of language or images. In some cases, adaptation may use transfer learning techniques, where you freeze large portions of a pre-trained model to retain general patterns while updating only certain layers to focus on specialized tasks. The intensity of this customization can range from full end-to-end training on a massive dataset to lighter **prompt engineering** or **low-rank adaptation** (**LoRA**) for scenarios with limited compute resources. All these techniques need a vast amount of compute resources and careful coordination of various jobs. K8s and tools such as **Kubeflow**, **Ray**, and **Argo Workflows** can greatly streamline the adaptation phase by providing a consistent, containerized environment that supports distributed training, automated hyperparameter tuning, and scalable fine-tuning workflows.

- **Model serving**: This is the final stage of the GenAI pipeline, where trained model artifacts are deployed to deliver inference in real time or through batch processing. In the real-time scenario, a microservices-based architecture is typically used to expose the model via REST or gRPC endpoints. This setup enables load balancing, auto-scaling, and integration with continuous deployment strategies such as canary releases and A/B testing. To handle large volumes of inference requests efficiently, tools such as **KServe**, **Ray Serve**, and **Seldon Core** can help manage model deployments on K8s. For batch processing, workflows can be orchestrated to periodically load a dataset, run inference at scale, and write out results to object storage services such as Amazon S3. In both methods, it is crucial to enable monitoring and logging to track latency, throughput, and potential errors. By combining these practices, we can ensure GenAI models remain performant, stable, and ready to handle dynamic production workloads.

- **Model monitoring**: Continuous monitoring of the model's performance is essential in a production environment to ensure it meets evolving business and technical requirements. **Key performance indicators** (**KPIs**) should be tracked in real time, coupled with alerts or dashboards for faster issue identification. Whenever a model's performance dips or distribution shifts are detected (e.g., data drift or concept drift), feedback loops kick in to trigger retraining or fine-tuning. This iterative approach allows the model to adapt to new patterns, maintaining both relevance and reliability.

  Beyond raw metrics, model monitoring also includes bias detection and adherence to guardrails, ensuring outputs remain fair, compliant, and aligned with domain-specific constraints. Integrating model monitoring with your broader MLOps infrastructure enables automated rollbacks or canary deployments if a new model version underperforms. By incorporating periodic ground truth reviews and regularly updating datasets, we can continuously improve the model's accuracy and trustworthiness throughout its life cycle.

Now that we've covered the key steps of the GenAIOps pipeline, let's dive deeper into some of the common tools and workflow engines used in the K8s environment.

GenAIOps on K8s

K8s provides the scalability and flexibility required for complex tasks such as workflow orchestration, model training, and experiment tracking, enabling organizations to deploy and iterate faster. Within the K8s ecosystem, tools such as **Kubeflow**, **MLflow**, **JupyterHub**, **Argo Workflows**, and **Ray** bring unique capabilities to support everything from experimentation and automated pipeline execution to distributed computing. In this section, we will delve into how these platforms integrate with K8s, highlighting their key features and comparing their approaches to address the diverse needs of GenAIOps. We already discussed JupyterHub in detail in *Chapter 5*, so we will cover the rest of the tools here.

KubeFlow

Kubeflow (`https://www.kubeflow.org/`) is an important tool for managing and executing GenAI models in K8s environments. GenAI applications require significant computational resources and distributed workflows, areas where Kubeflow adds immense value.

Kubeflow provides distributed training for large models by integrating with frameworks such as TensorFlow and PyTorch, supporting parallel processing across multiple GPUs or custom accelerators. This reduces training time for massive datasets and enables efficient resource utilization. By leveraging K8s' orchestration capabilities, Kubeflow dynamically scales resources up or down based on workload demand, ensuring efficient GPU utilization and minimizing idle resources. This elasticity is important for GenAI workloads with fluctuating computational needs during different stages of training and inference. *Figure 11.2* gives an overview of the Kubeflow ecosystem and how it relates to the wider K8s and AI/ML landscapes. Refer to Kubeflow's *Getting Started* guide at `https://www.kubeflow.org/docs/started/installing-kubeflow/` for various deployment options and step-by-step instructions.

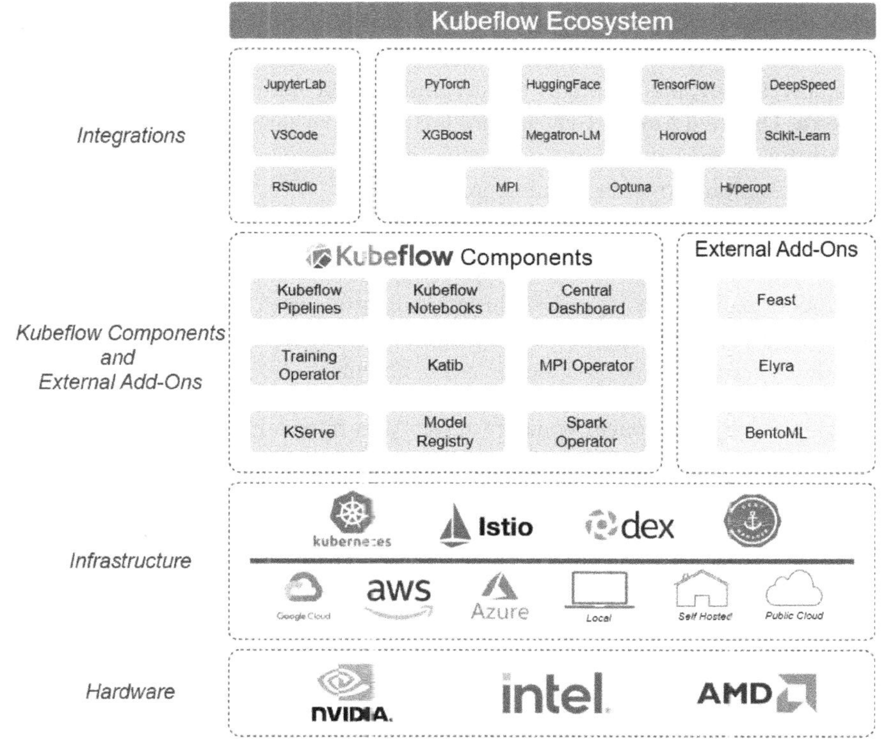

Figure 11.2 – The Kubeflow ecosystem

(Source: https://www.kubeflow.org/docs/started/architecture/)

The following are the key components of Kubeflow:

- **Kubeflow Notebooks** (`https://www.kubeflow.org/docs/components/notebooks/overview/`): This provides a robust, scalable, web-based development environment that is particularly well suited to the experimentation phase of GenAI projects. Data scientists and ML engineers can utilize Kubeflow Notebooks to spin up Jupyter notebooks within K8s-managed infrastructure, simplifying resource provisioning, especially for GPU-intensive workloads common to GenAI. Platform administrators can standardize notebook images for their organization by pre-installing the necessary packages and managing access control with Kubeflow's **role-based access control** (**RBAC**). This approach streamlines collaboration, ensuring that notebook sharing across the organization is both secure and efficient.
- **Katib** (`https://www.kubeflow.org/docs/components/katib/overview/`): Hyperparameter tuning is an essential component of GenAI model development, and Kubeflow provides Katib, an automated tuning tool, to optimize model configurations and architectures. Katib can run multiple tuning jobs concurrently, accelerating the process of finding the best-performing models.

- **Kubeflow Pipelines** (`https://www.kubeflow.org/docs/components/pipelines/overview/`): This automates complex workflows by orchestrating data preprocessing, model training, fine-tuning, and deployment, streamlining the entire ML life cycle. Pipelines are structured as **Directed Acyclic Graphs (DAGs)** (`https://www.kubeflow.org/docs/components/pipelines/concepts/graph/`), ensuring reproducibility and reducing manual intervention across the training process.
- **KServe** (`https://www.kubeflow.org/docs/external-add-ons/kserve/introduction/`): Once models are trained, Kubeflow's KServe component provides scalable, efficient model deployment across K8s clusters, supporting both batch and real-time inference. KServe offers dynamic scaling, A/B testing, and canary deployments, ensuring GenAI models can seamlessly transition into production environments.

Kubeflow also addresses the *data-intensive* nature of GenAI by integrating preprocessing steps, such as data augmentation and feature extraction, directly into its pipelines. This reduces errors and ensures that each run follows a consistent data preparation process. All artifacts, including datasets, models, and evaluation metrics, can be stored in Kubeflow's artifact repository, enabling reproducibility. Metadata tracking ensures that all pipeline runs, artifacts, and experiments are traceable, simplifying the process of debugging and retraining models when necessary.

Kubeflow provides templates for orchestrating LLM workflows, enabling efficient deployment and fine-tuning in K8s environments. By supporting multi-tenant environments and namespace isolation, Kubeflow ensures secure, compliant workflows across organizations, preventing resource conflicts between teams. Kubeflow is particularly valuable for GenAI projects requiring extensive experimentation, model retraining, and deployment pipelines. Its ability to automate the full ML life cycle, from data ingestion and distributed training to hyperparameter tuning, deployment, and monitoring, reduces the overhead for data scientists and DevOps teams.

MLflow

MLflow (`https://mlflow.org/`) is an open source platform that helps simplify the AI/ML life cycle and provides tools for experimentation, model versioning, and reproducibility. MLflow, along with K8s, provides scalability and orchestration capabilities to manage complex workflows in distributed environments.

The following are some of the core components of MLflow:

- **Mlflow Tracking** (`https://mlflow.org/docs/latest/tracking.html`) provides both an API and a user interface for logging parameters, code versions, metrics, and artifacts throughout the ML process. Centralizing details such as parameters, metrics, artifacts, data, and environment configurations gives teams valuable insight into their models' evolution over time. When deployed on K8s, it typically runs as a Pod with persistent storage (e.g., Amazon S3) to securely store artifacts and metadata.

- **MLflow Model Registry** (`https://mlflow.org/docs/latest/model-registry.html`) provides a systematic approach to model management and assists in handling different versions of the models that belong to different stages of the ML life cycle, such as staging, production, and archived with tracking. It also provides a centralized store, APIs, and a user interface for collaboratively managing model lineage, versioning, aliasing, tagging, and annotations. When deployed on K8s alongside the tracking server, it benefits from high availability and horizontal pod autoscaling for large-scale operations.
- **MLflow Projects** (`https://mlflow.org/docs/latest/projects.html`) provides a standardized format for packaging ML code and containerizing ML experiments, making them portable across environments. When deployed on K8s, these projects can be orchestrated as distributed jobs using tools such as Argo Workflows or Kubeflow Pipelines, enabling parallel execution for tasks such as hyperparameter tuning and model optimization.
- **MLflow Models** (`https://mlflow.org/docs/latest/models.html`) offers a standard format for packaging ML models that can be used in a variety of downstream tools, such as real-time serving through a REST API or batch inference on Apache Spark. In K8s environments, these models can be served through frameworks such as KServe, Seldon Core, or Ray Serve, leveraging K8s features for seamless scaling, load balancing, and integration with other K8s services.

For instance, in a real-world use case, MLflow can be used to track experiments as data scientists optimize hyperparameters, ensuring that each run's metrics, parameters, and artifacts are recorded for reproducibility and analysis. The best-performing models can then be registered in MLflow Model Registry, enabling streamlined deployment to KServe Pods for real-time serving. With K8s autoscaling, the deployed models can dynamically scale to handle increased user traffic during peak periods, ensuring robust and efficient performance.

Argo Workflows

Argo Workflows (`https://argo-workflows.readthedocs.io/en/latest/`) is an open source, K8s-native workflow engine designed to orchestrate complex pipelines in K8s environments. It allows users to define workflows as DAGs (`https://argo-workflows.readthedocs.io/en/latest/walk-through/dag/`) or step-by-step instructions. Each step of a DAG runs as a separate Pod in the K8s cluster. This architecture leverages K8s scalability and fault tolerance, making it a great solution for ML pipelines.

Argo Workflows is implemented using K8s **custom resource definition** (**CRD**) specification. Each workflow can dynamically pass data between steps, run tasks in parallel, and conditionally execute branches, making it highly adaptable.

One of the primary advantages of Argo Workflows is its ability to scale horizontally and orchestrate thousands of workflows concurrently without significant overhead. Features such as automated retries, error handling, artifact management, and resource monitoring simplify the Argo Workflow execution and improve its resilience. Many K8s ecosystem tools use Argo Workflows as the underlying workflow engine. Some examples include Kubeflow Pipelines, Seldon, Katib, and so on. Refer to the Argo Workflows *Getting Started* guide at `https://argo-workflows.readthedocs.io/en/latest/quick-start/` for detailed, step-by-step installation instructions.

Argo Workflows is a general-purpose workflow engine that can be leveraged in many use cases, including ML pipelines, data and batch processing, infrastructure automation, **continuous integration/continuous delivery** (**CI/CD**), and so on. Refer to the Argo Workflows documentation at `https://argo-workflows.readthedocs.io/en/latest/#use-cases` for a detailed walkthrough of each of those use cases.

Ray

Ray (`https://www.ray.io/`) is an open source framework designed for scalable and distributed computing, enabling the execution of Python-based applications across multiple nodes. Ray provides a unified interface for building distributed applications and offers a rich ecosystem of libraries, including **Ray Serve** (`https://docs.ray.io/en/latest/serve/index.html`) for scalable model serving, **Ray Tune** (`https://docs.ray.io/en/latest/tune/index.html`) for hyperparameter tuning, **Ray Train** (`https://docs.ray.io/en/latest/train/train.html`) for distributed training, **Ray RLlib** (`https://docs.ray.io/en/latest/rllib/index.html`) for scalable reinforcement learning, and **Ray Data** (`https://docs.ray.io/en/latest/data/data.html`) for distributed data preprocessing and loading. When deployed on K8s, Ray leverages K8s' orchestration capabilities to manage and scale distributed workloads efficiently.

Ray can be deployed on K8s using the **KubeRay** operator (`https://github.com/ray-project/kuberay`), as depicted in *Figure 11.3*, which provides a K8s-native approach to managing Ray clusters. A typical Ray cluster comprises a head node Pod and multiple worker node Pods. The KubeRay operator facilitates the creation, scaling, and management of these clusters, ensuring seamless integration with K8s environments.

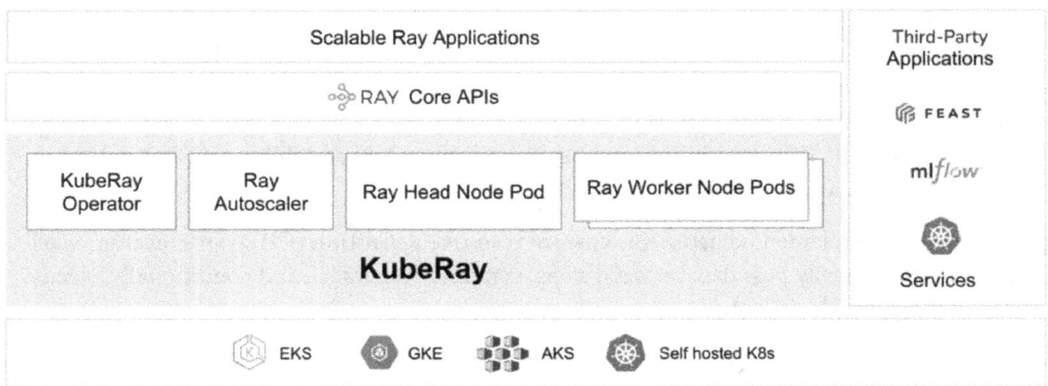

Figure 11.3 – The KubeRay architecture

(Source: https://docs.ray.io/en/latest/cluster/kubernetes/index.html)

KubeRay provides several CRDs to streamline Ray cluster management:

- **RayCluster** (`https://docs.ray.io/en/latest/cluster/kubernetes/getting-started/raycluster-quick-start.html`): Defines the desired state of a Ray cluster, including specifications for head and worker nodes. This CRD allows users to customize resource allocations, environment variables, and other configurations pertinent to the Ray cluster.
- **RayJob** (`https://docs.ray.io/en/latest/cluster/kubernetes/getting-started/rayjob-quick-start.html`): Enables the submission of Ray jobs to a Ray cluster. By specifying the job's entry point and runtime environment, users can execute distributed applications without manual intervention.
- **RayService** (`https://docs.ray.io/en/latest/cluster/kubernetes/getting-started/rayservice-quick-start.html`): Facilitates the deployment of Ray Serve applications, which are used for scalable model serving. This CRD manages the life cycle of Ray Serve deployments, ensuring high availability and seamless updates.

KubeRay offers autoscaling capabilities, allowing Ray clusters to adjust their size based on workload demands. This feature ensures efficient resource utilization by adding or removing Ray Pods as necessary, accommodating varying computational requirements. KubeRay supports heterogeneous compute environments, including nodes equipped with GPUs. This flexibility enables the execution of diverse workloads, from general-purpose computations to specialized tasks requiring hardware acceleration.

Deploying KubeRay on a K8s cluster

In this section, we will deploy the KubeRay operator in our EKS cluster setup. The KubeRay operator can be deployed as a Helm chart, which is available at the `kuberay-helm` (`https://github.com/ray-project/kuberay-helm`) repository. Let's update the Terraform code to install the KubeRay operator using Terraform Helm Provider. Add the following code to `aiml-addons.tf` (alternatively, you can download the complete file from the GitHub repository at `https://github.com/PacktPublishing/Kubernetes-for-Generative-AI-Solutions/blob/main/ch11/aiml-addons.tf`):

```
resource "helm_release" "kuberay-operator" {
  name       = "kuberay-operator"
  repository = "https://ray-project.github.io/kuberay-helm/"
  chart      = "kuberay-operator"
  namespace = "kuberay-operator"
  create_namespace = true
  depends_on = [
    module.eks
  ]
}
```

Execute the following commands to deploy the `kuberay-operator` Helm chart in the EKS cluster and verify the installation using the `kubectl` command. The output should confirm `kuberay-operator` to be deployed as a **Deployment** and that its Pods are in a `Running` status:

```
$ terraform init
$ terraform plan
$ terraform apply -auto-approve
$ kubectl get deploy,pods -n kuberay-operator
NAME                                   DESIRED   CURRENT   READY
deployment.apps/kuberay-operator       1         1         1
NAM                                   READY  STATUS    RESTARTS   AGE
pod/kuberay-operator-5dd6779f94-4tzsr 1/1    Running   0          84s
```

Now that we have successfully installed `kuberay-operator` in the EKS cluster, let's use some of the capabilities of Ray, such as Ray Serve, to serve the GenAI models. As discussed before, Ray Serve provides a scalable way of serving AI/ML models using the Ray framework. Using Ray Serve with a **vLLM** (`https://github.com/vllm-project/vllm`) backend for LLM inference offers several compelling benefits, particularly in terms of scalability, efficiency, and ease of deployment.

vLLM is an open source library designed to optimize LLM inference through more efficient memory management and parallelization strategies. It uses a novel **PagedAttention** (`https://huggingface.co/docs/text-generation-inference/en/conceptual/paged_attention`) mechanism, an innovative attention algorithm inspired by virtual memory paging in operating systems. It significantly reduces GPU memory fragmentation, allowing multiple inference requests to run concurrently with less overhead. In addition, vLLM employs continuous batching of incoming requests, grouping them together to optimize computational resources and improve inference speed. Another major advantage is vLLM's efficient memory sharing during parallel sampling, generating multiple output sequences from a single prompt, which reduces memory usage by up to 55% and boosts throughput by up to 2.2 times (`https://blog.vllm.ai/2023/06/20/vllm.html`). Taken together, these features enable to achieve higher throughput, lower latency, and reduced hardware costs when serving LLMs at scale. Moreover, vLLM integrates seamlessly with popular libraries such as **Hugging Face Transformers**, making it easy to adopt without extensive code changes.

In this section, we will deploy the Llama-3-8B model using Ray Serve with a vLLM backend on an Amazon EKS cluster. First, we need to create a K8s Secret resource containing our Hugging Face API key, which the Ray Serve deployment will use to download and host the Llama model. Execute the following command to create a K8s Secret named `hf-secret`:

```
$ export HF_TOKEN=<Your Hugging Face access token>
$ kubectl create secret generic hf-secret --from-literal=hf_api_
token=${HF_TOKEN}
secret/hf-secret created
```

Download `ray-service-vllm.yaml` from the GitHub repository (`https://github.com/PacktPublishing/Kubernetes-for-Generative-AI-Solutions/blob/main/ch11/ray-service-vllm.yaml`) and execute the following command to create a Ray Service:

```
$ kubectl apply -f ray-service-vllm.yaml
rayservice.ray.io/llama-31-8b created
```

This Ray Service example does the following:

- Creates a Ray cluster with head and worker nodes with the specified container images and resources
- Downloads and installs the code/dependencies needed for vLLM inference
- Starts Ray Serve using the **serveConfigSpecs** defined in the YAML
- Scales the Ray cluster and Ray Serve replicas automatically, depending on concurrency and resource usage

KubeRay will launch the head and worker nodes as K8s Pods. We can verify this by using `kubectl`:

```
$ kubectl get pods -l app.kubernetes.io/name=kuberay
NAME                                        READY   STATUS     RESTARTS   AGE
llama-3-8b-raycluster-vw671-gpu-group-worker-
r2n96    0/1      Pending    0           49s
llama-3-8b-raycluster-vw671-
head-94452                 0/1      Pending    0           49s
```

These K8s Pods may initially enter a `Pending` state if the EKS cluster lacks sufficient compute or GPU resources. Karpenter, running in the cluster, will automatically detect this and launch the Amazon EC2 instances based on the resource requests. As a result, it can take 10–15 minutes for the Pods to transition to the `Running` state:

```
$ kubectl wait --for=condition=Ready pods -l app.kubernetes.io/
name=kuberay --timeout=900s
pod/llama-3-8b-raycluster-vw671-gpu-group-worker-r2n96 condition met
pod/llama-3-8b-raycluster-vw671-head-94452 condition met
```

Finally, let's verify inference on the Llama 3 model by port-forwarding to the Ray Service on port `8000`. Use the following commands to set up the port-forward for the Ray Serve application and then send a test prompt to the inference endpoint:

```
$ kubectl port-forward svc/$(kubectl get svc -l app.kubernetes.io/
name=kuberay,ray.io/node-type=head -o jsonpath='{.items[0].metadata.
name}') 8000:8000
Forwarding from 127.0.0.1:8000 -> 8000
Forwarding from [::1]:8000 -> 8000
$ curl http://localhost:8000/v1/chat/completions -H "Content-Type:
application/json" -d '{
```

```
"model": "meta-llama/Meta-Llama-3-8B-Instruct",
       "messages": [
         {"role": "system", "content": "You are a helpful assistant."},
         {"role": "user", "content": "Provide a brief sentence 
describing the Ray open-source project."}
       ],
       "temperature": 0.7
     }'
```

Additionally, we can connect to the **Ray Dashboard** (`https://docs.ray.io/en/latest/ray-observability/getting-started.html`) running on port `8265` to view metrics, logs, and overall cluster status. The Ray Dashboard provides *real-time metrics* on resource utilization, active actors, and running tasks within the cluster. We can also use it to inspect logs, monitor autoscaling events, and manage Ray Serve deployments, making it easier to debug and optimize your applications.

```
$ kubectl port-forward svc/$(kubectl get svc -l app.kubernetes.io/
name=kuberay,ray.io/node-type=head -o jsonpath='{.items[0].metadata.
name}') 8265:8265
Forwarding from 127.0.0.1:8265 -> 8265
Forwarding from [::1]:8265 -> 8265
```

Navigate to `http://localhost:8265` in your browser to access the Ray Dashboard.

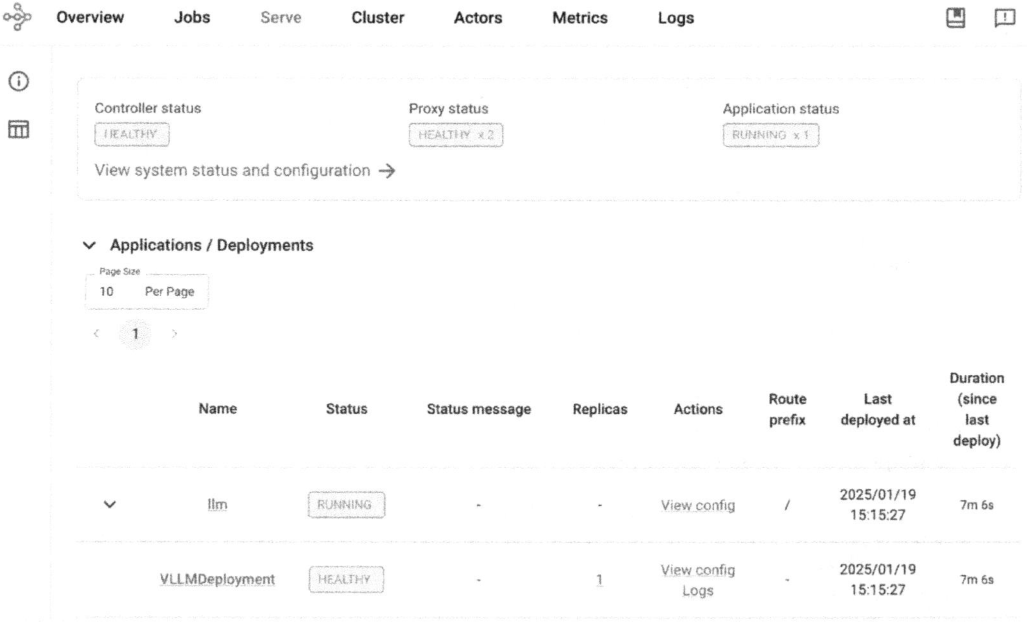

Figure 11.4 – The Ray Dashboard

In this section, we covered how to deploy KubeRay within a K8s environment. In the following section, we will compare Kubeflow, MLFlow, and Ray, three frameworks that are commonly used for MLOps deployment.

Comparing KubeFlow, MLFlow, and Ray

Kubeflow, MLflow, and Ray are open source frameworks designed for building AI/ML pipelines and facilitating MLOps. The following is a comparison table highlighting their unique features, which can guide you in selecting the right framework for your specific use case:

Features	**Kubeflow**	**MLflow**	**Ray**
Key application	Orchestrating and managing end-to-end ML workflows	Experiment tracking, model versioning, and life cycle management	Distributed computing, scalable training, and serving solutions for ML applications
Core strength	Workflow orchestration and multi-user environments	Experiment tracking and model registry	Distributed execution, hyperparameter tuning, and serving
Integration with K8s	K8s-native with seamless resource scaling	Can run in K8s for scalability	Integrates well with K8s for distributed workloads
Model registry	Basic tracking via metadata and outputs	Centralized registry for models and life cycle management	No native model registry; integrates with external tools such as MLflow for life cycle management
Deployment	Supports model deployment through KServe or custom workflows	Supports deployment to cloud, edge, and local environments	Distributed model serving with Ray Serve
Hyperparameter tuning	Integrated via Katib for AutoML	Limited; external libraries required	Native support through Ray Tune
Framework compatibility	Supports TensorFlow, PyTorch, XGBoost, and more	Framework-agnostic	Supports TensorFlow, PyTorch, XGBoost, and custom Python

Features	Kubeflow	MLflow	Ray
Monitoring	Monitoring via K8s tools (e.g., Prometheus)	Custom monitoring required for deployment	Native observability via the Ray Dashboard and customizable integrations with third-party tools
Ideal for	Teams needing a K8s-native MLOps solution	Teams focused on tracking, managing, and deploying models	Teams building scalable, distributed AI/ML applications

Table 11.1 – Framework comparison: Kubeflow versus MLflow versus Ray for MLOps

In this section, we explored various tools in the K8s ecosystem that aid in implementing GenAI automation pipelines. Tools such as Kubeflow streamline ML pipelines, notebooks facilitate experimentation, MLflow provides robust experiment tracking and model management, Argo Workflows enables efficient automated pipeline execution, and Ray facilitates powerful distributed computing capabilities. Each of these platforms integrates seamlessly with the K8s ecosystem, bringing unique features that cater to the diverse and evolving needs of GenAIOps. We also deployed the KubeRay operator in the EKS cluster and hosted the Llama 3 model using the Ray Serve framework.

In the next section, let's explore data privacy and model monitoring to ensure that our GenAI workloads are not only efficient but also secure and trustworthy.

Data privacy, model bias, and drift monitoring

In the rapidly evolving landscape of GenAI, ensuring data privacy, addressing model bias, and monitoring for drift are critical in building trustworthy and reliable AI systems. This section explores the strategies and tools available within the K8s ecosystem to safeguard sensitive data, detect and mitigate biases in AI models, and continuously monitor model performance for signs of drift. By addressing these challenges, we can maintain compliance, enhance transparency, and ensure the GenAI solutions deliver consistent and fair outcomes in production environments.

Methods to test bias and variance

Testing for model bias and variance in K8s environments can be automated and streamlined by leveraging ML pipelines, specialized monitoring tools, and scalable distributed frameworks. Tools such as Kubeflow, MLflow, and Argo Workflows can integrate with bias detection libraries and statistical analysis frameworks to automate this process.

Fairness and explainability libraries

Libraries such as **IBM AI Fairness 360 (AIF360)**, **Fairlearn**, and **SHapley Additive exPlanations (SHAP)** can be integrated directly into AI/ML pipelines in K8s. If these tools are containerized, they can be scaled alongside model deployments. These libraries evaluate bias by comparing performance discrepancies across protected attributes such as race and gender.

Now, let's explore how AIF360 can be integrated into a K8s-based ML pipeline to assess and mitigate bias. Consider a financial institution developing an ML model to predict loan approvals based on features such as credit score, income, and age. To ensure the model does not exhibit bias against certain demographic groups (e.g., race or gender), AIF360 can be integrated into the pipeline to evaluate fairness. AIF360 can be containerized and deployed as a K8s Pod. This Pod retrieves predictions stored in a persistent storage shared between the model and the fairness-check Pod, along with any necessary test data. Using these inputs, AIF360 computes fairness metrics such as disparate impact and equal opportunity difference to evaluate bias across sensitive attributes. If bias is detected, the pipeline can trigger a retraining job that incorporates mitigation techniques such as reweighting, optimized preprocessing, adversarial debiasing, and so on, provided by AIF360. Additionally, AIF360 can be used during the data preprocessing stage to detect and address bias in training datasets before model development. Refer to the AIF360 documentation at `https://github.com/Trusted-AI/AIF360` for interactive demos.

Model drift monitoring and feedback loops

In the ML project life cycle, data drift can manifest in various forms, each impacting the models differently and potentially reducing their effectiveness. The following are some examples:

- **Covariate drift** occurs when the distribution of input features changes while the relationship between features and the target variable remains the same. See the following examples:
    - In e-commerce, seasonal changes may cause a spike in searches for clothes and gifts during the holidays, shifting the input data distribution
    - In healthcare, an aging population could lead to a higher average age in a dataset used for predicting disease risks
- **Label drift** occurs when the distribution of the target variable changes, even if the input feature distribution remains constant. The following is an example:
    - In retail, an economic boom might lead to an increased purchase rate for premium goods, altering the target variable distribution
- **Concept drift** occurs when the relationship between input features and the target variable changes. The following is an example:
    - In an ad-serving platform, user preferences might shift when a new competitor enters the market, reducing the effectiveness of a model predicting ad clicks

- **Temporal drift** reflects gradual changes in data distributions over time. The following is an example:
    - In social media analytics, trends in language usage or hashtags may evolve, impacting models used for sentiment analysis
- **Sampling drift** occurs when the data collection process changes, leading to a shift in the sample distribution. The following is an example:
    - In customer surveys, a change in survey methodology might begin targeting a different demographic group, altering the dataset's composition
- **Feature interaction drift** involves changes in how features interact with each other, even if individual feature distributions remain stable. The following is an example:
    - In retail, a promotion on one product might influence the sales of complementary products in unexpected ways

Understanding these different types of drift—covariate, label, concept, temporal, sampling, and feature interaction—is critical for ensuring models remain reliable and effective over time.

The following are some of the statistical methods commonly used to measure different types of drift:

- **Target drift detection** (**TDD**) helps identify changes in the target variable's distribution. For example, in a fraud detection system, TDD would detect a shift in the proportion of fraudulent versus non-fraudulent transactions. It uses statistical measures such as KL divergence, chi-square tests, and similar methods to compare the current target distribution to the historical distribution, alerting users to shifts that could impact model performance.
- The **Kolmogorov-Smirnov test** (**KS test**) is a statistical method used to compare two distributions and determine whether they differ significantly. It is useful for detecting covariate drift, which occurs when the input feature distributions change. The KS test measures the maximum difference between the **cumulative distribution functions** (**CDFs**) of two datasets, providing a test statistic and a p-value to quantify the extent and significance of the drift. For example, the KS test can reveal changes in user behavior for an e-commerce platform, where feature distributions such as purchase frequency and product preferences may evolve over time.
- **Concept drift detection** (**CDD**) focuses on changes in the relationship between input features and the target variable. It identifies situations where the same inputs lead to different outcomes, signaling that the model's assumptions about the data are no longer valid. Concept drift is critical in applications such as recommendation systems, where customer preferences evolve over time, and credit scoring systems, where regulatory changes alter what constitutes a creditworthy individual.

Drift detection and remediation

When data drift is detected by a model monitoring component and exceeds a configured threshold, an event-driven workflow, using a tool such as Argo Workflows or Kubeflow, can be used to initiate a new retraining job. This retraining job can pull the latest version of the production data, typically stored in a data lake such as Amazon S3, and launch a model training or fine-tuning task using a pre-defined container image or a custom training job CRD. Bias and explainability checks using tools such as AIF360, SHAP, and Fairlearn can be embedded as an intermediate step in the pipeline to ensure the updated model not only meets performance requirements but also complies with fairness policies.

After retraining, the model is validated against established baselines, and metrics such as accuracy and F1 score are compared to those of previous versions. If the new model meets acceptance criteria, it is packaged as a container and pushed to a container registry. Deployment then occurs through a blue-green or canary rollout strategy.

All events and model artifacts are logged and stored in versioned buckets or databases, enabling root-cause analysis and debugging, as shown in *Figure 11.5*.

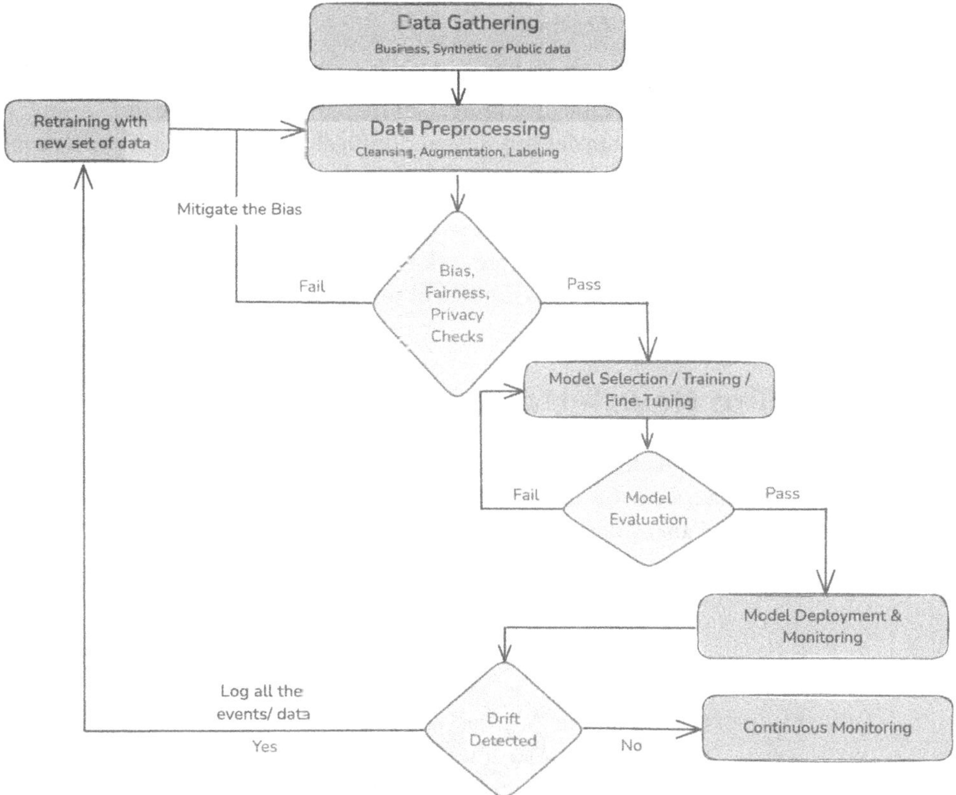

Figure 11.5 – An automated drift response flow in a GenAI pipeline

This kind of implementation promotes robustness, fairness, and resilience in GenAI model deployments without requiring constant manual oversight.

Summary

In this chapter, we explored the foundational concepts of GenAIOps, focusing on the tools and workflows required to deploy, monitor, and optimize GenAI models. It addressed challenges unique to GenAI workloads, such as automating data pipelines, ensuring data privacy, managing model bias, and maintaining life cycle optimization.

The process begins with data preparation. Model experimentation involves prototyping and testing different models to determine the optimal approach for specific business objectives. Collaborative tools such as Jupyter Notebook and Kubeflow Notebooks facilitate exploratory analysis. During model optimization, hyperparameter tuning and neural architecture search can be performed using tools such as Katib and Ray Tune. Model training and fine-tuning are performed across distributed systems using frameworks such as TensorFlow or PyTorch. Once models are trained, they can be deployed for inference in real-time or batch settings. Continuous monitoring then ensures that model performance remains robust as data patterns evolve over time.

K8s-native tools such as Argo Workflows, Kubeflow, and MLflow streamline pipeline orchestration, enabling distributed training, hyperparameter tuning, and model serving. These tools seamlessly integrate fairness and explainability libraries to assess and mitigate model bias and enable robust workflows to detect and address data drift, ensuring models remain reliable over time.

This holistic approach to GenAIOps balances performance optimization with ethical considerations, creating a scalable, repeatable, and trustworthy framework for GenAIOps. In the next chapter, we will build upon these concepts, delving deeper into the K8s observability stack to enhance monitoring and troubleshooting capabilities.

Join the CloudPro Newsletter with 44000+ Subscribers

Want to know what's happening in cloud computing, DevOps, IT administration, networking, and more? Scan the QR code to subscribe to **CloudPro**, our weekly newsletter for 44,000+ tech professionals who want to stay informed and ahead of the curve.

`https://packt.link/cloudpro`

12 Observability – Getting Visibility into GenAI on K8s

In this chapter, we will cover key observability concepts for monitoring GenAI applications in **Kubernetes** (**K8s**). We'll dive into why monitoring is critical for optimizing GenAI workloads, examining both system-level metrics and application-specific signals. By integrating tools such as **Prometheus** for metrics collection and **Grafana** for visualization, and leveraging the debugging capabilities of **LangChain**, you'll learn how to construct a comprehensive monitoring framework that provides real-time and actionable insights.

In this chapter, we're going to cover the following main topics:

- Observability key concepts
- Monitoring tools in K8s
- Visualization and debugging

Observability key concepts

Observability is the foundational framework for identifying, investigating, and remediating issues in a system, as shown in *Figure 12.1*. It provides a holistic view of system behavior and performance. Observability is built on three core pillars: **logs**, **metrics**, and **traces**. Logs capture detailed event information, metrics quantify system performance, and traces provide an end-to-end view of request flows. Together, these components enable efficient monitoring and troubleshooting of complex distributed systems. This integration ensures actionable insights for maintaining system reliability and performance.

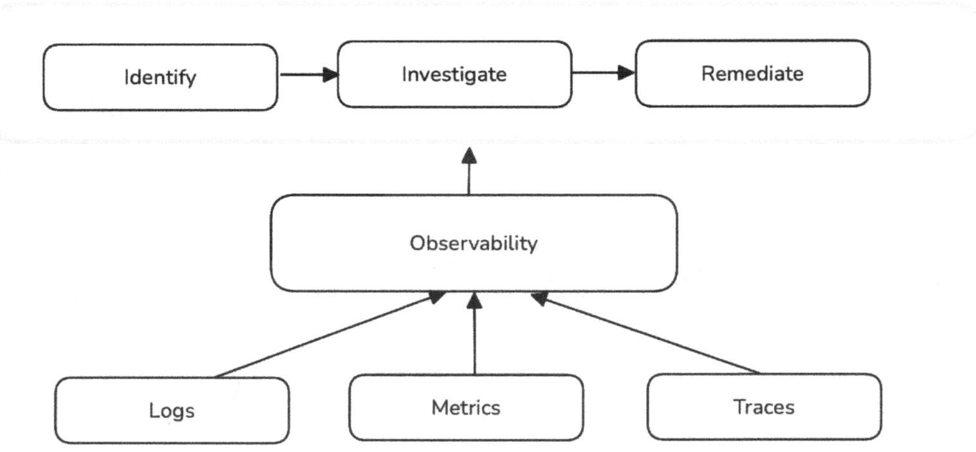

Figure 12.1 – Observability framework

Logs

System logs cover events such as transactions, system errors, and user actions. K8s generates logs at different layers, such as container logs, node logs, and cluster-level logs. You can use the following command to see logs for a Pod:

```
$ kubectl logs <pod-name>
```

If the Pod has multiple containers, a specific container log can be observed with the following:

```
$ kubectl logs <pod-name> -c <container-name>
```

By default, logs in K8s are ephemeral and are lost when Pods restart. To persist logs, one can use sidecar containers or logging agents that forward logs to a centralized storage backend such as **Amazon CloudWatch Logs**, **Elasticsearch**, or **Loki**.

K8s does not provide cluster-wide logging by default. To implement logging at the cluster level, one can use solutions such as Loki or managed services such as **Datadog**, **Splunk**, **Amazon CloudWatch**, and **New Relic**.

Standard logs provide great insights into pod-level events and errors; however, they don't cover a complete trace of an API response. That's where K8s audit logs come in, offering a more granular view of API interactions for security and compliance purposes. We will cover K8s audit logs in the next section.

K8s audit logs

K8s provides *audit log capabilities* to track all API requests made to the K8s API server. This provides a detailed record of actions performed by users, service accounts, and controllers and can help with security, compliance, and troubleshooting.

To enable audit logs, modify the K8s API server configuration by adding the following:

```
--audit-log-path=/var/log/kubernetes/kube-apiserver-audit.log
--audit-policy-file=/etc/kubernetes/audit-policy.yaml
```

The following YAML shows a sample audit policy that will log the request metadata without the request body:

```
apiVersion: audit.k8s.io/v1
kind: Policy
rules:
  - level: Metadata
```

In managed K8s offerings such as Amazon EKS, control plane audit logs can be configured to stream to Amazon CloudWatch Logs. Refer to the EKS documentation at `https://docs.aws.amazon.com/eks/latest/userguide/control-plane-logs.html` for instructions on how to set up the audit logs.

While logs provide a detailed view of discrete events, such as errors, system activity, and user actions, metrics offer a complementary perspective by capturing continuous performance data over time. In the next section, we shift our focus from event-based insights to performance monitoring using metrics.

Metrics

Metrics involve *time-series data* that tracks system performance indicators such as memory usage and latency. In K8s, metrics provide real-time performance data about the cluster, nodes, Pods, and containers. These metrics help with monitoring, scaling, and troubleshooting workloads running inside a K8s cluster.

Metrics in K8s are collected at different layers:

- **Node metrics**, such as CPU, memory, disk, and network usage at the node level
- **Pod and container metrics**, such as resource consumption of each Pod and container
- **Cluster-level metrics**, such as the overall health and performance of the cluster
- **Application-level metrics**, which are custom application metrics such as request latency and error rates

In *Chapter 6*, we covered the key metrics that are critical for application scaling and end user experiences. We covered both conventional metrics, such as CPU and memory usage, and custom metrics, such as queue length and HTTP request rates. Prometheus is a common way of collecting metrics in the K8s environment; we will discuss this in a later section.

Traces

Traces provide a visual representation of how a single request flows through a distributed system, tracking its interactions with various services, APIs, databases, and components. Tracing in K8s helps track requests as they propagate through different services, containers, and nodes within a distributed system. Traces provide end-to-end visibility into the lifecycle of a request, allowing developers and operators to understand latency issues, failures, and dependencies in microservices architectures.

In K8s, tracing is crucial because applications often consist of multiple microservices communicating over the network. Unlike logs and metrics, which provide snapshots of system behavior, tracing provides contextual insights into request flows.

OpenTelemetry (**OTel**) (`https://opentelemetry.io/`) is a common framework used for collecting traces. Once collected, OTel can export the traces to **Zipkin** (`https://zipkin.io/`), **Jaeger** (`https://www.jaegertracing.io/`), and **AWS X-Ray** (`https://aws.amazon.com/xray/`). We will cover OTel in detail in later sections.

In this section, we explored the fundamentals of observability in K8s and the three core pillars – logs, metrics, and traces. In the next section, we will explore various tools in the K8s landscape to monitor GenAI workloads.

Monitoring tools in K8s

Achieving true observability in K8s requires a holistic approach that integrates logs, metrics, and traces. Each pillar offers unique strengths and is suited for specific use cases. By adopting the best practices for combining logs, metrics, and traces, one can optimize monitoring strategies and achieve better system reliability and resilience, ultimately enhancing the user experience.

The following is a sample stack for observability, as depicted in *Figure 12.2*:

- **Fluentd and Fluent Bit** collect logs from Kubernetes nodes, Pods, and applications and forwards them to Amazon CloudWatch/Loki/OpenSearch for storage.
- **OTel** collects traces and application-specific metrics, exporting them to Prometheus (for metrics) and Jaeger/AWS X-Ray/Zipkin (for traces).
- **Grafana** provides a single interface to visualize logs (from Loki), metrics (from Prometheus), and traces (from AWS X-Ray). Developers and operators use Grafana dashboards to analyze performance, debug issues, and set up alerts based on logs, metrics, and traces.

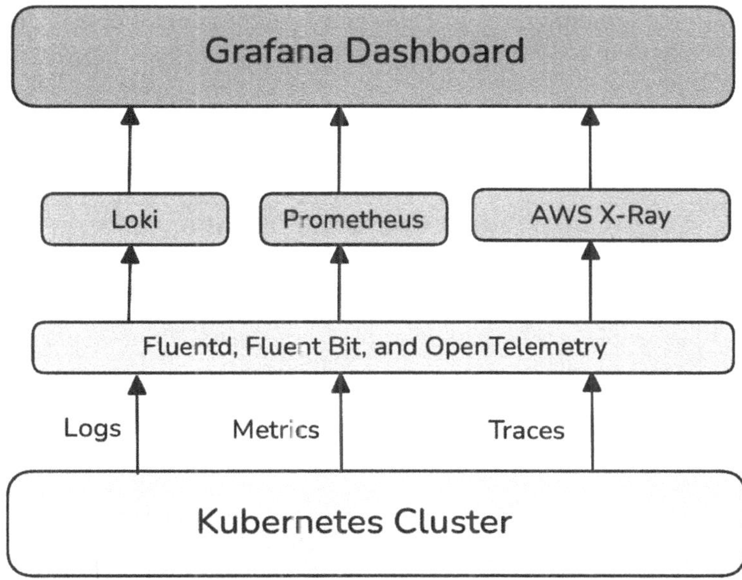

Figure 12.2 – Observability stack in K8s

We will discuss each of these tools in the following sections.

Fluentd and Fluent Bit

Fluentd (`https://www.fluentd.org/`) is a lightweight and scalable log aggregator that is widely used in K8s for collecting, processing, and forwarding logs to various backends. In a K8s cluster, Fluentd is typically deployed as a DaemonSet, ensuring that each node has an agent responsible for collecting logs from all running Pods and containers. Fluentd can gather logs from multiple sources, including container logs from `/var/log/containers`, K8s API server events, and system logs. It then parses, filters, and routes these logs to destinations such as Elasticsearch, Loki, Splunk, Amazon S3, and cloud-based logging solutions such as Amazon CloudWatch.

Fluentd is highly configurable through a plugin-based architecture. There are 100+ plugins available to support different log formats and backends (`https://www.fluentd.org/plugins`). It uses a structured logging approach, allowing logs to be processed in JSON format for better searchability and indexing. Fluentd supports log enrichment by attaching K8s metadata, such as the namespace or Pod/container name, before sending logs to a storage system. It also supports log filtering, buffering, and compression, which helps in optimizing resource usage in large-scale K8s environments. In K8s logging pipelines, Fluentd is often used alongside Loki (for efficient log storage) or Elasticsearch (for full-text log searching).

Fluent Bit (`https://fluentbit.io/`) is a lightweight version of Fluentd, optimized for low-resource environments and edge computing with much smaller memory footprint requirements. The following table provides a high-level comparison of Fluentd and Fluent Bit, highlighting their key differences and typical use cases:

Features	**Fluentd**	**Fluent Bit**
Resource usage	Significant CPU and memory usage	Lightweight; minimal CPU and memory usage
Architecture	Written in Ruby and C	Written in C
Plugin ecosystem	Large plugin library with more than 1,000 external plugins	Over 100 built-in plugins
Deployment model	Deployed as a K8s DaemonSet or sidecar with multiple plugins	Deployed as a K8s DaemonSet or sidecar with multiple plugins
Scalability	Requires more resources at scale	Very scalable in environments with constrained resources
Use cases	Containers/servers	Embedded Linux/containers/servers

Loki

Loki (`https://github.com/grafana/loki`) is a lightweight, scalable log aggregation system designed for the K8s environment. Unlike traditional log management systems such as Elasticsearch, Loki indexes only metadata (labels) instead of the full log content, making it efficient and cost-effective for large-scale deployments. Loki integrates with Prometheus and Grafana, allowing users to correlate logs with metrics for better troubleshooting and observability.

Loki collects logs from K8s Pods using agents such as Fluentd or Fluent Bit, which run as DaemonSets to forward logs to Loki for storage and querying, as shown in *Figure 12.3*. This enables developers and operators to search logs efficiently using **log query language** (**LogQL**) (`https://grafana.com/docs/loki/latest/query/`), filter logs by namespace, Pod, or container, and visualize them in Grafana.

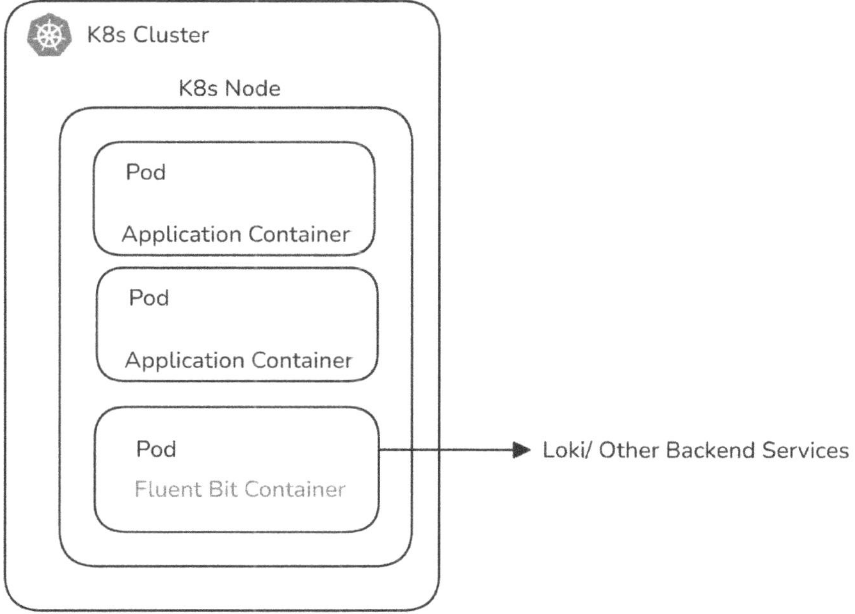

Figure 12.3 – Fluent Bit/Loki deployment in K8s

OpenTelemetry

OTel is a collection of APIs, SDKs, and tools that you can use to instrument, generate, collect, and export telemetry data (metrics, logs, and traces). It is commonly used for collecting and exporting telemetry data to various backend services, such as Prometheus, Jaeger, Datadog, and AWS X-Ray.

In K8s, OTel enables unified observability by collecting metrics, traces, and logs, which can be collected from Pods, containers, or nodes. It supports multiple backends for data storage and works with auto-instrumentation for programming languages such as Go, Java, Python, and Node.js. Refer to the OTel documentation at `https://opentelemetry.io/docs/platforms/kubernetes/operator/automatic/` for a detailed walkthrough of auto-instrumentation.

OTel collectors (`https://opentelemetry.io/docs/collector/`) act as central agents that receive, process, and export telemetry data. These collectors support all three telemetry signals (metrics, traces, and logs), making it a powerful unified observability solution. **OTel exporters** (`https://opentelemetry.io/docs/languages/go/exporters/`) are used to send collected data to backend systems such as Prometheus, Jaeger, and Datadog.

To deploy OTel in K8s, one can start by installing OTel collectors using a Helm chart and configure the collectors to define the receivers, processors, and exporters for telemetry data. Please visit the documentation at `https://opentelemetry.io/docs/demo/kubernetes-deployment/`

for OTel deployment in K8s. Alternatively, you can use the AWS distribution of the OTel project – **AWS Distro for OpenTelemetry** (**ADOT**) (`https://aws-otel.github.io/`) – for a secure, production-ready, open source distribution with predictable performance. To deploy ADOT on Amazon EKS, install the ADOT-managed add-on and configure collectors to forward observability data to your preferred destinations. Refer to the ADOT documentation at `https://aws-otel.github.io/docs/getting-started/adot-eks-add-on` for detailed installation instructions.

Prometheus

Prometheus (`https://prometheus.io/`) is an open source monitoring and alerting tool designed for collecting and querying time-series metrics. It was originally built by **SoundCloud** (`https://soundcloud.com/`) in 2012, to address the challenges of dynamic and distributed systems, and later joined the **Cloud Native Computing Foundation** (**CNCF**) in 2016 as the second hosted project after K8s. Prometheus collects and stores metrics as time-series data, where each data point is recorded with a timestamp and key-value pairs known as labels. It is widely used in K8s environments to provide real-time insights into system performance and resource utilization. In *Chapter 10*, we briefly discussed the Prometheus agent and adapters; let's take a deeper look now.

The following diagram illustrates the high-level architecture of Prometheus and some of the key components in its ecosystem:

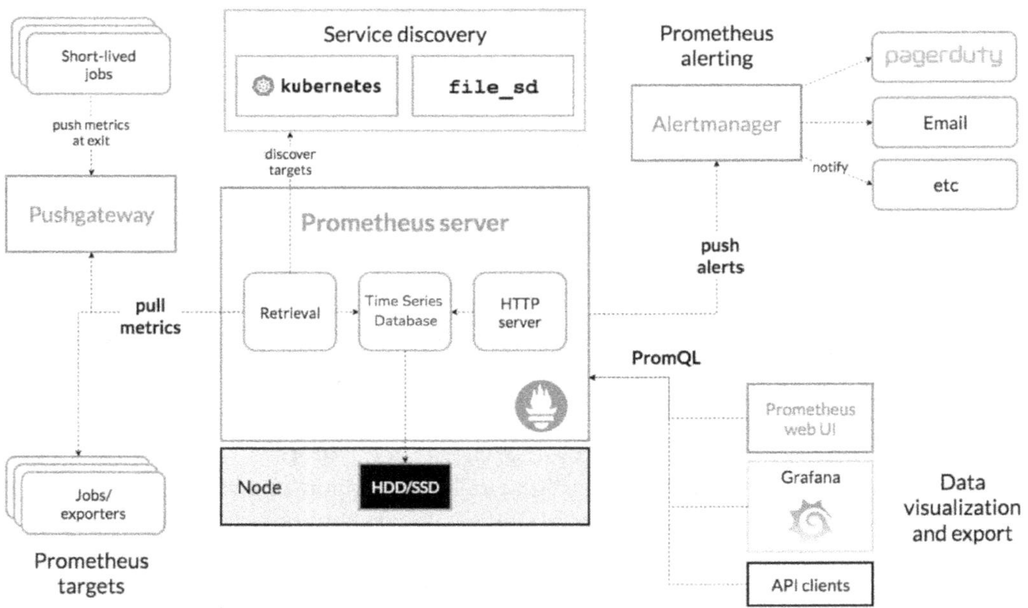

Figure 12.4 – Prometheus architecture

The following are the key components of the Prometheus architecture:

- **Prometheus server** (`https://github.com/prometheus/prometheus`): The Prometheus server is a central component that scrapes metrics from configured endpoints, such as nodes, Pods, or services. It stores these metrics in a time-series database, which can be queried using **Prometheus Query Language** (**PromQL**). Prometheus performs automatic target discovery in K8s to simplify monitoring in dynamic, containerized environments. Instead of manually specifying the endpoints for monitoring, Prometheus uses K8s APIs to dynamically discover targets such as Pods, Endpoints, and Services. This ensures that as workloads scale or shift within the cluster, Prometheus automatically adjusts to continue monitoring them without requiring configuration changes.
- **Prometheus exporters** (`https://prometheus.io/docs/instrumenting/exporters/`): Prometheus exporters are libraries that expose metrics in a format compatible with Prometheus. Exporters are essential for integrating Prometheus with systems or applications that do not natively expose metrics in the Prometheus format. They act as intermediaries, collecting data from the target system and exposing it on an HTTP endpoint for Prometheus to scrape. In K8s, exporters are widely used to monitor various components of the cluster, including nodes, applications, and external systems. For GenAI workloads, exporters are especially critical for monitoring GPUs, inference latency, and resource utilization. **NVIDIA DCGM exporter** exposes GPU metrics such as utilization, memory usage, temperature, and power consumption, critical for monitoring GPU workloads. We deployed this add-on on our EKS cluster setup in *Chapter 10*.
- **Prometheus Alertmanager** (`https://prometheus.io/docs/alerting/latest/overview/`): Prometheus Alertmanager handles alerts generated by Prometheus, sending notifications to different channels such as **Slack** (`https://slack.com/`), email, or **PagerDuty** (`https://www.pagerduty.com/`). It can be configured for GenAI use cases such as resource saturation alerts or higher inference latency. Prometheus Alertmanager supports deduplication, which consolidates duplicate alerts generated by multiple Prometheus instances to prevent notification flooding, and alert grouping, which groups similar alerts into a single notification for better readability.
- **Prometheus Pushgateway** (`https://prometheus.io/docs/instrumenting/pushing/`): This is a component of the Prometheus ecosystem that lets short-lived jobs push their metrics to Prometheus. This is especially useful for ephemeral workloads, such as short GenAI tasks, that cannot be directly scraped by Prometheus. In K8s environments, the Pushgateway acts as an intermediary, allowing batch jobs, cron jobs, and other transient workloads to publish metrics to a persistent endpoint. Prometheus then scrapes this endpoint at regular intervals.

- **PromQL** (`https://prometheus.io/docs/prometheus/latest/querying/basics/`): PromQL is a powerful and flexible query language used to extract and analyze time-series data stored in the Prometheus ecosystem, such as the Prometheus server itself or tools that rely on Prometheus as a backend, such as Grafana. It allows users to perform computations on metrics, filter and aggregate them based on labels, and derive insights through queries.

Now that we have covered the key components of the Prometheus stack, let's discuss how to deploy it within the K8s environment.

Deploying the Prometheus stack

In K8s, it is recommended to deploy the Prometheus server as a **StatefulSet**. A StatefulSet is a K8s controller used to manage stateful applications that require stable identities and persistent storage. Unlike Deployments, which treat Pods as interchangeable, StatefulSets assign each Pod a unique, stable hostname and ensure that storage volumes persist across Pod restarts. This ensures consistency and reliability for workloads that rely on maintaining state across restarts or rescheduling. Deploying the Prometheus server as a StatefulSet ensures that it has persistent storage access for metrics, using a **PersistentVolumeClaim** (**PVC**).

To streamline the K8s setup, the Prometheus community has developed Helm charts to deploy all essential components, which are available at `https://github.com/prometheus-community/helm-charts`. In our setup, we will deploy `kube-prometheus-stack` using the **Terraform Helm provider**. This Helm chart deploys Prometheus and Grafana instances in our EKS cluster, as shown in *Figure 12.5*. After deployment, we will configure Prometheus to scrape metrics from various components within the cluster, such as the NVIDIA DCGM exporter, Qdrant vector database, Ray Serve deployments, and so on. Prometheus automatically discovers the relevant target endpoints and collects metrics at regular intervals. Using the Grafana web console, we can then visualize and query these metrics, build and import interactive dashboards, and define alerting rules.

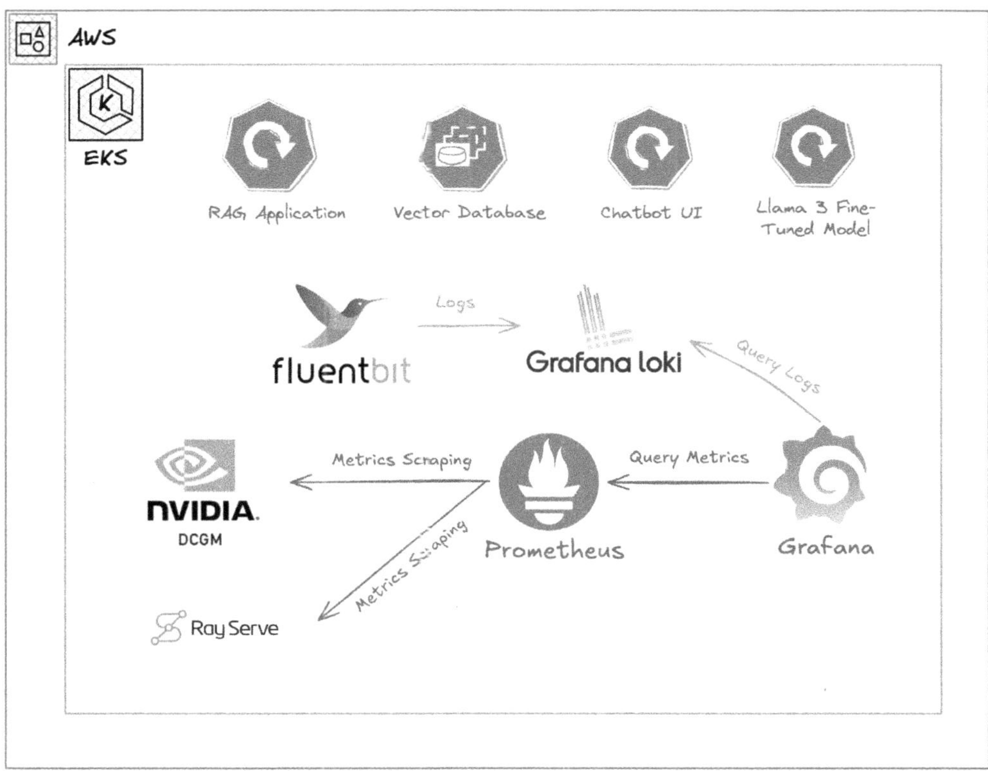

Figure 12.5 – Prometheus and Grafana setup in EKS cluster

To get started, download the `addons.tf` and `kube-prometheus.yaml` files from the GitHub repository at `https://github.com/PacktPublishing/Kubernetes-for-Gen-AI-Models/tree/main/ch12/`. The `kube-prometheus-stack` Helm chart, along with `prometheus-adapter`, will be deployed in the *monitoring* namespace, as shown in the following code snippet:

```
module "eks_blueprints_addons" {
  source = "aws-ia/eks-blueprints-addons/aws"
  ...
  enable_kube_prometheus_stack = true
  kube_prometheus_stack = {
    namespace = "monitoring"
    values = [
      templatefile("${path.module}/kube-prometheus.yaml", {
        storage_class_type = kubernetes_storage_class.default_gp3.id
      })]
```

```
  ...
  helm_releases = {
    "prometheus-adapter" = {
      repository = "https://prometheus-community.github.io/helm-
charts"
      chart      = "prometheus-adapter"
      namespace = module.eks_blueprints_addons.kube_prometheus_stack.
namespace
...
```

The Prometheus setup is customized using the `kube-prometheus.yaml` Helm values file. It does the following things:

- **Prometheus configuration**:
  - Configures the scrape interval and evaluation interval to 30 seconds
  - Specifies a scrape timeout of 10 seconds for targets
  - Sets a data retention of 5 hours and provisions 50Gi of PVC of the `gp3` storage class
- **Alertmanager configuration**:
  - Disables the Alertmanager component in this deployment; you can enable it by setting the `alertmanager.enabled` value to `true`
- **Grafana configuration**:
  - Deploys Grafana and enables the default monitoring dashboards

Execute the following `terraform` commands to deploy the `kube-prometheus-stack` and `prometheus-adapter` Helm charts in the EKS cluster:

```
$ terraform init
$ terraform plan
$ terraform apply -auto-approve
```

Verify the installation using the following `kubectl` command. The output should confirm that the Prometheus StatefulSet, node exporter DaemonSet, Grafana, `kube-state-metrics`, `prometheus-adapter`, and `prometheus-operator` deployments are in a **READY** status:

```
$ kubectl get ds -n monitoring
NAME                                              READY
kube-prometheus-stack-prometheus-node-exporter    6
$ kubectl get deploy -n monitoring
NAME                                        READY
kube-prometheus-stack-grafana               1/1
```

```
kube-prometheus-stack-kube-state-metrics    1/1
kube-prometheus-stack-operator              1/1
prometheus-adapter                          1/1
$ kubectl get sts -n monitoring
NAME                                           READY
prometheus-kube-prometheus-stack-prometheus    1/1
```

In larger environments, it is recommended to assign sufficient CPU and memory resources and use appropriate scrape intervals for different metrics to optimize resource usage. For example, for critical metrics such as CPU or memory utilization, it is recommended to use intervals of 10 to 15 seconds, whereas for less critical metrics, this interval could be in minutes.

In this section, we covered how to deploy the Prometheus stack in an EKS cluster. However, to gain deeper insights into GPU performance (critical for AI/ML workloads), we need to enable metric scraping for GPUs. In the next section, we'll cover integrating NVIDIA's DCGM exporter with Prometheus by configuring Service monitors.

Enabling GPU monitoring

In *Chapter 10*, we deployed the **NVIDIA DCGM Exporter add-on** to gain visibility into GPU utilization metrics. During the setup, we disabled the service monitors that enable Prometheus to scrape the metrics at regular intervals. **Prometheus Service Monitors** (`https://prometheus-operator.dev/docs/developer/getting-started/#using-servicemonitors`) and **Pod Monitors** (`https://prometheus-operator.dev/docs/developer/getting-started/#using-podmonitors`) are **CustomResourceDefinitions** (**CRDs**) that allow the Prometheus Operator to automatically discover and configure monitoring targets within a K8s cluster. By leveraging label selectors on K8s services and Pods, these monitors streamline the process of collecting metrics.

Let's update the Terraform code to enable the scraping of `dcgm-exporter` metrics using Service Monitors. Begin by downloading `aiml-addons.tf` from the GitHub repository at `https://github.com/PacktPublishing/Kubernetes-for-Generative-AI-Solutions/blob/main/ch12/aiml-addons.tf`:

```
resource "helm_release" "dcgm_exporter" {
  name        = "dcgm-exporter"
...
  values = [
      <<-EOT
        serviceMonitor:
          enabled: true
```

Execute the following `terraform` commands to update the NVIDIA DCGM exporter Helm chart in the EKS cluster:

```
$ terraform init
$ terraform plan
$ terraform apply -auto-approve
```

We can verify the scraping status by launching the Prometheus dashboard and checking the scraping target's health. By default, the Prometheus service is internal and not exposed outside of the cluster, so let's use the `kubectl port-forward` mechanism to connect to it from the local machine. Run the following command to initiate a port-forward connection from local port `9090` to Prometheus service port `9090` in the `monitoring` namespace:

```
$ kubectl port-forward svc/kube-prometheus-stack-prometheus -n
monitoring 9090:9090
Forwarding from 127.0.0.1:9090 -> 9090
Forwarding from [::1]:9090 -> 9090
```

Now, launch the `http://localhost:9090/targets?search=dcgm-exporter` URL in your browser to check the health of the DCGM exporter targets. *Figure 12.6* shows that all three `dcgm-exporter` endpoints are in the **UP** state, with each corresponding to a GPU worker node in the cluster:

serviceMonitor/dcgm-exporter/dcgm-exporter/0 3 / 3 up

Endpoint	Labels	Last scrape		State
http://10.0.45.150:9400/metrics	container="exporter" endpoint="metrics" instance="10.0.45.150:9400" job="dcgm-exporter" namespace="dcgm-exporter" pod="dcgm-exporter-5tcwl" service="dcgm-exporter"	3.434s ago	1ms	UP
http://10.0.34.35:9400/metrics	container="exporter" endpoint="metrics" instance="10.0.34.35:9400" job="dcgm-exporter" namespace="dcgm-exporter" pod="dcgm-exporter-vlbn8" service="dcgm-exporter"	9.685s ago	1ms	UP
http://10.0.28.203:9400/metrics	container="exporter" endpoint="metrics" instance="10.0.28.203:9400" job="dcgm-exporter" namespace="dcgm-exporter" pod="dcgm-exporter-jwwjk" service="dcgm-exporter"	12.178s ago	1ms	UP

Figure 12.6 – Prometheus target health status

Next, we can query the `dcgm-exporter` metrics using PromQL. For example, *Figure 12.7* shows the average GPU utilization across multiple GPUs over the past minute grouped by the K8s Pod, where `DCGM_FI_DEV_GPU_UTIL` is the metric exposed by `dcgm-exporter`.

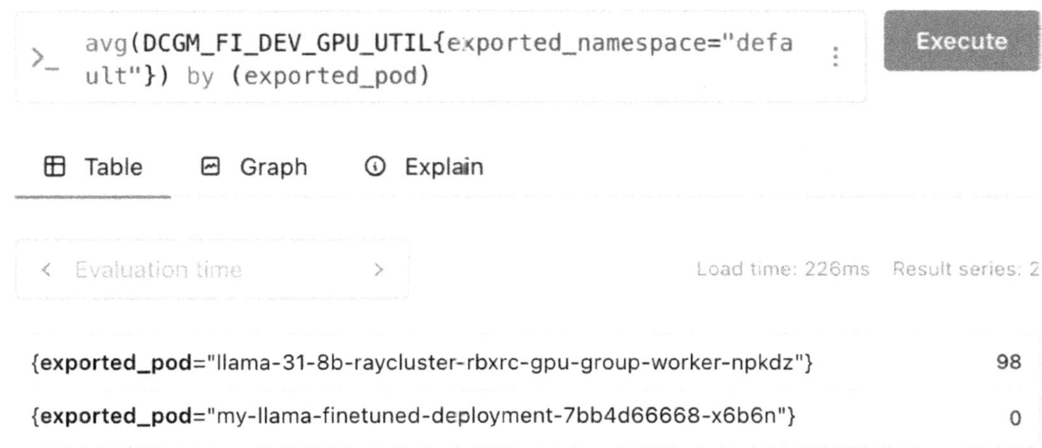

Figure 12.7 – Querying GPU metrics using PromQL

Similarly, we will create additional Service Monitors to collect metrics from both the Ray Serve cluster deployed in *Chapter 11* and various e-commerce chatbot application components. You can download the corresponding K8s manifest files from the GitHub repository at `https://github.com/PacktPublishing/Kubernetes-for-Generative-AI-Solutions/tree/main/ch12/monitoring` and apply each file using the `kubectl apply -f` command to deploy them to the EKS cluster:

```
$ kubectl apply -f <replace with service monitor file name>
```

After applying the files, navigate to the Prometheus dashboard and verify the status of the newly discovered scraping targets. You will notice both `ray-workers` and `ray-head` Pod targets in the dashboard, as shown in *Figure 12.8*.

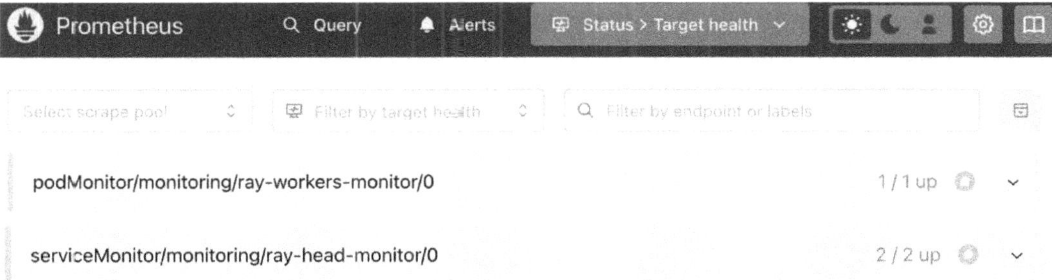

Figure 12.8 – Prometheus target health status

In this section, we explored various tools to monitor GenAI applications in K8s, such as Fluentd, Fluent Bit, Loki, OTel, and Prometheus. We also deployed `kube-prometheus-stack` in the EKS cluster and set up the Service/Pod monitors to collect metrics from `dcgm-exporter` and other application components in our EKS cluster. In the next section, we will dive into visualization tools such as Grafana to view these metrics.

Visualization and debugging

In this section, we will explore key practices for enhancing the observability of GenAI applications deployed on K8s. We will begin by demonstrating how Grafana can be used to visualize essential metrics such as GPU utilization, system performance, and the status of GenAI applications, to provide real-time operational insights. Additionally, we will dive into debugging strategies for Gen AI workloads by examining tools such as **Langfuse** (`https://github.com/langfuse/langfuse`), an open source LLM engineering platform designed to aid in debugging and the analysis of LLM applications.

Grafana

Grafana (`https://grafana.com/`) is an open source visualization and analytics platform widely used for monitoring K8s environments. It provides a centralized interface for querying, visualizing, and alerting on metrics collected from various data sources, such as Prometheus, Amazon CloudWatch, and Azure Monitor.

Grafana provides prebuilt and customizable dashboards to monitor K8s components such as API servers, etcd databases, nodes, Pods, and namespaces. These dashboards help visualize metrics such as CPU and memory utilization, network activity, and application-specific metrics. Grafana allows users to configure alerts with notifications sent to channels such as Slack, email, PagerDuty, or **Microsoft Teams**. Alerts are typically based on threshold conditions, though you can also implement anomaly detection through custom queries or external integrations.

Grafana provides the ability to define roles and permissions using **role-based access control** (**RBAC**), allowing fine-grained control over who can view or edit dashboards and alerts. Grafana supports a wide range of community-contributed plugins (`https://grafana.com/grafana/plugins/`), custom visualization panels (`https://grafana.com/grafana/plugins/panel-plugins/`), and dashboards (`https://grafana.com/grafana/dashboards/`), enabling users to extend its functionality and adapt it to specific use cases.

Grafana best practices

The following lists some Grafana best practices:

- Ensure Grafana dashboards and settings persist across Pod restarts by using a **Persistent Volume** (**PV**) and a PVC. This helps maintain the state even when Grafana Pods are rescheduled.
- Automate dashboard provisioning using ConfigMaps or **infrastructure as code** (**IaC**) tools, such as Terraform, to maintain consistent observability setups across environments.

- Enable robust authentication mechanisms (`https://grafana.com/docs/grafana/latest/setup-grafana/configure-security/configure-authentication/`) such as OAuth, SAML, and LDAP, to control user access. Use RBAC to manage user permissions effectively.
- When exposing the Grafana dashboard outside the cluster, use an Ingress controller with TLS termination to secure network communications.
- Leverage Grafana's rich plugin ecosystem to integrate with external data sources and specialized visualizations.
- Enhance observability by combining metrics, logs, and traces. Integrate Grafana with Loki for centralized K8s logging alongside metrics visualization.
- Monitor Grafana's resource usage and performance within the K8s cluster. This includes setting up alerts for abnormal behavior, which helps maintain optimal performance and availability.
- Use managed Grafana offerings such as **Amazon Managed Grafana** (`https://aws.amazon.com/grafana/`), **Grafana Cloud** (`https://grafana.com/products/cloud/`), and **Azure Managed Grafana** (`https://azure.microsoft.com/en-us/products/managed-grafana`) to offload operational tasks such as scaling, patching, and security management. This enables us to focus on creating dashboards and analyzing data. These services also provide seamless cloud-native integrations, auto-scaling capabilities, and cost efficiencies.

Setting up Grafana dashboards

In our setup, we deployed Grafana as part of the `kube-prometheus-stack` installation earlier in this chapter. Alternatively, Grafana Helm charts can be leveraged to deploy as a standalone option in K8s; refer to `https://grafana.com/docs/grafana/latest/setup-grafana/installation/helm/` for step-by-step instructions. By default, the Grafana service is accessible within the cluster unless it is exposed outside via the K8s `LoadBalancer` service type or an Ingress resource. So, let's use the `kubectl port-forward` mechanism to connect to the Grafana console:

```
$ kubectl port-forward svc/kube-prometheus-stack-grafana -n monitoring
8080:80
Forwarding from 127.0.0.1:8080 -> 80
Forwarding from [::1]:8080 -> 80
```

Now, open `http://localhost:8080/` in your browser to access the Grafana console. When prompted for credentials, note that a default admin user is automatically created during the Helm chart installation. You can retrieve the credentials from the K8s secret named `kube-prometheus-stack-grafana` in the `monitoring` namespace by running the following command:

```
$ kubectl get secret kube-prometheus-stack-grafana -n monitoring
-o go-template='{{printf "Username: %s\nPassword: %s\n" (index
.data "admin-user" | base64decode) (index .data "admin-password" |
base64decode)}}'
```

Once logged in to the Grafana console, navigate to **Connections** | **Data sources** in the left side menu bar to view and manage the connected data sources. You will notice the local Prometheus server is already added to the data sources, as shown in *Figure 12.9*.

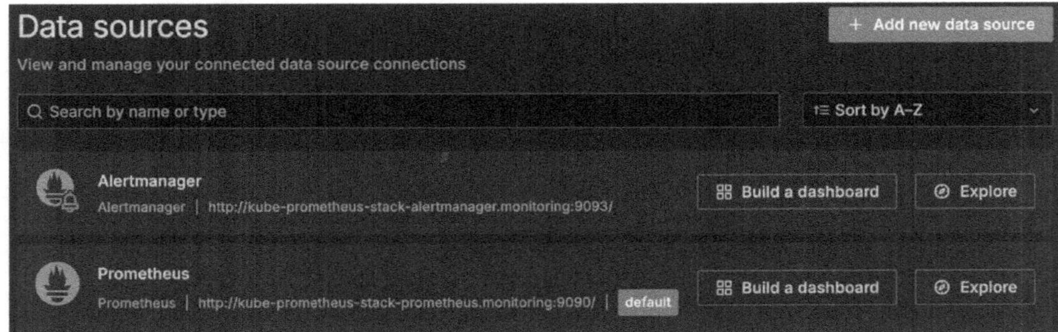

Figure 12.9 – Grafana connected data sources

As Grafana has access to Prometheus metrics, let's start exploring the Grafana dashboards. Navigate to **Dashboards** in the left side menu bar to view and manage the Grafana dashboards. You will notice a list of pre-existing dashboards that were already created by our `kube-prometheus-stack` installation, as shown in *Figure 12.10*.

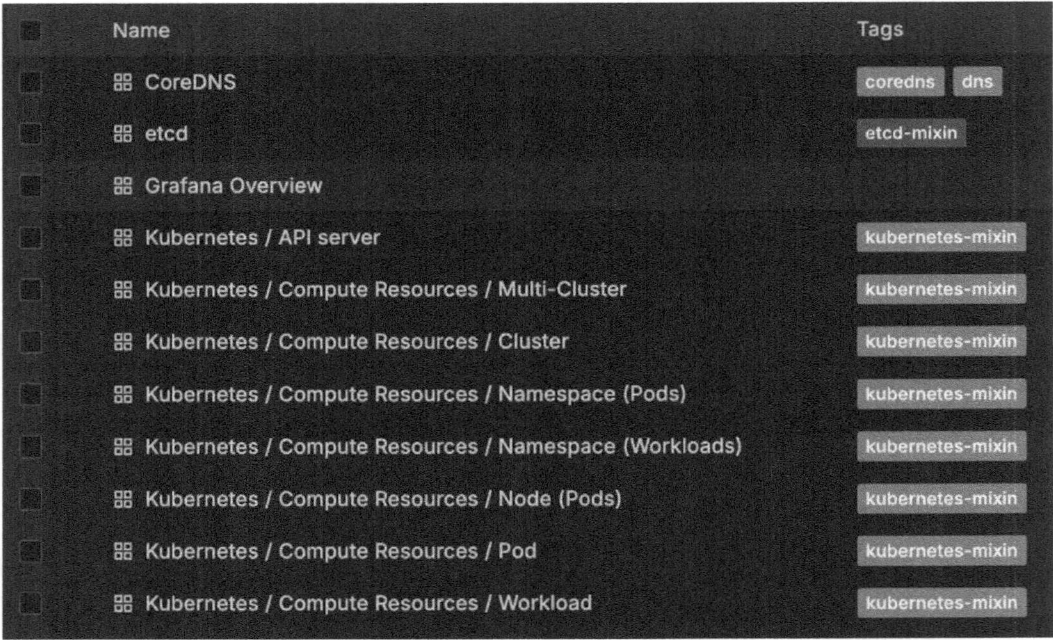

Figure 12.10 – Grafana dashboards list

These Grafana dashboards provide preconfigured monitoring views tailored for various K8s components, such as **CoreDNS**, **API server**, **Namespace**, **Pod**, **Workload**, **Node**, **Scheduler**, **Controller Manager**, and **kubelet**. You can select and explore these dashboards to gain insights into the performance, resource usage, and health of the K8s environments. For example, select the **Kubernetes | Compute Resources | Cluster** dashboard to view an overview of resource utilization, including CPU, memory, and storage metrics across the entire K8s cluster, helping you monitor and optimize cluster performance, as shown in *Figure 12.11*.

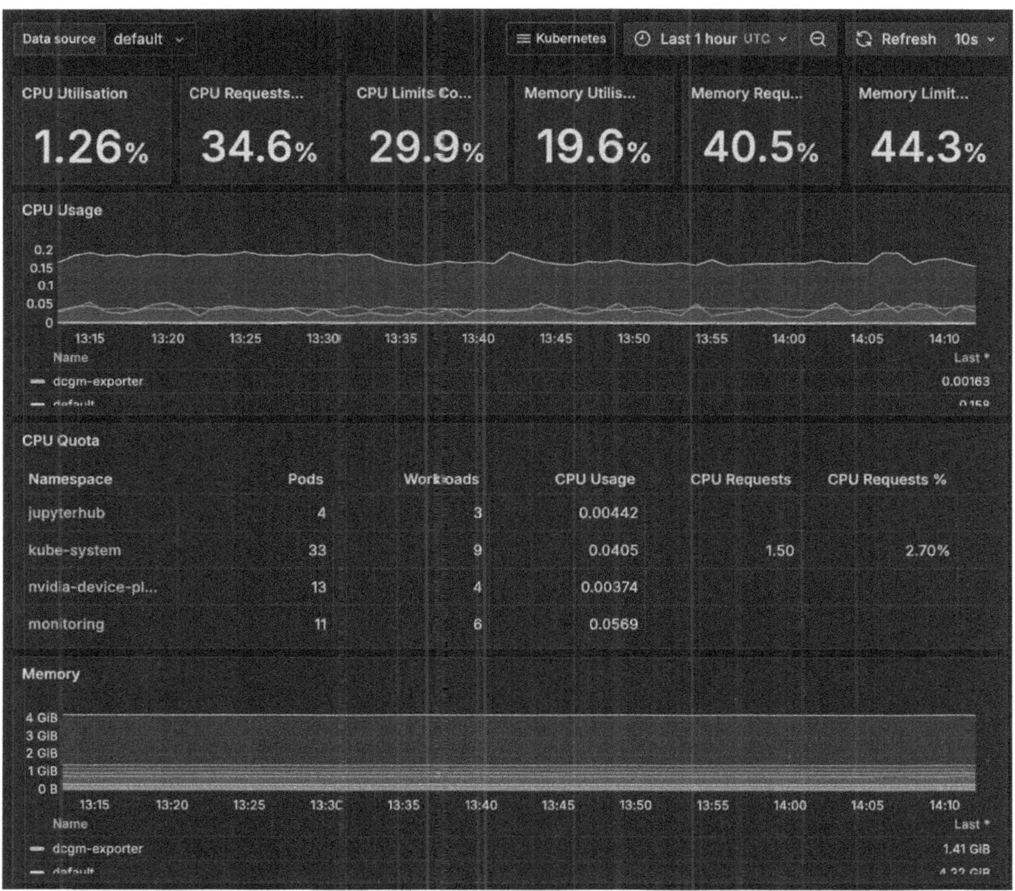

Figure 12.11 – Kubernetes Compute Resources dashboard

In this dashboard, we can see the CPU, memory quota, and usage metrics aggregated by each K8s namespace at the cluster level.

While the default dashboards offer comprehensive insights into core K8s components, you may also need visibility into specialized resources, depending on your workload. Now, let's take a look at how to visualize GPU metrics using the NVIDIA DCGM exporter dashboard.

NVIDIA DCGM dashboard

Earlier in this chapter, we enabled metrics collection from the NVIDIA DCGM exporter add-on using Prometheus Service Monitor resources. Now, we will visualize these metrics using Grafana dashboards. NVIDIA published a Grafana dashboard at `https://grafana.com/grafana/dashboards/12239-nvidia-dcgm-exporter-dashboard/` to monitor GPU utilization metrics.

You can import this dashboard to your Grafana instance using the instructions at `https://grafana.com/docs/grafana/latest/dashboards/build-dashboards/import-dashboards/`. Once the import is successful, you will be able to visualize the GPU metrics, as shown in *Figure 12.12*.

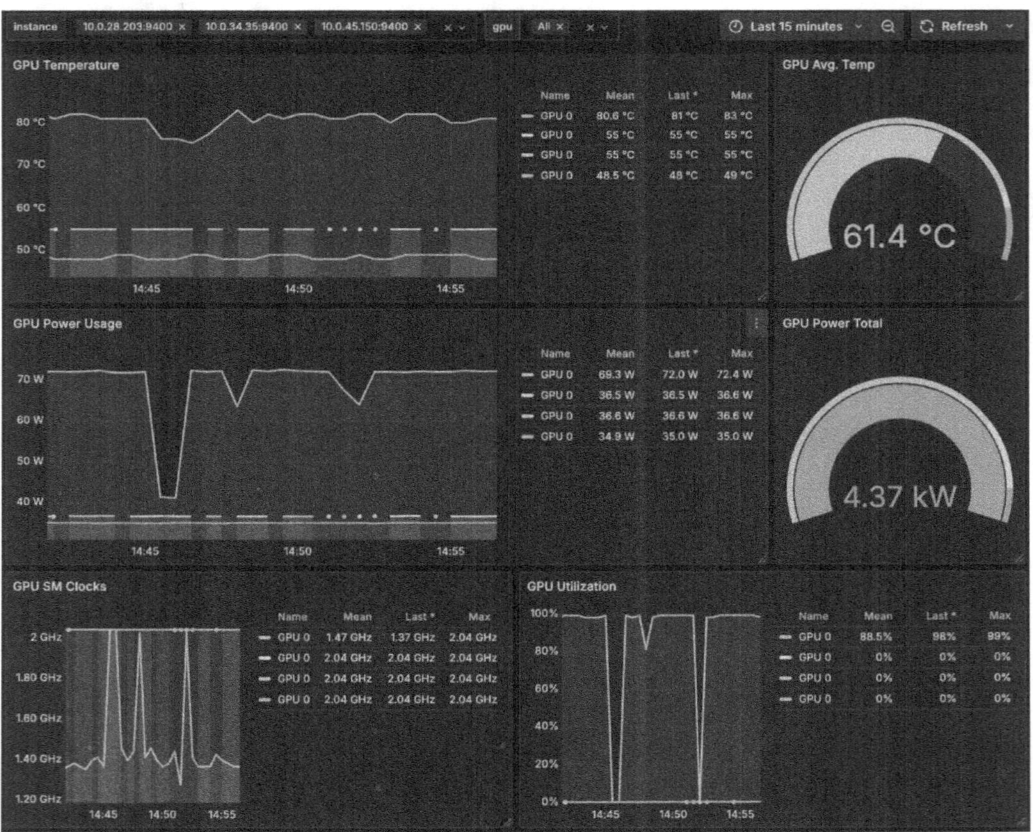

Figure 12.12 – DCGM exporter Grafana dashboard

This dashboard provides real-time visibility into key GPU performance metrics such as temperature, power usage, clock speeds, and utilization. With this information, you can quickly identify performance bottlenecks, detect potential issues, and optimize resource usage.

In addition to dashboards, we can also define Prometheus alerting rules to monitor GPU health and performance. For example, we can create a **Prometheus rule** (`https://prometheus.io/docs/prometheus/latest/configuration/alerting_rules/`) to trigger alerts based on various conditions such as high and low GPU utilization, elevated GPU temperature, or critical GPU errors. To create these rules, download `gpu-rules.yaml` from our GitHub repository at `https://github.com/PacktPublishing/Kubernetes-for-Generative-AI-Solutions/blob/main/ch12/monitoring/gpu-rules.yaml` and run the following command to configure them in our setup:

```
$ kubectl apply -f gpu-rules.yaml
```

Once deployed, we can visualize the rules in the Prometheus or Grafana console. In the Grafana console, navigate to **Alerting** | **Alert rules** in the left side menu bar to view the status of the alert rules, as shown in *Figure 12.13*.

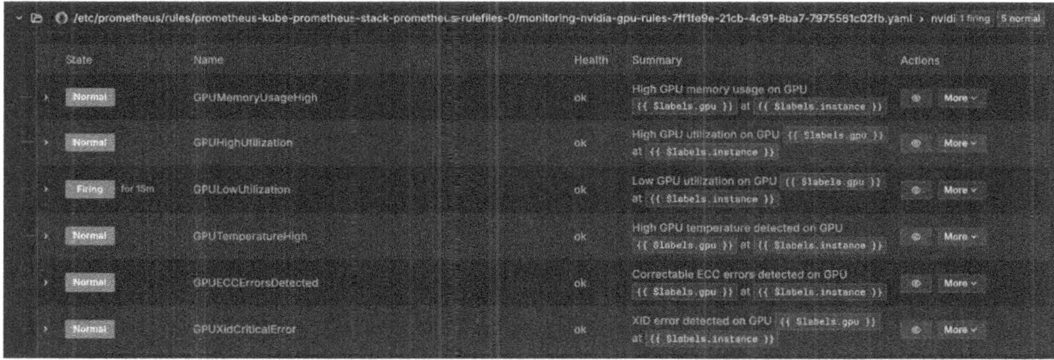

Figure 12.13 – NVIDIA GPU alert rules in the Grafana console

As shown in *Figure 12.13*, one of the GPU alerting rules is in a **Firing** state due to low GPU utilization on one of our worker nodes. To investigate further, we can expand the alert rule to view detailed information such as the worker node, GPU identifier, and the associated K8s Pod, as illustrated in *Figure 12.14*.

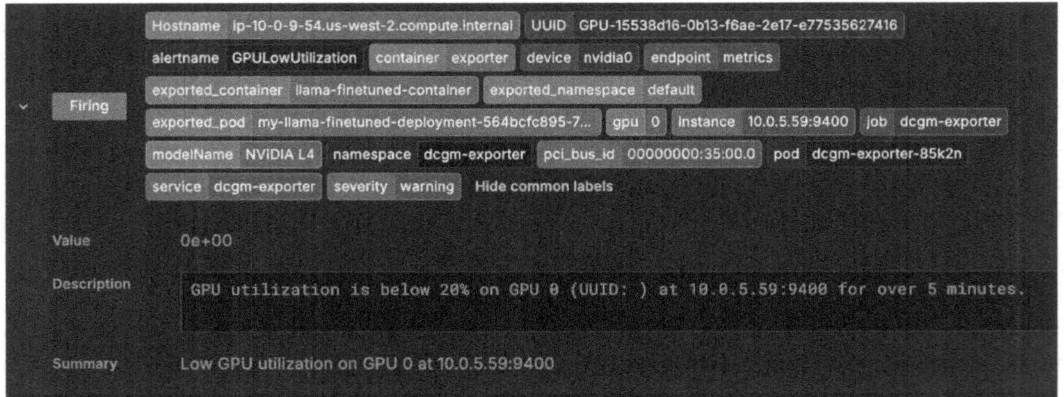

Figure 12.14 – GPU alert rule details in the Grafana console

While the DCGM dashboard provides deep visibility into GPU performance, it's also important to monitor the higher-level services that rely on these resources, especially in GenAI workloads. One such example is Ray Serve, which plays a key role in serving models such as Llama 3 in our deployment. Let's now set up a dedicated Grafana dashboard to monitor the performance and resource usage of Ray Serve components.

Ray Serve dashboard

In *Chapter 11*, we deployed a Ray cluster in our EKS cluster and used the Ray Serve framework to expose the Llama 3 model. Earlier in this chapter, we also created Prometheus Service and Pod Monitor resources to gather metrics from both the Ray cluster and Ray Serve deployments. Now, we will create a **Ray monitoring dashboard** to visualize key metrics such as request throughput, latency, ongoing HTTP connections, and resource utilization. To do this, download the Grafana dashboard JSON file (`ray-serve-dashboard.json`) from our GitHub repository at `https://github.com/PacktPublishing/Kubernetes-for-Generative-AI-Solutions/tree/main/ch12/dashboards`.

Open the Grafana console, navigate to the **Dashboards** page, and choose the **New** | **Import** option. Upload the `ray-serve-dashboard.json` file from your local filesystem and click the **Import** button. Once imported, select **Ray Serve Dashboard** from the dashboards list to view real-time information about your Ray Serve deployments, helping you identify bottlenecks and optimize performance, as shown in *Figure 12.15*.

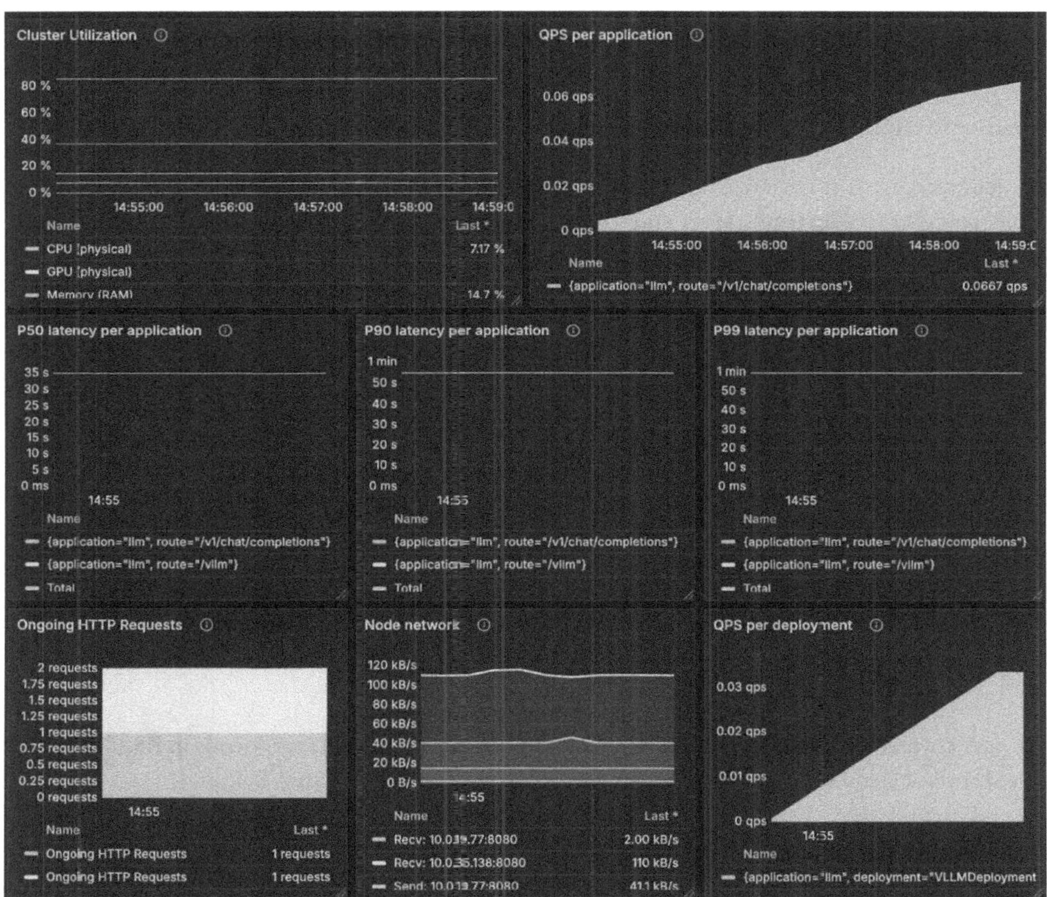

Figure 12.15 – Ray Serve Grafana dashboard

Just like GPU alerting rules in the previous section, we can also define Prometheus alerting rules to monitor the health and performance of Ray Serve deployments. For example, we can configure a Prometheus rule to trigger alerts based on conditions such as high error rates, increased latency, Ray worker node failures, response latency spikes, or low throughput. To create these rules, download the `ray-serve-rules.yaml` file from our GitHub repository at `https://github.com/PacktPublishing/Kubernetes-for-Generative-AI-Solutions/blob/main/ch12/monitoring/ray-serve-rules.yaml` and run the following command to configure them in our setup:

```
$ kubectl apply -f ray-serve-rules.yaml
```

Once deployed, we can visualize the rules in the Prometheus or Grafana console. In the Grafana console, navigate to **Alerting** | **Alert rules** in the left side menu bar to view the status of the alert rules, as shown in *Figure 12.16*.

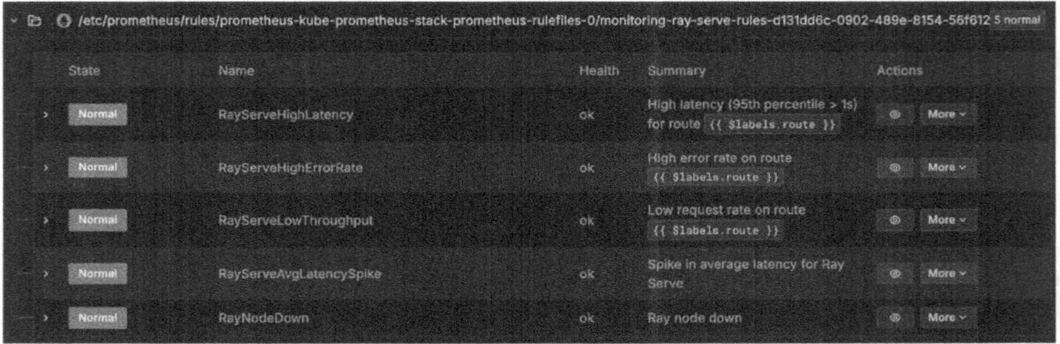

Figure 12.16 – Ray Serve alert rules in Grafana

As we have covered the different observability tools for monitoring GenAI workloads in K8s, let's now explore how to extend these concepts for GenAI frameworks, such as LangChain.

LangChain observability

LangChain (`https://github.com/langchain-ai/langchain`) is a framework for building applications with LLMs, which we covered in *Chapter 4*. It integrates with various tools to enable observability and debugging.

LangChain provides built-in capabilities to log and trace the execution of chains, agents, and tools. These features allow developers and operators to understand how prompts, responses, and workflows behave during execution. The **verbose mode** in LangChain enables detailed logs of intermediate steps, such as input prompts, output responses, and tool invocations, by setting `verbose=True` in chains, agents, or tools.

LangChain can integrate with **LangChainTracer** to collect execution data, including steps, timing information, errors, and retries. The tracer can be used via **LangSmith** (`https://www.langchain.com/langsmith`) or deployed as a self-hosted server in K8s.

The following code snippet defines a custom debugging and observability callback handler for LangChain, which helps track the execution flow of a chain. It logs when a chain starts, when it completes, and the time taken for execution, and handles errors gracefully:

```
import time
from langchain.callbacks.base import BaseCallbackHandler
from langchain.chains import LLMChain
from langchain_openai import OpenAI
from langchain.prompts import PromptTemplate
class DebugCallbackHandler(BaseCallbackHandler):
    def __init__(self):
        self.start_time = None

    def on_chain_start(self, inputs, **kwargs):
        """Triggered when the chain starts execution."""
        self.start_time = time.time()
        print("\n[DEBUG] Chain started...")
        print(f" Inputs: {inputs}")

    def on_chain_end(self, outputs, **kwargs):
        """Triggered when the chain successfully completes
execution."""
        elapsed_time = time.time() - self.start_time
        print(f"\n[DEBUG] Chain finished in {elapsed_time:.2f}
seconds")
        print(f"Outputs: {outputs}")

    def on_chain_error(self, error, **kwargs):
        print("\n [ERROR] Chain encountered an error!")
        print(f"  Error Message: {error}")
debug_handler = DebugCallbackHandler()
```

The `DebugCallbackHandler` class extends `BaseCallbackHandler`, making it compatible with LangChain's callback system. The constructor initializes a `self.start_time` variable, which is used to track the execution duration.

The `on_chain_error` method is called when an error occurs during chain execution. It prints an error message along with details about the encountered exception.

This callback handler is useful for debugging and performance monitoring in LangChain applications by providing real-time logs for execution tracking, timing analysis, and error handling.

While LangChain's built-in logging and tracing capabilities provide a solid foundation for understanding the internal workings of LLM chains and agents, there are scenarios where more advanced observability tools are needed, especially for production-grade applications. This is where platforms such as LangFuse come into play, offering richer insights, distributed tracing, and powerful dashboards tailored for LLM workflows. Let's take a closer look at how LangFuse enhances observability for GenAI applications in the next section.

LangFuse

LangFuse (`https://langfuse.com/`) is an open source observability and monitoring platform tailored for LLM applications. It provides deep insights into the execution of AI workflows by tracking user interactions, prompts, responses, and application performance. LangFuse supports key observability features such as logging, tracing, metrics collection, and visualization, making it invaluable for debugging and optimizing LLM-based applications.

LangFuse benefits from K8s-native capabilities such as scalability, auto-healing, and seamless integration with managed services. LangFuse collects and visualizes critical metrics and traces related to prompts, model latency, response accuracy, and system health. It supports distributed tracing, allowing developers to trace user interactions across multiple components, such as API gateways, vector databases, and LLM endpoints, to diagnose performance bottlenecks or errors.

Key features of LangFuse include the following:

- It logs detailed information about requests, including the input prompt, LLM-generated responses, and associated metadata such as token usage and model-specific parameters
- It captures the end-to-end lifecycle of interactions, enabling you to monitor every step in workflows, from user input to database queries and LLM outputs
- It provides interactive dashboards to visualize system performance, latency trends, error rates, and other **key performance indicators** (**KPIs**)
- It links errors or delays in AI pipelines to specific users, prompts, or workflows for faster debugging and resolution
- It easily integrates with Prometheus, Grafana, OTel, and other K8s monitoring tools to enhance existing observability stacks

For K8s deployments, LangFuse offers flexibility in deployment configurations, enabling you to run the observability stack alongside your AI workloads. It is compatible with Helm charts, ensuring smooth deployment and configuration in cloud-native environments. Detailed deployment instructions and configurations for K8s and EKS are available in the LangFuse documentation at `https://langfuse.com/self-hosting/kubernetes-helm`.

In this section, we explored various visualization and debugging tools for monitoring GenAI applications in K8s, including Grafana, LangChain, and LangFuse. We deployed Grafana in our EKS cluster and imported prebuilt dashboards to view the key performance metrics of various components, such as the API server, Ray Serve deployments, and so on. Additionally, LangChain and LangFuse provide advanced debugging and observability features for GenAI workloads, enabling you to trace LLM calls, monitor model outputs, and optimize prompt configurations.

Summary

In this chapter, we covered key observability concepts for monitoring GenAI applications in K8s. We understood why monitoring is critical for optimizing GenAI workloads, examining both system-level metrics and application-specific signals. We explored a comprehensive monitoring framework using tools such as Prometheus for metrics collection, Grafana for visualization, and LangFuse and LangChain for debugging.

In K8s, various tools cater to different facets of the observability framework. Prometheus excels at collecting and querying time-series metrics, offering built-in alerting capabilities and seamless integration with K8s. Fluentd and Fluent Bit serve as a unified logging layer, collecting data from diverse sources and routing it to multiple destinations. OpenTelemetry provides a vendor-neutral set of APIs and libraries for generating and processing telemetry data, spanning metrics, logs, and traces.

Grafana provides an intuitive interface to view and analyze metrics, logs, and traces, making it easy to detect anomalies and investigate performance bottlenecks. LangFuse specializes in detailed logging and observability of LLM-based requests, capturing prompts, responses, and metadata to facilitate faster debugging. LangChain offers a framework for orchestrating and experimenting with LLM workflows, helping us better understand and refine prompt engineering, chaining logic, and model responses.

In the next chapter, we will explore how to set up high availability and disaster recovery for GenAI applications on K8s.

13
High Availability and Disaster Recovery for GenAI Applications

In this chapter, we explore the concepts of **high availability** (**HA**) and **disaster recovery** (**DR**) tailored for GenAI applications deployed on **Kubernetes** (**K8s**) clusters. Given the dynamic and resource-intensive nature of GenAI applications, achieving seamless scalability and robust resiliency is essential for high-quality production deployments. We will discuss various architectural patterns and configurations that empower GenAI workloads to automatically scale based on usage demand while ensuring continuous service, even in the event of a disaster such as a regional outage.

In this chapter, we're going to cover the following main topics:

- Designing for HA and DR
- Resiliency in K8s
- DR strategies in K8s

Designing for HA and DR

HA (`https://docs.aws.amazon.com/whitepapers/latest/disaster-recovery-workloads-on-aws/high-availability-is-not-disaster-recovery.html`) ensures that a system remains operational with minimal downtime by eliminating single points of failure. It relies on *redundancy* across nodes, regions, or clusters and aims to maintain continuous service. HA is measured by uptime percentage, failover time, and system redundancy. For example, a system with 99.99% uptime allows only ~53 minutes of downtime per year. In the context of GenAI, where foundational models often drive critical business operations such as customer support, real-time text and image analysis, and so on, downtime can be expensive. HA ensures the following:

- Inference endpoints remain consistently responsive, meeting the business availability requirements
- Training jobs can handle node or service failures without crashing mid-way

DR (`https://docs.aws.amazon.com/whitepapers/latest/disaster-recovery-workloads-on-aws/disaster-recovery-options-in-the-cloud.html`) is focused on restoring services after catastrophic failures such as hardware malfunctions, cyberattacks, or natural disasters. It ensures that data is backed up and can be restored quickly to resume operations. DR strategies involve regular data backups, redundancy, and automated recovery workflows. Unlike HA, which prevents downtime, DR accepts some level of downtime and data loss but ensures that systems can be restored efficiently.

Three key metrics that define HA and DR are the **recovery point objective** (**RPO**), **recovery time objective** (**RTO**), and **maximum tolerable downtime** (**MTD**):

- RPO represents the maximum allowable data loss before recovery. A system with an RPO of 0 requires real-time data replication to ensure no data is lost, whereas an RPO of several hours may use periodic backups instead. The lower the RPO, the more advanced the backup mechanisms need to be.
- RTO determines the acceptable downtime before services must be restored. A low RTO of seconds or minutes requires active-active failover with redundant systems always on standby, while a higher RTO allows for manual intervention and restoration from backups.
- MTD is the longest period a service can be unavailable before causing unacceptable consequences to an organization. It defines the threshold for downtime beyond which service can suffer operational or financial challenges. MTD is a key component of **business continuity planning** (**BCP**) and DR strategies.

  Figure 13.1 illustrates these key metrics – RTO, RPO, and MTD in the context of data loss and system downtime following a failure event.

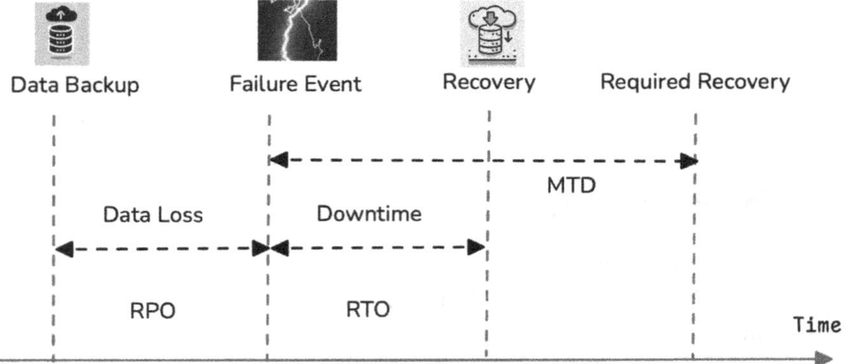

Figure 13.1 – Different recovery objectives

A highly available application should be able to withstand failures and maintain continuous operation despite partial network outages or hardware failures. It requires that the application has no single point of failure and workloads are distributed across multiple isolated failure domains, such as nodes, **Availability Zones** (**AZs**), and clusters.

Redundancy at various levels helps to handle potential failures. Key tenets of K8s that help to achieve HA include the following:

- **Redundancy**: Avoid single points of failure in both application components and infrastructure. Deploying multiple replicas of the applications using K8s Deployment or ReplicaSet objects can ensure redundancy in case of failures.
- **Autoscaling**: K8s **Horizontal Pod Autoscaling** (**HPA**) can help adjust the number of Pod replicas based on demand, ensuring that the application can handle varying loads efficiently. Additionally, Cluster Autoscaler and Karpenter can help manage the scaling of worker nodes in response to the scheduling needs of Pods.
- **Self-healing**: Deploying applications using K8s Deployment allows K8s to automatically replace failed Pods, maintaining the desired state of the application.
- **Safer upgrades and rollbacks**: By adopting application deployment strategies such as blue/green and canary deployments, you can ensure that new versions of applications are introduced safely. These strategies enable the testing of new versions with a subset of users before a full rollout, reducing the risk of widespread issues.
- **Chaos engineering**: Periodically simulate failures in your applications to validate the HA setup. Review and improve runbooks and operational guidelines based on simulated incidents.
- **Observability**: Collect the logs, metrics, and traces for real-time visibility into the infrastructure and the application's health and performance. Configure alerts to detect early signs of failures such as latency, error rate, and so on.

In this section, we discussed the importance of HA and DR for GenAI applications, which are uniquely sensitive to downtime and performance degradation. We also highlighted the key metrics that define HA and DR, such as RTO, RPO, and MTD, alongside the key K8s tenets that help achieve HA.

In the next section, we will delve deeper into these concepts by focusing on resiliency in K8s.

Resiliency in K8s

GenAI applications are resource-intensive, requiring fault tolerance and scalability to handle model training, large-scale inference, and real-time AI workloads. GenAI models usually require GPUs for accelerated inference and training, making GPU dependency and availability a critical factor in deployment. These workloads often experience unpredictable resource spikes, leading to scalability challenges that require dynamic provisioning. Additionally, data availability and consistency are essential, as large AI models rely on distributed storage and caching to maintain performance across multiple nodes. Long-running processes further complicate resilience, as model training can take hours or even days.

K8s provides a robust foundation for managing GenAI workloads, but ensuring resiliency requires specialized configurations and best practices at every layer of K8s, as shown in *Figure 13.2*.

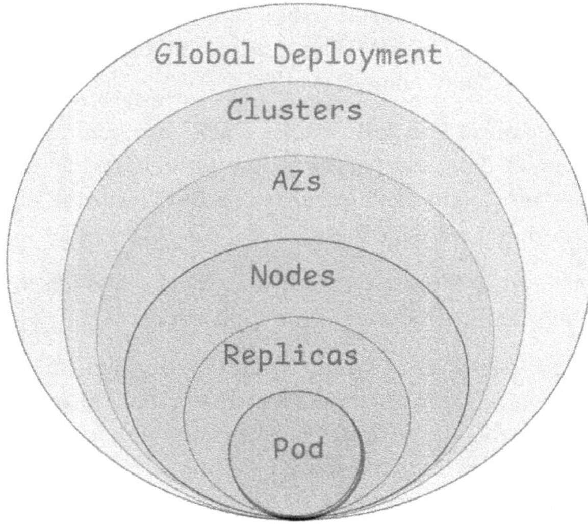

Figure 13.2 – K8s resiliency across different layers

These layers help ensure that applications remain highly available and can recover from failures. Let's cover each layer, starting from the innermost layer at the Pod level:

- **Pod level**: A Pod is the smallest deployable unit in K8s, consisting of one or more containers that share storage and networking. Pods are ephemeral, meaning that if one fails, K8s can restart or reschedule it elsewhere. To enhance resilience at this level, K8s provides liveness and readiness probes, ensuring that unhealthy Pods are restarted automatically and ready to serve the traffic respectively.

  Additionally, using resource requests and limits helps prevent resource exhaustion that could lead to Pod failures, and configuring graceful shutdown intervals can allow Pods to gracefully close the inflight requests. The following code snippet shows an example K8s manifest with *liveness probes*, *readiness probes*, and *resource requests* configured on our Llama inference endpoint. The liveness probe is configured to check the `/healthz` endpoint every 10 seconds on port `80`; similarly, the readiness probe is configured to check the `/readyz` endpoint:

  ```
  apiVersion: apps/v1
  kind: Deployment
  metadata:
    name: my-llama32-deployment
  ...
    terminationGracePeriodSeconds: 60
  ```

```
    containers:
    - name: my-llama32-container
  ...
      resources:
        requests:
          nvidia.com/gpu: 1
        limits:
          nvidia.com/gpu: 1
      livenessProbe:
        httpGet:
          path: /healthz
          port: 80
        initialDelaySeconds: 60
        periodSeconds: 10
      readinessProbe:
        httpGet:
          path: /readyz
          port: 80
        initialDelaySeconds: 60
        periodSeconds: 10
```

- **Replica level**: A replica is an identical copy of a Pod managed by a K8s controller, such as a **ReplicaSet** or **Deployment**, as covered in previous chapters. Having multiple replicas ensures that even if one Pod fails, other instances remain available to handle requests. It is especially important for AI model servers, such as **TensorFlow Serving** or **Triton Inference Server**, to ensure that inference requests can meet the SLA as the demand increases. Deployments should define a suitable number of replicas based on workload needs and traffic demands. HPA can dynamically adjust the number of replicas based on CPU, memory, and GPU usage, providing flexibility during high-load scenarios.

  For inference workloads, it is a good idea to have a minimum number of GenAI inference/model-serving Pods remain available during updates or disruptions by using **PodDisruptionBudget** (`https://kubernetes.io/docs/tasks/run-application/configure-pdb/`), as shown in the following K8s manifest:

```
  apiVersion: policy/v1
  kind: PodDisruptionBudget
  metadata:
    name: my-llama32-pdb
  spec:
    minAvailable: 2
    selector:
      matchLabels:
        app.kubernetes.io/name: my-llama32
```

- **Node level**: A node is a physical or virtual machine that runs Pods in a K8s cluster. Workloads should be distributed across multiple nodes to prevent a single machine failure from impacting application availability. If a node becomes unhealthy or unresponsive, K8s can automatically evict the affected Pods and reschedule them onto healthy nodes. Implementing K8s compute autoscaling solutions, such as Cluster Autoscaler and Karpenter, ensures that if additional capacity is needed, new nodes are provisioned, while underutilized nodes can be decommissioned to optimize resource usage.

  Additionally, spreading replicas across multiple nodes using topology spread scheduling constraints prevents a single-node failure from taking down all instances of an application. The following is an example of `topologySpreadConstraints` to spread Pod replicas across multiple nodes:

```
...
topologySpreadConstraints:
  - labelSelector:
      matchLabels:
        app.kubernetes.io/name: my-llama32
    maxSkew: 1
    topologyKey: kubernetes.io/hostname
    whenUnsatisfiable: ScheduleAnyway
```

  At the node level, K8s ensures basic resilience through health checks and eviction policies. However, for production-grade GenAI workloads, you often need additional safeguards and automatic recovery. You can leverage the K8s `node-problem-detector` (`https://github.com/kubernetes/node-problem-detector`) add-on, which makes various node problems visible to the upstream layers in the cluster management stack. It runs as a **DaemonSet** Pod on every worker node to scan for failures and reports them to *apiserver*.

  Amazon EKS introduced a **Node monitoring agent** (`https://docs.aws.amazon.com/eks/latest/userguide/node-health.html`) add-on that automatically reads node logs to detect certain health issues and adds *NodeCondition* accordingly. This can be combined with **Node auto repair** (`https://docs.aws.amazon.com/eks/latest/userguide/node-health.html#node-auto-repair`), which monitors the health of nodes, automatically reacting to detected problems and replacing nodes when possible. For example, when **Xid errors** (`https://docs.nvidia.com/deploy/xid-errors/index.html#topic_5_1`) are detected on GPU nodes, it automatically replaces them after 10 minutes and evicts the Pods to get them scheduled on healthy nodes. Xid errors are error codes generated by NVIDIA GPU drivers indicating that the GPU has encountered an issue, such as a hang, reset, or memory fault.

- **AZ level**: AZs are isolated data centers within a cloud provider's region. Running workloads across multiple AZs provides higher fault tolerance, protecting against failures at the data center level. K8s clusters deployed in a multi-AZ configuration ensure that even if an entire AZ experiences an outage, applications continue running in another AZ. You can leverage K8s *topologySpreadConstraints* scheduling constraints to distribute the Pods managed by a ReplicaSet or StatefulSet across different failure domains, such as AZs, to ensure protection against AZ issues. Combine it with nodes for an additional layer of resiliency:

```
...
topologySpreadConstraints:
  - labelSelector:
      matchLabels:
         app.kubernetes.io/name: my-llama32
    maxSkew: 1
    topologyKey: topology.kubernetes.io/zone
    whenUnsatisfiable: ScheduleAnyway
  - labelSelector:
      matchLabels:
         app.kubernetes.io/name: my-llama32
    maxSkew: 1
    topologyKey: kubernetes.io/hostname
    whenUnsatisfiable: ScheduleAnyway
```

  Additionally, Amazon EKS supports Amazon **Application Recovery Controller** (**ARC**) zonal shift and zonal autoshift (`https://aws.amazon.com/application-recovery-controller/`). ARC helps you to manage and coordinate the recovery of applications across AZs and AWS Regions. With zonal shift, you can temporarily mitigate issues and incidents by triggering a shift and redirecting in-cluster network traffic to a healthy AZ. For a fully automated experience, you can authorize AWS to manage this shift on your behalf using zonal autoshift. With zonal autoshift, you can configure practice runs to test that your cluster environment functions as expected with one less AZ. Refer to the AWS documentation at `https://docs.aws.amazon.com/eks/latest/userguide/zone-shift.html` to learn more about this feature and find instructions to enable it on your EKS cluster.

- **Multi-cluster deployment**: A multi-cluster architecture involves running workloads across multiple independent K8s clusters. This approach is useful for mitigating failures at the cluster level, ensuring that if one cluster fails due to a control plane issue or networking disruption, another cluster can take over the workload. Multi-cluster deployments are often used for active-active, DR, and geo-distributed applications. You can leverage services such as **Amazon Route 53** (`https://aws.amazon.com/route53/`) and **AWS Global Accelerator** (`https://aws.amazon.com/global-accelerator/`) to perform health checks and route the traffic in a multi-cluster setup.

- **Global deployment**: At the highest level, deploying workloads across multiple geographic regions ensures that applications remain available even if an entire AWS Region experiences an outage. This approach not only enhances DR capabilities but also provides low-latency access to users in different locations. However, multi-region architectures require careful management of data consistency, replication, and failover processes to guarantee seamless recovery when regional failures occur. Because Amazon EKS is a regional service, you must provision a separate EKS cluster in each AWS Region to achieve a truly global deployment.

Each of these layers contributes to overall system resilience in K8s. By implementing redundancy at different levels, organizations can build highly available, fault-tolerant applications that withstand various types of failures, from individual Pod crashes to full-scale regional outages.

Other K8s options for resiliency and HA are load balancing and service discovery:

- **Load balancing**: K8s services provide built-in load balancing to distribute network traffic across multiple Pod instances. By defining a service, you can expose an application running on a set of Pods as a network service, with K8s handling the distribution of traffic to ensure no single Pod becomes a bottleneck.
- **Service discovery**: K8s offers service discovery mechanisms that allow applications and services to locate and communicate with each other efficiently, even as instances are created or terminated. This dynamic discovery is facilitated through environment variables or DNS, enabling seamless interaction between services within the cluster.

In this section, we discussed how resiliency can be implemented at various layers in K8s environments, from the individual Pods to multi-AZ, multi-cluster, and multi-region architectures. In the next section, we will explore various DR strategies and how they can be applied to K8s workloads.

DR strategies in K8s

DR focuses on restoring services and data after catastrophic events such as natural disasters, security breaches, and significant system failures. An effective DR plan for K8s should aim to minimize data loss (RPO) and reduce downtime (RTO).

Figure 13.3 highlights four different DR strategies in the cloud, as highlighted in the AWS white paper for DR: `https://docs.aws.amazon.com/whitepapers/latest/disaster-recovery-workloads-on-aws/disaster-recovery-options-in-the-cloud.html`.

As we move from backup and restore to multi-site active/active, the RPO and RTO time shrinks from hours to minutes. However, complexity, orchestration, and cloud spend increase.

Choose a DR strategy based on the business application's uptime requirements and use case.

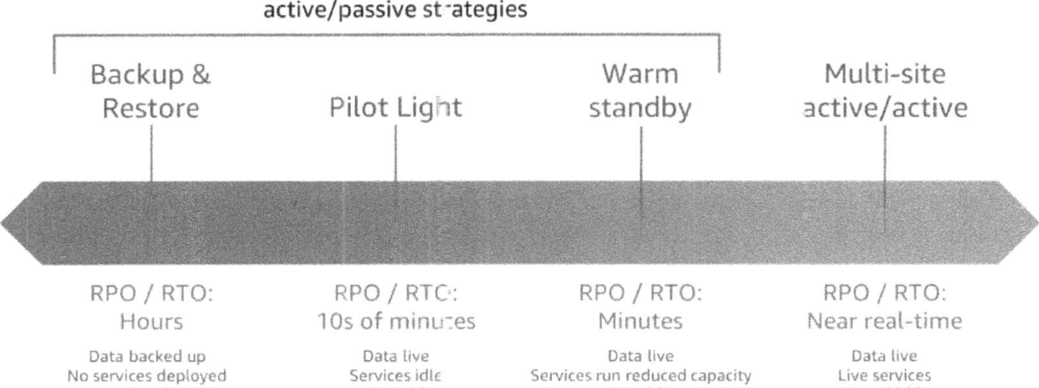

Figure 13.3 – Disaster recovery strategies

Let's explore a high-level perspective on architecting these DR strategies in K8s environments:

- **Backup and restore** (**RPO/RTO time in hours**): In K8s, backup and restore strategies are essential for lower-priority workloads where some downtime is acceptable. This approach involves periodically backing up data stored in **PersistentVolumes** (**PVs**) and other cluster resources such as **ConfigMaps**, **Secrets**, and **role-based access control** (**RBAC**) policies. During a disaster, all K8s resources must be provisioned again, and the backed-up data is restored. This method is cost-effective but results in longer recovery times, as restoring backups and re-provisioning the cluster can take hours. While this approach is viable for non-mission-critical applications, it does not meet the HA needs of production workloads.

  Open source tools such as **Velero** (`https://velero.io/`) and commercial solutions such as **Trilio for Kubernetes** (`https://trilio.io/products/kubernetes-backup-and-recovery/`) and **Portworx Backup** (`https://portworx.com/kubernetes-backup/`) provide automated backup and restore capabilities.

  Velero is an open source backup and restore solution designed for K8s workloads. It supports cloud-native environments, including AWS, Azure, and Google Cloud. Velero allows on-demand and scheduled backups of K8s clusters, covering Pods, deployments, and persistent volumes. It allows namespace-level and full-cluster backups, providing fine-grained control over data protection. One of Velero's strengths is its DR and cluster migration capabilities. Its scheduling features allow users to define periodic backups using cron-based scheduling, ensuring compliance with recovery and data retention policies. The tool is designed for multi-cloud environments, making it easier to implement hybrid cloud strategies. Additionally, Velero supports encryption for secure backup storage and uses RBAC to enforce security best practice.

Besides data, it's also essential to restore the cluster configuration, Secrets, and RBAC policies. These configurations can either be backed up using the same tooling or deployed using **infrastructure as code** (**IaC**) or **GitOps** (`https://about.gitlab.com/topics/gitops/`) tools. This enables the quick restoration of a K8s environment in case of failure.

- **Pilot light (RPO/RTO: 10s of minutes)**: The pilot light strategy keeps essential data and minimal K8s infrastructure live while leaving most services idle until a disaster occurs. This allows for quicker recovery compared to backup and restore, as some resources are already running and do not need to be provisioned from scratch. Persistent storage remains active, ensuring that stateful applications retain their critical data. However, the remaining workloads, such as application services and networking configurations, only become active when a failure is detected. This approach strikes a balance between cost and recovery speed by requiring only a fraction of the resources to be continuously available. Tools such as Velero, which support namespace-level and cluster-scoped backups, enable this setup by ensuring that key K8s objects and data are readily available for rapid scaling when needed.
- **Warm standby (RPO/RTO: minutes)**: A warm standby configuration ensures that a smaller-scale version of the production environment is always running, reducing recovery time to minutes. This approach is best suited for business-critical applications where downtime must be minimal, but maintaining a full-scale duplicate environment would be cost-prohibitive. The warm standby cluster continuously runs with scaled-down replicas of workloads, allowing immediate failover and rapid horizontal scaling when a disaster occurs. Additionally, real-time data replication solutions such as Portworx and Trilio for Kubernetes keep persistent storage synchronized across clusters, ensuring data consistency. This approach significantly reduces downtime while maintaining cost efficiency compared to a fully active environment.
- **Multi-site active/active (RPO/RTO: near real time)**: The multi-site active/active strategy offers the highest level of resilience by running multiple K8s clusters in different regions or cloud providers in real time. This setup ensures zero downtime and near-zero data loss, making it ideal for mission-critical services that demand continuous availability. Unlike other approaches, this strategy requires full redundancy, meaning that all workloads and data are replicated and running across multiple clusters simultaneously. Cross-region cluster deployment and cloud load balancers dynamically distribute traffic, ensuring seamless operation even if one cluster experiences an outage. Service mesh solutions such as **Istio** facilitate secure communication between clusters, while database replication strategies keep persistent data synchronized. Though this strategy incurs significant infrastructure costs, it provides the most reliable DR solution for organizations that cannot afford any service disruptions.

Let's consider a scenario where you have a GenAI application running in the AWS US-EAST-1 Region, which is your primary region. To ensure HA, you maintain a warm standby cluster in the US-WEST-2 region with a minimal compute footprint.

In the event of a regional outage in US-EAST-1, the following steps detail how the failover process would occur:

- Cloud monitoring, such as Amazon Route 53 health checks and CloudWatch alarms, detects that services in US-EAST-1 are unavailable. Application-level readiness and liveness probes start failing, indicating service degradation.
- DNS failover mechanisms, such as the **Amazon Route 53 failover routing** (`https://docs.aws.amazon.com/Route53/latest/DeveloperGuide/routing-policy-failover.html`) policy, automatically redirect traffic to the US-WEST-2 standby cluster.
- HPA/Cluster Autoscaler in the standby cluster triggers scale-up events. GenAI application endpoints and underlying worker nodes scale out to handle the production load.
- The standby cluster switches from passive to active mode, serving production traffic.
- Once US-EAST-1 is available again, evaluate data integrity and sync any missed transactions or logs. Once resynced, demote US-WEST-2 back to standby mode and resume normal operations in the primary region.

Additional K8s DR considerations

In this section, we explore the importance of automating DR using chaos engineering to validate the system's resilience and implementing proactive monitoring to detect outages early:

- **DR automation and testing**: Automating DR processes significantly reduces human error and accelerates recovery times. Using IaC tools such as Terraform ensures that K8s clusters can be redeployed quickly and consistently in the event of an outage. Automated failover solutions, such as Amazon Route 53 health checks, detect failures and reroute traffic to healthy instances automatically. To validate DR readiness, organizations should regularly conduct DR testing and drills.

  Chaos engineering tools include **Chaos Mesh** (`https://chaos-mesh.org/`), a cloud-native, open source K8s chaos engineering platform that allows users to simulate various failure scenarios within K8s clusters. It supports fine-grained chaos experiments at multiple levels, including the Pod, network, and storage levels. It can inject Pod failures, network disruptions, and node crashes in K8s Deployment. It also supports **CustomResourceDefinition** (**CRDs**) to define chaos experiments declaratively.

- **Monitoring and observability**: Proactive monitoring and observability help detect issues before they escalate into major outages. K8s provides built-in health checks through liveness and readiness probes, which restart unhealthy Pods to prevent failures from impacting the entire system. Logging and metrics collection tools such as Prometheus, Grafana, Fluentd, and Elasticsearch enable real-time visibility into cluster performance and system health. Implementing an alerting system integrated with PagerDuty or Slack ensures that incidents trigger immediate notifications, allowing response teams to act quickly and mitigate potential disruptions. A well-configured observability stack is crucial for diagnosing issues and optimizing DR strategies.

Summary

In this chapter, we covered the key concepts for HA and DR for GenAI applications deployed on K8s. Given the resource-intensive nature of GenAI workloads, it is critical to have scalability and resilience against hardware failures and regional outages.

HA minimizes downtime by eliminating single points of failure through redundancy across nodes, clusters, and regions. Key HA strategies in K8s include auto-scaling, self-healing, multi-cluster deployments, and load balancing.

DR focuses on restoring services after failures such as hardware malfunctions, cyberattacks, and natural disasters. Key DR metrics include RPO, RTO, and MTD. Various DR strategies include backup and restore (slow recovery but cost-effective), pilot light (minimal infrastructure remaining active for quicker recovery), warm standby (scaled-down live environment that quickly scales up), and multi-site active/active deployment (fully redundant clusters ensuring near-zero downtime).

Additionally, chaos engineering, automation, monitoring, and observability are crucial for enhancing HA and DR.

In the next chapter, we will cover a few other advanced GenAI topics related to K8s.

14

Wrapping Up: GenAI Coding Assistants and Further Reading

In the last few years, GenAI has significantly evolved, and there are now numerous GenAI-based coding assistants that can help with creating, launching, and monitoring K8s clusters. Since the field is evolving at a rapid pace, in this chapter, we will cover some of the coding assistants, evolving trends, and good references to read for further information.

In this chapter, we're going to cover the following main topics:

- GenAI-powered coding assistants
- GenAI-powered observability and optimization
- Amazon Q Developer walk-through with Amazon EKS
- References for further reading

Technical requirements

In this chapter, we will be using the following services, some of which require you to set up an account:

- `AWS` (`https://signin.aws.amazon.com/signup?request_type=register`)
- `Docker Desktop` (`https://www.docker.com/products/docker-desktop/`) or `Finch` (`https://runfinch.com/`)

GenAI-powered coding assistants

GenAI-powered assistants are transforming K8s cluster creation, deployment, and management by automating config file creation, workload scaling, and monitoring. Some GenAI-based coding assistants that can help with K8s clusters are the following:

- `Amazon Q Developer` (`https://aws.amazon.com/q/developer/`): This is Amazon's GenAI assistant, designed to help with cloud-based development, including K8s management on **Amazon Elastic Kubernetes Service** (**EKS**). It simplifies writing deployment manifests, automating **infrastructure as code** (**IaC**), and diagnosing issues in K8s deployment. It can also assist with optimizing cluster configurations by providing recommendations for resource allocation, autoscaling settings, and networking configurations. In this chapter, we will provide a walk-through on how to use AWS Q Developer for an EKS cluster deployment. We chose Amazon Q Developer for the walk-through since we are operating in an AWS environment.
- `GitHub Copilot` (`https://github.com/features/copilot`): This is an AI-powered coding assistant that can integrate into IDEs, such as Visual Studio Code and JetBrains. It can create K8s deployment code, such as deployment manifests, Helm charts, and CI/CD pipeline configurations. By providing inline suggestions and auto-completion, Copilot can accelerate K8s automation and ensure adherence to best practices.
- `Google Gemini Code Assist` (`https://codeassist.google/products/business`): This coding assistant can work across the software development life cycle. It can help with K8s workload optimization and infrastructure management and provide insights into scaling policies, cluster health, and performance tuning. By leveraging AI, Gemini suggests ways to optimize cost efficiency and minimize downtime, especially for GKE clusters.
- `Microsoft Copilot in Azure` (`https://azure.microsoft.com/en-us/products/copilot`): This can assist developers working with **Azure Kubernetes Service** (**AKS**). It provides recommendations for cluster scaling, node pool configurations, and security policies. Azure AI Copilot also integrates with Terraform and Bicep, allowing DevOps teams to automate K8s infrastructure provisioning efficiently.
- `IBM watsonx Code Assistant` (`https://www.ibm.com/products/watsonx-code-assistant`): This is particularly useful for teams using OpenShift and K8s in hybrid cloud environments. It automates application containerization, suggesting optimizations for container images, network policies, and security hardening. It also integrates with Red Hat OpenShift GitOps, allowing AI-driven automation of CI/CD pipelines and application deployment strategies.

- `K8sGPT` (`https://k8sgpt.ai/`): This is an open source tool that brings AI-powered diagnostics to K8s clusters by leveraging GenAI to identify, analyze, and explain issues. It can be run locally using a CLI or deployed in a K8s cluster for continuous analysis. It supports a variety of AI backends, including OpenAI, or even local LLMs through tools such as Ollama or LangChain, giving teams flexibility based on their data privacy needs. It scans various K8s resources, such as Pods, Services, Deployments, and Nodes, and detects problems such as crash loops, configuration errors, or failed health checks. Instead of K8s error messages, K8sGPT can provide clear, human-readable explanations along with suggested remediation steps, making it especially helpful for developers and SREs troubleshooting complex environments.

  For example, instead of a vague `CrashLoopBackOff` error, K8sGPT might explain that a Pod is crashing because it's missing a required secret or has a misconfigured environment variable.

In this section, we explored several GenAI-powered coding assistants that aid in software deployment, generating IaC, and debugging K8s clusters. However, when working with AI-generated configurations, such as Amazon Q Developer or any other GenAI assistant, it's essential to validate output manually and test it in a staging environment before deployment. Tools such as `terraform plan`, `docker scan`, and `kubeval` can help verify syntactic correctness and highlight configuration issues. Consider using policy-as-code frameworks, such as **Open Policy Agent** (**OPA**), to enforce security standards automatically.

In the next section, we will discuss how GenAI is transforming the K8s observability and optimization landscape.

GenAI-powered observability and optimization

Besides generating the K8s manifest files, GenAI is also transforming K8s operations by automating security, monitoring, and optimization. These AI-powered solutions are making K8s environments more efficient, cost-effective, and self-healing. Some good examples are the following:

- **AI-powered K8s autoscaling**: Traditional K8s autoscalers rely on CPU and memory thresholds, but AI-powered autoscalers predict workload demands and dynamically adjust resources to optimize performance and costs. Tools such as `StormForge` (`https://stormforge.io/`) and `PredictKube` (`https://dysnix.com/predictkube`) leverage **machine learning** (**ML**) to enhance autoscaling strategies, preventing over-provisioning while ensuring availability during traffic spikes.

- **AI-assisted K8s governance and policy enforcement**: AI-driven governance tools enforce compliance and security policies in K8s clusters. By integrating ML models trained in historical data and policy violations, one can go beyond static rule definitions. For example, one can analyze historical policy violations and detect patterns, such as which resources are most affected and under what conditions. Based on learned patterns, AI can suggest new rules to tighten access beyond the static rules for policy enforcers, such as OPA.
- **GenAI for K8s workflows and observability**: AI-powered observability tools analyze logs, metrics, and traces to identify anomalies before they impact applications. Solutions such as `New Relic AI` (`https://newrelic.com/platform/new-relic-ai`) and `Dynatrace Davis AI` (`https://www.dynatrace.com/platform/artificial-intelligence/`) can automate root cause analysis and alert prioritization, helping DevOps reduce downtime and improve troubleshooting efficiency. Prometheus with AI models enhances smart alerting by filtering out non-critical events and focusing on actionable insights.
- **Envoy AI Gateway** (`https://aigateway.envoyproxy.io/docs/`): This was developed to simplify the increasingly complex task of connecting modern applications to GenAI services. Built on Envoy Proxy, the project offers a unified layer to manage LLM/AI traffic at scale. Key goals of the project include providing seamless routing and policy control for GenAI workloads, supporting automatic failover for resilient service delivery, securing AI traffic with upstream authorization, and enabling usage limits through a flexible policy framework. At its core, Envoy AI Gateway aims to make GenAI infrastructure easier to integrate and safer to operate. To use Envoy AI Gateway's observability capabilities, users can configure Prometheus to scrape metrics exposed by the gateway, which include AI-specific insights such as token usage, time to first token, and per-token latency. These metrics follow OpenTelemetry's GenAI semantic conventions and are designed to give visibility into how GenAI models are performing in production.
- **Generative AI for K8s IaC**: AI-powered assistants accelerate K8s infrastructure deployment by automatically generating YAML, Terraform, and Helm configurations. Tools such as Amazon Q Developer enable teams to describe their desired infrastructure in plain language and receive optimized configurations.
- **AI-powered K8s cost optimization (FinOps)**: Optimizing cloud costs in K8s environments is challenging due to the dynamic nature of workloads. AI-powered FinOps solutions such as `Harness` (`https://www.harness.io/solutions/finops-excellence`) and `Cast AI` (`https://cast.ai/`) can analyze cluster utilization, suggest cost-saving measures, and adjust resource allocations to minimize waste. These tools help organizations optimize their K8s spending while maintaining application performance.

- **GenAI-powered K8s ChatOps**: AI-driven ChatOps tools enhance K8s management by enabling conversational interactions within platforms such as Slack and Microsoft Teams. `Botkube AI Assistant` (`https://botkube.io/`) allows users to query K8s clusters and execute commands via chat, while K8sGPT functions as an AI-powered K8s SRE, diagnosing and resolving cluster issues autonomously. AI-driven self-healing mechanisms can detect failures, restart Pods, and proactively fix issues without manual intervention.

In this section, we explored various AI-powered tools that can help transform K8s environments. These tools can be leveraged to automate key K8s operations such as autoscaling, security, cost optimization, and observability. In the next section, we'll walk through how to use a GenAI assistant to simplify the development of K8s applications.

Amazon Q Developer walk-through with EKS

In this section, we will explore how GenAI-powered assistants, such as Amazon Q Developer, can simplify the development of GenAI applications, streamline the creation and management of K8s clusters, and simplify deployments. Amazon Q Developer introduced a new *agentic experience* directly within the **command-line interface** (**CLI**), offering a dynamic and interactive coding experience. Agentic experiences refer to systems that actively assist users by understanding context, offering suggestions, and helping guide task completion. Amazon Q Developer iteratively refines changes based on your feedback and leverages information from your CLI environment to assist with local file operations, querying AWS resources, writing code, and automatically debugging issues.

> **Important note**
>
> When using GenAI-powered assistants for coding and executing local tasks such as running commands, always review generated code and commands thoroughly. Ensure they are secure, appropriate for your environment, and won't unintentionally affect critical resources or data.

Let's get started:

Install *Amazon Q Developer for command line* by following the instructions at `https://docs.aws.amazon.com/amazonq/latest/qdeveloper-ug/command-line-installing.html`.

Open a terminal or command-line application and initiate a conversation with Amazon Q Developer using the following command:

```
$ q chat
```

You will be directed to the **AWS Builder ID** login page (`https://docs.aws.amazon.com/signin/latest/userguide/sign-in-aws_builder_id.html`) to allow permission to Amazon Q Developer for command line.

Type the following query in the CLI. Amazon Q Developer will process your input, considering the provided context, call the **Amazon Bedrock API**, and respond with an output as shown in *Figure 14.1*:

```
> Write the command to list pods in a kubernetes cluster

To list pods in a Kubernetes cluster, you can use the following command:

bash
kubectl get pods


This will list all pods in the default namespace. If you want to list pods in a
specific namespace, you can use:

bash
kubectl get pods -n <namespace>
```

Figure 14.1 – Kubectl command generation using Amazon Q Developer

Now, let's ask the GenAI assistant to create the IaC templates for creating a new Amazon EKS cluster along with a VPC, private and public subnets, and so on. Use the following prompt in the CLI:

```
$ Generate Terraform code for an Amazon EKS cluster with:
- Cluster name "eks-genai-demo" in us-west-2 region using EKS v1.32
- Dedicated VPC (CIDR 10.0.0.0/16) with public/private subnets across
3 AZs
- 1 NAT gateway for internet access from private subnets
- Standard EKS Managed add-ons (Amazon VPC CNI, CoreDNS, kube-proxy)
- Output cluster endpoint and access information
Provide modular, well-commented code with appropriate provider
configurations and use open-source terraform modules where possible.
```

Within a few seconds, Amazon Q Developer will generate Terraform code to create an Amazon VPC, EKS cluster, and so on, along with Terraform provider configuration, input variables, and outputs, as shown in *Figure 14.2*:

```
I've created a complete Terraform configuration for an Amazon EKS cluster with the specifications you requested.
 The configuration is organized into multiple
files for better maintainability:

1. main.tf - Contains the main infrastructure configuration including:
   • AWS provider configuration
   • Kubernetes provider configuration for post-deployment management
   • VPC module configuration with public/private subnets across 3 AZs
   • EKS cluster configuration with managed node groups and add-ons

2. variables.tf - Defines all variables used in the configuration with sensible defaults:
   • Region set to us-west-2
   • Cluster name "eks-genai-demo"
   • Kubernetes version 1.32
   • VPC CIDR 10.0.0.0/16 with appropriate subnet CIDRs

3. outputs.tf - Provides useful outputs after deployment:
   • Cluster endpoint
   • Security group information
   • VPC and subnet IDs
   • Command to configure kubectl

4. versions.tf - Specifies required Terraform and provider versions

5. README.md - Documentation with usage instructions

Key features of this configuration:

• Uses the official AWS Terraform modules for VPC and EKS
• Configures a single NAT gateway for cost optimization
• Sets up proper tagging for Kubernetes integration with the AWS load balancer controller
• Configures standard EKS managed add-ons (VPC CNI, CoreDNS, kube-proxy)
• Creates an EKS managed node group with m5.large instances
• Provides proper authentication configuration for kubectl

To deploy this cluster:
1. Run terraform init to initialize the providers and modules
2. Run terraform plan to preview the changes
3. Run terraform apply to create the infrastructure
4. Use the output command to configure kubectl

The configuration is designed to be easily customizable through variables, and you can extend it by adding more
node groups or enabling additional EKS add-ons as
needed.
```

Figure 14.2 – Terraform code generation using Amazon Q Developer

We ran this prompt and uploaded the generated files to the GitHub repository at `https://github.com/PacktPublishing/Kubernetes-for-Generative-AI-Solutions/tree/main/ch14/amazon-q-demo`.

GenAI-powered coding assistants may use older versions of Terraform providers or modules, based on their training data. In the generated code, it used `Terraform version >= 1.0.0`, `AWS provider >= 5.0.0`, and so on. We can also give a follow-up prompt to use specific versions of these providers, as shown here:

```
$ Update the previous EKS cluster Terraform code to use the following
provider versions:
- Terraform version >= 1.9
- AWS provider >= 5.63
- Helm provider >= 2.15
- Kubernetes provider >= 2.32
Ensure all provider configurations are explicitly defined with these
version constraints in the required_providers block, and the code
remains compatible with these newer versions.
```

Amazon Q Developer will reason the prompt, start reading the Terraform files from the local filesystem, and suggest the changes, as shown in Figure 14.3:

```
Write to filesystem

Path: versions.tf

    1,  1: /**
    2,  2:  * Terraform and provider versions
+       3:  *
+       4:  * Updated to use specific minimum versions for compatibility
    3,  5:  */
    4,  6:
    5,  7: terraform {
-   6    :   required_version = ">= 1.0.0"
+       8:   required_version = ">= 1.9.0"
    7,  9:
    8, 10:   required_providers {
    9, 11:     aws = {
   10, 12:       source  = "hashicorp/aws"
-  11    :       version = ">= 5.0.0"
+      13:       version = ">= 5.63.0"
   12, 14:     }
   13, 15:     kubernetes = {
   14, 16:       source  = "hashicorp/kubernetes"
-  15    :       version = ">= 2.10.0"
+      17:       version = ">= 2.32.0"
+      18:     }
+      19:     helm = {
+      20:       source  = "hashicorp/helm"
+      21:       version = ">= 2.15.0"
   16, 22:     }
   17, 23:   }
   18, 24: }


Enter y to run this tool, otherwise continue chatting.
```

Figure 14.3 – Output of Amazon Q Developer

You can review the generated Terraform code and ask the agent to plan and deploy it to the AWS account using natural language prompts.

Similarly, you can use Amazon Q Developer to automatically generate complete project code from the ground up, such as for a to-do application that provides basic functionality to manage to-do tasks. Run the following prompt in an empty directory to generate a to-do application:

```
$ Please create a simple TODO application with the following
specifications:
Functionality
- Create new tasks with title and description
- Mark tasks as complete/incomplete
- Delete tasks
- View all tasks
Technical Requirements
- Create a single application
- Use in-memory storage for tasks (no need for a database)
- Follow good coding practices with appropriate comments
Docker Requirements
- Create a Dockerfile to containerize the application
- The Dockerfile should follow best practices
- Make it simple to build and run.
```

Within no time, Amazon Q Developer will start creating a hierarchal project structure, source code files, Dockerfile for containerization, documentation, and so on. We executed this prompt and provided the generated files in the GitHub repository at `https://github.com/PacktPublishing/Kubernetes-for-Generative-AI-Solutions/tree/main/ch14/todo-app`. It created the project structure and files shown in Figure 14.4:

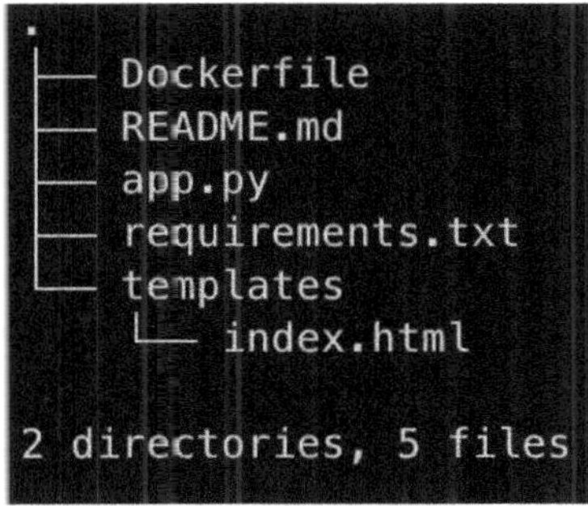
.
├── Dockerfile
├── README.md
├── app.py
├── requirements.txt
└── templates
    └── index.html

2 directories, 5 files

Figure 14.4 – Output of Amazon Q Developer

Review the generated files. To test the application locally, we can prompt Amazon Q Developer to build the container image and run it using Docker or Finch. Use the following prompt to build and run the container image:

```
$ Build and run the container image locally using Docker.
```

On a different terminal, you use the following commands to verify the container image and running container:

```
$ docker images
$ docker ps
```

Finally, we can take this a step further by asking the AI assistant to create the necessary K8s manifest files and deploy the application to a K8s cluster. Use the following prompt to create the K8s Deployment and Service resources:

```
$ Create necessary manifest files to deploy this application to a
kubernetes cluster. Run two replicas of this app and expose it via
ClusterIP service.
```

Within a few seconds, Amazon Q Developer will generate K8s deployment, service, and namespace manifest files, among others, to deploy the to-do application to a K8s cluster, as shown in Figure 14.5:

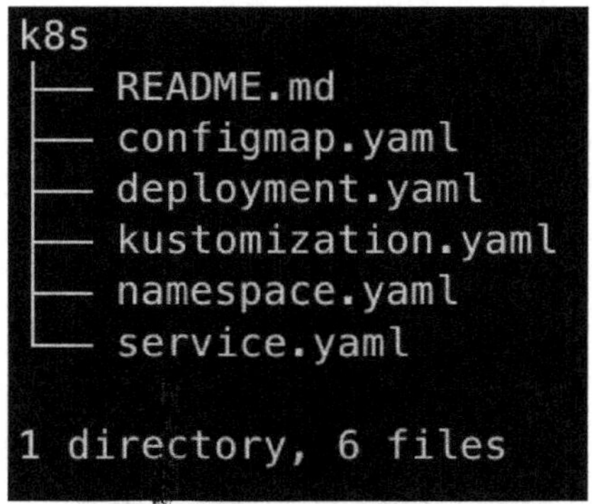

k8s
├── README.md
├── configmap.yaml
├── deployment.yaml
├── kustomization.yaml
├── namespace.yaml
└── service.yaml
1 directory, 6 files

Figure 14.5 – K8s manifest files created by Amazon Q Developer

In this section, we have explored how AI coding assistants such as Amazon Q Developer simplify software development tasks, including generating K8s configuration files and IaC templates for creating AWS and EKS resources. We have interacted with these assistants using natural language prompts, instructing them to perform various tasks such as building a container image, running applications locally, and modifying the generated code to meet specific requirements. In the next section, we will provide references for further reading on this topic.

References for further reading

- `https://kubernetes.io/docs/`: Official Kubernetes documentation, always up to date and comprehensive
- `https://github.com/kubernetes/kubernetes`: The core Kubernetes GitHub repo with source code
- `https://training.linuxfoundation.org/certification/`: The Linux Foundation, in partnership with the **Cloud Native Computing Foundation** (**CNCF**), offers three key K8s certifications – `Certified Kubernetes Administrator` (CKA), `Certified Kubernetes Application Developer` (CKAD), and `Certified Kubernetes Security Specialist` (CKS)
- `https://kubernetes.io/blog/`: The official blog with updates, best practices, and use cases
- `https://kubernetes.io/community/`: Community hub for contributing, SIGs, events, and getting involved
- `https://www.cncf.io/projects/kubernetes/`: K8s page on CNCF – project status, governance, and landscape
- `https://github.com/aws-ia/terraform-aws-eks-blueprints`: Official EKS blueprints using Terraform – modular and production-ready
- `https://awslabs.github.io/data-on-eks/`: Data on EKS is a tool to build, deploy, and scale Data & ML platforms on EKS
- `https://aws.github.io/aws-eks-best-practices/`: Official *Amazon EKS Best Practices Guide*, covering security, networking, scaling, GitOps, and more
- `https://wellarchitectedlabs.com/architecture-guides/containers/eks-best-practices/`: *AWS Well-Architected Labs* guide for EKS with practical labs and architecture reviews

Summary

In this chapter, we covered how GenAI-based coding assistants are transforming the way K8s clusters are being built, deployed, and monitored. These tools automate IaC, optimize workloads, and enhance observability. Key assistants include Amazon Q Developer, GitHub Copilot, Google Gemini Code Assist, Microsoft Azure Copilot, IBM watsonx Code Assistant, and K8sGPT. They support everything from writing deployment manifests and Terraform configurations to real-time diagnostics and optimization of cluster performance.

GenAI tools also boost observability, security, and cost efficiency through AI-powered autoscaling, anomaly detection, and policy enforcement. Tools such as StormForge, PredictKube, and Dynatrace Davis AI automate root cause analysis and resource scaling, while others, such as Harness and Cast AI, assist with K8s FinOps.

Amazon Q Developer offers CLI-based support to generate and refine Terraform templates, build Docker containers, and deploy complete applications using simple natural language prompts. It supports creating modular IaC for EKS clusters and enables fast iteration through intelligent suggestions.

Lastly, we provided a curated list of references for deeper learning. These include official K8s documentation, GitHub repositories, and blogs offering best practices, patterns, and community resources. It also highlights certification programs from the Linux Foundation and CNCF. Together, these resources offer valuable guidance for mastering K8s and effectively using GenAI-powered tools in production environments. We hope you enjoyed reading this book and we will look forward to getting your feedback on how we can improve in future editions.

Stay Sharp in Cloud and DevOps – Join 44,000+ Subscribers of CloudPro

CloudPro is a weekly newsletter for cloud professionals who want to stay current on the fast-evolving world of cloud computing, DevOps, and infrastructure engineering.

Every issue delivers focused, high-signal content on topics like:

- AWS, GCP & multi-cloud architecture
- Containers, Kubernetes & orchestration
- Infrastructure as Code (IaC) with Terraform, Pulumi, etc.
- Platform engineering & automation workflows
- Observability, performance tuning, and reliability best practices

Whether you're a cloud engineer, SRE, DevOps practitioner, or platform lead, CloudPro helps you stay on top of what matters, without the noise.

Scan the QR code to join for free and get weekly insights straight to your inbox:

https://packt.link/cloudpro

15

Unlock Your Exclusive Benefits

Your copy of this book includes the following exclusive benefit:

- Next-gen Packt Reader
- DRM-free PDF/ePub downloads

Follow the guide below to unlock them. The process takes only a few minutes and needs to be completed once.

Unlock this Book's Free Benefits in 3 Easy Steps

Step 1

Keep your purchase invoice ready for *Step 3*. If you have a physical copy, scan it using your phone and save it as a PDF, JPG, or PNG.

For more help on finding your invoice, visit `https://www.packtpub.com/unlock-benefits/help`.

> **Note**
>
> If you bought this book directly from Packt, no invoice is required. After *Step 2*, you can access your exclusive content right away.

Step 2

Scan the QR code or go to `packtpub.com/unlock`.

On the page that opens (similar to *Figure 15 .1* on desktop), search for this book by name and select the correct edition.

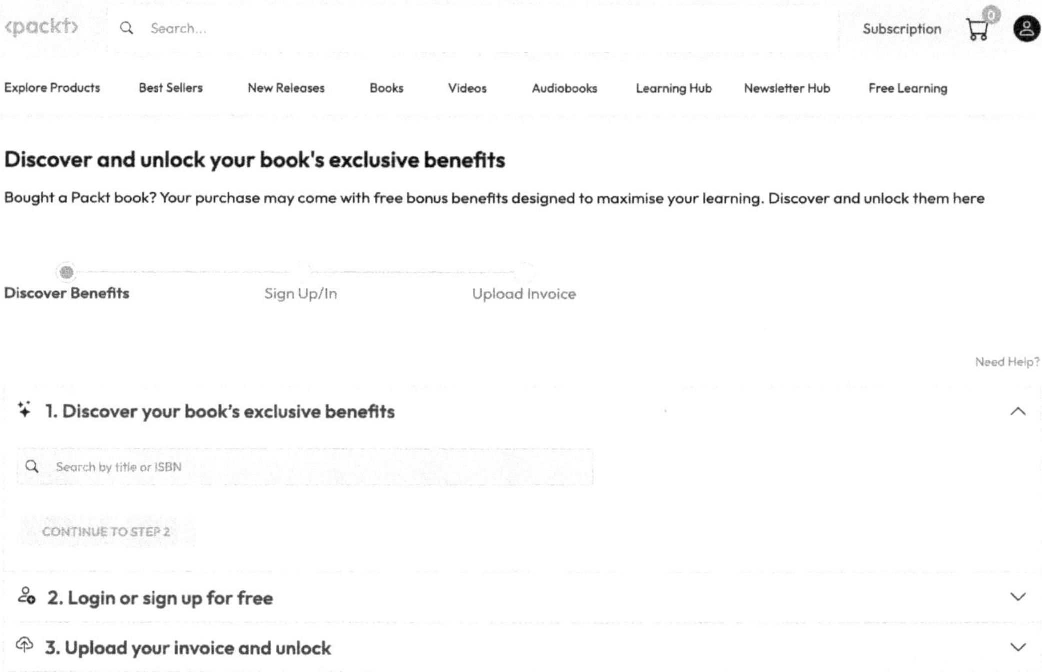

Figure 15.1: Packt unlock landing page on desktop

Step 3

After selecting your book, sign in to your Packt account or create one for free. Then upload your invoice (PDF, PNG, or JPG, up to 10 MB). Follow the on-screen instructions to finish the process.

Need help?

If you get stuck and need help, visit `https://www.packtpub.com/unlock-benefits/help` for a detailed FAQ on how to find your invoices and more. This QR code will take you to the help page.

> **Note**
>
> If you are still facing issues, reach out to `customercare@packt.com`.

Index

A

A/B testing
- reference link 159

adapter-based tuning 77

add-on software components
- CNI plugin 40
- CoreDNS 40
- CSI plugin 40
- device plugins 40
- monitoring plugins 40

Advanced Encryption Standard (AES) encryption algorithm 189

agent 5

Alpine Linux
- reference link 176

Amazon Bedrock 69
- URL 111

Amazon CloudWatch 240

Amazon CloudWatch Logs 240

Amazon EBS CSI driver add-on 89

Amazon EC2
- URL 49

Amazon EC2 Capacity Blocks for ML
- reference link 218

Amazon EC2 placement groups
- cluster 169
- partition 169
- reference link 169
- spread 169

Amazon EC2 Trn1 instances
- reference link 199

Amazon EC2 Trn2 instances 199

Amazon EC2 UltraClusters
- reference link 218

Amazon ECR
- URL 177

Amazon EKS 46

Amazon EKS Blueprints Addons module
- reference link 50

Amazon EKS cluster
- provisioning 51-58

Amazon Elastic Block Store (Amazon EBS) 136, 179

Amazon Elastic Container Registry (Amazon ECR)
- URL 60

Amazon Elastic Container Service 35

Amazon Elastic Kubernetes Service
- reference link 35

Amazon Inspector
reference link 178
Amazon Managed Grafana
reference link 255
Amazon Q Developer
walk-through, with EKS 283-288
Amazon Route 53
URL 273
Amazon Route 53 failover routing
reference link 277
Amazon S3 97, 223
Amazon S3 bucket 97, 184
Amazon SQS 118
Amazon VPC CNI
reference link 155
Ambient Mesh 161
Ampere 207
Anaconda 89
Anthropic Claude
URL 111
Antrea
reference link 155
Apache Mesos
reference link 35
Apache Spark
reference link 222
AppArmor
URL 180
Application Load Balancer (ALB) 188
Application Recovery Controller (ARC) 273
application scaling, metrics 117
conventional metrics 118
custom metrics 118, 119
application-specific integrated circuits (ASICs)
URL 199
Aqua Security
reference link 181
URL 47
Argo Workflows 223, 224, 227
reference link 227
artificial Intelligence (AI)
versus GenAI 3-6
Auto Scaling group (ASG) 49
Availability Zones (AZs) 47, 268
AWS Certificate Manager (ACM)
reference link 188
AWS Distro for OpenTelemetry (ADOT)
reference link 246
AWS EKS Terraform module
reference link 50
AWS Global Accelerator
URL 273
AWS Identity and Access Management (AWS IAM) 178
AWS Inferentia 199
AWS Key Management Service (AWS KMS) 178
aws-load-balancer-controller 61, 159
AWS Network Load Balancer 112
AWS Provider 52
AWS Secrets Manager
reference link 178
AWS Security Token Service (STS) 186
AWS Signer
reference link 177
AWS Systems Manager (SSM)
reference link 179
AWS Trainium
URL 199
AWS VPC Terraform module
reference link 50

AWS WAF
reference link 189
AWS X-Ray
reference link 242
Azure Container Apps
reference link 35
Azure Kubernetes Service (AKS) 45, 280
reference link 35
Azure Managed Grafana
reference link 255

B

bare-metal machines 18
Bidirectional Encoder Representations from Transformers (BERT) 8
Bilingual Evaluation Understudy (BLEU) 14
block storage system 18
Bottlerocket 175
business continuity planning (BCP) 268

C

Calico
reference link 155, 165
canary releases
reference link 159
Capacity Blocks 218
Cgroups
reference link 27
Chaos Mesh
URL 277
chatbot 89
deploying, on K8s 112-114
security best practices, implementing 190-194
Chatbot UI component 112
Chroma
URL 106
Cilium
reference link 155, 165
Classless Inter-Domain Routing (CIDR)
reference link 52
cloud-controller-manager
node controller 39
service controller 39
Cloud Native Computing Foundation (CNCF) 36, 246, 289
Cluster Autoscaler (CA) 127, 128, 145
Cluster Autoscaling 42
ClusterIP 157
reference link 60
service 94
CNI plugin 40
command-line interface (CLI) 283
community-contributed plugins
reference link 254
compute
best practices 140-144
compute instance ID 208
concept drift 235
concept drift detection (CDD) 236
ConfigMap 213, 275
container image 27
characteristics 27
creating 28, 29
Container Network Interface (CNI) 37, 153, 155
reference link 154
Container Orchestrators
benefits 34, 35
container registry 27
container runtime 27, 39
Container Runtime Interface (CRI) 155
reference link 154

containers 18, 25-27
container security 175
containers, for GenAI models
dependency management 30
model versioning and updates 31
need for 29, 30
resource access 31
security 31
Container Storage Interface (CSI) volume 193
container supply chain 176
container terminology 27, 28
container 27
container image 27
container registry 27
container runtime 27
content delivery network (CDN) 136
continuous integration/continuous delivery (CI/CD) 228
controller 119
control plane 47
control plane components
etcd 38
kube-apiserver 38
kube-controller-manager 38
conventional metrics 118
Convolutional Neural Networks (CNNs) 6, 8
CoreDNS 40
CoreDNS deployment 164
CoreDNS managed add-on
reference link 168
cost components 135, 136
cost optimization, techniques 140
compute best practices 140-144
networking best practices 144-146
storage best practices 146-150
covariate drift 235
CSI plugin 40
cumulative distribution functions (CDFs) 236
custom accelerators 198, 199
custom metrics 118, 119
custom resource definition (CRD) 177, 227, 251, 277
custom visualization panels
reference link 254

D

DaemonSet 200, 272
reference link 198
Dash
URL 112
Data Center GPU Manager (DCGM)
URL 203
Datadog 240
URL 47
Datadog Cluster Agent 119
data management 222
Data on Amazon EKS (DoEKS)
reference link 222
data plane components
container runtime 39
kubelet 39
kube-proxy 39
data privacy 234
DCGM-Exporter 119, 204
Deep Learning (DL) 3, 6
DeepSeek
reference link 63
defense in depth 174, 175
denial-of-service (DoS) attacks 180
deny-by-default model 162
device plugins 40
reference link 198
Directed Acyclic Graphs (DAGs) 226

Direct Preference Optimization (DPO) 14
disaster recovery (DR)
designing 267-269
strategies, in K8s 274-277
distroless
reference link 176
DNS-over-HTTPS
reference link 182
DNS-over-TLS
reference link 182
DNSSEC
reference link 182
DocArray 72
DocArrayInMemorySearch 72
Docker daemon 28
Docker Desktop for Linux
reference link 28
Docker Desktop for Mac
reference link 28
Docker Desktop for Windows
reference link 28
Docker Hub
reference link 27
DockerSlim
reference link 176
Docker's networking model 154
Docker Swarm
reference link 35
domain-specific optimization 68
drift monitoring 234
DR strategies, in K8s
considerations 277

E

egress costs 136
egress rules 162
eks-blueprints-addons 57
EKS documentation
reference link 241
EKS Pod Identity 187, 188
reference link 184
Elastic Fabric Adapter (EFA) 170
reference link 153
Elastic Kubernetes Service (EKS) 45, 280
used, for walk-through Amazon Q Developer 284-288
used, for walk-through Amazon Q Developer 283
Elasticsearch 240
encoder-decoder 9
end-of-sequence (EOS) 79
EndpointSlice
reference link 154
Envoy
reference link 160
Envoy AI Gateway
reference link 282
etcd 183
event-driven architecture (EDA) 118
experimentation
with JupyterHub 89-96
extended Berkeley Packet Filter (eBPF) 165
reference link 167
ExternalName
reference link 60

F

Facebook AI Similarity Search (FAISS) 72
Fairlearn 235
Falco 175
reference link 181
Falcon
reference link 63
FastAPI 102

feature interaction drift 236
field-programmable gate arrays (FPGAs) 199
file storage system 18
fine-tuned Llama 3 model
deploying, on K8s 102-105
fine-tuning 13, 68
Flask
URL 112
Flink
reference link 222
Fluent Bit
reference link 244
Fluentd 242
plugins 243
reference link 243
foundational models (FMs) 6, 221
Fully Sharded Data Parallel (FSDP) 19

G

Gated Recurrent Units (GRUs) 8
Gateway API
reference link 160
Gateway Controller 160
GDPR 47
GenAI 3, 6
container image, building 31-34
deployment stack 16-19
deployment stack, layers 17
use cases 19-21
use cases, for e-commerce 88, 89
versus Artificial Intelligence (AI) 3-6
GenAI apps, security considerations 184
Amazon EKS Pod Identity 187, 188
data privacy and compliance 184
IAM Roles, for Service Accounts 184-186
model endpoints security 188, 189
GenAI model
deploying, in K8s cluster 59-63
GenAI pipelines
data management 222
experimentation 223
model adaptation 223
model monitoring 224
model serving 223
overview 222
GenAI-powered
observability and optimization 281-283
GenAI-powered coding assistants 280-282
GenAI project life cycle
stage 12-15
GenAI workloads
securing, with Kubernetes' network policies 162
Generative AI operations (GenAIOps) 221
on K8s 224
GitOps 276
Goldilocks
reference link 140
Google Artifact Registry
reference link 27
Google Cloud Platform (GCP) 46
Google Colab 89
Google Kubernetes Engine (GKE) 45
reference link 35
Google TPUs 199
GPT-3.5 Turbo 108
GPU instance ID 208
GPUs, in K8s clusters
NVIDIA NIM 217
scaling and optimization considerations 216, 217
GPU time-slicing 206, 212-216
reference link 197

GPU utilization 203
challenges 206, 207
DCGM 203-206
Gradio
URL 112
Grafana 242
best practices 254, 255
reference link 254
Grafana Cloud
reference link 255
Grafana dashboards
NVIDIA DCGM dashboard 258-260
Ray Serve dashboard 260-262
reference link 254
setting up 255-258
graphics processing unit (GPU) 198, 199
availability, in cloud 218
partitioning and sharing techniques 207
reference link 197
resources, allocating in K8s 200-203
GUPs, partitioning and sharing techniques
NVIDIA MIG 207-209
NVIDIA MPS 210-212
time-slicing 212-216

H

HAProxy Ingress 159
hard disk drives (HDDs) 136
HashiCorp
URL 50
HashiCorp Configuration Language (HCL) 50
HashiCorp Vault
reference link 178
Helm
URL 52
Helm provider
reference link 52
high availability (HA)
designing 267-269
HIPPA 47
Honesty, Harmlessness, and Helpfulness (3H) 14
Horizontal Pod Autoscaler (HPA) 41, 119-122, 216
combining, with VPA 124
Hugging Face 98, 178
reference link 31, 221
Hugging Face Transformers 230

I

IAM permissions 89
IAM Roles for Service Accounts (IRSA)
reference link 184
IBM AI Fairness 360 (AIF360)
reference link 235
IIPTables
reference link 155
IMDSv2
reference link 179
immutable tag 176
inference endpoints 188
Inferentia
reference link 198
Infrastructure as Code (IaC) 48, 254, 276, 280
Ingress API 159
Ingress controllers
reference link 159
ingress-nginx 159
ingress rules 162
int 4 precision 78

Integrated Development Environment (IDE) 19
IP Address Management (IPAM)
reference link 155
IPTables mode 166
IPv6 addressing 167
IP Virtual Server (IPVS) 166
Istio 182, 276
Istio Ingress 159

J

Jaeger
reference link 242
JAX
URL 199
JupyterHub
for experimentation 89-96
JupyterHub-based playground 89
JupyterHub Workflows 224
Jupyter Notebook 42, 223
URL 89

K

K8s cluster
GenAI model, deploying in 59-63
used, for deploying KubeRay 229-233
K8s clusters, in cloud
advantages 46-48
Amazon EKS cluster, provisioning 51-58
setting up 48-50
setting up, prerequisites 51
K8s' networking model
reference link 154
tenets 154
K8s network policies
versus service mesh 165
K8s security considerations 175
container runtime security 180, 181
host security 179, 180
network security 182
secrets management 183, 184
supply chain security 176
Karpenter 128-134
URL 57
Katib
reference link 225
key performance indicators (KPIs) 224, 264
k-means clustering algorithm 5
knowledge integration 68
Kolmogorov-Smirnov test (KS test) 236
KServe 223, 226
reference link 226
kube-apiserver 38
kube-controller-manager
cloud-controller-manager 39
deployment controller 38
kube-scheduler 39
Kubecost 136-138
setting up 138-140
URL 47
Kubeflow 42
versus KubeRay 233, 234
versus MLFlow 233, 234
Kubeflow components
Kubeflow Notebooks 225
Kubeflow Notebooks
reference link 225
Kubeflow Pipelines
reference link 226
Kubeflow Workflows 223-226
kubelet 39, 154
kube-proxy 39, 166
reference link 166

KubeRay
deploying, on K8s cluster 229-233
versus Kubeflow 233, 234
versus MLflow 233, 234
KubeRay, cluster management
RayCluster 229
RayJob 229
RayService 229
KubeRay Workflows 223, 228
reference link 228
Kubernetes
reference link 35
Kubernetes Event-Driven Autoscaler (KEDA) 124-127
URL 125
Kubernetes (K8s) 19, 25, 36, 45, 153, 173
Argo Workflows 227
audit logs 241
chatbot, deploying on 112-114
ClusterIP 157
DR strategies 274-277
experiment tracking 224
factors 36, 37
fine-tuned model, deploying on 102-105
Generative AI operations (GenAIOps) 224
GPU resources, allocating 200-203
Katib 225
KServe 226
Kubeflow Pipelines 226
Kubeflow Workflows 224-226
KubeRay Workflows 228
MLflow Workflows 226
model training 224
monitoring tools 242, 243
NodePort 157
RAG application, deploying on 105-111
resiliency 269, 270
resiliency, across different layers 270-274
service implementation 157
workflow orchestration 224
Kubernetes (K8s), architecture 37
add-on software components 40
control plane components 38
data plane components 39
Kubernetes (K8s), for GenAI models
advantages 41, 42
challenges 41
need for 40
Kubernetes networking model 154, 155
CNI networking mode, selecting for Gen AI application 156
service health checks 158
service implementation, in k8S 157
Kubernetes Secrets
reference link 178

L

label-based targeting 162
label drift 235
labels 246
LangChain
observability 262-264
verbose mode 262
LangChain framework
key capabilities 69-71
LangChainTracer 263
LangFuse
features 264
reference link 254, 264
LangSmith 263
Large Language Models (LLMs) 6, 68, 221
response generation process 105
selection 69
Lifetime Value (LTV) 13
Linkerd 182

Linux Namespace
reference link 27
Llama 2
reference link 31
Llama-3-8B-Instruct model
reference link 221
Llama 3 fine-tuning job 96
container image, creating 97-99
data preparation 97
deploying 99-101
llama.cpp
reference link 31
LoadBalancer 94, 157
reference link 60
log query language (LogQL)
reference link 244
Loki 240, 244
reference link 244
Long Short-Term Memory (LSTM) 8
Low-Rank Adaptation (LoRA) 13, 77, 223
Lustre 18

M

Machine Learning (ML) 3, 4, 221, 281
evolution 6-9
massively parallel processing (MPP) 198
maximum tolerable downtime (MTD) 268
McKinsey
reference link 19
memory coherence 18
Meta
reference link 31
Meta's Llama-3.2-1B
reference link 215
metrics
application-level metrics 241
cluster-level metrics 241
node metrics 241
pod and container metrics 241
Microsoft Teams 254
MIG profiles
reference link 208
Mistral
reference link 63
mixed MIG strategy
reference link 209
MLFlow
versus Kubeflow 233, 234
versus KubeRay 233, 234
MLflow components
MLflow Model Registry 227
MLflow Models 227
MLflow Projects 227
Mlflow Tracking 226
MLflow Model Registry
reference link 227
MLflow Models
reference link 227
MLflow Projects
reference link 227
Mlflow Tracking
reference link 226
MLflow Workflows 226
model bias 234
model bias and variance
drift detection and remediation 237, 238
drift monitoring and feedback loops 235
fairness and explainability libraries 235
methods, testing 234
model fine-tuning 76
example 77-84
LoRA 77
uses 76
model hallucinations 76
Model Hub 31

monitoring plugins 40
monitoring tools, K8s
Fluent Bit 242-244
Fluentd 242-244
Grafana 242
Loki 244
OpenTelemetry (OTel) 242, 245
Prometheus 246-248
Multi-Instance GPU (MIG)
reference link 197
multiple node-specific configuration
using 215
Multi-Process Service (MPS)
reference link 197
multi-stage build
reference link 176

N

namespaces 182
native networking
versus overlay networks 156
Natural Language Processing (NLP) 6
Network Address Translation (NAT) 154
networking
best practices 144-146
Network Interface Card (NIC) 167
Network Load Balancer (NLB) 157, 188
reference link 59
network performance optimization, for GenAI 165, 166
CoreDNS 168
custom networking 166
eBPF 167
IP address exhaustion issues 166
Kube-Proxy 166
network latency and throughput enhancements 168
SR-IOV 167
network policies
implementing, in chatbot applications 163, 164
used, for securing GenAI workloads 162, 163
Neuron device plugin 200
Neuron SDK
reference link 199
New Relic 240
URL 47
n-grams 14
NiceGUI
URL 112
node classes
reference link 129
node controller 39
NodeLocal DNSCache
reference link 168
NodePools
reference link 129
NodePort
reference link 60
NodePort Service 157
nodes types
control plane 37
data plane/worker nodes 37
NVIDIA Collective Communications Library (NCCL) 170
nvidia-container-toolkit 200
nvidia/cuda 99
NVIDIA Data Center GPU Manager (DCGM) 203-206
exporter 247
NVIDIA device plugin for Kubernetes 200
reference link 198
NVIDIA device plugin Helm chart 201

NVIDIA documentation
reference link 204
NVIDIA GPU Operator 204, 208
NVIDIA GPUs 119
NVIDIA Inference Microservices (NIM) 217
NVIDIA MIG 207-209
NVIDIA MPS 210-212
NVMe instance store 179

O

observability
metrics 241
pillars 239
system logs 240
traces 242
OPA Gatekeeper
reference link 177
OpenAI 178
reference link 25
URL 3
OpenID Connect (OIDC) 182
Open Policy Agent (OPA) 177, 281
OpenSearch
URL 106
OpenTelemetry (OTel)
reference link 242, 245
Operating Systems (OSes) 25
operator pattern 204
Oracle Cloud Infrastructure (OCI) 47
OTel collectors
reference link 245
OTel exporters
reference link 245
overlay networks
versus native networking 156

P

PagedAttention 230
PagerDuty
reference link 247
Parameter-Efficient Fine-Tuning (PEFT) 77
PCI DSS 47
Performance-Efficient Fine Tuning (PEFT) 13
PersistentVolumeClaim (PVC) 95, 248
PersistentVolumes (PVs) 254, 275
personally identifiable information (PII) 174
Pinecone
URL 106
Pod
reference link 59
PodDisruptionBudget
reference link 271
Pod Monitors
reference link 251
Pod Security Standards (PSS) 42
Portworx Backup
reference link 275
Principal Component Analysis (PCA) 5, 73
Prisma Cloud's Container Security
reference link 181
Prometheus 118, 159, 246
architecture 247
GPU monitoring, enabling 251-254
reference link 246
prometheus-adapter 119
Prometheus adapter 206
Prometheus Alertmanager
reference link 247
Prometheus exporters
reference link 247

Prometheus Pushgateway
reference link 247
Prometheus Query Language (PromQL) 247
Prometheus rule
reference link 259
Prometheus server
reference link 247
Prometheus stack
deploying 248-251
prompt engineering 15, 68, 223
prompt tuning 13
PromQL
reference link 248
Python Flask API
reference link 32
Python Package Index
URL 89
PythonREPLTool 70
PyTorch 42
URL 199

Q

Qdrant
URL 106
Quantized Lower Rank Adoption (QLoRA) 13

R

RabbitMQ 118
RAG pipelines 217
RAG system 89
Ray
reference link 222
Ray Data
reference link 228
Ray RLlib
reference link 228
Ray Serve 223
reference link 228
Ray Train
reference link 228
Ray Tune
reference link 228
Recall-Oriented Understudy for Gisting Evaluation (ROUGE) 14
recovery point objective (RPO) 268
recovery time objective (RTO) 268
Recurrent Neural Networks (RNNs) 6, 8
RedHat OpenShift
reference link 35
Regions 47
reinforcement learning 5
Reinforcement Learning from Human Feedback (RLHF) 13
Remote Direct Memory Access (RDMA) 18, 170
ReplicaSet 271
ReplicaSets 60
Reserved Instances (RIs) 142
Retrieval Augmentation Generation (RAG) 15, 71
deploying, on K8s 105-111
implementing 72
query, running 72-76
Return on Investment (ROI) 12
robust authentication mechanisms
reference link 255
Role-Based Access Control (RBAC) 42, 177, 225, 254, 275

S

sampling drift 236
ScaledObject 125
scale-down 128
scalers 125
scale-up 128
scratch
reference link 176
seccomp
reference link 180
Secrets 183, 275
secrets-store-csi-driver
reference link 178
security best practices 174
implementing, in chatbot app 189-194
security information and event management (SIEM) 184
Seldon Core 223
SELinux
reference link 180
semi-supervised learning 5
service account identity 184
service controller 39
service-level agreements (SLAs) 47
service mesh
control plane 160
data plane 161
resilience and fault tolerance policies 160
security policies 160
traffic management policies 160
using, in traffic management 160, 161
versus K8s network policies 165
service mesh, implementations
Istio 161
Linkerd 161
SHapley Additive exPlanations (SHAP) 235
sidecar containers 161
single MIG strategy
reference link 209
Single Root Input/Output Virtualization (SR-IOV) 165, 167
Slack
reference link 247
Snyk
URL 177
SOC 47
solid state disks (SSDs) 136
SoundCloud
reference link 246
special interest groups (SIGs) 36
Splunk 240
URL 47
StatefulSet 248
state-of-the-art (SOTA) 206
statistical methods
concept drift detection (CDD) 236
target drift detection (TDD) 236
storage
best practices 146-150
StorageClass 90
StormForge
reference link 140
Streamlit
URL 112
supervised learning (SL) 4
supply chain security 176
build phase 176
encrypt phase 177
scan phase 178
store phase 177
test phase 177
Support Vector Machines (SVMs) 8
system logs 240
K8s audit logs 241

T

target drift detection (TDD) 236
temporal drift 236
TensorFlow 42, 199
TensorFlow Serving 271
tensor processing units (TPUs)
  reference link 198
Terraform
  reference link 50
Terraform Helm provider 248
Terraform provider 52
third-party (3P) tools 47
traces 242
traffic management
  with service mesh 160, 161
Trainium 199
  reference link 198
Trainium-powered instances
  reference link 199
transformer architecture 9-11
  concepts 10
transformer model 9
Trilio for Kubernetes
  reference link 275
Triton Inference Server 271
Trivy
  reference link 178
Trn2 UltraServers
  reference link 199

U

unsupervised learning (UL) 5
uvicorn
  URL 110

V

vector database 106
Velero
  URL 275
Vertical Pod Autoscaler (VPA) 42, 122-124, 216
  combining, with HPA 124
  operating modes 122
virtual functions 167
Virtual Machine (VM) 18, 25
Volta architecture
  reference link 211
VPC flow logs 166

W

Weave Net
  reference link 155
web application firewalls (WAFs) 182
Wiz container security
  reference link 181

X

XGBoost
  reference link 198

Z

Zipkin
  reference link 242

www.packtpub.com

Subscribe to our online digital library for full access to over 7,000 books and videos, as well as industry leading tools to help you plan your personal development and advance your career. For more information, please visit our website.

Why subscribe?

- Spend less time learning and more time coding with practical eBooks and Videos from over 4,000 industry professionals
- Improve your learning with Skill Plans built especially for you
- Get a free eBook or video every month
- Fully searchable for easy access to vital information
- Copy and paste, print, and bookmark content

Did you know that Packt offers eBook versions of every book published, with PDF and ePub files available? You can upgrade to the eBook version at packtpub.com and as a print book customer, you are entitled to a discount on the eBook copy. Get in touch with us at customercare@packtpub.com for more details.

At www.packtpub.com, you can also read a collection of free technical articles, sign up for a range of free newsletters, and receive exclusive discounts and offers on Packt books and eBooks.

Other Books You May Enjoy

If you enjoyed this book, you may be interested in these other books by Packt:

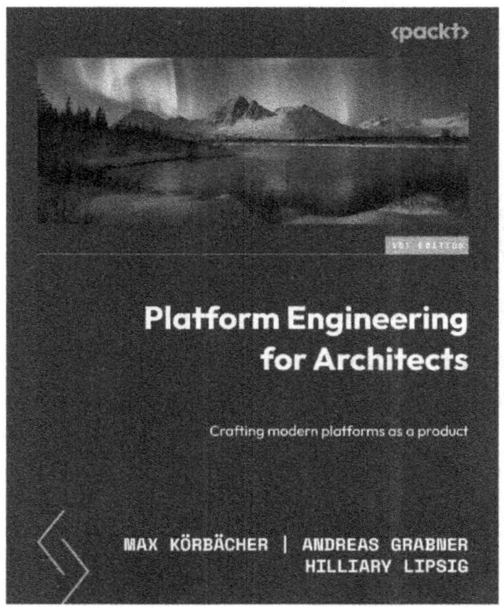

Platform Engineering for Architects

Max Körbächer, Andreas Grabner, Hilliary Lipsig

ISBN: 978-1-83620-359-9

- Make informed decisions aligned with your organization's platform needs
- Identify missing platform capabilities and manage that technical debt effectively
- Develop critical user journeys to enhance platform functionality
- Define platform purpose, principles, and key performance indicators
- Use data-driven insights to guide product decisions
- Design and implement platform reference and target architectures

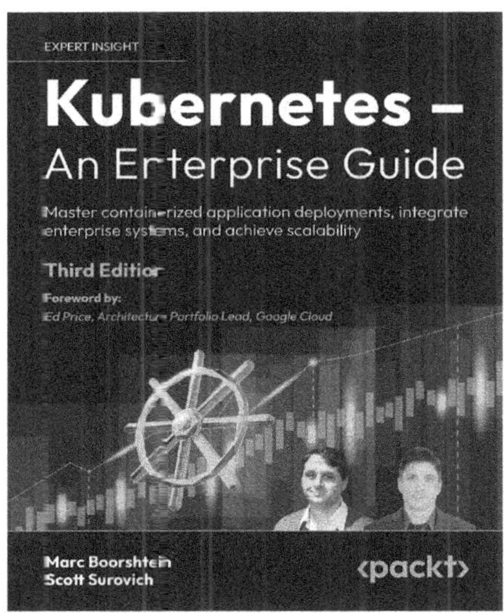

Kubernetes – An Enterprise Guide – Third Edition

Marc Boorshtein, Scott Surovich

ISBN: 978-1-83508-695-7

- Manage secrets securely using Vault and External Secret Operator
- Create multitenant clusters with vCluster for isolated environments
- Monitor Kubernetes clusters with Prometheus and visualize metrics using Grafana
- Aggregate and analyze logs centrally with OpenSearch for deeper insights
- Build a CI/CD developer platform by integrating GitLab and ArgoCD
- Deploy applications in an Istio service mesh and enforce security with OPA and GateKeeper
- Secure container runtimes and prevent attacks using KubeArmor

Packt is searching for authors like you

If you're interested in becoming an author for Packt, please visit `authors.packtpub.com` and apply today. We have worked with thousands of developers and tech professionals, just like you, to help them share their insight with the global tech community. You can make a general application, apply for a specific hot topic that we are recruiting an author for, or submit your own idea.

Share Your Thoughts

Now you've finished *Kubernetes for Generative AI Solutions*, we'd love to hear your thoughts! Scan the QR code below to go straight to the Amazon review page for this book and share your feedback or leave a review on the site that you purchased it from.

`https://packt.link/r/1-836-20993-2`

Your review is important to us and the tech community and will help us make sure we're delivering excellent quality content.

www.ingramcontent.com/pod-product-compliance
Lightning Source LLC
Chambersburg PA
CBHW081050220326
41598CB00038B/7045

9781836209935